THE ACKNOWLEDGED CHRIST
OF THE INDIAN RENAISSANCE

M. M. THOMAS

The Acknowledged Christ
of the
Indian Renaissance

SCM PRESS LTD
LONDON

TO
PENNAMMA

334 00008 4
First published 1969
by SCM Press Ltd
56 Bloomsbury Street London WC1
© SCM Press Ltd 1969
Printed in Great Britain by
Western Printing Services Ltd Bristol

CONTENTS

Preface   ix

I   Rammohan Roy: The Christ of 'The Precepts'   1
1. A New Look at an Old Controversy: Rammohan Roy and Dr Joshua Marshman
2. Sources of the Knowledge of God
3. The Nature of the Moral Teachings of Jesus
4. The Person and Work of Christ
   A. *Marshman's 'seven positions'*
   B. *The natural inferiority of the Son to the Father*
      (i) The Son dependent and subject
      (ii) Unity of will, not identity of being
      (iii) Mediator and Messiah as First-born of creatures
   C. *Marshman's defence and the Raja's rejoinder*
      (i) The Son's nature and office
      (ii) Unity of nature, distinction of Persons
      (iii) First-born, not first-created
      (iv) The Atonement
      (v) The Trinity
5. A Critical Evaluation
   The Idea of God and Divine Nature

II   Some Indian Christian Defences against Brahmoism: Lal Behari Day and Nehemiah Goreh   38
1. The Sources of the Knowledge of God
2. The Doctrine of Atonement
3. The Idea of a National Church
4. A Critical Evaluation

III   Keshub Chunder Sen: The Doctrine of Divine Humanity   56
1. The Doctrine of Christ and Uni-Trinity
   J. N. Farquhar and M. C. Parekh on Keshub's Christology
2. Universal Christ and Indigenous Church
   A. *The meaning of apostolic authority*
   B. *'The Hindu Church of Christ'*
   C. *Parekh on Keshub Chunder Sen and Bishop Azariah's reply*

Contents

IV P. C. Mozoomdar: The Oriental Christ and the Unfolding Spirit   82
  1. The Framework of Theology: The Divine Spirit
     A. *A revised pantheism*
     B. *The doctrine of the Spirit*
     C. *A critique of Christianity*
  2. The Spirit in Jesus Christ
     A. *The manifestation of the divine character*
     B. *The uniqueness of Jesus Christ*
  3. Other Aspects of the Spirit
     A. *Law and Spirit*
     B. *The Spirit and the Church*
     C. *The Spirit and universal religion*
  4. A Critical Evaluation

V Brahmobandhav Upadhyaya: Christ as *Chit*   99

VI Vivekananda: Christ as *Jivanmukta*   111
  1. Sri Ramakrishna
  2. Swami Vivekananda
     A. *Vedanta as the only universal religion*
     B. *Christ and Christianity interpreted*
  3. Some Christian Critiques
     A. *C. F. Andrews on Vivekananda*
     B. *J. R. Chandran on Christian apologetics*
     C. *Bishop Appasamy's doctrine of immanence and mysticism*
  4. An Evaluation

VII Radhakrishnan: The Mystic Christ   150
  1. The Framework
  2. The Meaning of Christ
  3. An Interpretative History of Christianity
  4. Universal Religion
  5. Christian Evaluations
     A. *Religious protest against the 'absolute': P. Chenchiah*
     B. *The struggle to provide a spiritual basis for the new India: P. D. Devanandan*
     C. *Philosophical criticism of the doctrine of the equality of religions: D. G. Moses*
     D. *Christology in terms of dynamic monism: Surjit Singh*

E. *Questioning the doctrine of mysticism: Lesslie Newbigin and Stanley Samartha*
F. *A theology of Christian non-dualism: Mark Sunder Rao*
6. Comment

VIII Mahatma Gandhi: Jesus, the Supreme Satyagrahi   193
1. The Framework of Gandhism
2. The Message and Person of Jesus
3. Religion and Religions
   A. *Equality of religions*
   B. *Swadeshi in religion*
   C. *Communication of things of the Spirit*
4. A Reinterpretation of Christianity
   Two Christian statements
5. Some Christian Responses
   A. *Christians of the inner Gandhi circle: S. K. George and C. F. Andrews*
   B. *E. Stanley Jones' interpretation*
   C. *Paul D. Devanandan on Gandhi's critique*
6. An Evaluation

IX The Theology of National Renaissance   239
1. The Idea of Divine Providence
2. *Praeparatio Evangelica*
3. The Gospel as a Message of Fellowship
4. The Meaning and Relevance of Jesus Christ
5. The Structure of the Church for Service and Mission

X Epilogue: Criteria of an Indian Christian Theology   284
1. The Nature and Function of Theology
   A. *The nature of faith*
   B. *The expressions of faith*
   C. *The function of theology*
2. The Changeless and the Changing Aspects of Theology
   The role of pre-understanding
3. Criteria of a Living Theology
4. Some Relevant Indian Discussions

Appendix I: Short biographical notes   319
Appendix II: Movements mentioned in the book   332

Index   337

PREFACE

I am innocent of any ambition to be a systematic theologian. Neither by training nor by inclination have I a vocation along that line. Nevertheless, I am deeply concerned with men's reflections on the truth of Jesus Christ in the context of their grappling with the meaning of life in concrete situations of history. These reflections may be fragmentary and unsystematic, but they constitute living theology, the raw material of theological systems. The theological fragments of this book relate to one historical situation, namely the awakening of Indian nationalism in the nineteenth and the early part of the twentieth century.

What I have done in this study is to survey how some of the foremost spiritual leaders of the Indian renaissance, especially of Neo-Hinduism, sought to understand the meaning of Jesus Christ and Christianity for religion and society in renascent India. The leaders I have selected are Raja Rammohan Roy the prophet of Indian nationalism, Keshub Chunder Sen and P. C. Mozoomdar of the Brahmo Samaj, Swami Vivekananda and Dr S. Radhakrishnan representing the Neo-Advaita movement and Mahatma Gandhi the Father of the Nation. As part of the survey, I have also tried to study how the Indian Church, in the thought of some of its theologically-minded representatives, has attempted to enter into dialogue with the ideas of these leaders and to formulate its own faith in Christ and the meaning of Indian nationalism. In the selection of Christian thinkers, I have been guided primarily by the need to bring out what the Indian Church has thought and said in dialogic response to the leaders of Neo-Hinduism whose understanding of Christ and Christianity I have surveyed. Even here the selection is by no means exhaustive and I have not been guided by any order of honour or of importance to the development of Indian Christian theology. In fact, I am very conscious of serious omission of theologically important Western and Indian names. Some important names are only mentioned in passing. I have inclined more towards some men who have taken seriously the dialogical situation created by Indian nationalism and who are likely to be neglected by historians of theology. But then my justification is that Indian Christian theological thought is being studied more adequately by competent people in India and elsewhere. The danger of too great a concentration on the theologians or even on the Christian group is that it lends itself to the false idea that Christian theology is a matter only of the inner life of the Church.

Raymond Panikkar has spoken of *The Unknown Christ of Hinduism*, and as a parallel to it, I am speaking in this book of the Acknowledged Christ, not of Traditional Hinduism but of Renascent Hinduism, seen as part of the total renaissance of India. The acknowledgment of Christ in India, whether by Hindu leaders or Christian men, is no doubt partial and very inadequate. But I am persuaded that the mission of the Church in the religion and life of India, and the development of an Indian Christian theology serving that mission require that the crucial issues and terms of Christ's dialogue with India underlying the nature of these partial acknowledgments be properly understood and evaluated. This book is a beginning in that direction, but no more than a beginning. In the final analysis, Christ's confrontation with the heart of India is the basis of Christian mission and missionary theology.

The Epilogue deals with some of my personal reflections on the principles which should guide the task of building an Indian Christian theology. I have written it reluctantly. My knowledge of the contemporary theological debate in the West is rather superficial. My reading of the theologians from the West whom I have mentioned is not wide, deep or up-to-date enough to give my comments on them real value in the continuing debate. These comments should be seen as no more than expressing my own approach. The reason for including them is that some clarification of the assumptions behind the interpretative survey of the rest of the study seemed called for.

It was when I spent a sabbatical-year in 1966–67 as Henry Luce Visiting Professor in the Union Theological Seminary, New York, and had to teach, that I thought of doing a course in the Second Semester on 'The Theological Task in India'. Thus, I started collecting the material which is used here. But the writing itself had to be done in the midst of my teaching and travel in America that year and of my other activities in India and abroad afterwards. I am most conscious of the inadequacies of the book. If I have succeeded in sharing some of my concern for a relevant Indian Christian theology through these pages, I shall be amply rewarded.

I acknowledge my indebtedness to President John Bennett of the Union Theological Seminary, New York for the invitation he extended to me to spend an academic year at the Union. This made possible some contacts with currents of modern theological thought as they found expression among the professors and the students of the Seminary my indebtedness to whom is explicit at many points in this book. It also gave me opportunities for some personal theological research and reflections. The Librarians of the Missionary Research Library, New York, have been most generous in rendering help. I acknowledge my thanks also to the Rev. Richard W. Taylor, Mr T. K. Thomas and Dr Leroy S. Rounder for reading through parts of the manuscript and giving me suggestions; to Rev. P. T. Thomas for his help in preparing the Appendix; and to Mrs Dorothy Fernāndez, Miss Bunty Simmons and Mr R. Ramasubramonia Iyer for patiently typing out the manuscript from an illegible hand. I am greatly indebted to Rev. John S. Bowden of the SCM Press for undertaking the publication of the book in England, and to the Christian Literature Society of Madras for bringing out an Indian edition.

My wife, perhaps, contributed most to seeing this book through. She insisted on my beginning the process of writing a book on my own, during my sabbatical leave in New York. And, at times, when I was tempted to give it up as impossible, she encouraged me to continue, though it often meant preoccupation with writing even during the few days we had together. And it was during the anxious three months of our stay at the Vellore Hospital for her treatment that she persuaded me to do the chapters which were yet to be written. The struggle against cancer and its ultimate threat to a loved one is not necessarily a bad context for reflection on the meaning of the Gospel of the Resurrection, but it is hardly the best occasion for writing. But I took it because after the immediate crisis had passed, Pennamma (Elizabeth) was eager that I should finish the writing before we left Vellore. And I did. There is, therefore, a special relevance in my dedicating the book to her. I do so however in gratitude for her constant concern for the Christ-centredness of my vocation amidst my many wanderings among men, ideologies and theologies and for her intuitive spiritual discernment on which I have grown increasingly to rely.

M. M. Thomas

Christian Institute for the Study of Religion and Society
Bangalore
15 December 1968

CHAPTER ONE

Rammohan Roy: The Christ of 'The Precepts'

1. A NEW LOOK AT AN OLD CONTROVERSY: RAMMOHAN ROY AND DR JOSHUA MARSHMAN

Raja Rammohan Roy has been called the prophet of Indian nationalism and the pioneer of liberal reform in Hindu religion and society. Many studies of his life and thought and his contribution to the Indian renaissance exist, as does the history of the Brahmo Samaj which he founded. It is important for us to know this whole background.[1] But we shall confine ourselves to examining the theology of Rammohan Roy, and of the Serampore missionaries who entered into controversy with him to establish the orthodoxy of the faith of the Church.

The story of the controversy may be summarized as follows:[2] In 1820 Raja Rammohan Roy published extracts from the Gospels containing the Teachings of Jesus, especially sermons and parables. The title of the publication was *The Precepts of Jesus The Guide to Peace and Happiness, extracted from the Books of the New Testament, ascribed to the four evangelists* (with translations into Sanscrit and Bengalese). Dr Marshman, one of the Baptist missionaries of Serampore, writing editorially in the *Friend of India* No. XX (February 1820) commented critically on the manner in which only a part of the Gospels was published, and said that it 'may greatly injure the cause of truth'. In response to this, Rammohan Roy published *An Appeal to the Christian Public in Defence of the Precepts of Jesus by a Friend of Truth*. To this Dr Marshman published in the *Friend of India* No. XXIII (May 1820) his 'Remarks on Certain Observations in *An Appeal* etc.' and followed it in the *Friend of India*, Quarterly Series No. I (September 1820) with his 'Observations on Certain Ideas contained in the Introduction to *The Precepts of Jesus* etc.' Rammohan Roy replied with *A Second Appeal to the Christian Public in Defence of the Precepts of Jesus*. Dr Marshman came out in 1822 with *A Defence of the Deity and Atonement of Jesus Christ in reply to Rammohan Roy of Calcutta*.[3] To this, Rammohan Roy replied in 1823 with his *Final Appeal to the Christian Public in Defence of the Precepts of Jesus*. The first Appeal is 18 pages long, the second 112 and the third nearly 200.[4]

As this controversy was going on, Mr William Adam, one of the Serampore missionaries who was translating the New Testament into Bengali with the help of Rammohan Roy, confessed Unitarianism in 1821. This incident added heat to the controversy.

Some other writings of Rammohan Roy have a bearing on his ideas on Christianity. Of these, special mention may be made of his writings under the pseudonym 'Shivaprasad Sarma' on 'The Missionary and the Brahman' in the *Brahminical Magazine*, which appeared occasionally between 1821 and 1823; and under the pseudonym of Ram Doss in which he entered into a public controversy with Dr Tytler on Hinduism and Christianity.

When we look at the debate from our vantage point, some theological issues stand out. We may spell out some of the main ones.

2. SOURCES OF THE KNOWLEDGE OF GOD

It is rather surprising that the first Christian intellectual encounter of a serious theological nature in India took place not with traditional Hinduism but with a Hinduism liberating itself under the impact of Western rationalism and social morality. Rammohan Roy had three fundamental ideas in his religion: first, a monotheistic faith in the unity of God inspired fundamentally perhaps by Islam; secondly, the conviction that morality is the essence of true religion; that moral degradation is the accompaniment of polytheism and idolatrous worship; and, thirdly, a certain rationalism which, while conscious of its limits, still demands that religion should hold only to beliefs which are reasonable, and that reason should serve to purify religion of superstitition and unnecessary mysteries and miracles. These ideas are basic to an understanding of the structure of Rammohan Roy's religion. It is made abundantly clear in his early writings. His first publication, *Tuhfat-ul-Muwathiddin* (*A Present to the*

Believers in One God) was a treatise in Persian with a preface in the Arabic language.[5] He published *Vedanta Sutra* in Bengali, translated into English with the title: 'The Vedanta or the Resolution of all the Vedas, the most Celebrated and Revered Work of Brahminical Theology, Establishing the Unity of the Supreme Being, and that He alone is the Object of Propitiation and Worship.' In this he argues two points, that the terms *Om, Tat* and *Sat* 'simply affirm that one unknown true being is the creator, preserver and destroyer of the universe', and that 'moral principle is part of the adoration of God'.[6] In his 'Defence of the monotheistic system of the Vedas in reply to an apology for the present state of Hindu worship' he prays that the hearts of his countrymen may be led to 'that pure morality which is inseparable from the true worship of Him'.[7] Probably the relation between immorality and idolatry, and between right morality and monotheism is established most clearly in his Introdiction to the 'Translation of the Isopanishad, one of the Chapters of Yajur Ved, according to the Commentary of the Celebrated Shankaracharya; Establishing the Unity and Incomprehensibility of the Supreme Being, and that his Worship Alone can lead to Eternal Beatitude'.[8] In this Introduction he says:

I have never ceased to contemplate with the strongest feelings of regret the obstinate adherence of my countrymen to their fatal system of idolatry, inducing, for the sake of propitiating their supposed Deities, the violation of every humane and social feeling, and to view in [this system] the moral debasement of a race, ... I pray that [Hindus may come to] a conviction of the rationality of believing and adoring the Supreme Being only; together with a complete perception and practice of that grand and comprehensive moral principle: Do unto others as ye would be done by.[9]

Here the influences of Christian moral principles and Western deistic rationalism are evident.

It is interesting to note that the young Raja Rammohan Roy in fact starts in *A Present to the Believers in One God* with a strong rationalistic protest against all religions and an attempt to build a natural theology on the basis of the authority of reason. At the end of the treatise he divides the religious people of the world into four:

a class of deceivers, a class of deceived people, ... a class of people who are deceivers and also deceived, [and] ... those who by the help of Almighty God are neither deceivers nor deceived.

And earlier he declares:

There is a strong hope that [any person of sound mind] will be able to distinguish the truth from untruth and true propositions from fallacious ones, and ..., becoming free from the useless restraints of religion, which sometimes become sources of prejudice ... and causes of physical and mental troubles, will turn to the One Being who is the fountain of the harmonious organization of the universe, and will pay attention to the good of society.[10]

He later recognized to a greater degree the limitations of reason, pointing to 'a conviction in the mind of its total ignorance of the nature and of the specific attributes of the Godhead, and a sense of doubt respecting the real essence of the soul'. And this consciousness of the inability of reason to understand the nature and essence of ultimate realities, led him to leave speculative doctrines of religion aside and adhere to the notion, rationally arrived at, 'of the existence of a supreme superintending power, the Author and Preserver of this harmonious system' and to concentrate on the discovery of a morality which will 'reconcile us to human nature, and ... render our existence agreeable to ourselves and profitable to mankind'.[11] This in a sense is a movement away from religion as understood as mystical and metaphysical gnosis to religion understood as ethical existence. In Rammohan Roy, the Christian Church was dealing with the modern secular temper in an Indian form.

Inevitably there was a conflict between the principles of natural theology which Rammohan Roy held and those of evangelical theology which Marshman held. It may be useful to define the agreements and disagreements between them on the nature of authority in theology. We may mention a few of the points specially worthy of note.

Rammohan Roy has shown in many of his writings his aversion to what he called 'speculative doctrines and creeds' and 'metaphysical arguments'.[12] About God, he affirmed that man cannot know or contemplate the nature of the deity;[13] he can only 'read His existence' in 'the works of nature',[14] including, we should suppose, the works of the moral nature of man and society. Marshman would certainly go with Roy in the affirmation that 'we know nothing of the Godhead', but would add, 'but what God himself has revealed' and supported by 'Divine Testimony' by which he means the Scriptures of the Old and New Testaments.[15]

Rammohan Roy in defence of his freedom from prejudices and his objectivity in approaching the truths of Christianity, claims that he has not been spoiled by 'a parent or tutor' and therefore by 'the powerful effects of early religious impression' and that he had gone directly to 'the words of the Author of this religion and the undisputed instructions of his holy Apostles', i.e. the Scriptures.[16] While Marshman approves the Raja's going directly to the Scriptures for the authoritative divine testimony, he rejects the idea that 'the most certain way of enabling anyone to discover in a superior manner the truths and doctrines of Christianity is to leave him till the age of thirty or forty without any religious impression'.[17] Indeed Marshman seems to set a high value on the attestation of divine testimony given in Scripture by the Church across the ages; and he criticizes Rammohan Roy for teaching 'doctrines opposed to those held by the mass of real Christians in every age'.[18]

Marshman however goes on to point out the fundamental source of prejudice and blindness which is present in every man, namely the false orientation of the self. Here he discusses the nature of what we have now come to recognize in modern language as 'ideology' perverting every man's approach to truth.

> Is not the human heart the fabricator of its own prejudices? The partiality of friendship will often so blind a man's eyes as to prevent his crediting the clearest facts relative to an opposite party, though completely within the reach of investigation. Of this we have examples not only in political matters, where truths and facts received by one side are treated with the utmost contempt by the other; but in private disputes in which facts come under our own view. ... Above all, does not that principle of self-righteousness which cleaves to all by nature, often blind man to the clearest truths, because they are unpalatable? If this be the case, may it not be wise in our author to examine whether some secret bias of this kind may not have caused him to mistake respecting doctrines in their own nature of the most humbling tendency.[19]

This insight of a self-transcending reason, and therefore of false orientation of self making rational objectivity impossible, is basic. In a sense, it is affirming that the discovery of ultimate truth is not a rational pursuit, but must follow the faith-response to the Truth one seeks to understand. And probably it is here that Marshman sees humbling submission to revelation, as given in Scriptural testimony, as the only source of the knowledge of God and his truth.

At this point, he declares his belief that the Scriptures are the only test of the truth of traditions in the Church, which may be considered as of little value when we have the Scriptures themselves. He is reluctant 'even to enquire' the opinion of the Fathers on doctrinal matters.

In doctrine and practice therefore men in the first three centuries may have adhered to the Scripture or they may have swerved from them; but as this can be known only by bringing them to the Scripture as the test, they are of no value while we have the Scriptures themselves.[20]

As for the nature of the authority of the Scriptures Marshman insists that 'a real Christian' should believe 'the Divine authority of the whole of the Holy Scriptures' and receive them as 'the Word of God'.

If a part of them alone be received because it contains valuable precepts, while the rest is esteemed scarcely worthy of notice, . . . they are stripped of their peculiar majesty and authority and degraded to a level with the writings of men; . . . they are no longer the power of God unto salvation.[21]

As Rammohan Roy however points out:

Christian churches have selected passages from the Bible, which they conceive particularly excellent and well adapted for the constant perusal and study of the people of their respective churches.[22]

Marshman is therefore forced to qualify his earlier wholesale disapproval of Rammohan Roy's selection of parts of the Bible for publication, by saying that it is not the selection that he criticizes but the basis of the selection. It is certainly not wrong to select and publish a part of the Bible, even to publish only the precepts of Jesus; but it should be done as

a sample of the whole Scriptures, and representing them as according indubitable proof of the authencity of its narratives and the reasonableness and importance of its doctrines, [instead of separating them] from that

Gospel, of which they form so important a part . . . an idea which perverts the grand design of the Gospel, and frustrates the grace of God in the salvation of men. . . . We not only think that Rammohan Roy had a fair right to fix on the preceptive part, that such a compilation might have been highly useful. But it is of importance that every compilation be given us as a *sample* of the Sacred Writings in all their excellence and importance, and not as a substitute for the whole; in such a way as to create a deep reverence for every part of the Scriptures; and not so as to deprecate the rest of the Word of God.[23]

Indeed Marshman emphasizes that the theme of the whole Bible is salvation by faith expressing itself in obedience; and therefore, like Rammohan Roy himself, it is not interested in speculation. All the doctrines of the Bible including 'even that which relates to the being of God' are

intended less for speculation than for that faith and cordial obedience which renovate the heart and produce the fruits of righteousness. The gratification of mere curiosity seems never to have been the object of Divine Revelation. Hence of historical facts, we are told just as much as will be profitable to the mind. . . . Hence we have scarcely a full creed given us in any part of the Scriptures. He who would believe to the saving of the soul, must in the very act unite to faith cordial obedience, in doing which he finds at length that he has a complete creed given him in those precepts which he has been obeying from the heart. So just is that saying of our Lord's, 'He that *will do his will* shall know the doctrine, whether it be of God or whether I speak of myself.' Doctrines delivered in the form of divine commands however involve in themselves a far stronger kind of evidence than as though delivered merely as speculative axioms.[24]

Marshman thus underlines the non-speculative nature and soteriological function of doctrines. Whether he remembers these principles in his controversy is another question.

Both Marshman and Rammohan Roy accepted the principle of interpreting the Old Testament and the New in the light of each other, and of discovering the meaning of one passage in correspondence to similar usages elsewhere. But Marshman once objected to the exegesis of John 10.30 in the light of John 17.11, 22 because their contexts were different, and for this Rammohan Roy replied that it was a 'universally adopted rule, that passages of Scripture should be explained by their reference to one another'.[25] On the whole,

Rammohan Roy had a critical rational approach to the text of the Bible and recognized that 'certain passages' of the Bible had 'undergone human distortions'.[26] He, however, considered the whole of the Old and New Testaments to be the foundation of theology. Marshman was committed to belief in the verbal inspiration of the Scriptures, of which 'all is the dictate of the Holy Spirit', and considered all parts of the Bible as 'equal in authenticity but differing in clearness and fulness'.[27] It was in this sense that he saw it as 'natural to expect that [the doctrine of the atonement] will be either expressed or implied in the Old Testament'. To him, the Old Testament, the 'declaration' of Jesus, the 'declaration' of the Evangelists, 'the writings' of the Apostles and the book of Revelation 'originating in a different source' – all these 'five different sources' were 'equal in authenticity' as sources of Christian doctrine. Certainly Marshman reads the New Testament too fully in the Old; and Rammohan Roy frankly states that he is unable to follow Marshman in some of these readings. Marshman also reads into the New Testament the Trinitarian and Atonement doctrines developed after New Testament times.

With respect to 'historical and some other passages' in the Gospel, Rammohan Roy says 'they are liable to disputes and doubts of free thinkers and anti-Christians'; especially the story of miracles. At one point, the Raja claims that he is himself not sceptical about them, but there is no doubt that they have little spiritual or theological significance to him except as mythologies helpful to preserve the precepts of Jesus. It is here that we are brought to the heart of the controversy between Marshman and Rammohan Roy, namely the relation between morality and salvation in Christianity.

3. THE NATURE OF THE MORAL TEACHINGS OF JESUS

Rammohan Roy was a Protestant Hindu moving away from the amoral and monistic/polytheistic tendencies of traditional Hinduism under the influence of Western liberalism. The appeal of Jesus Christ to him was primarily to his Protestant Hindu soul. Jesus' ethics and monotheism attracted him. In a letter which he wrote to Mr John Digby in 1815, he says:

The consequence of my long and uninterrupted researches into religious truth has been that I have found the doctrine of Christ more conducive to moral principles and better adapted for the use of rational beings than any others which have come to my knowledge.[28]

In the introduction to *The Precepts of Jesus*, he says that 'though [the moral law] is partially taught also in every system of religion, with which I am acquainted, [it] is principally inculcated by Christianity'; and he interprets it as the 'essential characteristic of the Christian religion'. His reaction against metaphysics and his concern for a religion which answers the moral and spiritual problems of human existence on earth are evident when he writes about the Precepts of Jesus:

Moral doctrines ... are beyond the reach of metaphysical perversion, and intelligible alike to the learned and the unlearned. This simple code of religion and morality is so admirably calculated to elevate men's ideas to high and liberal notions of God, who has equally submitted all living creatures, without distinction of caste, rank or wealth to change, disappointment, pain and death and has equally admitted all to be partakers of the bountiful mercies which he has lavished over nature and is also so well fitted to regulate the conduct of the human race in the discharge of their various duties to themselves and to society. ...

So, like liberals elsewhere, he separates the teaching of Jesus Christ from the historical events of his life, death and resurrection and their biblical interpretation and publishes them as sufficient to 'reconcile us to human nature and render our existence agreeable to ourselves and profitable to the rest of mankind'. He goes on:

I feel persuaded that by separating from the other matters contained in the New Testament the moral principles found in that book, these will be more likely to produce the desirable effect of improving the hearts and minds of men of different persuasions and degrees of understanding. For historical and some other passages are liable to disputes and doubts of free thinkers and anti-Christians, especially miraculous relations, which are much less wonderful than the fabricated tales handed down to the natives of Asia, and consequently would be apt, at best, to carry little weight with them.[29]

Later in the argument he affirmed that this omission was not meant to 'express doubts of their authenticity' but because it had little importance in his own eyes to authenticate the moral teachings of Jesus.

These precepts separated from the mysterious dogmas and historical records appear, on the contrary, to the compiler to contain not only the essence of all that is necessary to instruct mankind in their civil duties, but also the best and only means of obtaining the forgiveness of sins, the favour of God and strength to overcome our passions and to keep his commandments.[30]

It is significant that in contrast to many other Indian thinkers who came after him, he is attracted more by the Synoptic Gospels with their emphasis on Jesus' teachings than by the Gospel of St John with its meditations on Jesus and similarity to traditional *bhakti* or mystic religious experience; and his extracts are almost totally from the Synoptic Gospels. Rammohan Roy says that 'nothing but the sublimity of the precepts of Jesus' first drew him to Jesus and it was evident that, in his understanding, knowledge of the moral law had in it its own power to reconcile men to God and empower them to lead the moral life.

It was the doctrine of the sufficiency of law to justify and sanctify men, implied in Rammohan Roy's conscious omission of the historical and doctrinal parts of the Gospels in *The Precepts of Jesus*, that Marshman wanted to challenge, to point out man's need of grace, the act of God in Jesus Christ, to atone and reconcile man to God, and to enable him to live the moral law. The concern of Marshman indeed was right.[31] Marshman gives the impression however that the doctrines of the Deity and Atonement of Jesus Christ, which he rightly urges as central to the Christian religion, stand in a way separate from the moral teachings. At least the point that his concern for salvation in Christ is integrally related to the moral life and its problems at depth is not well made, so that some of the arguments of Marshman must have appeared to Rammohan Roy as extraneous to his primary concern for a true moral life and as pushing him into religious and metaphysical speculation. Indeed this has always remained one of the dangers in the communication of the Gospel in India. Men awakened through the Gospel from the metaphysical to the ethical apprehension of reality as central, do not want to be deflected from the ethical field; the meaning of Jesus Christ must come to them in terms of the ethical; therefore the communication of the Gospel of salvation has to be in terms of the nature and fulfilment of the moral life. The Gospel as salvation and the

Gospel as ethics cannot be separated, even from a purely evangelistic point of view. Indeed, many Indians have come to accept Jesus Christ as Saviour precisely through the Sermon on the Mount, which has awakened them not only to a new moral law but also to the prophetic awareness of the tragedy inherent in the law and the need of man for divine redemption and God's answer in the Gospel of Jesus Christ.

To give examples, Nehemiah Goreh's conversion to Christ was the culmination of a process which began with his being 'much struck by the beauty of Christ's teaching, and example, especially by the doctrines of the Sermon on the Mount'.[32] Mathura Nath Bose began his pilgrimage to Christ with *The Precepts of Jesus* compiled by Rammohan Roy. S. K. Datta gives the story of how, at the Brahmo Samaj, Bose

heard extracts read from a book compiled by the founder, Rammohan Roy, and they seemed to bring to him a spiritual message. He obtained a copy and read it with great eagerness. The work was entitled *The Precepts of Jesus, the Guide to Life* and contained voluminous extracts from the Sermon of the Mount. He found Christ and was baptized after two years of consideration and preparation.[33]

In the case of the Christian poet of Maharashtra, Narayana Vamana Tilak, also, the first impact came from the Sermon on the Mount, in which he found 'answers to the most abstruse problems of Hindu philosophy'; and saw that 'the most profound problems were completely solved'. And among the five points in Jesus Christ which appealed to Tilak two or three of them were related to his ethical humanity:

Five points in regard to Jesus Christ impressed me deeply. First, I found in Him the ideal man, Second, it is He, and He alone, who makes love to God and to man of the same importance. Third, His perfect identification with His Father. Fourth, His inconceivable faith in Himself as the life and light of the world. Fifth His Cross and the whole story of His crucifixion.[34]

It is not an uncommon development for a Hindu to go through the moral ideal of Jesus to the secret of his personality and his work of salvation. Indeed Rammohan Roy himself gives a piece of advice to the missionaries in this connection: 'It has been owing to their beginning with the introduction of mysterious dogmas and relations that at first sight appear incredible that notwithstanding every exertion on the part of our divines', few Muslims and Hindus are converted to the Christian religion.[35] Rammohan Roy's insight has to be seriously taken into account. In fact Marshman himself sees the truth that the teaching of Jesus bears the imprint of salvation in Christ, that 'the most obnoxious of all the dogmas of Christianity' are contained in 'the teaching of Jesus himself' and that emptied of these doctrines, his teaching does not have 'truth sufficient to form a teacher'.[36] In the controversy Marshman does not seem to follow this path of digging into morality to its spiritual dimension.

When we come to discuss the development of the understanding of Jesus Christ in Keshub Chunder Sen and P. C. Mozoomdar in the Brahmo Samaj itself, we shall see a deeper movement from the Teachings to the Teacher, though they do not make the whole pilgrimage as the poet Tilak did. And it is significant that Manilal C. Parekh, who from the impact of the theology of Rammohan Roy, Keshub Chunder Sen and P. C. Mozoomdar went through to the reality of salvation in Jesus Christ, has the following comment to make on Rammohan Roy's stopping at the precepts of Jesus.

There is not the least doubt that the Precepts of Jesus commend themselves easily and spontaneously to the mind of unsophisticated humanity as no other system of morality does.... But the main question is whether this is the whole of Christianity. From the very first, whether it was due to these unsurpassable or unequalled 'words' of his, or to his 'works', these miracles of mercy which he performed as a part of his daily life, or to the manner of his speaking his 'words' and doing his 'works', that 'authority' with which he spoke, and that 'grace and truth' with which his Person was full, or whether it was due to all these combined, each contributing its share to the general result, there is not the least doubt that the question as to his Person has been from the very first inextricably involved in that of his Precepts.... The question continually forced itself upon the mind of both his friends and enemies as to who he was, as we learn from not one but all the four Gospels. It was on this question that his disciples staked their all and followed him, and that Jesus himself staked his all, even his life as well as the future of his work. He sealed the Precepts with his blood and through the love that he thus showed invested them with not only that authority but even divine power, without which they would have been but a dead letter or what is worse an infinitude of burden which no human being could bear for a moment.[37]

For Marshman, the deity of Jesus Christ and his work of atonement provide what Parekh calls 'authority' and even 'divine power' to his moral teachings.[38] On the whole, however, he sees it in the reverse order. He looks at the excellence of the moral teachings of Jesus primarily as a proof of the doctrine of salvation through Christ; and therefore as having a secondary instrumental character. His evangelicalism is challenged to find that Rammohan Roy gives priority to the moral rather than the doctrinal, that Rammohan Roy's book

instead of [exhibiting these precepts] . . . as affording indubitable proof of the authenticity of its narratives and the reasonableness and importance of its doctrines, were in reality separated from that Gospel of which they form so important a part, and held up as forming of themselves the way of life, an idea which perverts the grand design of the Gospel and frustrates the grace of God in the salvation of man, the apostolic axiom applying with as great force now as ever, 'If righteousness comes by the law, Christ is dead in vain.'[39]

And he sums up the two 'leading doctrines of the New Testament' thus:

That God views all sin as so abominable that the death of Jesus Christ alone can expiate its guilt; and that the human heart is so corrupt that it must be renewed by the Divine Spirit before a man enter heaven. . . . Without these two dogmas, what is the Gospel?[40]

The primary concern is here formulated as to how to 'enter heaven', while Rammohan Roy's was 'peace and happiness' in earthly existence. There was a connection. But it was not properly made by Marshman.

4. THE PERSON AND WORK OF CHRIST

The main theological issue in the controversy centres round the doctrine of the person and work of Jesus Christ. As already stated, Marshman's emphasis on right doctrine is based not on love of speculative axioms or a formulated creed, but on their integral relation to salvation by faith in the saving grace of God in Jesus Christ. He approaches them as 'doctrines necessary for salvation'. Reference has already been made to the eloquent passage in which he makes explicit the unsystematic character of theological beliefs in the Bible, and the relation of belief to Christian existence. It is worth quoting in full here:

The evidence given in Scripture to the existence of the Triune God, the Deity of the Son, and the Atonement of Christ for the sons of men, is to be found less in definition and simple declaration, than as interwoven in precepts and commands, which is the case even with that which relates to the being of God, all these doctrines being intended less for speculation than for that faith and cordial obedience which renovate the heart and produce the fruits of righteousness.[41]

Marshman would have been on sound theological grounds if he kept to this insight into the functional and therefore flexible character of Christian doctrines. The tragedy was that he sought to impose a whole systematically formulated creed in all its fullness as necessary for salvation and righteousness. Actually the Christological and Trinitarian dogmas he was defending were those which came to their present form in the course of many centuries after the New Testament period; but Marshman sought to defend the credal definitions themselves as being given in the Bible. They certainly may be defended as an expression of and growth from the biblical faith or as preserving it, but, by defending those formulations as contained in the Bible and therefore absolutely necessary for salvation, Marshman failed to distinguish between the responses of faith, seeking to express itself in unsystematic formulations in the Bible, and the formulations of systematic theology which developed later. This had two results. Marshman's defence identified faith-response with assent to doctrines and thereby suppressed whatever faith-response to Jesus Christ existed in Rammohan Roy. Secondly, it pushed Rammohan Roy into premature definition of the 'nature' of Jesus Christ. As we have already said, he was moving away from the metaphysical to the moral and rational. He did not come to recognize the historical dimension of faith, which would make it possible for him to speak of an act of God in history. And he reacts to the pressure of Marshman in the debate with two parallel approaches, first by affirming his moral interpretation which becomes moralistic in self-defence; and second by falling back on the ontological categories of Deism. This probably hindered Rammohan Roy from digging through the moral to the historical-prophetic interpretation of God, Christ and Salvation.

Writing to a friend in September 1820, Rammohan Roy gives his reaction to the first stage of the controversy as an unfortunate journey into incomprehensible metaphysics. After indicating that he never attempted to oppose Christian dogmas presented in liberal terms, he says:

> I regret only that the followers of Jesus, in general, should have paid much greater attention to enquiries after his nature than to the observance of his commandments, when we are well aware that no human acquirements can ever discover the nature even of the most common and visible things and moreover that such enquiries are not enjoined by the divine revelation.[42]

Of course, it is clear that Rammohan Roy here confuses the soteriological-historical dimension of life with the mystical-metaphysical dimension which he rejects, nor does he see it as related in any sense to the depths of the rational-moral dimension which he accepts. Indeed he had scrupulously avoided using the Gospel of John in his *Precepts*, because of its mystical-metaphysical character; it is only to reply to Marshman that he is compelled to give his own exegesis of several passages of that Gospel.

It may be useful at this stage to survey briefly the theological content of Rammohan Roy's understanding of Jesus Christ and the points at which Marshman found it necessary to oppose him.

The basic debate revolves round the affirmation of Marshman that 'Jesus is Jehovah God' and the manner in which the deity or divinity of the man Jesus of Nazareth is understood.

A. *Marshman's 'Seven Positions'*

Marshman advances 'seven positions' on the authority of the Scriptures to prove the deity of Jesus, and all these seven are refuted by the Raja on his own exegesis of the same Scripture passages used by Marshman. Marshman's seven positions are summarized by Rammohan Roy as follows:

1. That Jesus was possessed of ubiquity, an attribute peculiar to God alone.
2. That he declared that a knowledge of his nature was equally incomprehensible with that of the nature of God.

3. That he exercised the power of forgiving sins, the peculiar prerogative of God.
4. That he claimed almighty power 'in the most unequivocal manner'.
5. That his heavenly Father had committed to him the final judgment of all who have lived since the creation.
6. That he received worship due to God alone.
7. That he associated his own name with that of God the Father in the sacred rite of baptism.[43]

They are intended to prove the divinity of Jesus of Nazareth by showing that Jesus as he lived on earth as man was omniscient, omnipotent and omnipresent. Here, of course, Marshman, is clearly affirming the divinity of Jesus at the cost of denying in Jesus the limitations of finiteness, human growth and spiritual dependence on God, which are basic to his full humanity. In fact, the exegesis to prove his seven arguments is extremely strained; and the Raja had no difficulty in puncturing them on the authority of Scripture itself. The arguments to and fro are too uninteresting and monotonous to be given here in full detail. As an example we shall summarize the basic points in relation to the first position of Marshman.

He asserted that 'no being possesses ubiquity but God Himself', and Jesus had it. Did not Jesus tell Nicodemus that the Son of Man who is talking to Nicodemus at the same time *'is* in heaven' (John 3.13). Or again, Jesus says 'Where two or three are gathered together in my name, there *am I* in the midst of them.' In both these, Jesus claims omnipresence. Rammohan Roy contends that, in the Bible, there is frequent use of the present tense which must be understood in the past or the future tense e.g., John 11.8: 'Before Abraham was *I am*' (to be understood as past tense); John 16.32: 'Ye shall be scattered every man to his own, and shall leave me alone, yet *I am* not alone' (to be understood as future tense). There are many passages where Jesus himself speaks of his own coming from God and going to God, descent from heaven and ascent to heaven of the Son of Man, for instance, John, 6.62; 16.7; 5.28; 13.36, etc. He contends that 'the attribute of omnipresence is quite inconsistent with the human notion of the ascent and descent effected by the Son of Man'. He further argues from Greek linguistic practice and gives his own translation of the passage thus: 'And no one except the descender from heaven, the Son of Man, the being in heaven, hath ascended unto heaven.' The claim of ubiquity in Matt. 18.20 is similar to that claimed for Moses and the prophets in Luke 16.21, where it is said, 'They have Moses and the prophets'.[44]

In reply Marshman expresses his gladness that Raja Rammohan Roy approves the pre-existence of Jesus in heaven and asks him how he could interpret it except in terms of his eternal deity. Further he says that the Scripture speaks of Jehovah also as coming and going (Gen. 11.5; 8.33).

A little further acquaintance with the Scriptures might have convinced him that Jehovah, who upholdeth all things by the word of his power, can never be absent from any place, and that when he is said to descend to any particular place, it is meant that he then manifests his presence in a more evident manner than in other places.

He does not see any inconsistency therefore between omnipresence and the idea of God's descent and ascent. 'He who upholds all things must necessarily be present with all things.' He also seeks to counter the argument from grammar.

Were this criticism perfectly correct, it would not be of the least service to the author as 'he being in heaven' is precisely the same as 'he who is in heaven'. . . . The fact is that John is more accurate in the choice of his participles than even our English translators.

In many of the passages, the rendering of the present sense in a past tense would make for 'consummate absurdity, not to say falsehood of doctrine and fact'. Regarding the presence of Moses and the prophets, it is certainly the presence of 'the writings', but Jesus could not have meant any of his writings; it is his own presence that is intended.[45]

To this Rammohan Roy replies in detail supporting his arguments still further with more scriptural passages. As for the pre-existence of Jesus, he interprets it in terms of I Peter 1.20 and II Tim 1.7, but he does not see any eternal deity in pre-existence.

B. *The Natural Inferiority of the Son to the Father*

The proof of this point is the core of Rammohan Roy's argument.

(i) *The Son Dependent and Subject*

Jesus was dependent and subject as Son to the Father. Rammohan Roy says:

For, admitting for a moment that the positions of the Editor [i.e. Marshman] are well founded, and that the Saviour was in possession of attributes and powers ascribed to God; have we not his own express and often repeated avowal that all the powers he manifested were committed to him as the Son by the Father of the Universe? And does not reason force us to infer that a being who owes to another all his power and authority, however extensive and high, should be in reality considered inferior to that other? Surely therefore, those who believe God to be supreme, possessing the perfection of all attributes, independently of all other beings, must necessarily deny the identity of Christ with God.

And he gives passages specially from the Gospel of John 'to illustrate the entire dependence of the Son of God and his inferiority and subjection to and his living by him'. He quotes I Cor. 15.24–28 to show that when all things are subjected to Christ, God is excepted, and that, in the end, the Son shall deliver the Kingdom to the Father and shall himself be subject to God that God may be all in all – as clearly indicating dependence and inferiority of the Son in relation to the Father. He translates Col. 1.15 as 'the image of the invisible God, the first-born of every *creature*'. According to Rammohan Roy these passages show Jesus 'as the Messiah, Christ or anointed Son of God', and not God himself.

Jesus spoke of himself throughout all the Scriptures only as the promised Messiah, vested with high glory from the beginning of the world (John 17.5; 6.24; 9.35–37; 17.1, 2; 1.34, 42). ... and in numerous passages Jesus declares that before he assumed the office of the Messiah in the world, he was entirely subject to and obedient to the Father, from whom he received the commission to come to this world for the salvation of mankind.... he tells them (John 14.28): 'The Father is greater than I.'[46]

(ii) *Unity of Will, not identity of Being*

Rammohan Roy defines the unity between God and Jesus 'as a subsisting concord of will and design ... and not identity of being'. The words 'I and my Father are one' should be defined in terms of 'that they may be one as we are one' (John 10.30; 17.11, 20–23). 'The Saviour meant unity in design and will by the assertion also, that he was in God or dwelt in God and God in him (John 10.38).' Here Rammohan Roy says that once we grant that the unity of God and Christ is of the same character as Christ and his apostles, there are only three choices left for defining the unity:

First as conveying the doctrine that the Supreme Being, the Son and the Apostles were to be absorbed mutually as drops of water into one whole; which is conformable to the doctrine of that sect of Hindu metaphysics who maintain that in the end the human soul is absorbed into the Godhead, but is quite inconsistent with the faith of all denominations of Christians.

Secondly, as proving an identity of nature, with distinction of person, between the Father, the Son and the Apostles, a doctrine equally inconsistent with the belief of every Christian, as multiplying the number of persons of the Godhead far beyond what has ever been proposed by any sect.

Thirdly, as expressing that unity which is said to exist wherever there are found perfect concord, harmony, love and obedience such as the Son evinced towards the Father, and taught the disciples to display towards the Divine will. That the language of the Saviour can be understood in this last sense solely, will, I trust, be readily acknowledged by every candid expounder of the sacred writings, as being the only one alike warranted by the common use of words, and capable of apprehension by the human understanding.[47]

(iii) *Mediator and Messiah as First-Born of Creatures*

To Rammohan Roy therefore, Jesus is 'the first-born of every creature' pre-existing in heaven with God, and sent to the earth as the Christ or the Messiah. Thus

the epithet Son of God with the definite article prefixed is appropriate to Christ, the first-born of every creature, as a distinct mark of honour which he alone deserves.[48]

He ends the chapter on the 'Natural Inferiority of the Son' by declaring his faith in Jesus Christ as pre-existent (i.e. as existing from the beginning of time) himself being the first-born of creatures, and supreme above all creatures including the angels.[49]

The Scriptures indeed in several places declare that the Son was superior even to the angels in heaven living from the beginning of the world to eternity, and that the Father created all things by him and for him. At the same time, I must, in conformity to those very authorities, believe him as produced by the Supreme Deity among created Beings (John 5.26, Col. 1.15).[50]

c. *Marshman's Defence and the Raja's Rejoinder*

At the heart of his theology, Marshman is concerned with proving that God alone and no creature, even if he is first-born, can atone for man's sin and reconcile man to Him; it is this that compels him to defend the thesis that Jesus Christ is by nature, not by adoption or achievement, God. He puts the question this way:

> ... Divine justice required a sacrifice through whom God *could be just*, while the justifier of the sinner ... the blood of no mere creature could take away sin. We are *solemnly assured* that it was Jehovah, the unchangeable God, the Creator of heaven and earth, for whom the Father prepared a body ... that it is Jehovah who is our righteousness and in whom the seed of Israel are justified and glory – and who being King of God's spiritual Israel, rules in the hearts as the omniscient and almighty saviour.... The sole question then is, whether the Son be *by nature God*, bringing omnipotence, omniscience and omnipresence to his work as well as infinite rectitude and mercy – or whether he be a mere creature, elevated to a state to which by nature he had not the least right. In other words, did he *humble himself* by becoming in our nature the Mediator between God and man, or did he by this act *really exalt himself* and attain a rank in the universe for which his original nature furnished him with neither pretension nor capacity.[51]

Marshman goes through the expectations of the Messiah in the Pentateuch, the Psalms and the Prophets and their fulfilment in the New Testament to give evidence for his thesis that Jesus is 'Jehovah God'; and then he passes on to an examination of the main arguments of Rammohan Roy given in the chapter on 'The Natural Inferiority of the Son to the Father'.

(i) *The Son's Nature and Office*

Were not all the powers manifested by Jesus 'committed to him as the Son by the Father of the Universe?', Rammohan Roy had asked. Marshman replies:

> To this we at once answer: *No*. That he was appoined by the Father to act as Mediator between Him and sinners, we have already seen.... But that he even as Mediator possessed a single power, perfection, or attribute which was not eternally inherent in his Divine Nature, we ... deny.

The distinction between the mediatorial 'office' given to him and his inherent eternal divine 'nature' is basic for Marshman. For the sake of the former the Son had to 'empty himself of his glory by assuming our nature; and his mediatorial kingdom is only for a season'; the Father's glorifying the Son is giving him the glory which by nature belonged to him; and it is the 'mediatorial kingdom' which he delivers up to his Father in I Cor. 15.[52] Though he does not like to substitute human arguments for scriptural testimony, he is forced to give two analogies:

1. Among men the son may be inferior to the father in years, in knowledge, in office, but a *oneness of nature* with his father he must possess. Our question is indeed only about the *nature* of the Son.[53]
2. Common sense can easily understand how one *equal in nature* to another may yet be *subordinate in office*.[54]

To this, Rammohan Roy answers by showing the inconsistencies between 'any rational idea of the nature of the Deity' and God being subject to God to act the part of the Mediator. He asks

whether it is not most foreign to the notion of the immutable God, that circumstances could produce such a change in the condition of the Deity, as that he should have not only been divested of his glory for more than thirty years, but even subjected to servitude? Are not the ideas of supreme dominion and that of subjection, just as remote as the east from the west. Yet, the Editor says, that while he was stripping himself of his glory, and taking upon himself the form of a servant, he was just as much Jehovah as before.[55]

And he goes on to show that 'the peculiar attributes of God' like supremacy, omnipotence, omniscience were never ascribed to Jesus in the Scripture (Matt. 20.23; 26.23; John 11.41; Mark 13.32). He adds that even in the creed of the orthodox Trinitarians, God alone is 'described as self-existent having proceeded from none', while the Son is 'represented as proceeding from the Father'. And he gives more scriptural passages to prove the 'subordination' of Jesus to God and asks whether they 'do not prove the entire humanity of the Son, or a complete change in his divine nature, if he was ever possessed of it'.

The Editor may perhaps say, after the example of his orthodox friends, that these as well as other sayings to the same effect proceeded from Jesus in his human capacity; I shall then entreat the Editor to show me any authority of the Scriptures, distinguishing one class of sayings of Jesus Christ as man, from another set of the same author as God. Supposing Jesus was of a two-fold nature, divine and human, as the Editor believes him to be, his divine nature in this case, before his appearance in this world, must be acknowledged perfectly pure and unadulterated by humanity. But after he had become incarnate, according to the Editor, was he not made of a mixed nature, God and man, possessing at one time both opposite sorts of consciousness and capacity? Was there not a *change of a pure nature into a mixed one*?[56]

His exegesis of Phil. 2 is also relevant in order to understand Rammohan Roy. He makes a clear distinction between 'being in the form of God' and 'being God'. The form does not involve essence. But if 'form of God' and 'form of a servant' both refer to essences, then it means 'that Christ was possessed of the real essence of God and the real essence of a servant. How can we reconcile real Godhead with real servitude, even for a moment?'[57]

Indeed what the Raja rejects absolutely is the belief in incarnation, either one or many, because he cannot see it except as idolatry, doing violence to the unity of the Godhead, and 'the immense distance between the human and divine nature'. This is the basic foundation of all his approaches to religion. Writing under his pseudonym Sivaprasad Sarma in the *Brahminical Magazine* he asks,

Is it conformable to the nature of *the Supreme Ruler* of the universe *to take the form of a servant*, though only for a season? Is this the true idea of God which the Editor maintains? Even idolators among Hindus have more plausible excuses for their polytheism ... both of them being equally and solely protected by the shield of mystery.[58]

And in this context he sees Trinitarian Christianity as expressing 'ideas of divine nature so gross' as to be able to 'consider God as having been born, circumcised, as having grown, and been subject to parental authority, as eating and drinking, and even as dying, and as having been totally annihilated (though for three days only; the period intervening from the crucifixion of Christ to his resurrection)'.[59] And the question is, how anyone can believe 'that an object confined to a small portion of the earth comprehends literally all the fulness of the Deity bodily and spreads over the whole universe'.[60] It is similar to a Hindu's belief in his Thakor, since both are 'founded on the same sacred basis viz. the manifestation of God in the flesh'.[61]

(ii) *Unity of Nature, Distinction of Persons*

Regarding the three alternatives (1) monism without distinction, (2) unity of nature with distinction of persons, (3) unity of will, which Raja Rammohan Roy sets forth in his exegesis of the verse 'I and my Father are one', Marshman chooses the second with a clear understanding of the difference between the nature of Christ's unity with the Father and that of the unity of Christians in Christ.

The oneness which Christ prayed they might obtain was a oneness among themselves in Him and his heavenly Father, of which he proposed the union between himself and his Father as the grand exemplar.

He goes to affirm that even the unity of Christians in Christ is not merely that of will and design but of nature, and redeemed human nature:

Does not this very comparison necessarily imply a *Oneness of Nature* between the Father and the Son? What is the basis of that union between the followers of Christ which he prayed might become as perfect as that between the Son and the Father? Is it not a common human nature? Further, what completes their perfect union as Christians? Is it not their partaking of *one renewed nature* – nay, is it not their union perfected in exact proportion as they *equally* partake of this renewed nature? ... Instead of proving our author's point, therefore, this passage decidedly proves that, with a Distinctness of Person, the most perfect Equality of Nature, essence and holiness must subsist between the Father and the Son. They are equally Jehovah, equally righteous and holy.[62]

To this Rammohan Roy answers:

Jesus could not mean in praying for his apostles (v. 11) an unity in nature among them whence we might have inferred unity in nature between him and his God; since they were long before this prayer created in the one human nature; nor could he pray for a renewed spiritual nature to be given to them (as the Editor thinks to be the case), because they were already endowed with that spiritual union, as is evident from the passage of the very chapter (17.6, 8, 16, 22). ... Besides, unity in spiritual nature is not the same kind of unity which subsists between the individuals of one nature. By the unity so prayed for, cannot be meant anything else than unity of will and design. Although that unity may not be of the same degree that subsisted between him and the Father, yet the force of the conjunction 'as' shews that it is of the same kind.[63]

(iii) *First-born, not First-created*

Marshman quotes Dr Owen's argument against Unitarianism,

based on the Colossian passage, which speaks of 'first-born' and not 'first-created'; so that

Christ is so the *first-born* as to be the *only begotten* Son of God, He is so the first-born of every creature, that he is *before* them all, *above* them all, *heir* to them all, and so *no one* of them.[64]

And Marshman rhetorically asks how a creature could be the mediator of all creation and the Saviour and Judge of all mankind according to the witness of the Scriptures.

How was it that he did not feel struck with the absurdity of a *creature's* creating all things and upholding them by the word of his power – of a *creature's* being the God of Abraham, Isaac and Jacob – of the highest archangels being commanded to worship a *creature* – of the Father, declaring a *creature* Jehovah, the immutable God – of a *creature's* declaring himself the Almighty, the searcher of hearts?[65]

Marshman gives an exegesis of the first chapter of St John's Gospel to show how the apostle gives there 'that fulness of evidence respecting Christ's deity and humanity which will never be successfully impugned to the end of time'.

The very first clause, 'In the beginning was the Word' ... demonstrates his Godhead, he who is necessarily existent from eternity being the Eternal God. His distinct *personality* is then shown, 'the Word was *with* God'; and lastly his *Deity*, 'the Word was God'. But the apostle does not stop here; he demonstrates his Divine Nature from his *works*. 'All things were made by him and without him was not anything made that was made.' He then describes his *Humanity*, 'The Word was made flesh and dwelt among us and we beheld his glory, the glory as of the *Only* begotten of the Father', thus drawing a line of infinite distinction between him and all others termed the sons of God. This passage alone is an answer to everything relative to Christ's being subordinate to the Father, his growing in knowledge etc. If he condescended to be made flesh, it became him to become an infant of days, and to be in all things like unto us, yet without sin.[66]

It is relevant at this point also to introduce the conversion of one of the Serampore missionaries, William Adam by name, to Unitarianism, through the discussions he had with Yates and Rammohan Roy on the translation of the third verse of the first chapter of the Gospel of John. This is how Collet gives the story.

At first, Dr Yates agreed to translate 'All things were made *through* him', but by the next session of the Committee he had discovered in the substitution of *through* for *by* a suggestion of Arianism and on the following day withdrew from the enterprise altogether on account of the tendency toward heresy which had transpired. During these discussions Mr Adam tells us, Rammohan Roy 'sat pen in hand, in dignified reticence, looking on, listening, observing all, but saying nothing'. This project and the manner of its termination naturally drew 'heretic' and 'heathen' into an intimacy more frequent and confidential, with the result that Mr Adam finally renounced his belief in the doctrine of Trinity and avowed himself a Unitarian.[67]

As for Rammohan Roy, he will go so far as to accept that Jesus was Messiah, in the sense of the supreme messenger of God, who 'lived in the divine purpose and decree', but definitely as creature, not Creator. Even supposing that the doctrine is true that

he like Adam lived with God before his coming into this world . . . and afterwards was sent to the world in the body of Jesus, for effecting human salvation . . ., this does not preclude us from rejecting the idea of a twofold nature of God and man.[68]

The doctrine of Jesus as the unfallen Adam, incarnate to save mankind, is suggested here. But the one point he would not compromise is his conviction of the creation of the Son in the beginning, as contrasted with his eternal generation. He would have admitted

that the Son of God is God in the same way as the son of a man is man,

if it was not coupled with the assertion of the coeval existence or

equal duration of the Son with the Father; for every son, whatever may be his nature, must have existence originating subsequently to that of his own father.[69]

(iv) *The Atonement*

This brings us to the controversy about the atonement. The different elements contained in this doctrine as seen by Marshman relate to Jesus' *expiating sin by his death*, his giving life to those who believe on him, his interceding with God for sinners and his forming of the *only medium* through which man can approach God.

For Marshman the doctrine of the atonement 'follows' that of the deity of Jesus Christ. The question revolves round the meaning of the word 'Saviour', as used by Rammohan Roy and Marshman. Marshman asks:

Is [Jesus Christ] called the Saviour of men because he gave them moral precepts by obeying which they might obtain the Divine favour, with the enjoyment of heaven as their just desert; or because he died in their stead, to atone for their sins and procure for them every blessing, even his Spirit to enable them to trust in his death and merits for salvation, and from a principle of love cordially obey his precepts to the end of life?

Evidently he stands for the second meaning. If he is only a Teacher we must honour Moses more, since 'it was in reality *his* law that [Jesus] explained and established'.[70] The Raja replies by saying that though St Paul speaks of the powerlessness of the law and the necessity of the Cross for 'righteousness', there is no 'single passage pronounced by Jesus enjoining a refuge in such a doctrine of the cross, as all-sufficient and indispensable for salvation'. In his thinking, the 'the blessings of pardon' are available 'from the merciful Father through repentance, which is declared the only means of procuring forgiveness of our failures'.[71]

In his *Final Appeal* Rammohan Roy argues that the Old Testament prophets enjoin justice and mercy as more acceptable to God than sacrifices (Micah 6.7–8; Hos. 6.6; Isa. 1.11, 16–18 etc.). Therefore it would be more in keeping with the 'pure religion of Jesus' to understand the cross and the ideas of sacrifice in the New Testament in terms of

Jesus the spiritual Lord and King of Jews and Gentiles [exposing] his own life in fulfilment of the duties of his mission ... and [persevering] in executing the commands of God, even to the undergoing of bodily suffering in the miserable death of the cross – a self-devotion or sacrifice of which no Jewish high priest had offered an example.

To him, the several concepts of justice inherent in the doctrine of atonement are inadequate. For instance,

Would it be consistent with common notions of justice to afflict an innocent man with the death of the cross, for sins committed by others, even supposing the innocent man should voluntarily offer his life in behalf of those others?

In fact, the apostles' use of the categories of the sacrificial system is understandable because they had to speak to Jews in the religious language of the Jews of their day.

We may easily account for the adoption of the apostles, with respect to him, of such terms as sacrifice and atonement for sin, and their representing Jesus as the high priest, engaged to take away the sins of the world by means of his blood. These were modes of speech made use of in allusion to the sacrifices and blood-offerings which the Jews and their high priest used to make for the remission of sins; and the apostles wisely accommodated their instructions to the ideas and forms of language familiar to those whom they addressed.[72]

The task today is to recover the meaning of Jesus Christ from its accommodation to categories of the Jewish sacrificial system and translate it 'in a spiritual sense', [73] that is, in moral and rational terms. This is what Rammohan Roy has done.

(v) *The Trinity*

The subject of Trinity need not detain us a great deal. The main controversy between Rammohan Roy and the missionaries was on the deity and the atonement of Jesus Christ and only secondarily throughout on the doctrine of the Holy Spirit and consequently the doctrine of the Trinity.

In the *Second Appeal*, Rammohan Roy opposes Marshman's scriptural proofs for the personality and deity of the Holy Spirit and defines the Holy Spirit as synonymous with 'the prevailing influence of God'.[74] He sees no mention of the Holy Spirit in the primitive sermons of the apostles recorded in the Acts of the Apostles, and points out on the authority of

the *Ecclesiastical History* of Mosheim, a celebrated author among Trinitarians, ... that the doctrine of the Trinity, so zealously maintained as fundamental by the generality of modern Christians made not its appearance as an essential or even secondary article of Christian faith, until the commencement of the fourth century;

that till that time opinions about it were aired among Christian doctors 'with the utmost liberty'. He adds:

I beg leave to remark that if, in the first and purest ages of Christianity, the followers of Christ entertained such different opinions on the subject of the distinction between Father, Son and Holy Spirit, without incurring the charge of heresy and heterodoxy, and without even breaking the tie of Christian affection towards each other, it is a melancholy contrast that the same freedom of opinion on this subject is not now allowed, nor the same mental forbearance maintained among those who call themselves Christians.[75]

And he argues that the Council of Nicea may have favoured the doctrine of the Trinity, as an accommodation to the polytheism to which the Gentile converts in that age were accustomed.[76] He then takes up and refutes the modes of reasonings which Trinitarians use to support their faith as monotheistic.[77]

To this Marshman replies with more scriptural evidences establishing the personality and deity of the Holy Spirit and contends that 'the doctrine of the Ever-blessed Trinity needs no further confirmation: it follows of course.' He closes by citing three scriptural passages including one from Isa. 48 to 'bring the sacred Three fully into view'.

All that can be fairly deduced from Mosheim is that in the first three centuries, they had formed *no specific creed* but simply believed what the Scriptures revealed respecting the Sacred Three – precisely like the Editors of this article.[78]

The Raja follows with more arguments controverting Marshman and gives his own exegesis of the Trinitarian formula in II Cor. 13.13 as follows:

Here the apostle prays that the guidance of Jesus Christ, the love of God, and the constant operation of the holy influence of God, may be with Christians, since without the guidance of Jesus, no one can be thoroughly impressed with the love of the Deity under the Christian dispensation, nor can the love of God continue to exist unless preserved by divine influence.[79]

Rammohan Roy takes up the controversy further in the *Brahminical Magazine*. He summarizes the explanations of the theologians of the time on the Trinity and asks:

Are not these explanations . . . sufficient to puzzle any man, if not drive him to atheism? . . . If we set out on this irrational career where are we to stop?[80]

His answer to Marshman's final invitation to accept the doctrine of the Trinity may be quoted:

After I have long relinquished every idea of a plurality of gods or of the persons of the Godhead, taught under different systems of modern Hinduism, I cannot conscientiously and consistently embrace one of a similar nature, though greatly refined by the religious reformations of modern times; since whatever arguments can be adduced against a plurality of persons of the Godhead, and on the other hand whatever excuse may be pleaded in favour of a plurality of persons of the Deity, can be offered with equal propriety in defence of Polytheism.[81]

5. A CRITICAL EVALUATION

We have surveyed the content of the theologies of the Serampore missionaries and Raja Rammohan Roy as they have found expression in the controversy between them. They may be seen in part as the struggle of modern India to define the truth and meaning of Jesus Christ in terms relevant to its life and thought, and in part as the Church's witness to its faith in dialogue with a segment of the Indian mind. The history of the later development of the theology of the Brahmo Samaj and the Christian Church in India may be considered as containing within them their own critical evaluation, and attempts to correct them and surpass them. Nevertheless it is necessary for us to give a critical evaluation of them briefly from our standpoint.

The development of Brahmo theology, especially later by Keshub Chunder Sen, contained two criticisms of Rammohan Roy's position taken in the controversy. First, his secular approach to religion made him incapable of appreciating mystic spirituality and bhakti cults in any religion. Keshub introduced Chaitanya into Brahmo religious practice and gave it a new turn away from the Raja's dry rationalism and its total rejection of emotions in the exercise of religion. Secondly, the Raja's deistic or unitarian faith considered the idea of Divine incarnation (avatarism) in any religion as a compromise of monotheism and as an inevitable source of personal and social demoralization. Manilal C. Parekh, who came to a positive acceptance of Christianity and appreciation of its Trinitarian theology through Brahmoism, found in these two reactions of Keshub against the Raja's rational and moralist secularism a bridge to take him to Jesus Christ; and therefore in his own evaluation of Raja Rammohan Roy's theology he follows the lead of Keshub. He assails the Raja's rationalism as making for 'an inherent incapacity' to appreciate 'the mystic teaching' of St Paul and St John and 'even to understand their standpoint and vital experience which was behind it, much less accept it'.[82] As for the similarity between Hinduism and Christianity in their common doctrine of incarnation, 'instead of being a stumbling-block', which it was to the Brahmo Samaj, it is 'a stepping-stone to a real synthesis or harmony of the two faiths'. Parekh adds this significant autobiographical note:

> The present writer might add in all humility that in his own case the cycle has been completed inasmuch as in his spiritual development along the line of thought laid down by Keshub Chander Sen, it was through his study of Vaishnavaism, the spiritual school of Hinduism which believes in Incarnation, that he came to see the truth of the perfect Incarnation of God in Christ Jesus. While the similarity of the two faiths interested and attracted him to both of them, it was the dissimilarity between the two examples held out in both these as the supreme Incarnation that made him prefer Christianity to Vaishnavaism. This was undoubtedly due to the same ethical feeling which made Rammohan Roy even in this controversy take Ram as the typical Avatar and not Krishna, though Hinduism as a whole has looked upon the latter as the typical and perfect Avatar.[83]

Parekh thus seemed to have moved with Rammohan Roy's ethical concern into a new appreciation of the bhakti-mysticism and the idea of the divine incarnation, and come to a belief in Jesus Christ as the perfect incarnation of the one Holy God.

While the validity of Parekh's spiritual development and of his evaluation of Rammohan Roy's theology may be granted, we have to raise some questions in this connection. Firstly, does it mean that modern men imbued with the rational ethical secular temper like that of Rammohan Roy, cannot apprehend the truth and meaning of Jesus Christ unless they revert to a religious-mystical experience or version of reality? Is there not a path to understand and encounter Jesus Christ as the ground and salvation of reason and morality within a secular framework without a return to traditional religiosity? This is an important enquiry in modern Christian theology. Secondly, does not 'the ethical feeling' which made Rammohan Roy prefer Rama to Krishna as the perfect incarnation get weakened by the emphasis on 'religious faiths'. It is a moot question whether the eclectic religion of Keshub or the more Christ-centred inter-religious synthesis of Manilal Parekh has preserved the same ethical passion for personal holiness and social righteousness which characterized Rammohan Roy. Indeed as we shall see, the later writings of Parekh show a spirituality with a total accommodation to caste-system. It is possible to argue that the movement of return to mystic spirituality and avatarism under Keshub has not been an unmixed gain for the apprehension of the fullness of Jesus Christ by modern India.

In fact, in another comment on Rammohan Roy's rejection of the doctrines of the Atonement, the Deity of Jesus Christ and the Trinity, Manilal Parekh himself comes, to my mind, to the central issue which is the bridge between the rational moral temper and the reality of Jesus Christ, namely, love as the starting point and key of all Christology and theology. On atonement, Parekh says:

Love is the last term in the moral and religious vocabulary of man, and all true love logically ends [in] or is synonymous with sacrifice, and it is by this that the death of Jesus Christ has to be interpreted and understood. The Cross is the consummation of the life of Jesus, and it is by that that His whole life is to be understood and not *vice versa* as that would be explaining the higher by the lower. The vicarious death of Jesus is a new category in the religious thinking of the world and as such it explains not only his whole life better but gives a meaning to a very large part of the inner history of man, explaining at the same time the work of God therein.[84]

So also with the Incarnation and the Trinity:

... It was at this fundamental fact which is the foundation of Christianity' viz. God's humiliation of Himself in His love of man, that Rammohan Roy along with so many philosophers in the past as well as in the present stumbled. This was the rock of offence and a stone of stumbling to him. The same thing that is said of love with regard to atonement in the last paragraph may be said with regard to this also, and whether we think of Incarnation or Atonement which are the actions of God with regard to Man, or of the Trinity which pertains to the inner life of God within Himself, it is love that will supply the key wherewith we may open the secrets of these mysterious and wonderful problems. Such a verse as this, wherein it is said that 'he laid aside his glory and took on himself the form of a servant' can be understood only when one understands the true meaning of love. It is of its very essence to humiliate itself to come down and to go lower than the level of those who are its objects. St John says, God is love. He is Love more than Power, Wisdom etc. and it is of this inmost life and essence that we have the manifestation in the life and above all in the death of Christ Jesus.[85]

This statement of Parekh, it seems to me, could be the basis of a proper evaluation of the theology, not only of Raja Rammohan Roy but also of Marshman.

The Idea of God and Divine Nature

Rammohan Roy has its own distinctive theism as the starting point of all his theological reflections. It is a version of the idea of Brahman revised in the light of the philosophical categories of the natural theology of monotheism and rational Deism from the West, and conceives the moral law as the will of God. And he is seeking to interpret Jesus Christ in the light of this prior understanding of God and divine nature. Given the nature of an immutable God, transcending all creation and all creatures, and upholding them by his moral law, any kind of a dynamic of movement in God or from God to the world is ruled out. Within this framework of thought, Rammohan Roy can interpret the most spiritual unity between Jesus and God only as one of 'will and design'. This is the limit beyond which his philosophical monotheism will simply break down. We do not know whether this 'beyond' was possible for Rammohan Roy himself. But if it ever came, it could come only by digging into the nature of morality and God and their relation in terms essentially of love. This would have meant a new vision of the centrality of the Cross of Jesus Christ, at least as the symbol of God in the midst of mankind, and probably leading to a fuller faith in Jesus as God's self-disclosure to man.

Marshman himself did not help in this process. He could not. In the first place, as Collet has said, he identified faith-response to Christ with a set of rigid doctrines. Theoretically he did not do this. He himself says that in the first centuries Christians 'had formed no specific creed' and that in the New Testament the doctrinal assumptions are flexible and mixed in an unsystematic way with moral and spiritual teachings and commands. But in practice he was too rigid and identified saving faith with assent to a 'specific creed'. In the second place, Marshman's own ideas of God and divine nature were a mixture of the Old Testament concepts of the 'unchangeable Jehovah', 'the Eternal I Am', 'Jehovah God, Creator of the universe' and the philosophical concepts of classical theism, embedded in the creeds of the Church. This was in one sense inevitable, but instead of correcting his concept of God and the divine nature, by the life, death and resurrection of Jesus Christ, he sought to define the divinity of Jesus Christ by the norms of divinity he had from elsewhere. And in so doing he could not see love as belonging to the central essence of the Godhead. So he directed all his arguments to prove that Jesus the Incarnate Son still possessed omnipotence, omniscience and omnipresence, rather than to affirm that the self-emptying and self-sacrificing love of Christ Jesus was itself the disclosure of the nature of divinity as Love, and that the other aspects of divinity, omniscience, omnipotence and omnipresence themselves, must be interpreted in the light of Christ in terms of Infinite Being in Love. Marshman seems in many places to interpret the incarnation of the Son almost as a suspension rather than as a disclosure of divinity. He says:

The season when he laid aside his glory and took on himself the form of a servant, was not the fittest to furnish proofs of his Deity; since his infinite love and faithfulness would constrain him to act perfectly as a servant, a character as opposite to that of deity, to which belongs supreme dominion, as the east is to the west. Hence while thus emptying himself of his glory he of course gave no further indication of his deity than circumstances absolutely required.[86]

No doubt, servanthood and dominion, infinite love and divine sovereignty are opposed to each other in many theistic conceptions. But is it necessarily so in the Christian understanding of God as the Father of our Lord Jesus Christ, as Almighty Love? Here certainly, Marshman's dominant concept of omnipotence is not integrally related to the Cross of Christ. Or is he being influenced a little too much by the tradition of interpreting the *kenosis* in Phil. 2, as a giving up of divine glory.[87] Certainly at other sundry places, Marshman is conscious that the infinite love disclosed in Christ is itself an epiphany of Christ's divinity; but looking at the whole controversy, he puts it almost as an afterthought, and also as separate from the genuine divinity of Christ which he seeks to defend in terms of omniscience, omnipotence and omnipresence. The following passage shows him vacillating between interpreting incarnation as sacrifice and as revelation of divine glory:

Still while thus incarnate, he was the Almighty Creator, upholding all things by the Word of his power. In thus condescending to lay aside his glory and dwell in clay, indeed, he demonstrated his Godhead no less by his Almighty love and pity than by his Almighty power and wisdom, in creating and upholding all things.[88]

But he knows that the humble Christian comes to the knowledge of Christ's divinity intuitively through his experience of divine love in salvation. In his closing pages he not only combines omniscience with love but even goes as far as to define omni-attributes in terms of love:

The humble Christian at the present day, who has perhaps never heard a single argument formally advanced in support of his Deity, lives almost intuitively on his Saviour as God over all blessed for evermore. His omniscience, his omnipresence, and almighty power, his infinite love, his boundless mercy and pity are ever present to his mind. He realizes his Great Intercessor with the Father as acquainted with his inmost thoughts his most secret desires, as sending him help in every time of trouble, as strengthening his faith, his hope, his love, his godly fear and forming him after his own image.[89]

This approach of interpreting omni-attributes in terms of love is present also in the body of the *Defence*. But he does not make it the foundation of his Christology. Principal S.K. Rudra of St Stephen's College, Delhi, writing in 1911, saw this essential connection between Divine Glory and Christ's humility most clearly. He says:

The Pauline statement that Christ emptied himself of His divine glory is equally true and parallel with the Johannine statement that when the 'Word became flesh and dwelt among us, we beheld His glory, the glory as of the only-begotten of the Father full of grace and truth.' The humiliation, the weakness, the Cross, are to the Christian the exhibition of the mystery and the majesty of the Eternal God. The ultimate conception of God is not in terms of power and force, not in terms such as 'the Unknown, the Unknowable', but in terms of the humiliation of the Cross, in terms of deathless love, for God is love.[90]

The significance of much of the modern theological ferment lies precisely in interpreting the *kenosis* of Jesus not as an emptying of divinity but of the self to disclose true divinity of love. To quote a modern writer; Bishop J. A. T. Robinson:

It is in Jesus, and Jesus alone, that there is nothing of self to be seen, but solely the ultimate, unconditional love of God. It is as he emptied himself utterly of himself that he became the carrier of 'the name which is above every name', the revealer of the Father's glory – for that name and that glory is simply Love. The 'kenotic' theory of Christology based on this conception of self-emptying is, I am persuaded, the only one that offers much hope of relating at all satisfactorily the divine and the human in Christ.[91]

At this point probably we are criticizing not Marshman, but the classical formulations of Christology which sought to conceive Christ in terms of the categories of classical theism. As Schubert Ogden has shown in *The Reality of God*, the philosophical theism so far used to define Christology has suffered from the inability to combine supreme dominion with infinite love, otherness with infinite relatedness. Marshman does not therefore stand alone in his difficulties of interpreting Jesus Christ. And having pushed the controversy to the extent of making Rammohan Roy commit himself to a sort of Unitarianism or Arianism, he had no choice except to answer it, because more than the future of a doctrine, the substance of faith itself, was at stake.

In so doing however, Marshman was not true to the insights of the Nicene Fathers, regarding the distinctive way in which they spoke of Jesus as God, differentiating him from God the Father. Raja Rammohan Roy himself remarks that Marshman's 'frequent repetition of such phrase as "Jesus is Jehovah God" '[92] cannot carry conviction in a discussion within the categories of classical theism, which are more or less assumed by the two parties. Indeed Rammohan Roy rightly points out that Marshman is overlooking the Nicene creed which describes God as 'self-existent, having proceeded from none' and represents 'the Son as proceeding from the Father', thus ascribing 'the attributes of self-existence to the Father of the Universe alone'.[93] What the fathers affirmed was that 'while the Word is *true God*, he is *God from God*, God eternally begotten by God unbegotten'.[94] Yates in refusing to translate John 1.3 as 'All things were made *through* him' instead of '*by* him' indicates that the Serampore missionaries were not prepared to make the distinction between God who created the world and the Word as the agent of Creation. The Nicene Fathers certainly made this distinction between God the Father and Jesus Christ.

NOTES

1. For a short biographical note and bibliography see Appendix I.
2. A fuller account is given by Sophia Dobson Collet in *The Life and Letters of Raha Rammohun Roy*, London, 1900, in the chapter entitled 'Regular and Irregular Campaigns against Trinitatian Orthodoxy', pp. 36–61.
3. These four articles were reprinted in one volume under the title of the fourth, *A Defence of the Deity and Atonement of Jesus Christ* . . ., and published in London in 1822. Quotations and references which follow are taken from this volume.
4. In the collected *English Works of Raja Rammohun Roy*, Allahabad, 1906. Quotations and references below are taken from this edition.
5. Translated in *English Works*, pp. 941ff.   6 *Ib.*, pp. 17, 14.
7. *Ib.*, p. 126.   8 *Ib.*, p. 61.
9. *Ib.*, p. 74.   10 *Ib.*, pp. 958, 947.
11. *Ib.*, p. 483 (Introduction to the *Precepts of Jesus*).
12. *Ib.*, pp. 572, 636.   13 *Ib.*, p. 194.
14. M. C. Parekh, *Rajarshi Ram Mohan Roy*, Rajkot, 1927, p. 29.
15. *Defence*, p. 146.
16. *Second Appeal*, cited by Marshman, *Defence*, p. 66.
17. *Defence*, p. 67.   18 *Ib.*, p. 68.
19. *Ib.*, pp. 67f.   20 *Ib.*, p. 251.
21. *Ib.*, pp. 7f.   22 *English Works*, p. 559.
23. *Defence*, pp. 18–20.   24 *Ib.*, pp. 80f.
25. *English Works*, p. 820.   26 *Ib.*, p. 823.
27. *Defence*, p. 82.   28 Parekh, *op. cit.*, p. 34.
29. *English Works*, pp. 483ff.   30 *Ib.*, p. 552.
31. We shall not discuss the manner in which he pursued the controversy. C. F. Andrews, (*The Renaissance in India: its Missionary Aspect*, London, 1912, p. 112) called it 'ungracious and short-sighted'. Collet, *op. cit.*, p. 39, says that Marshman's dogmatism arose from holding the doctrine of the Atonement in its harshest form, and regarding 'that alone as "the Gospel" '. J. R. Chandran concurs with this opinion when he says that the controversy 'became unpleasant mainly because of the attitude taken by Marshman and the other missionaries that those who interpreted Christ differently from their interpretation were enemies of the Gospel' (*Union Seminary Quarterly Review*, 1964/65, p. 251).
32. C. E. Gardner, *Life of Father Goreh*, London, 1900. See the biographical note in Appendix I.
33. S. K. Datta, The *Desire of India*, London, 1908, pp. 246f. See biographical note in Appendix I.
34. J. C. Winslow, *Narayana Vamana Tilak*, Calcutta, 1923, p. 21f.
35. *English Works*. p. 557.   36 *Defence*, p. 51.
37. M. C. Parekh, *op. cit.*, pp. 56f.   38 *Defence*, pp. 23ff.
39. *Ib.*, p. 18.   40 *Ib.*, p. 10.
41. *Ib.*, p. 80.   42 Collet, *op. cit.*, p. 41.
43. *English Works*, p. 572.   44 *Defence*, pp. 23f.; *English Works*, pp. 585ff.
45. *Defence*, pp. 218–26.   46 *English Works*, pp. 573–77.
47. *Ib.*, pp. 577f.   48 *Ib.*, p. 577.
49. Thomas Rees, the Secretary of the Unitarian Society, publishing in London in 1825 Rammohan Roy's *Precepts of Jesus and First and Second Appeals to the Christian Public*, felt obliged to say in the Preface: 'They [the Unitarian Society] are aware that, holding as they do the strict and proper humanity of Christ as one of their fundamental tenets, they may possibly be charged with a dereliction of principle in thus circulating under their authority a work which maintains his pre-existence and super-angelic rank and dignity. But they rest their defence upon the peculiar nature of the case' (p. xiv).

50 *English Works*, pp. 583f.
52 *Ib.*, pp. 195–7.
54 *Ib.*, p. 211.
56 *Ib.*, pp. 805–8.
58 *Ib.*, p. 172.
60 *Ib.*, p. 192.
62 *Defence*, pp. 205f.
64 *Defence*, p. 198.
66 *Ib.*, pp. 211f.
68 *English Works*, p. 815.
70 *Defence*, pp. 34f.
72 *Ib.*, pp. 700–5.
74 *Ib.*, p. 622.
76 *Ib.*, p. 629.
78 *Defence*, pp. 249–52.
80 *Ib.*, pp. 191, 193.
51 *Defence*, pp. 144f.
53 *Ib.*, p. 202.
55 *English Works*, p. 803.
57 *Ib.*, p. 811.
59 *Ib.*, p. 184.
61 *Ib.*, p. 892.
63 *English Works*. pp. 820f.
65 *Ib.*, p. 207.
67 Collet, *op. cit.*, p. 44.
69 *Ib.*, p. 168.
71 *English Works*, pp. 570–2.
73 *Ib.*, p. 725.
75 *Ib.*, pp. 627f.
77 *Ib.*, pp. 632–6.
79 *English Works*, p. 866.
81 *Ib.*, p. 874.
82 Parekh, *op. cit.*, pp. 91f. On Parekh himself see the biographical note in Appendix I.
83 *Ib.*, pp. 103f.   84 *Ib.*, pp. 89f.
85 *Ib.*, pp. 90f.   86 *Defence*, p. 195.
87 R. H. Fuller accepts the traditional interpretation of Phil. 2 and contrasts it with the idea of 'the incarnate life as an *epiphany* of the divine glory' in Col. 1.15–20; I Tim. 3.16; I Peter 3.18–22; Heb. 1.1–4; John 1.1–14 (see *The Foundations of New Testament Christology*, London, 1965, ch. VIII, pp. 203f.). E. L. Mascall and J. A. T. Robinson see the meaning of the Philippians passage differently.
88 *Defence*, p. 112.   89 *Ib.*, p. 254.
90 S. K. Rudra, *The Christian Idea of the Incarnation*, Madras, 1911, p. 14. For a biographical note on Rudra see Appendix I.
91 J. A. T. Robinson, *Honest to God*, London, 1963, p. 74.
92 *English Works*, p. 820.   93 *Ib.*, p. 805.
94 E. L. Mascall, *The Secularisation of Christianity*, London, 1965, p. 150.

CHAPTER TWO

Some Indian Christian Defences against Brahmoism: Lal Behari Day and Nehemiah Goreh

In the wake of the Bengal renaissance, and contributing to it, there were three intellectual centres in Calcutta – the Brahmo Samaj of Rammohan Roy representing Hindu monotheism, the Hindu College of Mr Hare, propagating a creed of antitheistic liberal Rationalism, and the Christian College of Alexander Duff, grounded on the Christian faith. The educated Hindus liberated from traditional Hinduism were drawn to one or other of these centres, and the controversies among the three creeds formed the substance of the cultural renaissance of Bengal at that period. Indeed, they were influenced by the renaissance and were involved in its credal controversies. Each of these creeds had to justify its validity before its own members and the educated public in general by studies and lessons which entered into controversy with the other two. These studies and tracts and lectures are a source of insights for Indian Christian theology. We do not mean only the content of the Christian arguments but of others as well. Some of the educated Hindus were converted to Christianity at this time; there were others who joined them without making the final commitment. Undoubtedly the manner and content of the arguments through which they justified Christianity to the reason and conscience of themselves and others, are of special interest to us. In this connection, the controversies conducted by Lal Behari Day and Krishna Mohan Banerjee in Bengal and Nehemiah Goreh and Pandita Ramabai in Poona with Brahmo theology are of special significance. They sought not only to establish the Christian truth against Brahmoism, but also showed a positive response to the Brahmo demand for a National Christianity. In this discussion, we shall refer mainly to the Lectures[1] which Day gave between 1863 and 1866 in Calcutta and Nehemiah Goreh's several writings, especially *Theism and Christianity*[2] and *The Brahmos: Their Idea of Sin*.[3]

The three theological issues which the Indian Christian writers deal with are (1) The source and authority of religious knowledge (2) Sin and salvation and (3) National Christianity.

I. THE SOURCES OF THE KNOWLEDGE OF GOD

We have already seen what Raja Rammohan Roy thought of the source of the human knowledge of God, when we considered his controversy with Marshman. After the Brahmo Samaj was formed, and with the change in its leadership from Raja Rammohan Roy to Debendranath Tagore, there was a good deal of rethinking on the question of the authority of religion and the source of saving religious truth.

Lal Behari Day in his *Lectures* discusses the changes in the foundation of Brahmoism, from Vedism, through Naturalism to Intuitionalism. For a long time, the belief in 'the Divine authority and inspiration of the Vedas' was its 'fixed dogma'. Babu Devendra Nath Tagore, the President of the Brahmo Samaj, wrote in 1846 that the Brahmo Samaj considered 'the Vedas and the Vedas alone as the standard of our faith and principles'.[4] In 1850

> the Brahmos publicly declared that they acknowledged no other revelation than the volume of nature, [which is] open to all, and which contains a revelation, clearly teaching, in strong and legible characters, the great truths of religion and morality.

And now Brahmoism is said to be founded on 'common sense' or in the language of a Brahmo tract-writer, whom Day quotes, on 'the rock of intuition'[5]. Referring to the Brahmo tract, *Exposition of the Principles and Creed of the Brahma Dharma*, Day says:

> I find the principle stated that ... *common sense* or *intuition* is the source of all our religious knowledge – This then is a fundamental principle of the Brahma Samaj, the principle namely, that a Divine revelation, in the ordinary sense of the term, is not necessary to communicate to us the knowledge of God and the means of salvation ... that is, the light of nature or the light of reason or common sense, or intuition being sufficient for the purpose. I maintain this principle to be essentially false.[6]

A little further on he gives his reason:

Great as is the mind of man, it cannot, especially with the blight of sin upon it, come near the unapproachable Deity – it cannot enter the cabinet of the Divine counsels. ... The world in its Wisdom did not know God, till God himself was pleased to send us a teacher from heaven, in the person of His Own Son, to impart to us the knowledge of Himself and to show us the way of everlasting happiness.[7]

He regards 'the human mind as a superb display of Divine power'. Something 'concerning God and our duty can be known from the light of nature, of reason and of conscience'. For instance,

I believe with the Hebrew poet that 'the heavens declare the glory of God....' I believe with St Paul that 'the invisible things of Him, from the creation of the world, are clearly seen, being understood by the things that are made, even His eternal power and Godhead'. And I also agree with the same writer when he says, that 'where the Gentiles which have not the law, do by nature things contained in the law' ... they do most assuredly give us some light. But what I maintain is that that Light is not sufficient to guide us to the path of eternal happiness. But if the combined illumination of nature, reason and conscience be such a feeble glimmer, how faint must be the rays, if any, which mere unaided intuition can dart upon us.[8]

Though the truth of God is 'not discoverable by reason' when revelation discovers it, 'it may be easy to show that it is conformable to human reason',[9] and 'in harmony with the laws of the human mind'.[10]

When life and immortality are brought to light by the Gospel – when Christianity reveals to men the justest notions of God and man, it is doubtless easy for subsequent writers to show, that those just notions and doctrines are quite in accordance with the dictates of reason and conscience.

Further, 'the human intellect can give arguments for proving the existence and attributes of God'.[11] But revelation has been the only source of religious truth.

It was the God-man that illumined the moral and religious world. It was Jesus Christ that compassed this marvellous revolution in the moral and religious world. Since that time no progress has been made in the development of religious truth. ... And for the last eighteen hundred years since the appearance of Christ upon earth, human intuition and human education have been again and again at work, but not *one* *Truth*, I mean moral and religious truth, has been discovered which Jesus did not teach.[12]

Day is profuse in his appreciation of the good in Brahmoism. But he is sure that it is not the fruit of unaided reason or intuition. The 'belief in the existence of God, the creator of heaven and earth', in the 'future state of existence', in the sinfulness of man and his need of deliverance from it, in the need of 'purity of heart' for man to enter heaven – all those tenets of Brahmoism with which a Christian can agree, are 'borrowed either directly or indirectly from the Bible'.[13] Day is sure that Brahmoism has 'a mission to fulfil in the present state of the country', and if he reads the signs of the times aright, he does not doubt that 'that mission will eventually prove favourable to the propagation of the only true religion, namely Christianity'.[14] He values Brahmoism 'as a protest against idolatry', 'as an inspiration of social reform in our country' and 'as an index of that spirit of religious enquiry which has begun to manifest itself in some of our educated countrymen'.[15] The truths that show themselves in all these respects of Brahmoism are derived from the biblical revelation; but then they are separated from the revelation. As long as Brahmoism does not acknowledge the divine inspiration of the Bible and the foundation to be the 'rock Christ' instead of the 'rock intuition',[16] Brahmoism 'as a system of religion' is 'baseless', 'uncertain', and 'unauthoritative'.[17] Day uses the whole of his final Lecture to expand this lack of basis, certainty and authority in the Brahmo religion. A religion should be based on revelation and not human reason. It should be 'founded on a written revelation' to have 'certainty about its leading doctrines'. There may be different ways of interpreting the written word, but those different interpretations could only affect the non-essential parts of the system. Neither could there be, in such a case, the possibility of 'organic changes in the system' as it has been happening with Brahmoism which changed its foundations too easily.[18] In fact Brahmoism considers 'unbounded speculation'[19] as a mark of its liberality, but it is actually a mark of its uncertainty. More than this, Brahmoism has no divine authority for its truths, to command the conscience of man, since it is founded on 'mere human opinion' and cannot say: 'Thus Saith the Lord'.[20] Day contrasts this with Christianity thus:

Christianity is not a baseless religion; it is founded on the Word of God, which was committed to writing by inspired men, who spake as they were moved by the Holy Spirit, and gave unquestionable proof of their Divine Commission. Christianity is not uncertain; like its Divine Founder, it is independent of all changes of human opinions, of all revolutions in philosophy and science, of all conflicts between sectaries; its institutes are all written down in a book, the most wonderful book in the world, which is intelligible to all, though some of the things contained in it have baffled the intellects of the deepest thinkers of the human race. Christianity is not unauthoritative, it is not founded on human opinion, or vague surmises on the thinking of individual men, on the deduction of human reason; it is founded on Divine authority, for it has God for its Author; and whether speaking in a voice of thunder or in accents of love, it always begins with: 'Thus Saith the Lord.'[21]

Lacking this divine authority, Brahmoism is 'of no worth at all' as regards 'the salvation of the soul'.[22]

Nehemiah Goreh follows more or less the same pattern of arguments to show that divine revelation is the only source of sure knowledge of God. Day in his first lecture on Brahmoism had said:

Rammohan Roy was right when he taught that there is but one God, he was wrong when he maintained that that was the invariable teaching of the Hindu sastras.[23]

It is this theme that Goreh expands in his discussion on *Theism and Christianity*. His thesis is clearly this: Hindu sastras are essentially pantheistic or monistic, and theism, wherever and in whatever form found, has its source in the divine revelation as recorded in the Old and New Testaments. Only the impact of the revealed religion of Christianity has produced Brahmo monotheism and Brahmo ideas of morality based on such theism; and therefore Brahmos have no choice other than that of accepting in full the revealed religion and ethics of Christianity or of reverting to the monism/polytheism and moral corruption of traditional Hinduism.

Goreh criticizes Max Muller for holding up the life of Rammohan Roy as 'a sample of the fruits of the Veda', when as is well-known

His 'character and ideas' [were shaped] by the powerful influence of Christianity under which he was brought up by studying the Christian Scriptures themselves – as well as English books in which all that is about

God or morality or other truths of religion has come from Christianity. . . . [Roy] had no idea of what the Veda really was.

Goreh says elsewhere:

Pure Theism is a great light and it is Christianity that emits that light. It is Christianity that so enlightens men's minds that they begin to get pure notions of God and of other truths of religion, and are enabled to know the pure Natural Religion, which men's darkened reason has never been able to find out, and the false religions issuing from the darkened reason of man have never enabled them to know.[24]

In *Theism and Christianity* he takes up 'the chief points of Brahmoism' – belief in one God, holy, almighty and most merciful, the notion of God as Creator of all, the Ten Commandments of morality, belief in personal immortality, punishment of sin and divine forgiveness, and everlasting life – and seeks to prove that 'they are not to be found in the religious books of our country and have not been known to our countrymen'. Goreh refers to the idea that religion in India 'began to be corrupted in the later days only, say from the times of the Puranas, but that Theism was the faith of our forefathers in more ancient times'. He adds: 'But where is the proof, I ask, for such an assertion?' and he goes on to refute it. And after his long essay on all the points his conclusion is as follows:

This examination alone ought to make us pretty sure that a correct knowledge of religious truths is not attainable by human reason. For this great country of ours is a world in itself, and our forefathers were not inferior to any nation in the world, in learning, cleverness, and power of reasoning. And in one respect, namely, in possessing a religious and pious disposition, they appear to me far superior to all other people, except those in whom the influence of Divine Revelation has produced such a disposition. And such a disposition has made our forefathers and countrymen fitted to show whether man ever acquires correct knowledge of religious truths by his own reason without the light of revelation. I say then that (it) is unattainable by human reason.

This does not mean that reason has no place in religion. It is 'impotent and dark with regard to matters of faith'; but reason is 'a gracious gift of God' and is 'most serviceable in Religion in its own place'. Goreh himself has written a great deal both to refute Hindu religious systems and to defend Christianity as the true revealed religion by rational arguments. But his point is that reason 'leads us to the right faith, though after that it must retire'.[25] Revelation remains the sole authoritative source of the knowledge of God and true religion.

2. THE DOCTRINE OF ATONEMENT

It is in controverting 'the doctrine of Brahma repentance' which is 'the cornerstone of the whole edifice of Brahmoism',[26] that Day spends the best part of three of his lectures. In fact, this doctrine is a continuation of the ideas of Rammohan Roy, as we have already seen, but now reaffirmed by Debendranath Tagore, the President. Here is this central teaching:

The question is how can man regain the lost favour of God? ... Here is the answer of the Brahma Samaj through its President – 'Repentance – genuine repentance is itself the expiation of sin. God is not merely a just king. He is also a merciful Father... Will He when He sees their penitent hearts withhold from them the gift of His pardon? Never' ... (i.e.) – repentance is *all* that is necessary for pardon of sin.[27]

The Brahmo Tract on Atonement explains this doctrine more fully. It says that 'atonement scientifically considered' is nothing more than a return to God renouncing sin 'to enjoy the blessings of His company'. Hence the turning back to God is the whole philosophy of atonement. Hence our belief that 'repentance is atonement'.[28]

Since our God is absolute love, everlasting and abiding love immutable as His nature, [he] loveth always. He changeth not, though we change. Our virtues and vices do not modify His nature. ... The whole change which sin brings on is in ourselves, not in him; so likewise the change consequent on atonement.

Indeed, there is no Divine punishment for sin apart from its natural consequences, which are inherently connected to it. And in their purpose 'all His inflictions are remedial and salutary'. Thus in the very act of punishment, 'justice and mercy instead of running counter to each other, most beautifully harmonize'. Salvation is deliverance not 'from punishment', but 'from sin'.[29]

Day rejects all this as 'one mass of misconception'. He controverts the Brahmo doctrine as a denial of the true idea both of God's nature and divine government of the world; and also as misunderstanding the nature of man and human sin. His main arguments are as follows:

First, the Brahmo doctrine that God is

incapable of being displeased with a sinner, [represents him] as abstracted from the affairs of the world and feeling no concern in the obedience or disobedience which His creatures rendered to Him [and shows] an erroneous view of the holiness of God.[30]

Day emphasizes the sense of the wrath of God as a fact of the history of the pagan religions of propitiation and sacrifice and in the voice of conscience; it is a working of Divine holiness.

'The anger, wrath and displeasure of God' in the language of a Christian theology are not [anthropomorphic] passions or affections of the Divine nature, resembling those which receive the same names in man. They are terms denoting the necessary opposition of the Divine rectitude to such as have violated the holy Law of the righteous Lord who loveth righteousness. ... It is the language of *government*, not of *passion*. ... God is holy – essentially, necessarily, eternally and absolutely holy. ... – He hates sin universally, intensely and necessarily. ... The primary object of His displeasure is *sin*; He is not displeased with the nature of man *as man*, for that was derived from Him, but He is displeased with the nature of man as sinful, which is from the sinner himself.[31]

Therefore atonement should be such as to make a change in the attitude of God to the sinners. It is necessary that 'His views undergo a change'.[32]

Secondly, the Brahmo theory of atonement is founded on an erroneous idea of punishment in the Divine government. Punishment is not merely a 'natural and necessary consequence of sin'. There are such consequences, but Divine government requires 'other punishments than remorse of conscience'.[33] Nor is all punishment 'remedial'. Tagore is wrong in thinking that 'the only aim of the Divine government is the promotion of our happiness' and 'the reformation of the criminal'.[34] 'Punishment' should not be confused with 'chastisement'.[35] 'The vindication of God's honour' and 'the manifestation of His Majesty' are the dominant aims of punishment inflicted as Divine justice.

Thirdly, Brahmoism has a shallow view of sin and the justice of

God. The evil of sin, being infinite, demands 'an infinite punishment – infinite, either in nature or in duration'. This is not because of God's will but because of his nature which is 'the ultimate source of morality'. A finite creature cannot bear this infinite punishment.

Whence it follows that if sin is to be punished agreeable to its desert and yet the sinner saved, it must meet this punishment in the person of one who can sustain an infliction which is infinite in nature.[36]

Fourthly, man needs not only 'freedom from sin' but also 'remission of sin'. Indeed Brahmoism tells us that I 'may have to suffer for my sins for endless ages'. Thus without the concern for salvation from eternal punishment for sins and guilt it is concerned with only a 'half-salvation'. And when freedom from punishment for the past sins and the guilt related to them are taken seriously, it is clear that dutifulness and sorrow for the past cannot remove demerit and present regret cannot burn former guilt.[37]

And fifthly, the Brahmo doctrine of repentance is of no use to man, since 'I cannot repent by my own power'. When men have 'neither the will nor the power to reform; for true repentance is nothing less', the Brahmo theory of atonement is 'impracticable and inefficacious'.[38]

Nehemiah Goreh also discusses, in his short tract, *The Brahmos: their Idea of Sin*, the same Brahmo tract *Atonement and Salvation* which is examined by Lal Behari Day in his lectures. By following their own reason instead of revelation, Brahmos have fallen into error regarding 'the nature of sin' and the meaning of divine punishment, and this has cut at the very root of religion. Goreh quotes approvingly the statement from a Brahmo tract which says: 'That the frightful nature of sin *deserves* a punishment whose severity is beyond the reach of conception, no one can venture to question.' But he says, this truth is contradicted by statements which say:

God may visit us with the direst of torments: *but* such torments are intended for our welfare and will continue till they effect this object. . . . God punishes sinners *for their good*, . . . all these inflictions are *remedial and salutary*.

Goreh comments:

Thus looking exclusively to the attributes of God's mercy and goodness, they have completely annihilated the notion of another great truth, namely

His justice. The writer of that pamphlet has simply turned God's justice into His mercy.

In his definition,

Justice is ... simply to render to a person his due and *because it is his due*, and *not from any consideration of benefiting that person*.

And therefore to make the good of the sinners the only legitimate object of punishment and for that reason to rule out eternal punishment, is to deny God's justice which demands that the sinner be given a punishment which he deserves. Goreh accepts as true that many avail themselves of God's punishment and amend their ways; but

Punishment is simply *due* to sin; and if justice *demands* that punishment ..., then there can be no mercy on God's part in giving that punishment to sinners.

Goreh further grants that 'there is both justice as well as mercy in the *temporal* punishments that sinners receive *in this life*'; but he rejects the Brahmo idea that all punishment whether here or hereafter is remedial only, which therefore rules out eternal punishment. Indeed, Goreh says that in the Brahmo idea, there is no conception of punishment meted out to sinners in justice. This means that Brahmoism turns sin

from being a *moral* evil into a mere *natural* evil, from being an act of wickedness and deserving detestation, into a disease deserving kindness ... [or] a *misfortune* like a bad wound in a diseased body which deserves kind treatment.

And the real problem is that it does violence to the concept of man as a free moral agent:

For if man is a free agent and does what he does by his will and choice his wicked acts cannot but be considered as wicked acts; and he deserving blame and punishment. But if his wicked acts do not deserve punishment and consequently are not wicked acts, he must be supposed to have perpetuated them, not by his free will and choice but from necessity. Man is then a machine and not a free agent, and a responsible being. In other words, he is not a *rational* soul, but a material machine. This is Materialism.[39]

And he continues to spell out its implications:

In that case there is no more virtue, no moral Government of God, and in short no religion. [The Brahmo's] ... erroneous notion of the mercy and goodness of God has proved to be the whirlpool.

It is relevant to point out that the doctrine of Eternal Punishment played a crucial role in Goreh's conversion to Christianity. It was allied to his Christian understanding of God's holiness, God's moral government of the world in justice and man's character as a free moral agent. And Goreh argues out the truth of the doctrine against Brahmos in another of his writings.[40] He raises the question about the infinite love of God raised by the doctrine thus:

But you will say that 'such a notion is irreconcilable with the infinite goodness and love of God; that the God of infinite love will, by His Almighty Power, and by some contrivance or other, make sooner or later His chastisement effectual to the conversion of all moral beings; that they may be saved; and that none of his creatures should perish eternally.'

And Goreh's rejoinder is that if men as moral agents can by moral decision and practice of virtue 'at last arrive at such a degree of moral strength that their nature becomes therefore incapable of being turned towards sin', will it not be equally possible for moral beings to go on so obstinately in the course of sin that

they will at last arrive at such a degree of moral wickedness and corruption that it will therefore be impossible for them to turn towards God. [And conversely, while] God being merciful always remembers His mercy in the midst of His justice, and makes the deserved punishment of the sinner also remedial to him *while it is possible*, [there may even be] cases of sinners in which no room is left for the exercise of Divine Mercy and consequently they should be left to suffer punishment, which they have most justly deserved, as punishment only.

The Christian doctrines of the Incarnation and Atonement naturally follow. They show, to quote Day

how the second person of the adorable Trinity satisfied, on behalf of man, the Divine justice, by Himself suffering the punishment due to man's sin; how He magnified and made honourable the law of God by rendering to it, on the behalf of man, a perfect obedience; how the obstructions to the full flow of the Divine mercy were removed by Him; and how justice and mercy have met together in the Christian system, and righteousness and peace have kissed each other; and what admirable provision there is made for the purification of human nature by the inward operation of the mighty Spirit of God.[41]

Day speaks of his experience of conversion from Brahmoism to Christ:

> I myself was once a Brahmo, though not in name, yet in reality. I ... believed that repentance was a sufficient expiation for sin. ... He opened my eyes and showed to me Christ, in all the lustre of His mediatorial glory and the charms of His ineffable Love. ... I then saw that Christ, not repentance, was the propitiation of my sins, and not of my sins only, but the sins of the whole world. It was then that I realized what I perceived, how true penitence was created in the human heart, not by its own ability, but the gracious influences of the Holy Spirit.[42]

3. THE IDEA OF A NATIONAL CHURCH

It is clear from what has already been said, that Day and Goreh rejected the Brahmo idea of basing religious knowledge and experience on the shifting foundation of human reason and intuition and their unbounded speculations and affirmed the divine revelation attested by Scripture as the only foundation of true religion and the knowledge of salvation. They were also unable to accept the Brahmo approach that the natural religious consciousness of man and the religions and philosophies which it has produced in India were a preparation and help to attain the true knowledge of God. These two truths are stated in the clearest terms by Pandita Ramabai who moved from the Prarthana Samaj of Poona to Christianity. She says that she rejected Brahmo religion because it was

> nothing but what a man makes for himself. He chooses and gathers whatever seems good to him from all religions for his own use. The Brahmo religion has no other foundation than man's own natural light, and the sense of right and wrong which he possesses with all mankind. It could not and did not satisfy me; still I liked and believed a good deal of it that was better than what the Orthodox Hindu religion taught.[43]

She elsewhere affirms that

> the natural religious consciousness, oriental or occidental, is in no way a help to understand the mind of God and to know Him.[44]

Goreh could not understand the Brahmo emphasis on the Oriental

Christ and on interpreting Christ within the categories of Hindu religious and philosophical thought even when they were reformed to comprehend theism. In his opinion the essential Hinduism is in the last analysis pantheistic/monistic and cannot provide the framework for Christian truth. Day however realized the value of Hindu religiousness and its 'spirit of religious enquiry' for Christian evangelism. He once wrote:

A Hindu is the most religious being in existence. He puts up his bed religiously, anoints his body religiously, washes religiously, dresses religiously, sits religiously, stands religiously, learns religiously, remains ignorant religiously and becomes irreligious religiously. It is this religiousness, forming so prominent a part of the Hindu character, and called into activity by the combined influence of English education and Christian missions, which has created that spirit of religious enquiry over which I am now rejoicing.[45]

Krishna Mohan Banerjee, the Bengali colleague of Day, went much further in relating Christianity to what he saw as the divine witness in Hinduism. Though he started with the refutation of Hindu philosophy and religion as error,[46] in his later writings[47] he recognized Christianity as having a more positive relation to Vedic religion and Christ the Lamb slain from the foundation of the world as the true Prajapati.[48] But he was very much a pioneer in giving such a positive response to the Brahmo idea of relating Jesus Christ to Hinduism.

Day and Banerjee are however seen together in advocating the idea of a National Church of Bengal. The plan was that of Day. For Day, the 'saving doctrines' constituted the essence of the Church. He was also concerned with the right form of the Church which is in accordance with Scripture. In his opinion,

One form [of the Church] is more scriptural in its constitution than another; and to know which is most scriptural is an important point.[49]

Nevertheless the form of the Church 'loses its significance when compared with the saving doctrines of Christianity'. And his plan was for the various denominations of Christianity, including the Roman Catholics, to unite on the common foundation of the fundamental doctrines declared in the Apostles' Creed. As a result, he addressed to the authorities of the Missions a memorandum on 'The Desirableness and Practicability of organizing a National Church in Bengal'. The ecumenical spirit which breathes in the document may be evident in the following passage from it:

> I would construct the United National Church of Bengal on the broadest possible basis, so as to include in its communion a great variety of opinions. And I know not a broader creed than what is called the Apostles' Creed or The Creed by way of eminence. That it was composed by the inspired apostles themselves I do not believe; nevertheless it is sufficient for us to know that it embodies within its brief compass the essential teaching of the Holy Scriptures, that it comprises a summary of those articles of belief which is necessary for salvation, that it was the *symbolum* of the primitive Church, and that in the days of the apostolical fathers, it was put into the hands of catechumens who recited it at their baptism as their confession of faith ... By founding the United Church of Bengal on so broad and catholic a basis, we should be in communion with every Church in Christendom, the Greek and Latin Churches not excepted. I for one would rejoice if our brethren of the Native Roman Catholic Church of Bengal could unite with us in the formation of a National Church, which they could do by adjuring the dogmas of the infallibility of the Pope and the insufficiency of the holy Scriptures as a rule of faith; for I look upon the Roman Catholic Church, though disfigured with corruption, as a branch of the true visible Church of Christ.[50]

4. A CRITICAL EVALUATION

The concern to establish the divine initiative and authority in man's knowledge of God and his salvation through repentance and faith is central to Christian theological enterprise. The alternative is a subjectivisim which has no grounds for its certainty other than human self-assurance. Day and Goreh are right therefore in affirming that true saving religious knowledge and experience cannot be based on human reason or intuition, but require divine revelation met by the response of faith. But valid questions could be raised regarding the relation between reason or intuition on the one hand and revelation-faith on the other. On the whole Day avoids the danger of identifying faith in an objective Divine act of revelation and salvation with intellectual assent to doctrines about it, because of his understanding of creed as a '*symbolum*' of an existential commitment of the self to the divine initiative in the depth of the human spirit. In fact, in a letter Day wrote to a Hindu friend, Mr G. M. Tagore, while he points out that while 'my spirit was overjoyed' to know that Tagore believed in the doctrine of the atonement, he adds:

> But dear sir, allow me to impress upon you a common but nevertheless all-important truth, that a mere *intellectual* and *speculative* faith in the doctrine of the Bible can never save a man. I might believe *historically* in Jesus Christ, *intellectually* in the doctrine of the atonement . . . Yet I might not be saved.[51]

Perhaps Goreh did not clearly make this distinction between doctrinal belief and saving faith, and exaggerated doctrines themselves as literal truths rather than symbolic expressions of it. On one point however both were very much children of their day, namely, in not differentiating between the saving *act* of God in Jesus Christ, its *record* in the Bible (which Day calls book-revelation) and the saving *doctrines* of Christianity abstracted from it. Perhaps it is not easy to differentiate them, but it is a necessary task of theology.

On the relation between Christianity and religious and philosophical Hinduism, Indian Christian thought in the nineteenth century generally followed the evangelical missionary attitude, too easily contrasting them as light to darkness. Nehemiah Goreh, Lal Behari Day and Pandita Ramabai saw the Hindu theism of the Brahmos as the result of a reformation of Hinduism through the impact of the notions of Christianity and in that sense as indicating a movement of evangelical enlightenment. And Goreh was right in affirming that Brahmo theism, as a half-way house, had no stability of its own and that it would have to move forward to a fuller apprehension of Christ and Christianity or backward to the traditional Advaita. We can see from the decline of Brahmoism and the resurgence of Advaita Vedanta to influence in modern India, that history has also proved Goreh right. But he was certainly not right in his too absolute rejection of all efforts to discover the hidden work of Christ in Hinduism and to affirm points of contact and continuity between Christianity and Hinduism in the Indian context. This is where Krishna Mohan Banerjee became a pioneer. Whether his reading of the work of Christ in the Vedic religion was right or not, his effort to look for the 'Aryan Witness' to Christ opened a new line in Indian Christian thought.

The arguments to establish the necessity of the Incarnation and the death of Jesus Christ to atone for human sin can never be adequate.

The relation between love and justice in the economy of salvation remains a mystery, which the consecrated intellect can fathom only 'as in a glass darkly'. Brahmos no doubt had a shallow view of sin and the wrath of God against it and were advocating a forgiveness without the cost of the atoning suffering and sacrifice of God in Christ. But Day and Goreh seem to interpret God's wrath against sin almost wholly in the categories of a holiness which is completely unrelated to His love, and speak of God's punishment of sin in the Divine Government purely in terms of vindication of God's honour and justice without any relation to the Divine will to redeem the sinner. Indeed, the idea of 'punishment' is taken almost entirely from the criminal penal codes. Certainly, they have not happily worked out the relation between God's holy nature and God's saving will. In fact at certain points the Brahmo arguments have better grounds. Dorothy Sayers once said that the word 'punishment' might very well be left out of the Christian idea of judgment; and there is today a greater appreciation of the fact that God's wrath and judgment are the other face of God's love; perhaps it is even the subjectivity of man who spurns the reality of holy love. Indeed it is not less real for that matter, and Goreh is right that the Christian concept of man as moral agent and sin as moral evil goes with the possibility of man's closing the door on the love of God even eternally. But then it goes also with the hope that the infinity of God's love cannot fail. The idea of eternal 'punishment' is different and is revolting. But compared with the passion of Day and Goreh to assert this Gospel of the act of God in the death of Christ as the condition for true repentance and realization of divine forgiveness and salvation, the inadequacies of their doctrine of atonement are not of major significance.

As for the vision of the National Church of Bengal which found expression in Day's Address to the Missions, it is a positive response to the challenge of the truth he saw in the Brahmoist passion for Indianness and Unity without compromising the fundamental saving truths of the Gospel. Indeed, the formation in 1868 of the Bengal Christian Association under the leadership of Krishna Mohan Banerjee, the Calcutta Christo Samaj in 1887 under the guidance of Kali Charan Banerjee, and the National Church of Madras in 1886 under the leadership of Parani Andy[52] have been the first stirrings of the movement expressing a common theological idea of the Church as transcending denominational divisions and capable of rootage in the Indian soil. But Day's idea of an indigenous Church was rooted in the universality of the Apostles' Creed, and broad enough to include all denominations, including Roman Catholics, not as they are but reformed in the light of Scripture. This vision of Church unity is daring and it will continue to inspire us in India and elsewhere.

NOTES

1. Published under the title: *An Antidote to Brahmoism in Four Lectures*, Calcutta, 1867 (cited as Day, *Lectures*).
2. N. Goreh, *Theism and Christianity* (Oxford Mission Occasional Papers), Calcutta, 1882, reprinted as *The Existence of Brahmoism itself a Proof of the Divine Origin of Christianity*, Allahabad, 1889.
3. N. Goreh, *The Brahmos, Their Idea of Sin*, Poona, 1882.
4. *The Englishman*, 24 October 1846, quoted by Day, *Lectures*, p. 10.
5. *Lectures*, p. 11.
6. *Ib.*, p. 17.
7. *Ib.*, pp. 24f.
8. *Ib.*, pp. 129f.
9. *Ib.*, p. 20.
10. *Ib.*, p. 131.
11. *Ib.*, p. 20.
12. *Ib.*, pp. 108f.
13. *Ib.*, p. 26.
14. *Ib.*, p. 42.
15. *Ib.*, pp. 123f.
16. *Ib.*, p. 58.
17. *Ib.*, p. 124.
18. *Ib.*, p. 131.
19. *Ib.*, p. 15.
20. *Ib.*, pp. 136f.
21. *Ib.*, p. 155.
22. *Ib.*, p. 46.
23. *Ib.*, p. 7.
24. N. Goreh, *Proofs of the Divinity of Our Lord*, Bombay, 1887, pp. 56f.
25. N. Goreh, *Objections to Catholic Doctrine*, Calcutta, 1868, pp. 144–6.
26. Day, *Lectures*, p. 40.
27. *Ib.*, pp. 26–8.
28. No. 13 in the English series, quoted by Day, *Lectures*, pp. 94f.
29. *Lectures*, pp. 95–7.
30. *Ib.*, pp. 97–9.
31. *Ib.*, pp. 102f.
32. *Ib.*, p. 82.
33. *Ib.*, pp. 104–8.
34. *Ib.*, p. 36.
35. *Ib.*, p. 108.
36. *Ib.*, p. 110.
37. *Ib.*, p. 114.
38. *Ib.*, pp. 39, 113.
39. These and other quotations from Goreh's writings are taken from Balwant A. M. Paradkar, *Theology of Nehemiah Goreh*, Bangalore, 1969.
40. Goreh, *Objections to Catholic Doctrine*, pp. 14–17.
41. Day, *Lectures*, p. 118.
42. *Ib.*, pp. 42f.
43. Pandita Ramabai, *A Testimony*, 2nd ed., Kedgaon, Poona, 1917, p. 18.
44. Supplement to *A Testimony*, p. 7.
45. Day, *Lectures*, p. 88, repeating an article from the *Calcutta Review*.
46. K. M. Banerjee, *Dialogues on Hindu Philosophy*, Calcutta and London, 1861.
47. *The Arian Witness: or the Testimony of Arian Scriptures in corroboration of Biblical History and the Rudiments of Christian Doctrine*, Calcutta, 1875; *The Relation between Christianity and Hinduism* (cited as *Essays*), Calcutta, 1881.
48. See K. Baago, 'The First Independence Movement Among Indian Christians', *Indian Church History Review*, June 1967. From the time of Rammohan Roy, Brahmoism had interpreted Vedic religion as monotheistic; and Vedism was the foundation of Brahmo

religion until, of course, they had to yield to closer students of the Vedas. The Arya Samaj also interpreted Vedas in monotheistic terms. Therefore it was natural for Banerjee under the influence of renascent Hindu thought of his time to reflect on the positive relation between Vedic religion and Christianity. And he set out in the *Arian Witness* to prove that 'while all Hindus who have been instructed in Western literature, science and history have departed from the faith derived from their immediate forefathers, Hindu Christians can alone have the satisfaction of knowing that the fundamental principles of the Gospel were recognized and acknowledged, both in theory and practice, by their primitive ancestors, the Brahminical Aryans of India, and that if the authors of the Vedas could by any possibility now return to the world, they would at once recognize the Indian Christians far more complacently as their own descendants than any other body of educated natives' (*Arian Witness* p. 10). And he goes on to explain 'the striking parallels between the Vedas and the Old Testament, e.g. with respect to the Creation, the Fall, the Deluge and the idea of Sacrifice'. The only difference between Vedic and biblical accounts of religion is 'the greater clearness and the still greater firmness and certainty of decision with which monotheism is upheld in Jewish Scriptures. Almost in all other respects the Vedas represent with equal clearness, the ideals of the patriarchal dispensation in the ages of Noah, of Abraham, of Melchisedec, of Job and of similar characters noticed in the Bible' (*Essays*, pp. 69f). And he saw in the Vedic idea of the Purusha Sacrifice and Prajapati the expectation of Jesus the Immanuel and the Sacrifice. He says: 'The Vedic writers say distinctly that the Lord of Creation himself a Purusha begotten in the beginning (or before all worlds) offered himself a sacrifice for the Devas, who by birth were mortals like men, but were translated to heaven "by path of sacrifice". They add that the same Lord of Creation was "half mortal, half immortal". This is still nearer an approach to the ideal of our Immanuel' (*Essays*, p. 70). In the history of Hinduism, no god has been given the throne of Prajapati; and 'no one can claim that throne and that crown in the hearts of the Hindus, true to the original teaching of the Vedas, so forcibly as the historical Jesus.' Thus 'Christianity fills up the vacuum – a most important vacuum – in the Vedic account of the sacrifice, by exhibiting the true *Prajapati* – the Lamb slain from the foundations of the world' (*Essays*, p. 79). (All quotations are taken from Baago's article.)

49 G. Macpherson, *Life of Lal Behari Day*, Edinburgh, 1900, p. 48.
50 *Ib.*, pp.49f.   51 *Ib.*, p. 47.   52 See Baago, *op. cit.*

CHAPTER THREE

Keshub Chunder Sen:
The Doctrine of Divine Humanity

Keshub Chunder Sen came to the leadership of the Brahmo Samaj and became the founder of the Church of the New Dispensation. Within Neo-Hinduism, he represented in many ways a movement away from the rationalism of Rammohan Roy and the Vedic Brahmoism of Debendranath Tagore, to a new appreciation of the traditional Hindu spirituality represented by Bhakti-mysticism, yogic discipline, invocation of divine names and incarnational theology. He was also an eclectic convinced of the harmony of religions. But he carried with both a devotion to Jesus Christ dissociated from historical Christianity and interpreted as the source of creative renewal of Hinduism and the concrete centre of a new universal religion of the Spirit. The theological significance of Keshub Chunder Sen may be seen along three lines. First, he led the country and Hinduism itself 'in some degree into discipleship to Christ'.[1] Secondly, he has introduced Jesus Christ to several Indians, some of whom came to a fuller vision of and commitment to him 'while going along the lines laid down by Keshub'.[2] And thirdly, Keshub has produced some original seminal ideas like his doctrines of Divine Humanity and a National Church, which found their fuller expression in the search for indigenous Christology and ecclesiology by Indian Christian leaders.

In this discussion we shall not consider Keshub's life and teachings in general, but confine ourselves to his ideas on three topics: Jesus Christ and the Trinity; the Church; and the relation between religions in the light of Christ.

1. THE DOCTRINE OF CHRIST AND UNI-TRINITY

The evolution of Keshub's thought on Jesus Christ and his relation to the Triune God may be traced through the series of annual lectures he gave in Calcutta. The first lecture was given in 1866 and the title was *Jesus Christ, Europe and Asia*. In it Keshub dwelt on the 'moral excellence' of Jesus – on the 'character of Jesus, and the lofty ideal of moral truth which he taught and lived',[3] 'his tenderness and humility, lamb-like meekness and sympathy, his heart full of mercy and forgiving kindness' coupled with 'his firm absolute unyielding adherence to truth'. Keshub 'then exclaimed in a breathless climax, "Verily Jesus was above ordinary humanity!" '[4] Parekh quotes another passage:

Tell me, brethren, whether you regard Jesus of Nazareth, the carpenter's son, as an ordinary man? Is there a single soul in this large assembly who would scruple to ascribe extraordinary greatness and supernatural moral heroism to Jesus Christ and him crucified? Was not he who by his wisdom illuminated, and by his power saved a dark and wicked world – was not he who has left us such a priceless legacy of divine truth, and whose blood has wrought such wonders for eighteen hundred years – was not he above ordinary humanity?[5]

Keshub spoke of 'forgiveness and self-sacrifice' as 'the two cardinal principles of Christian ethics, so utterly opposed to the wisdom of the world and so far exalted above its highest conceptions of rectitude' which are needed by all people for the 'reformation of their character'. And he held up the Cross as the exemplification of them:

I assure you, brethren, nothing short of self-sacrifice, of which Christ has furnished so bright an example, will regenerate India . . . And the better to stimulate you to a life of self-denial, I hold up to you the cross on which Jesus died.[6]

In this lecture, he speaks of Jesus' mission in these terms: 'Sent by Providence to reform and regenerate mankind he received from Providence wisdom and power for that great work.'[7] P. C. Mozoomdar who was already attracted to Jesus Christ says that he was 'agreeably struck with the high enthusiasm and deep appreciation Keshub displayed toward Jesus Christ as the Messiah'.[8] So he 'demanded to know Keshub's whole mind' on Christ, and Keshub replied in a letter that he would abide his time to develop his idea of Christ:

Of course I have my own ideas about Christ, but I am not bound to give them out in due form, until altered circumstances of the country gradually developed them out of my mind. Jesus is identical with self-sacrifice, and as he lived and preached in the fulness of time, so must he be in time preached in the fulness of time. The more is sacrifice needed in India, and the more it is made, the more will Jesus find a home in this land. I am, therefore, patiently waiting that I may grow with the age and the nation, and the spirit of Christ's sacrifice may grow therewith.[9]

This idea of a *kairos* for the communication of the Gospel, or depending upon the soil itself prepared to receive it through a life of service and self-sacrifice, is worth pondering. This is by the way. Mozoomdar tells us that during this period Seely's book *Ecce Homo*, lent to him by George Smith, then Editor of the *Friend of India*, made a deep impression on Keshub.

We discussed the book with interest and conspicuous benefit. But in course of time Keshub ceased to speak of *Ecce Homo* and drew his further views of Christ from Oriental ideals, which his own genius and spiritual experiences portrayed to him.[10]

Perhaps as a corrective to the impression Keshub gave through his glorification of Jesus Christ, he gave another lecture on the *Cult of Great Men and the National Church*, in which he warned against men binding themselves 'as slaves to any particular person as the only chosen prophet of God. For at sundry times and in diverse places, God spoke in time past unto the fathers by the prophets.' Partly following Carlyle, he included in the list of prophets, Luther, Mohammed, John Knox and Chaitanya. However he calls Jesus Christ 'the Prince of prophets'.

And though Jesus Christ, the Prince of Prophets, effected greater wonders, and did infinitely more good to the world than the others, and deserves therefore our profoundest reverence, we must not neglect that chain, or any single link in that chain of prophets that preceded him, and prepared the world for him; nor must we refuse honour to those who, coming after him, have carried on the blessed work of human regeneration for which he lived and died.[11]

In one lecture he said that the Future Church should have 'the gospel of mercy as represented in the parable of the Prodigal Son – unsurpassed in the literature of Divine Grace' as its basic creed.[12] In England, he spoke of the teachings of the Gospel as his spiritual nourishment. The London *Spectator* specially stated that he included not only the general teachings of the Gospel, but 'the sublime egotism of Christ' who 'constantly preached himself as "*the way*" to God'.[13]

In 1879 Keshub chose, as the topic for his annual lecture, *India Asks, Who is Christ?*

On all sides there are indications and signs which clearly ... prove that this question emanates from the 'very heart of the nation'.

This situation and his 'love for Christ' are his apology for choosing the subject. And he goes directly to the very crucial problem of the divinity of Jesus:

The divinity of Jesus – yes, that is the great subject on which I desire to discourse. ... I must proceed to give you some of those ideals and sentiments which for many long years I have cherished in the depth of my heart.

And he explains what he calls 'the doctrine of divine humanity'.

Christ struck the keynote of his doctrine where he announced his divinity in these words: 'I and my Father are one'; ... 'I can of my own self do nothing'; 'I am in my Father and my Father is in me.'

Jesus emptied his own self so utterly that he became the transparent medium in which God indwells and through which men can see God and know him:

He manifested this divine life in man as no other man had ever done before. There is Christ before us as a transparent crystal reservoir in which are the waters of divine life. There is no opaque self to obstruct our vision. The medium is transparent, and we clearly see through Christ the God of truth and holiness dwelling in him. When Jesus was asked by one of his disciples to show the Father, he wondered and said, 'You have seen me and yet you venture to say, you have not seen the Father' ... We see in Jesus perfect self-surrender and perfect asceticism. For if a man has renounced self, what more will he renounce? ... This unique character of complete self-surrender is the most striking miracle in [the] world's history which I have seen, and which it is possible for the mind to conceive.[14]

Indeed it is in the utter self-surrender and dependence of Jesus on God that he manifested the Father and showed himself as the Son.

And then he affirms the pre-existence of the Son as an idea in the Godhead and his incarnation in Jesus of Nazareth to teach us Sonship:

Did he not say distinctly, 'Before Abraham was, I am'? How then, and in what shape, did he exist in heaven? As an Idea, as a plan of life, as a predetermined dispensation yet to be realized, as purity of character, not concrete but abstract, as light not yet manifested ... In fact Christ was nothing but a manifestation on earth, in human form, of certain ideas and sentiments which lay before in the Godhead.

... In the Old Testament of the world's history, you see man's fall through disobedience; the New Testament shows the birth of the obedient child of God, who ever rejoices in doing his Father's will and so came down Jesus in all his glory from heaven to teach us sonship or true loyalty to the Father ... Thus it is that Christ existed in God before he was created. There is an uncreated Christ as also the created Christ, the idea of the son and the incarnate son drawing all his vitality and inspiration from the Father. This is the true doctrine of incarnation. Take away from Christ all that is divine, all that is God's, no Christ remains.[15]

And Keshub speaks of Christ's presence wherever men are swayed by the spirit of sonship in relation to God the Father. The Incarnate Son makes men aware of the presence of Christ in them. He says:

The time is coming and now is when India shall worship the Father in spirit and in truth. The time has come when you can no longer be inimical or indifferent to Christ. Say unto Christ as unto your best friend – welcome! I say emphatically and I say before you all, that Christ is already present in you. He is in you even when you are unconscious of his presence. Even if your lips deny Christ, your hearts have secretly accepted him. For Christ is 'the light that lighteth every man that cometh into the world'. If you have in you the spirit of truth and filial devotion and self-sacrifice that is Christ. What is in a name?[16]

It is in this lecture that Keshub shows how his theology is able to affirm a point of contact with the pattern of thought and experience of traditional Hinduism and to make it a point of departure to convey the idea and experience of sonship understood in the light of Jesus Christ. For instance, he takes the traditional Vedantic idea of mystic union and pantheism and transforms it into an active unity of will and communion through obedience to God and his righteousness. And he justifies India seeking to understand Christ in Indian patterns of thought and life. He only asks that it be true to the reality. He speaks of the doctrine of Divine Humanity as 'essentially a Hindu doctrine', and the picture of Christ's life and character he has drawn as 'altogether a picture of ideal Hindu life.' It is his belief that India will reach Christ through the Vedantic Hindu creed of absorption and immersion in the Deity, which prevails extensively in the country. He speaks of Christ's pantheism as contrasted with a false one.

But what is Hindu pantheism? Essentially it is nothing but the identification of all things with God. I do not mean that you should adopt pantheism as it exists in Hindu books. Far from it. Oh! there are mischievous errors and absurd ideas mixed with it, which you must eschew. Christ's pantheism is a pantheism of a loftier and more perfect type. It is the conscious union of the human with the Divine Spirit in truth, love and joy. The Hindu sage realizes this union only during meditation and contemplation, and he seeks unconscious absorption in his God, with all his faults and shortcomings about him. His will is not at one with the will of God. But Christ's communion is active and righteous; it combines purity of character with devotion. Hindu pantheism in its worst form is proud, being based upon the belief that man is God; it is quietism and trance. Christ's pantheism is the active self-surrender of the will. It is the union of the obedient, humble and loving son with the Father. In Christ you see true pantheism. And as the basis of early Hinduism is pantheism, you, my countrymen, cannot help accepting Christ in the spirit of your natural Scriptures.[17]

During the course of the lecture which we are discussing, Keshub grew lyrical in expressing his devotion to Jesus, and his words have been quoted on many occasions since.[18] And he ended this oration with a clarion call in which he uses the idea of 'the fulness of time' again.

Young men of India ... Believe and remember what Christ has said, and be ready to receive him. He is coming, and in the fulness of time, he will come to you ... The bridegroom is coming. Let India be ready in due season.[19]

The next lecture, on *God-Vision in the Nineteenth Century*, given in 1880, deals with his understanding of the Resurrection of Jesus Christ and his exaltation at the right hand of God. There is here correspondence to the modern process of demythologization and the affirmation of the truth of the myth as the believer's self-assurance in his inner being through faith, about the spiritual victory of the Cross of Christ. It is worth repeating in full.

God almighty, art Thou alone?... Now I ask Thee, O Spirit Supreme, is there anyone else with Thee, or art Thou alone sitting in solitary glory? Methinks, I see another being there. It is my Christ. Yes, it is my Christ who is there. There! where? on the right hand side of God? No, God has neither a right nor a left hand. When I say, Christ is there, do I mean the bodily Christ? No, Science tells me that the body is altogether decomposed in a few days after death. Surely the body cannot rise up; yet my Christ is there. Oh! it is the Spirit of Christ who is there, reclining on the bosom of the Lord. But the man Christ, they say, was cruelly and ignominiously persecuted and crucified unto death by his enemies, and then he was buried and heaps of stone were placed upon his body. But there was such a thing as Resurrection subsequently, so we are told in the Gospel narrative. Are you sure of it? Are you sure that Christ after he was buried soared up to the high heavens? Where is the testimony? Who are the witnesses? I am proud to be one of them, for I do verily believe and am prepared to testify that Christ has risen from his earthly grave. Do I speak with the authority of an eyewitness? Yes, I do. If you think Christ is in the grave, you are certainly dreaming. For where is he to be found on earth? Nowhere. Christ dead and decayed is a deception. Christ risen is Christ indeed. The Spirit of Christ has risen and returned to the Father... Surely thou livest. Thou art in heaven with thy Father, clinging to His bosom. Thy spirit is in Thy Father's Spirit. O Jesus, I again say, Christ has risen. It is no delusion, no dream but a reality, a reality which you can all behold and see... That glorious fact, the resurrection of Christ, every true believer can feel and realise within himself even today, aye at this very moment.... Whenever our hearts are drawn by Christ-force, we are drawn towards heaven, for Christ is not buried but risen. Not only has he risen, but everyone can rise with him and in his Spirit to the highest heaven....[20]

In a later lecture however he sees meaning in the bodily resurrection itself; namely the 'suggestion' of 'continuity of Christ's humanity', the permanent Man for men.

This brings us to the final important lecture by Keshub which we want to examine. It deals with *That Marvellous Mystery, the Trinity*.[21] In 1881 itself, in a letter to Max Muller, Keshub defined his position as 'that of a Uni-Trinitarian', that is, a position, as he understood it, 'between the orthodox Trinitarians on the one hand and the rationalistic Unitarians on the other'.

I set my face completely against the popular doctrine of Christianity, yet

I recognize 'divinity' in some form in Christ, in the sense in which the Son partakes of the Father's divine nature. We in India look upon the son as the father born again.... Hence the Hindu, while regarding the father and the son as distinct and separate persons, connects them in thought by some kind of identity. [In this way] we comprehend the divinity of Jesus as contra-distinguished from his 'Deity'. True sonship, such as it was in Christ, must be divine.[22]

But in the lecture he gives more or less his ultimate position on Christ and the Trinity, his doctrine of Christ as Divine Humanity, emerging as the end of the process of creation, within the mystery of the Triune God.

Keshub gives us a poetic picture of the world of nature, history, morality and love.

All came streaming from that one creative fiat – the Almighty Word. They call it *Logos* ... What was Creation but the Wisdom of God going out of its secret chambers, and taking a visible shape. His potential energy asserting itself in unending activities! The dormant Will stirred itself and as it stirred itself there came forth world after world leaping out of the bosom of God. ... That voice, once uttered, has ever since rolled backward and forward ... creating fresh forms of life and light, east, west, north and south. Creation means not a single act, but a continued process. It began, but has gone on increasingly through all ages ever since it began, ... a continued evolution of creative force, a ceaseless emanation of power and wisdom from the Divine Mind ... His speech, His Word, a continued breathing of force is creation. What a grand metaphor is the Logos!

Keshub connects this 'graduated development through ever-advancing stages of life' of the Logos with 'Indian Avatarism' on the one hand and the scientific theory of evolution on the other:

The Puranas speak of the different manifestations or incarnations of the Deity in different epochs of world's history. Lo! the Hindu avatar rises from the lowest scale of life through the fish, the tortoise and the hog up to the perfection of humanity. Indian Avatarism is indeed a crude representation of the ascending scale of Divine Creation. Such precisely is the modern theory of evolution.

This 'continued evolution of the Logos' culminates in Jesus Christ as its crown:

The New Testament commenced with the birth of the Son of God. The

Logos was the beginning of creation and its perfection too was the Logos – the culmination of humanity in the Divine Son. We have arrived at the last link in the series of created organism. The last expression of Divinity is Divine Humanity. Having exhibited itself in endless varieties of progressive existence the primary creative force at last took the form of the Son in Christ Jesus.

Keshub reflects on the divine-human nature of Jesus Christ. And his central emphasis is on the essential humanity of the Son. He has a human nature which is perfect because of its unity with the Divine nature. As has already been stated, the significance of the bodily resurrection

however untenable on scientific grounds, suggests a very important idea. It suggests the continuity of his humanity. . . . Here man remains man . . . he was intended and designed by Providence to be unto man a man, a pattern man, a God-man, and so he was, and so he is, and so he shall continue to be through endless ages. . . . He is humanity pure and simple in which Divinity dwells. In him we see human nature perfected by the affiliation to the Divine nature. And in this affiliation we see the fullest realization of the purpose of Christ's life and ministry. . . . What is Christianity but the Religion of Humanity – or shall I say the worship of Humanity. [Christianity is] Brother-worship! A strange doctrine! Yet perfectly logical. Christ . . . is our holy brother in flesh.

Creation however cannot stop here. The universalization of the divine sonship of Jesus Christ is the next stage in the creative process. Sonship is bound to develop itself in all humanity.

God sent His only begotten Son in order to make all his children, one and all, sons and heirs of God. . . . The problem of creation was not how to produce one Christ, but how to make every man Christ. Christ . . . was 'the way'. . . . He [went] through the whole length and breadth of humanity illuminating and sanctifying all generations of mankind with the radiance of Divinity.

And the divine sonship 'carrying all mankind heavenward' is the Holy Spirit who 'makes all mankind partakers of Divine Life'.

Thus it is the Holy Spirit that 'makes Christ, otherwise a mere historical character, a sanctifying power with us', establishing 'the Logos within us as the Divine Son subjectified'.

To the Holy Spirit belongs the glory of begetting and baptising the Son of

God, as scriptural history testifies; and to Him and Him alone belongs the power of converting all mankind into Sons of God.

So Keshub shows 'the complete triangular figure of the Trinity', with 'the whole of the economy of creation' and 'philosophy of salvation'. He says:

The apex is the very God Jehovah, the Supreme Brahma of the Vedas. Alone, in his own eternal glory He dwells. From him comes down the Son, in a direct line, an emanation from Divinity. Thus God descends and touches one end of the base of humanity; then running all along the base permeates the world and there by the power of the Holy Ghost drags up degenerated humanity to Himself. Divinity coming down to Humanity is the Son; Divinity carrying up humanity to heaven is the Holy Ghost.

J. N. Farquhar and M. C. Parekh on Keshub's Christology

J. N. Farquhar, writing in *Modern Religious Movements in India*, though critical of many aspects of Keshub's life and thought, gives the verdict that Keshub was moving forward 'steadily nearer an adequate account of Christ's person and His relation to God'. In his opinion,

Keshub's richest religious experience came from Christ, and, in consequence, in the latter part of his life, his deepest theological beliefs were fully Christian.[23]

Keshub's Christology moulded Manilal Parekh's mind and represented his own theological position for more than a decade while he was a member of the New Dispensation Church.[24] But as he moved to greater appreciation of the orthodox Christian position in Christology, Parekh became more critical of Keshub's Christology. Of his lecture on the Trinity Parekh says that it is full of inconsistencies.

It is neither more nor less than a shifting to and fro among ancient and exploded heresies; his position on the whole is akin to Arianism, ... though at times it approached what is called Semi-Arianism.

He recognizes however that Keshub has made 'a great advance' in his theological thinking on Christ, 'inasmuch as he identifies Christ with Logos', and sees Christ as the Word of God through whom God created the whole universe and continues the creative process. But Parekh is very critical of the total identification of the Word of God with the evolutionary process.

This view, wide as it was, lacked depth, inasmuch as Keshub ... failed to see the great gaps in that process of evolution. The fact is that Keshub ... does not take into account the awful abyss between man and God caused by sin, an abyss which can only be bridged by the love of God suffering on behalf of sinful man. It is this which we see in Christ, as he suffers in Gethsemane the agony and bloody sweat, and as he endures the awful solitude and shame and pain of the Cross. The divine humanity of Christ is not to be explained as merely a link in a process of Evolution, for though it brought a higher stage of life in the existence of man, it did this at the incalculable cost of what is known as the *kenosis* i.e. the self-emptying of God Himself. And it is in this remedial act on the part of God Himself, in this awful tragedy of sin and its outblotting, that the Holy Trinity reveals Itself. The self-revelations of the Trinity as described by Keshub under the figure of a triangle has in it no Cross, where the Son takes upon Himself the God-forsakenness of Humanity, and by separating Himself from God unites us to Him, and thereby reveals the depth of life and love in the Eternal Being of God. As represented by him, the process looks more like the *Vaishnavic Lila* or playful enjoyment of God, than the supreme tragedy of man's and consequently God's existence too which it is.[25]

This is well stated, and is justified in relation to the lecture on the Trinity, on which Parekh comments. But the criticism is exaggerated if we take Keshub's total approach. In the earlier lectures, he makes clear the total self-emptying in Jesus which made him the fullness of God, transparent to reveal and mediate divinity through his humanity. Parekh himself quotes Keshub's ideas on sin, atonement and reconciliation in Christ:

Man waged war with God, through atonement they are reconciled. Man waged war with man; they are reconciled through atonement. The atoning medium in each case is Jesus Christ, the Son of God. ... In his atoning blood, the most polluted of all ages and climes find a place. ... Once for all in history, the blessed atonement was consummated by Christ. The consummation was complete and absolute. Christ has offered himself, as an atonement for all flesh and for all eternity. It is done, it is done. He has given his precious blood for all of us, whether we believe it or not.[26]

Keshub criticized the orthodox Christians and the Church for preaching Jesus Christ as the Father 'appearing on earth in human shape like the avatars of Hinduism'; he called this 'idolatry and heresy', contrary to 'the early Fathers', 'Holy Writ' and Christ. Probably he had Marshman's description of Jesus as 'Jehovah God' in mind. In this Parekh sees both misunderstanding of the Church's teaching and confusion of thought on the part of Keshub.

'The Christian Church has never said that Christ is the incarnation of the Father; and to say so has been considered by it a heresy. Unfortunately Keshub made so sharp a distinction between the Father and the Son that he forgot that father and son are correlative terms and . . . it is the sonship of Christ which makes the fatherhood of God possible and vice versa. The Christian dispensation was nothing but a fuller revelation of God himself . . . The Christian revelation is the revelation of the Fatherhood of God, through the life of Sonship of Jesus Christ.[27]

Parekh also lists a great many contradictions contained in Keshub's statement about 'Christ's position within the Trinity'.

He calls him the Logos, the taking of the form of the primary creative Force, an emanation from Divinity, and the manifestation of the Lord of Heaven and earth. He again calls him the Father's begotten Son, a child, a creature. . . . In another place in the same lecture he says he upholds even the co-eternity of the Son with the Father, 'though not as a person but as a sleeping Logos', which lived potentially within the Father's bosom. He calls him the Reason of God begotten by the 'volition' of the Almighty. In another place, he calls Christ the second person of the Holy Trinity. All this is highly inconsistent with itself. . . .

He gives three reasons for all these inconsistencies. In his opinion Keshub had no 'coherent system of thought'; 'he was never at his best in philosophical speculation'; and further he carried with him the remnants of Unitarianism in his thought from the early days of Brahmoism. It was this last that made him fail to understand that the orthodox Trinitarian doctrine, instead of violating the unity of God, 'filled it with a content and reality, without which the idea of God becomes a mere abstraction. The whole question centres round the fact that God in his essence is love. Thus in many respects, Keshub's Christology was 'yet far from that full-orbed faith that shows forth from the Gospels and the Epistles, in the lives and teachings of the Apostles and Fathers, martyrs and saints'. Nevertheless Parekh is emphatic in affirming that 'Keshub had really arrived at a point which is in a way within the compass of Christianity.'[28]

Farquhar also asserts that 'Keshub was not a consistent thinker, far less a systematic theologian'.²⁹ However, it is unfair to judge a pioneer who sought to formulate a Christology which will do justice to his spiritual vision of Christ, and explain that vision in the context of a situation in which the currents of the rationalist, the biblical and Hindu thought met, except in terms of his theological intention. Certainly he was not consistent or systematic. It would have been difficult even for a better systematic thinker to succeed. His very failure in the effort to formulate his Christology in a language adequate to express the depth of his faith in Christ as the centre of his own spiritual life and the fulfilment of the Western and Indian religious heritages, had its magnificence. And the judgment of S. K. Datta, surveying Indian theology in the first decade of the twentieth century, that

The nearest approach to a distinctly Indian interpretation of Christ has come from a non-Christian sect, Brahmo Samaj,³⁰

is justified if we consider Keshub's idea of Christ as the Divine Humanity.

Keshub's doctrine of Divine Humanity which links the incarnation with the whole creative process has a certain theological quality which still remains to be explored by the Indian Church. It has similarities with the idea of Jesus Christ as the 'inhumanisation' of divinity, characteristic of some Russian Orthodox theologians, especially Solovyev. No doubt, as Parekh says, the discontinuity of sin and the centrality of the Lamb slain from the foundation of the world and the Cross of Christ did not find their proper emphasis. But this has been the characteristic danger in all theologies of the creative cosmic process with a Creation–Incarnation–Resurrection axis. We shall meet the same problem in P. Chenchiah's theology of the New Creation. The same feature exists in the theology of de Chardin. But the opposite danger exists in the theologies starting with the discontinuity of the Cross and eschatology from the process of nature and history. Christ never becomes fully involved in the process. These two theologies need to correct each other. But both types of formulation must be judged valid. And it is significant that Keshub does not forget the importance of the righteous will and ethical content of the gospel in his enthusiasm for the Divine Humanity; indeed he makes the surrender of the human will of Jesus to the will of the Father in love, the basis of his transparency for the manifestation of the Divine Sonship. Keshub here shows great depth of understanding about the relation between the moral and the spiritual dimensions of human existence. But in some of his christological formulations, especially when dealing with the universal reality of the Logos and the universal presence of Christ and the universal activity of the Holy Spirit, one has the suspicion that Keshub had given up the centrality of the historical Jesus as the Word Incarnate and as the basis and criterion of the Holy Spirit. In fact, Unitarians of Britain criticized the religion of Keshub's Church as 'a mass of mysticism, superstition and absurdity'.[31] If it is so, then Keshub's move away from the rational moral secularism of Rammojan Roy into religious ecstasy and metaphysics cannot be said to have been an unambiguous movement towards a fuller apprehension and appropriation of the truth of Jesus Christ. This however must be examined in relation to Keshub's approach to the relation of Jesus Christ to Christianity and Hinduism, and to the nature and function of the Church.

2. UNIVERSAL CHRIST AND INDIGENOUS CHURCH

There is in Keshub Chunder Sen an affirmation of the distinctively Asian heritage in religion, metaphysics and culture, not merely as a medium of communication of the meaning of Christ but as containing truth and value which should find fulfilment in Jesus Christ and his Universal Church. Even in his first lecture, Keshub presents Jesus Christ as revealing 'the grandeur of which Asiatic nature is susceptible' and his religion as 'altogether an oriental affair'.[32] Later he draws his picture of the Oriental Christ more vividly.

Behold, he cometh to us in his loose flowing garment, his dress and features altogether oriental, a perfect Asiatic in everything. Watch his movements and you will find genuine orientalism in all his habits and manners, in his uprising and down-sitting, his going forth and his coming in, his preaching and ministry, his very language, style and tone. Indeed, while reading the Gospel, we cannot but feel that we are quite at home when we are with Jesus, and that he is altogether one of us. Surely Jesus is our Jesus.[33]

No doubt, Christ is universal, and in him 'Europe and Asia, the East and the West may learn to find harmony and unity'. But he warns the 'native converts to Christianity' that they should not 'confound the spirit of Christianity with the fashions of Western civilization'. Christ must be seen within the universal framework and made indigenous. In his subsequent lectures he included Mohammed and Chaitanya among the prophets who prepared the way for Christ or continued his work after him and spoke of Sakhyamuni, Confucius and Zoroaster along with Christ at the right hand of God. Thus Christ was to be understood and appropriated in the context of all cultures and religions.[34]

The idea of Jesus Christ as the source of correction and fulfilment of Hinduism appears in several places in Keshub's lectures. 'In Christ you see true pantheism', and he is the criterion to judge and reform Hindu pantheism.

In accepting him ... you accept the spirit of a devout Yogi and loving Bhakta, the fulfilment of your national prophets and scriptures.[35]

If you have the true Christ in you, all truth, whether Jew or Gentile, Hindu or Christian, will pour into you through him, and you will be able to assimilate the wisdom and righteousness of each sect and denomination.[36] ... Christ is not Christianity. ... I have always disclaimed the Christian name and will not identify myself with the Christian Church, for I set my face completely against the popular doctrine of Christianity. ...[37] I repudiate the little Christ of popular theology, and stand up for a greater Christ, a fuller Christ, a more eternal Christ.[38]

He explains his 'Logos-Christ' thus:

Scattered in all men and women of the East and the West are multitudinous Christ-principles and fragments of Christ-life – one vast and identical Sonship diversely manifested. ... Thus all reason in man is Christ-reason, all love is Christ-love, all power is Christ-power. ... It exists even where it is not professed.[39]

And after the Son, this is the Dispensation of the Holy Spirit who universalizes Divine Humanity by leavening all mankind with the 'Christ-leaven' and establishing 'the Logos within us as the Divine Son subjectified'.[40]

Based on these theological principles, Keshub defines his concept of the future Church as both indigenous and universal:

The future Church of India must be thoroughly an Indian Church. The future religion of the world will be the common religion of all nations, but in each nation it will have an indigenous growth, and assume a peculiar and distinctive character.[41]

Certainly Keshub was an eclectic in religion. But we are here concerned with Keshub's theology of the relation between Christ, Christianity and other religions underlying his eclecticism. Though it is difficult to find one consistent theology of Keshub on this point, it is possible to detect three strands of his thought.

The first is 'a belief in the supremacy of Christ as the God-man',[47] which impelled him to see the harmony of religions in his 'Eclectic Church' as definitely Christ-centred. In 1883 he could say:

We preach not a new sect but the death of sectarianism and the universal reconciliation of all churches. But the very idea of an Eclectic Church, it will be contended, is anti-Christian. To mix Christ up with the hundred-and-one creeds of the world is to destroy and deny Christ. . . . [But] it is not a treaty of Christ with anti-Christ that is proposed, but the reconciliation of all in Christ. . . . Nay, I would go further and declare Christ to be the centre of this Broad Church.[43]

P. C. Mozoomdar remarks:

In Keshub's ideal of a National Church, the religion of Christ composed a very large element, nay more than half the substance.[44]

More than this, the selection of elements from national religions is made in the light of Christ. Thus to quote Mozoomdar again,

The growth of the Christian spirit in the New Dispensation revival thus became national, and the growth of national theistic religion was regulated by the Spirit and teachings of Christ.[45]

Second, we find the idea that all religions are equally true. Keshub has given expression to this doctrine in an article appearing in the *Sunday Mirror* on 23 October 1865.

Our position is not that truths are to be found in all religions [and to be gathered in Christ, with Christ as criterion], but that all the established religions of the world are true. . . . The glorious mission of the New Dispensation is to harmonize religions and revelations [and] to establish the truth of every particular dispensation.[46]

The third strand was Keshub's doctrine of *adesh* (Divine inspiration) in which he saw himself as divinely appointed and commissioned to be 'the leader of the New Dispensation in which all religions are harmonized and which all men are summoned to enter as their spiritual home'.[47] At this point he may possibly have seen the Holy Spirit mediated through his own *adesh* as the basis and criterion of truths in the various religions to be harmonized.

Parekh holds that the statement affirming Jesus Christ as 'the standard by which he wants to judge all the religions before selecting therefrom the Christian elements' (which was made in 1883 and referred to above) expressed Keshub's most mature conviction; and Parekh adds that it is 'purely Christian'. Farquhar is of the opinion that probably under the influence of Ramakrishna Paramahamsa, Keshub may have shifted from a Christ-centred harmony to the idea of the equality of all established religions. Of course, it remains still an open question whether Shri Ramakrishna influenced Keshub or *vice versa* at this point. In any case Keshub also attempted a unification of diverse religious beliefs and practices in the Church of the New Dispensation on the basis of the authority of his own *adesh*. Most probably these three theological criteria were mixed up in Keshub, 'crossed and hindered' by each other, with one or another of them coming to the forefront at different times, making 'his teaching about the New Dispensation' more inconsistent than some of his other teachings.

Inconsistency apart, the idea of a Christ-centred integration of the Indian and Western religious and cultural heritages expressing itself in an indigenous Christianity is highly relevant to the future of the Christian Church in India. In fact, the Church of South India has written into its constitution that it stands for a Church expressing the universality of Christ in indigenous thought-patterns and life-forms of the Indian people. In view of the rapid changes taking place in these thought-patterns and life-forms, it is necessary to say that the Church must become indigenous not to an India that is past, but to contemporary India in which the religious and cultural traditions of its hoary past are themselves seeking reintegration within the context of the struggle for a new humanism relevant to the developing secular pluralistic and open society. In fact not only Keshub Chunder Sen, but Rammohan Roy also is relevant at this point.

The concern for a Christ-centred integration of Christian and other traditions in India must be seen in contrast with the idea of building a universal religion based on the equality of all established religions. We shall examine this idea when we consider Ramakrishna Paramahamsa, Swami Vivekananda and Dr S. Radhakrishnan. It is in most cases the result of a basic mystic spiritual or exclusively ethical utilitarian devaluation of all historic religions; and in either approach, the idea of a unique divine act in history for the salvation of mankind has no central place or significance.

The doctrine of *adesh*, the inspiration of the Holy Spirit, has its proper place in any doctrine of the Church. It is the basis of creativity, reform and renewal of the Church, which must take place continually if the Church is to be a living one. But the Holy Spirit who inspires, guides and sanctifies is the spirit of Jesus Christ, recalling the Church to himself or revealing new truths of him and his will. But no new truth can be contradictory to the Christ-event recorded in the Scriptures and embedded in the tradition of the Church across the ages. Therefore *adesh* of the Holy Spirit must be anchored in the Scriptures, and work within the context of the living tradition of the continuity of faith, the historic Church of Christ. Outside this framework *adesh* has been productive of indiscipline and disunity in the Church across the ages; and, completely out of touch with the historic tradition of the Church, it did become sectarian and individualistic in Keshub. In fact, what Keshub's theology of the Church utterly lacked was the idea of a tradition giving the Church a historic continuity and unity based on common authority of faith, sacraments and ministry. In Keshub's definition of the Holy Spirit, the Church and *adesh*, there is a predominance of the mystical over the historical and of self-sufficient individualism over the discipline of a fellowship. This is the source of weakness in Keshub's theology.

A. *The Meaning of Apostolic Authority*

Indeed the Church of Christ today does not manifest its unity and continuity in an organically structured community, either within the nation or in the world as a whole. The *adesh* has found its expressions in the discontinuity and disunity of the Church; and it is significant that in 1883 Keshub wrote to the Metropolitan of India precisely on this point, asking the Bishops' Conference to consider the question of the unity of the Church of India as an urgent matter for the sake of an effective witness to Christ in India. He wrote to the Bishop of Calcutta, Edward Ralph Johnson:

Secondly: Unity in the Church of Christ. Sectarianism being a thing carnal is baneful at all times and in all positions. But here in India it greatly hinders the acceptance of Christ by the people. When so many churches and sects offer themselves and demand allegiance, India confounded and vexed asks, – Which is the true Church of Christ? Is it not possible, my Lord, to introduce greater harmony into the Christian community in India.[48]

This challenge has been behind the Church unity movements in India, leading to the Church of South India, and the scheme of Union of Northern India. But even where the Church remains fragmented, the fragments affirm some 'given elements', the deposit of faith, sacraments and ministry as the basis of the apostolic authority and continuity which they claim, and within which they remain. It is these 'given elements' as the source of authority which are lacking in the doctrine of authority claimed by Keshub Chunder Sen and the Church of the New Dispensation on the basis of *adesh*. It is no doubt hard for a divided Church, with each denomination claiming apostolic authority, somewhat exclusively of each other, to impress this point on Keshub Chunder Sen and to dismiss him and the Church of the New Dispensation as having no share in such authority. This is evident from a brief encounter which took place between Keshub and the Bishops of the Anglican and Roman Churches in Calcutta. Keshub Chunder Sen's 'Minister's Epistle' or New Year Message begins as follows:

Keshub Chunder Sen, a servant of God, called to be an apostle of the Church of the New Dispensation, which is in the holy city of Calcutta, the metropolis of Aryavarta, to all the great nations in the world and to the chief religious sects in the east and the west,
to the followers of Moses, of Jesus, of Buddha, of Confucius, of Zoroaster, of Mahmet, of Nanak and to the various branches of the Hindu Church, to the saints and sages, the bishops and the elders, the ministers and the missionaries of all these religious bodies,
Grace be unto you and peace everlasting.

And then the central message vouchsafed to Keshub:

Thus saith the Lord –

Sectarianism is an abomination unto me and unbrotherliness I will not
   tolerate....
These words hath the Lord our God spoken unto us, and His new gospel
   He hath revealed unto us, a gospel of exceeding joy.
The Church universal hath he already planted in this land, and therein
   are all prophets and all scriptures harmonized in beautiful synthesis....
Let Asia, Europe, Africa and America with divine instruments praise the
   New Dispensation, and sing the Fatherhood of God and the Brother-
   hood of Man.[49]

According to the comment on 'Three Messages' appearing in the *New Dispensation* of Sunday 29 July 1883,[50] this 'Ministers' Epistle' called forth 'two important documents' one the 'Message of the Church of England Bishops of India and Ceylon in Conference assembled in Calcutta' and 'A Reply' to Sen by the Roman Catholic Bishop Meurin, the Vicar Apostolic of Bombay, entitled 'the True Basis of Christian Fellowship'. All the three documents 'relate to fellowship', but it is the discussion on 'authority' raised by the Churches which is of special interest to us. Bishop Meurin seems to have argued that the Protestants have no divine message or credentials, and the self-assertion of Babu Sen is 'blasphemous arrogance and imposition', or the result of 'hallucination'. If God had elected Sen 'to be His apostle he would have endowed him with the gift of miracles or with that of prophecy or with both'. The editorial answer to these arguments is simple:

Dr Meurin does the same thing; the Anglican Bishops do the same thing. They hold their respective creeds to be divine and they therefore preach them as infallible and authoritative messages revealed by God, not the crotchets or invention of man's erring intellect. And if in so doing they are not guilty of imposition or hallucination why should the poor preacher of the New Dispensation be ridiculed or hated as such?

Further, as for miracles and prophecy, he asks:

If the divinity of his [the Babu's] own mission and message is considered doubtful for want of miracles and prophecies, what are the miracles or prophecies to authenticate the divinity of the eight Anglican Bishops' mission and message of fellowship. And may we not apply the same crucial test to the Catholic Bishop himself? Where are his credentials? What proof is there of the divinity of his mission and message?[50]

A significant fact is that the 'Comment' at one point distinguishes the source of authority Jesus had for his message and 'the inspiration or revelation' behind other claims, The former is 'supernatural' in origin but for all the rest, including the Anglican, the Roman and the New Dispensation, it is 'natural'.

In neither case is there anything beyond natural inspiration and command of conscience which is a command of God.[51]

We do not know how far this represents Keshub's own views or how it would square with his doctrine of the Holy Spirit. But this question of the apostolic authority of the Church and its relation to the authority of Jesus Christ, continued in the Holy Spirit and the authority of inspiration supernatural and natural, has remained in Indian Christian theology a most important subject for defining the nature of the election, which makes the people of Christ the divinely ordained medium of the universal mission of God in Christ. It is the *sui generis* character of Church authority that is here placed in question. This problem comes up again in the writing of the Rethinking Christianity Group in one form, and in the theological discussions on Church unity in another; and it continues to be with us in all our dialogues with those outside the organized Church of Christ.

B. *'The Hindu Church of Christ'*

Keshub's Church of the New Dispensation has also raised another theological issue in this whole debate, namely the Christian status, *vis-à-vis* the Church, of individuals and groups who have seen and met God in and through Jesus Christ, and are even prepared to accept him as their God and Saviour in some verbal confessional form, but are not convinced that they should leave the society, culture and religion of Hinduism, to join the social, cultural and religious structure of Christianity in India, which expresses the Church in the main line of continuity with the historic Church of Christ. There are three questions here. First, what is the Christian interpretation of the relation of Christian faith to non-Western cultures and societies, and non-Christian religions? and in what sense if any, do we consider them as having a divine purpose in the economy of God's creative and redemptive purposes? Many issues arise here. Do we seek the conversion of Hindus or the conversion of Hinduism? In the conversion of the Hindu to Christ, can Hinduism play any positive role? Can the Hindu who becomes Christian bring any new understanding of Christ to the world Church? Second, what is the Christian interpretation of the renaissance taking place among Hindus and in Hinduism, as a result of their positive response to Christianity as ethics, religion and/or spirit. Third, how far can a Hindu Christianity be considered an embodiment of Christ or at least a preparation for the conversion of Hindus and Hinduism to Christ and for the fuller development of a truly Indian Church?

These questions remain more acute today than ever before, and will come up over and over again in our enquiry regarding Christian theology in India today.

c. *Parekh on Keshub Chunder Sen and Azariah's Reply*

To highlight the theological issues underlying Keshub's ideas of the harmony of religions and the Hindu Church of Christ, we may take the article Parekh wrote in the *International Review of Missions* of 1928 on 'Keshub Chunder Sen: His Relation to Christianity' and the comment on it in the same issue of the magazine by Bishop Azariah of Dornakal under the title 'India and Christ'.[52]

Parekh notes the different elements of the positive responses within Hinduism to Christ – the crude form of adding Jesus Christ to the Hindu pantheon, Gandhi's acceptance of his moral teachings as authoritative and in some cases the acknowledgement by a few of Jesus Christ as Lord and Master, Saviour and God. Of course, many of those who have made such positive response, keep away from 'organized forms of Christianity of any kind', and are suspicious of all forms of proselytism by the missions. A corresponding positive response is growing among Christians expressed in the search for the 'good in Hinduism', the realization of Westcott that the mystic approach to Hinduism will help contribute to 'the interpretation of the inner meaning of the religion of Christ'. This double movement finds its expression in Keshub Chunder Sen's New Dispensation which was 'nothing less than the Christo-centric harmony of religions in general and of Hinduism and Christianity in particular'. He believed that

The higher and purer spirit [of Hinduism] will pass through the New

Dispensation into the life of Christ making true Hinduism and true Christianity one thing in God.

Parekh expressed his conviction that 'the affiliation of the mystic consciousness of the Hindu race to the Spirit of Christ through the establishment of the Hindu Church of Christ' which Keshub accomplished was a uniqe service to 'both Hinduism and Christianity', trying to 'reconcile them in Christ Jesus'.

Bishop Azariah in his reply notes 'the fact that India is wistfully turning her eyes towards Jesus Christ' today more than in the days of Keshub Chunder Sen. This, he sees as a strong argument to 'formulate in unequivocal language the Gospel we have to present to India at this interesting period of her history'. The Bishop goes on to point out, that Hinduism is essentially not a belief, but

> a scheme of life; it is a bundle of practices and observances that have caste as their centre and circumference . . .
> What Keshub said is indisputedly true: Hinduism is remarkably tolerant of heresies; the touch of the Musalman and the shadow of the Yavana is an abomination, and yet the orthodox Hindu has no scruples in offering homage to *pir* or in receiving Buddha as the ninth incarnation of Vishnu. Hinduism is certainly 'a vast and mighty absorbant'; as long as its social system is not disturbed it will patronize and absorb all rivals.[53]

And then he asks:

> What is Christianity? It is often said that Christianity is Christ. That is true; but it is also a way of life; . . . it is a scheme of life in a society; it is an organism, a family, a fellowship, a brotherhood – whose centre, radius and circumference is Christ.

The conflict between Christianity and Hinduism arises not primarily at the level of doctrines, but precisely as between rival 'schemes of life in society'; and there can be no compromise between Hinduism as caste and Christianity as fellowship in Christ.

The Hindu way of life stands for caste and exclusivism; the Christian way of life for catholicity and inclusiveness. In it there can be neither Jew nor Greek, neither circumcision nor uncircumcision, neither barbarian nor Scythian, neither bondman nor freeman, neither male nor female; all are one in Christ Jesus. The Hindu way of life culminates in personal mystic union with God; the Christian way is unselfish service for man. 'He saved others, himself he cannot save.' Here is irreconcilable conflict.[54]

The fact that the Church is not good enough for Indians to join, too organized for Indian genius, and divided in the doctrine or practice of the Sacraments, does not justify them in 'remaining outside organized Churches' as 'secret believers' or organizing a 'Hindu Church of Christ' or an 'Oriental Catholic Church'.

For the Church is not an association that individuals can or may organize for their own convenience. It is the Body of Christ, a new creation which came into being by His own creative act.

Into this 'new creation' men enter through 'the waters of baptism'. And baptism symbolizes a new scheme of life, within a new fellowship:

At baptism, men separated themselves from their old scheme of life – social, moral and religious – and entered a new way of life in a new fellowship.⁵⁵

And the common life of this fellowship is nurtured by

a common faith . . ., a common discipline . . ., a common task . . ., a common worship . . ., and . . . a common participation of Christ.

in the Sacrament of Holy Communion. In spite of its divisions, the Church is still, 'undoubtedly the one instrument of His Spirit's special operation in the world'.

What a presumption to call any association a Church that is not in fellowship with the One, Holy Catholic and Apostolic Church of which Jesus Christ Himself is the foundation and corner stone.

The significant thing in Azariah's article is his emphasis on faith in Christ primarily as participation in a universal fellowship which is continuous in history and which involves common sharing in a common mission and service to the world based on a corporate religious and social life. This understanding of faith is distinguished from faith understood as mystic vision or religious philosophy or caste.

Bishop Azariah's position represented the forward-looking wing of the established Protestant Churches in India. The debate raises some interesting questions. For example: What is the place of the mystic elements in the Christian scheme? This we shall consider when we come to examine the Christian response to the Ramakrishna movement. Again, in what sense can we equate Christ with a scheme of religious and social life, and the fellowship of divine *agape* with a social structure? and how far should Christ and *agape* be seen as transcending all schemes of religious life and social orders and able to judge and transform them all? In India, is the Christian fellowship to be seen as a social alternative to caste, and Christianity as a religious alternative to Hinduism? This would be to identify faith too fully with the Church and the Christian community. Though we are far from denying the partial historical realization both sacramentally and socially of the fellowship of *agape* in the Church, it must be seen as an eschatological reality which is never fully identified with any scheme of society or religion. It is this eschatological note that one misses in Bishop Azariah's necessary emphasis on the historical manifestation in the life of the Church as the essence of faith. If we have this eschatological approach, we shall certainly not absolutize Christian religion or Christian society. And if Christ transcends Christian religion and society, the question whether Christ and *agape* are to be seen also as a spiritual ferment working within the Hindu society and Hindu religion to convert them to Christ and to judge and redeem them in him without destroying them is not an irrelevant one. Further, Azariah has identified Hinduism with the caste scheme of life. But when Hinduism itself has rejected that scheme as inadequate and is engaged in a struggle to express a new idea of society more in tune with the Christian scheme, can this be considered in some sense a movement of Hinduism to Christ? Or again, when the trend in Hinduism is to seek to express spirituality more in moral and social than in metaphysical and mystical terms, what is our Christian estimate of such a search?

The eschatological and the historical are both essential characteristics of the Christian faith and must be kept together without either too radical a division between them or too radical an identification. This has serious implications for the Christian approach to Christianity and its relation to other religions, for the Christian understanding of traditional social structures and the Christian responsibility in them, and for defining the nature of the Church in the Indian setting. We shall revert to some of these implications as we go along.

NOTES

1 J. N. Farquhar, *Modern Religious Movements in India*, New York and London, 1915, p. 22.
2 M. C. Parekh, *Bramarshi Keshub Chunder Sen*, Rajkot, 1931, p. v.
3 *Ib.*, p. 21.
4 P. C. Mozoomdar, *The Life and Teachings of Keshub Chunder Sen*, Calcutta, 1887, pp. 176f.
5 Parekh, p. 22. 6 *Ib.*, pp. 26f.
7 Mozoomdar, p. 176. 8 *Ib.*, p. 178.
9 *Ib.*, p. 179. 10 *Ib.*, p. 180.
11 Parekh, p. 33. 12 Mozoomdar, p. 205.
13 Quoted by Mozoomdar, p. 224. 14 Parekh, pp. 98 f.
15 *Ib.*, pp. 99f. 16 *Ib.*, p. 103f.
17 *Ib.*, pp. 101f. Writing in the *Indian Mirror*, he comes to the same idea of a distinctive revision of pantheism in the light of Christ: 'Let the Indian pantheist behold God everywhere and everything in him, but let him also, through Christ, accept the distinct personality of manhood, and by separating himself from Divinity, learn that the only way to bridge the gulf between God and Man is not the total absorption of the human in the Divine essence, but to so surrender self that for once and for ever, his will may coincide with the Divine will.' (Quoted by Parekh, p. 110.)
18 For instance, (1) 'None but Jesus, none but Jesus ever deserved this bright, this precious diadem, India; and Jesus shall have it' (*Ib.* p. 94). (2) 'My Christ, my Sweet Christ, the brightest jewel of my heart, the necklace of my soul—for twenty years have I cherished him in my miserable heart . . . The mighty artillery of his love he levelled against me, and I was vanquished and I fell at his feet, saying – Blessed child of God, when shall others see the light that is in thee? Therefore I say, countrymen, be not as the unbelievers are, do not throw yourselves into the vortex of materialism and scepticism. Christ your friend is walking through the streets of this country, carrying the banners of God, the Most High . . .' (*Ib.*, p. 104).
19 *Ib.*, p. 105. 20 *Ib.*, pp. 113–15.
21 *Ib.*, pp. 150–70. The passages quoted below occur on pp. 154–9.
22 *Ib.*, pp. 149f. 23 Farquhar, *op. cit.*, pp. 66f.
24 Parekh, *op. cit.*, Preface. 25 *Ib.*, pp. 72f.
26 *Ib.*, pp. 194f. 27 *Ib.*, pp. 165, 173–5.
28 *Ib.*, pp. 171–4. 29 Farquhar, *op. cit.*, p. 63.
30 S. K. Datta, *The Desire of India*, London, 1908, pp. 255f.
31 *The Inquirer*, 12 May 1883, quoted in *The New Dispensation*, vol. II, 2nd ed., Calcutta, 1916, p. 222.
32 Parekh, pp. 24f. 33 *Ib.*, p. 95.
34 *Ib.*, pp. 25f., 33. 35 *Ib.*, pp. 102f.
36 *Ib.*, p. 133. 37 *Ib.*, p. 149.
38 *Ib.*, p. 160. 39 *Ib.*, p. 162–4.
40 *Ib.*, p. 167. 41 Mozoomdar, p. 205.
42 Farquhar, *op. cit.*, p. 56. 43 Parekh, pp. 188f.
44 Mozoomdar, p. 349, cited by Parekh, p. 120.
45 Mozoomdar, p. 361.
46 Quoted by Farquhar, *op. cit.*, p. 57.
47 Farquhar, p. 55.
48 *The New Dispensation*, vol. II, pp. 178–82. 49 *Ib.*, pp. 173–5.
50 *Ib.*, pp. 241–8; quotations below from p. 245.
51 *Ib.*, p. 247.
52 *International Review of Missions* 17, 1928, pp. 145–54 and 154–9.
53 *Ib.*, p. 155. 54 *Ib.*, p. 156. 55 *Ib.*, p. 157.

CHAPTER FOUR

P. C. Mozoomdar: The Oriental Christ and the Unfolding Spirit

The one colleague of Keshub Chunder Sen in the Church of the New Dispensation, who came nearest to him in his discipleship of Jesus Christ was Pratap Chander Mozoomdar. He was also the author of the *Life and Teachings of Keshub Chunder Sen*. He finished a book on Jesus Christ during his first visit to America and it was published in 1883. This book, *The Oriental Christ*, elucidates the understanding of Jesus Christ as Divine Humanity which he learned from Keshub. It is however significant that Mozoomdar places the primary emphasis on picturing Christ in the framework of oriental patterns of thought and spirituality. He says that the life and teachings of Jesus 'presented by Christian missionaries through the coloured medium of European ideals and European theology' had failed to make any point of contact with the distinctive 'spiritual instincts and national sympathies' of the Hindus.[1] Everything universal has also its indigenous character. Further if 'the light of oriental faith and mystic devotion' is allowed to fall upon 'the celestial figure of the sweet Prophet of Nazareth', that figure will be 'illumined with strange and unknown radiance'[2] This should add to the 'depth and variety of spiritual estimates' of him in the world and must be a 'gain to humanity'.[3] Therefore, he says, he has consciously 'tried to orientalize him [Christ] as much as possible'.[4] What does this orientalization mean? He contrasts the Eastern Christ with the Western Christ:

When we speak of an Eastern Christ, we speak of the incarnation of unbounded love and grace; and when we speak of the Western Christ we speak of the incarnation of theology, formalism, ethical and physical force.[5]

1. THE FRAMEWORK OF THEOLOGY: THE DIVINE SPIRIT

A. *A Revised Pantheism*

In seeking to discover an Indian spiritual and metaphysical framework for his understanding of Christ and his experience of him Mozoomdar relies in his 1883 writings on a revised pantheism. He explains that there are different kinds of pantheism. Mozoomdar makes clear what kind the Brahmo Samaj repudiates and what kind it accepts as an essential aspect of the 'spiritual instinct of India'. In this choice between pantheism and pantheism, Christ and Christian teachings themselves are presented as the criteria. Thus the Brahmo rejects a pantheism which is destructive of divine or human personality:

... Christ did not destroy his personality. Christ did not come to teach us to destroy our personality. Christ did not teach the miserable doctrine of absorption and annihilation: on the contrary, Christ has perpetuated and glorified his own personality and that of his followers by establishing between God and man the eternal relation of filial progress. Man's personality is then truly human and complete when it is not opposed to God, and being one with the Father is our genuine freedom.

To accuse the Brahmo Samaj ... of a pantheism which is soul-destroying and annihilates human personality is to do them a very great injustice. On the contrary, a too prominent insistence on man's personality is the distinguishing feature of [Brahmo] theism. ... That pantheism which identifies the universe with its Maker, and man with God, the Brahmo Samaj repudiates. That pantheism which takes away from the sinner's view the painful spectacle of his own sins, and leaves no field for repentance, progress, salvation and a personal sense of God's grace; that pantheism which ignores the difference between man and God, the Brahmo Samaj repudiates.[6]

Nevertheless, the Brahmo Samaj is not afraid of 'pantheism' and mysticism of another kind. For instance, it has always recognized 'the spirit of a presiding Providence in all things'. It sees 'the glory and wisdom of the Supreme Spirit' in the beauty of nature, bears his voice in 'the events of human life and history' and discerns his 'workings' in the life of prophets and saints.

The Divine Spirit permeates every pore of matter and of humanity, and yet is absolutely different from both. There is no flight of fowls to their evening home that is not directed by the unerring hand of Divine Love. There is no lily in the field and no rose in the valley whose blossom and fragrance do not come from the breath of Infinite Beauty. There is no beauty, no wisdom, no faithfulness, no purity, no piety and self-sacrifice that is not inspired by him. The goodness of all the good is a ray of reflection from him, the greatness of all the great points to his throne on high. If this be pantheism the Brahmo Samaj is not ashamed of it. . . . If this be mysticism, the Brahmo Samaj is proud of it. It is eminently the spiritual instinct of India.[7]

And in Mozoomdar's opinion, the person and work of Christ could be best interpreted within this framework:

Yes, Christ lived in God, loved in God, taught in God, suffered in God that we too might live and love, suffer and teach as he did. Christ's whole nature was swimming in the ocean of Divinity, as this visible universe of ours swims in the might and majesty of God.[8]

Mozoomdar would go behind the specific doctrines of pantheism and mysticism which declare God's 'identity' with the universe and men, and consider the 'instinct' which they represent and use it to interpret Christ. No doubt, it is easy to slip into the language of identity, as evidently he tends to do in this last quotation, but the theological intention of Mozoomdar is to apprehend Jesus Christ in relation to patterns of spirituality and understanding indigenous to the Orient. And he is careful at many points (not all) to repudiate a mystic vision which concentrates on unity of nature without conformity to the holy will of God. For instance he says this of *Samadhi:*

In communion and transcendental *Samadhi*, we can feel absorbed in his blessed nature and intense light. His peace goeth forward before us, and stilleth everything within and around. But does all that avail, if our character is dissimilar to his, and if in our deeds, thought, and wishes and practical purposes, we tread in other courses than those appointed by his holy will and eternal wisdom?[9]

B. *The Doctrine of the Spirit*

A decade later, in his treatise on the Spirit of God, he follows Keshub Chunder Sen's Doctrine of the Spirit further to explore and explain his synthesis of the Hindu and Christian conceptions of the Spirit which provides the framework for his understanding of Jesus Christ and God. He affirms that the universal background, ... the universal heart of things ... is surcharged with the Spirit and presence of God.[10]

But all things do not reveal the Spirit equally. There is an evolutionary movement of greater unfolding as we move from nature, humanity, saints and the Son of God. Speaking of the Incarnation of the Spirit he writes:

In continually higher, clearer, nearer revelations through all things does the Spirit approach our nature, till he makes his glorious abode in ourselves. We find our home in all objects, they find their home in us when God incarnates himself in what he has made. With all that is now knowable of him, he is here, all things show him, they are his forms, his thoughts, the features of his countenance deeply veiled. He lives in outward nature as the soul in an august body. He lives in man, the life of his physical form, the presiding Spirit of his mind, heart and soul. Humanity is his incarnation: the best among men are most like him. The Son of God is the type of that humanity.[11]

In nature, in life, in soul, in humanity, in revelation, in history secular and sacred, divine relations and dealings are unfolded and have to be discerned.[12]

The Spirit of God as 'the evolving principle' in the creative process, says Mozoomdar, is a fundamental doctrine of Hinduism.

Thus the presence of God in creation [Vedas] in the soul of man [Upanishads] and in his dealings with the types of the race, through religious and national dispensations [Puranas] discloses the marvellous analogy that there is between spiritual Hinduism and the characteristic doctrine of Christianity. The Spirit of God is the source and substance of all things, the evolving principle in all matter, and bears forth all souls. ... The Hindu conception of the Spirit is a pervasive presence.[13]

And he compares it with the Christian religion.

Generally speaking, the Old Testament corresponds to the Vedas, the Gospel to the Puranas, and the Epistles of St Paul to the Upanishads. But Christianity in the Old and New Testaments has mainly the dispensation of the Father and the dispensation of the Son, scarcely anything that can be called the dispensation of the Spirit. When the last finds adequate record, the analogy between the Hindu and Christian schemes will become complete.[14]

The Spirit also illumines the triune nature of God and the unity of humanity. It is in the light of the Spirit of God working in creation and in our souls that we know God to be a Trinity.

Three forces of the Divine nature have, according to Hindu wisdom, entered into the formation of all things. The first is the force whereby God holds his own being and gives being to others; the second is the force by which he has intelligence and gives intelligence to others; the third is the force whereby he has love and joy and confers love and joy upon others.

Thus existence, reason and joy in God correspond to his three well-known names Brahman, Paramatman and Bhagavan. And he adds:

Now, no possible conception of the Divine nature, ancient or modern, Eastern or Western, is possible beyond this threefold principle. The closest parallel between the Christian faith and Hindu conceptions of the threefold nature of God is here observable. The only difference is that in the Hindu evolution, the Spirit occupies the second and in the Christian system it occupies the third place in the self-revelation of God's nature.[15]

Where is mankind one? Mozoomdar answers: In the Spirit.

Poets, astronomers, prophets and founders are all cosmopolitans. The Spirit which animated them is the one universal Spirit who is the higher and better self in each of us. How the One Universal can detach himself into countless individualities, and again and often reunite these into the same Spirit, into the same undifferentiated humanity all the world over, as it were into an identity of thought, heart and aspiration, passes the understanding ... Thou O God art the all-inspiring medium! We live and have our being in Thee. Thus one great, true word spoken resounds in all nations.[16]

The ultimate fact is the Spirit who is 'never far, but always within our hearts', from whom it is impossible to flee, as the Psalmist cried, and to flee to whose embrace is as Augustine said, the ultimate destiny of man.[17] This is the spiritual source of humanity.

Thus, the Spirit active in the creative process, and illuminating the triune nature of God and providing the basis of the oneness of humanity and the destiny of man, gives the proper framework to interpret the meaning of Christ and Christianity in India and to India.

c. *A Critique of Christianity*

The Doctrine of the Holy Spirit in Christianity, as expounded by Mozoomdar, has its peculiar nuances. According to this doctrine

The relation of the Spirit to man is a . . . moral relation – the relation of responsibility, obedience, and voluntary self-subjection.[18]

Jesus himself has given central emphasis to the Holy Spirit. The Christian Scripture endlessly testifies to the personality of the Holy Spirit.

He was the abiding Presence, the constant Indweller, the all-suffering Comforter, the Supreme Interpreter, the source of all inspiration, to whom Christ led them up by all that he said and did, against whom whoever committed any sin was beyond the grace of forgiveness. . . . The Father is far above, the Son is far away: the Spirit abides with you always; and in the Spirit both the Father and the Son abide.[19]

And it is the Spirit that has led Mozoomdar himself to Christ.

By the light of the testimony of the indwelling Spirit alone have I recognized and loved and assimilated Christ, till he is my daily meat and drink.[20]

He sees also the work of the Spirit in the expansion of Christianity and in the life and mission of the Church in all the world. But the Christian Church has relegated the Holy Spirit to the margins.

Adoration, love, worship, have been offered to the Son . . . Behold the Spirit has no altar erected to him in all Christendom. . . . That personal Holy Spirit is scarcely anything more than ecclesiastical dogma. . . . The truth about [Him] has been practically exiled from the Christian's sanctuary, his home and his heart. . . . The living Spirit of God, if he ever appeared, seems to have retreated from the Church in the rage for popular Christology, or sublimated himself into an arithmetical supplement.[21]

And this has perverted the theology of the Church. Especially does he protest against the Christ-unitarianism characteristic of much of Christian theology.

In the history of the Christian Church believers have often accorded to the personality of Christ absolute Godhead, and thus tried to find satisfaction for every spiritual instinct. But this was never without some kind of protest: it was not natural; and the leading minds of early Christendom were forced, after a few centuries, to determine in public council what place should be assigned to the Spirit in the economy of Christian theology. How far the decision then made has answered the exigencies of spiritual development we would not say, though perhaps, theologically, it has quieted some people.[22]

Elsewhere, of course, Mozoomdar makes clear that the 'decision then made' was not fully satisfactory, because it did not conceive the primacy of the Holy Spirit in creation, in the spiritual development of mankind, in the manifestation of the Divine Humanity in Christ and in the building up of the Church in the Dispensation of the Spirit. Perhaps the stage was not reached for the true Doctrine of the Spirit to emege. But today, the Brahmo doctrine is a significant development in this regard. For,

We in the Brahmo-Samaj declare, with faith and force, that the Dispensation of the Spirit has come, that we are of it, and that it hath sealed our salvation. . . .[23] The process of that Holy Spirit has been through all the vast stages of the human evolution. The self-revelation of the Spirit seems to be at its last stage if it has any end at all. . . .[24]

The utmost glory of the world is at best a twilight, the clearest indication of material things is an enigma, the best of man is a semi-transparent medium, and even the revelation is a sealed book. The interpretation and light of everything is in the life that is luminous by living amidst the realities of the Dispensation of the Spirit of God.[25]

2. THE SPIRIT IN JESUS CHRIST

Within this framework of the Doctrine of the Divine Spirit and its procession through creation and history and through Christ and the age of the Spirit, Mozoomdar builds up the meaning of the Person and Work of Jesus Christ.

A. *The Manifestation of the Divine Character*

Writing in *The Oriental Christ*, he emphasizes Jesus Christ as the manifestation of Divine character. Following Keshub's idea of Christ as Divine Humanity and linking it with his own emphasis on moral character, Mozoomdar discusses the relation of Christ and God.

Christ then, as the Son of God, was the manifestation of divine character in humanity. . . . Who but the Eternal himself can reveal his character in relation to man? That character descends in Christ for the enlightenment, conversion, regeneration and adoption of all men. Therefore Christ is the Son of God and the Son of Man alike.[26]

Christ 'taught not only humanity, but also divinity' through humanity:

Trying to realize that Spirit (the Spirit of God) in himself, he felt he and his Father were one. Trying to realize it in his disciples, he felt that he was in them and they in him. This divinity descended unto him in such measure, that he said, 'He that hath seen me hath seen the Father.' Thus God can be seen in man.[27]

Is the Eternal, then, to be approached and thought of as a man thinks of a man? ... No; the Infinite is not man, but he is exceedingly manlike. Not in body, for God is a pure Spirit, but in nature and in soul. Unlike us in his immensity and unspeakable glory, in the unapproachable heights and unimaginable varieties of his being, he is exceedingly like us in those graces and blessed spiritual gifts with which he has filled our inner being. Because man's soul is exactly made in the divine image, therefore to know our true nature is to know as much of the Infinite as can be known on earth. ... God is the Absolute Whole. ... To be able to feel how far like and unlike the divine spark in us is to the eternal glory of the Spirit Father, it is necessary that we should be Christlike, and put on that sonship which he taught and practised.[28]

We can think of God at one level as manlike because man has the image of God in him. Knowing Christ's humanity and knowing ourselves in relation to it is therefore to know God himself as he is related to us without losing the mystery of his transcendent Being.

B. *The Uniqueness of Jesus Christ*

Mozoomdar has a chapter in *The Spirit of God* on 'The Spirit in Christ'. In it, he gives an idea of his Christology. He speaks of the uniqueness of Jesus Christ on several counts. Jesus Christ is unique, *first* because he completes all other partial and local incarnations and makes for a truly spiritual and universal incarnation of the Spirit, and provides an everlasting model of the divine order of humanity. Other incarnations

... stand for certain isolated principles of God's nature; ... the prophets of one country ..., the incarnations of one age, ... are partial, local, imperfect, bounded by time, nationality and circumstance. Socrates is for the Greeks, Moses for the Hebrews, Confucius for the Chinese, Krishna for the Hindus, and Mohamed for the Musalmans ... The need of man is for a central figure, a universal model, one who includes in himself all these various embodiments of God's self-manifestation. The need of man is for an incarnation in whom all other incarnations will be completed. Such an incarnation was Christ.[29]

According to Mozoomdar 'Jesus Christ was in spirit' in Socrates, Abraham and 'all the great and good ever reverenced in humanity'; he is 'the type of humanity', the Divine Man:

> He was as no other man ever was or shall be: this is his uniqueness. Christ is unique, not because his flesh was born of a virgin, but because he was the unity of all those who had preceded him in the divine order of humanity. . . . Christ is unique because in him the unity of all these shapes of divine excellence was first effected. Therefore we call him the Son of Man, and the history of the Christian religion is the history of the progress of humanity.
>
> Some day . . . the followers of Christ [will] realize that he does not supplant or abolish the prophets and incarnations of other religions but that they all and each have their place in him, that he completes and reconciles them.
>
> He is the type of all humanity. Humanity broken up before and after is bound up in him, so that he is the human centre and bond of union in the religious organizations of mankind. . . . Alas, what God meant to be all-inclusive [Christian ministers] have made all-exclusive!³⁰

Secondly, 'Christ is unique because he perfectly embodies the true and universal relation between God and man'. He revealed the Father-Son relationship which is 'the true relation between God and man' and 'taught us to be the Sons of God'.

> He is embodied as the image of the Spirit of God. We exclaim, with John, 'The Word was made flesh, and dwelt among us: and we saw his glory, as the glory of the only-begotten of the Father, full of grace and truth.' God and man became one, not in transcendent idealism, but in actual visible reality. Such was Christ.³¹

Christ transcended 'the limits of time and space' and this 'invests the central figure of Christ with a universality which has to be recognized even by those who decline to accept his religion'. But so far as Christians are concerned, 'this universality' has led many of them to 'ascribe to him the eternity and infinitude of the Godhead', and to exaggerate Christ as 'including and exhausting' God, the Veriest Supreme. Here Mozoomdar asks for an either-or choice between Theism and Christianity:

> Declare openly that Christ is all in all, that the absolute Godhead is included and exhausted in him; and let the so-called Supreme Being of the Theist retire for ever from the arena of practical and personal religion, or

like us (Brahmos) declare that God is all in all, that Christ is his spiritual manifestation only as the type ever growing into perfection.³²

He conceives of Christ as the most perfect manifestation possible of 'the eternal reason' and fatherly 'relation' of God which determines the goal of human history within the realm of finitehood:

So far as God's nature and relation could be shown within the limits of finite humanity, at a distant age and in imperfect human society, Christ showed it. Christ is an evolution from the transcendent state of undifferentiated consciousness of God. From the mystic depths of the Father's eternal reason, the Son sprang into personality as a fitting consummation here on earth of created things in the fulness of time becoming flesh.³³

Indeed, 'the indispensability' of Jesus Christ in Mozoomdar's Christology is integrally related to the necessity of divine love not for an infinite object but for the creation of the finite world and of mankind in it and for bringing them to perfection. Christ eternally is conceived as the crown of 'this marvellous structure of man'. Therefore Christ's is 'not an arbitrary infinitude, a co-eternal personality that makes two infinities, two eternals, two Gods'. Jesus said that his father was greater than he; 'dependence, love, trust and oneness ... make the very essence of Christ's nature'. It is necessary that 'the greater originates the less, includes the less, absorbs the less'.

If the Presence and Personality of the Son offered infinite satisfaction to the Love and other attributes of the Eternal one, what necessity for further objects is left behind? The whole creation with its marvels of love and intelligence becomes a pure redundancy. ... God creates us because ... he loves us, because we are necessities in the economy of his nature; and the divine humanity of Christ only crowns this marvellous structure of man. The indispensable necessity for Christ is the necessity for the creation of all things, the evolution and progress of all things, the perfection of things from the imperfect.³⁴

Mozoomdar continues to explain the life, death, resurrection and second coming of Jesus Christ in terms of the spiritual mission of the Divine Humanity. His mission was not individualistic;

He came to reveal the nature of the will of God, and in the light of that revelation to lay down the basis of a Kingdom, of a Society, of a divine household, wherein the relations of men and their Maker and their relations to each other should be as they had never been before.³⁵

The new human relations of Fellowship which Christ's life established are defined thus:

That men who looked upon each other as aliens, strangers, not unoften enemies, who, disliked, distrusted, deluded by each other, feared, ill-treated, made tools of, made toys of each other, should forsake such attitudes and look upon each other as members of the same household, brothers, equals, friends, children of the same Father, bound to cherish, help, edify, elevate, sanctify each other by the overmastering impulse of love, a mutual interest and a common yearning, an intense feeling of oneness, of *ownness*, is the principle which Jesus Christ came to establish.[36]

And the cross of Christ represents the passion, suffering, which was the other part of the Christ-life. The cross is the 'symbol of God's will ruling all the events of human life' bringing 'victory over nature, over sorrow, over want, over death', while of the Resurrection, he says:

It is substantial, not material: its substance is the same as the composition of the Spirit of God with whom we commune every day.[37]

Elsewhere he has said:

He [Christ] was spiritualized entirely; he was the Spirit made flesh. The glory of his transfiguration was spiritual glory. The glory of his crucifixion was spiritual glory: the material surroundings were mean and miserable. The glory of his resurrection was spiritual glory: it was no flesh and blood, but the spirit ascended with the Kingdom above. We materialize him because we have so little of the Spirit. We know nothing higher than flesh and blood; we naturally turn his resurrection into flesh and blood. The Spirit of God glorified himself in the Son.[38]

Mozoomdar affirms that 'Christ has not only risen but returned as he promised'[39] in the Holy Spirit. And therefore the Brahmo-Samaj declares the Dispensation of the Spirit, making possible an unceasing 'succession of divine humanity'.[40] This does not mean that 'the function of the Son' has ceased. No. 'I again say it shall never cease'.[41] And the consummation of Creation could be interpreted as his second coming:

The succession of divine humanity shall never cease; but no son of man shall ever be greater than Jesus and no name as his name – every knee shall bow to him. The past prefigured him, the future shall illustrate him, from him the present shall draw its inspiration. They talk of the second coming of Christ, and wait for the destruction of the world in that hope. The world does not hold out a prospect of speedy annihilation but of steady progress and prosperity; and if Christ's second advent is to take place, he shall come as the expected guest of the world's bridal chamber, not the avenging angel of its graveyard.[42]

3. OTHER ASPECTS OF THE SPIRIT

A. *Law and Spirit*

In exploring the spiritual depth of the problem of morality, Mozoomdar goes far beyond Rammohan Roy and Keshub Chunder Sen. He makes a clear distinction between a man obeying moral laws and his having a spirit which acts morally by its nature. At the lower level, man knows his alienation from the Spirit and the laws of righteousness. The words of St Paul, 'The good that I would I do not: but the evil that I would not, that I do', and the verse from the Vishnu Dharmottara,

I know what is righteousness, but I have not the readiness to perform it. I know what is unrighteousness, but have not the power to abstain from it.

– these are cries of every heart seeking a spiritual answer.[43] And that answer is the gift of the Spirit, of the 'supernatural', which is 'not unnatural' but 'nature beyond nature'[44] and which endows us with

the superhumanity of the Eternal, [which] gives us an accomplishment which in the highest sense is miraculous. It is thus that the humanity of man finds itself continually exalted to higher planes of trust and achievement; and thus also the sympathies and co-operations of God are proved to be intensely human and concrete. ... Only what is superhuman is accomplished by the devout in such a simple, modest, exceedingly human way that it seems to be a matter of course.[45]

This is the accomplishment of the Spirit of Sonship.

The doctrine of spiritual sonship which ... [Christ] taught ... enfolds within itself as an eternal potency the very source of the law-making faculty in human nature which adapts its moral deliverances for every occasion of duty and trial as it arises. ... There is the teacher who teacheth many things – every rule of life and every detail of conduct. There is also the teacher who saith little, teaching only that by learning which a man may instinctively do what is right and good. Lessons are endless, the spirit of man is one; and when the spirit is full of light, every part of life shineth out. The mission of the true teacher is therefore to teach only what kindles the spirit in man, and leave everything else to the man himself.[46]

There are three things that sum up morality and kindle the spirit – namely love, faith and holiness.

Humanity ... in faith, love, and holiness concentrates the whole spirit of the Sermon on the Mount.[47]

Christ was himself the realization of this 'humanity or true sonship'. The divine humanity became incarnate on earth within the Jewish tradition,[48] not only as fulfilment but also as judgment of the Mosaic law. And Christ has bequeathed to humanity 'the Holy Spirit who ... would ... suffice for all truth, all precept, all moral requirement'.[49]

B. *The Spirit and the Church*

Mozoomdar is deeply conscious of the spiritual perversions of those who claim the inspiration of the Spirit.

Like other great gifts, the gift of inspiration is claimed by the least worthy. But nevertheless religious impulses ought not to be discounted. Now and then [St Paul] rises to the height of identifying the indweller with the indwelt devotee as when he says, 'The Spirit searcheth all things and knoweth the mind of God'.

The prophets in the past and 'the Apostolic Church, the community of spiritual men' in the present have also rightly claimed to embody the Spirit and interpret the mind of God. But there is need of a test of the Spirit, to enable discrimination between false and true inspirations of the Spirit.

Thus we are brought face to face with three manifestations – the impulse in the heart and conscience, the unanimity in the Church and the voice of the dead recorded in the Scriptures. When these three voices speak in union, the testimony of the Spirit's coming is complete; when they disunite, the impulse may be for the man or the moment, never for all time.[50]

Mozoomdar speaks of other tests – the moral 'fruits of the Spirit', 'the power of transmitting it (the Spirit) to others' and the unity of the community.

The test of the Spirit is in the heart and in the conduct. ... The sure test of the Spirit is the power of transmitting it to others. The laying on of hands is a pregnant symbol... unity is the only test that God's spirit abides in a community. ... Unity is the seal of spiritual progress. Mutual subjection and mutual adjustment are the signs of the Spirit's work, all places and all functions distribute themselves naturally.[51]

c. *The Spirit and Universal Religion*

We have already seen how Mozoomdar sees Jesus Christ as completing and reconciling all the revelations of the Spirit in the religious history of mankind. This is the basis of his doctrine of the relation between religions in which he closely follows Keshub at certain points. He repudiates the idea of the equality of all religions on the one hand and the idea of any one religion as having a monopoly of inspiration of the Spirit on the other. In his opinion,

Each religion is the offspring of the Spirit according to the needs and nature of the people among whom it arose, but in the advancing progress and unity of mankind, it is observable there is a law of unity and progressive order in the rise and spread of all the great systems of truth.

What he sees is not merely a harmony of religions in the Spirit but the possibility of the emergence of a universal religion of the Spirit in the future.

A universal religion is always forming in the atmosphere. ... It has contributed slowly to the formation of a unity between man and man – at least creating aspirations for a common religion. ... The skeleton of all religions largely shows a common structure. Of course, the skeleton alone is not the living organism, and the other things that make it up differentiate one faith from another. But even this subsequent making up shows a connection and continuity. It is the same hand that lays down the rudiments and from the rudiments builds up the organic whole. ... Coming from common instincts, common truths, common processes, religion proves its source also is common; namely the Spirit of God. ...[52]

And he sees that in Brahmo Samaj the 'harmony' has already been realized, because for them 'the Spirit of God is all in all, both for worship and the sanctity of personal character'.[53] Therefore the Brahmo Samaj indicates the end towards which all religions are moving under the guidance of the Spirit.

4. A CRITICAL EVALUATION

Mozoomdar's theology stands in the line laid down by Keshub Chunder Sen and much of the appreciation and criticism of Keshub can be applied equally to Mozoomdar also. Several points may be made.

Firstly, Mozoomdar's interpretation of nature, history, incarnation and Jesus Christ as a continuous movement of evolutionary progress of the unfolding of the Divine Spirit recognizes Jesus Christ as the most perfect manifestation possible within the limits of the finitude of man and history, of the essential 'nature' of the Divine Spirit and its 'relation' to mankind. At this point Mozoomdar recognizes not only the uniqueness but, in a sense, also the ultimacy for man of the revelation of God in Jesus Christ. But equally with Keshub his idea of the evolution of the Spirit does not see the discontinuities created by human sin. The unfolding of the Divine Spirit in creation and history, through religions, to Christ and the universal religion of the Spirit is seen apart from the deeper tragedies of the spiritual freedom of man in historical existence, so that the Cross is not central enough to Mozoomdar's idea of Divine revelation and human salvation. This is the point raised by Manilal Parekh in criticism of Keshub and it is relevant here also.

Secondly, Mozoomdar makes the affirmation that the reality of God is not exhausted by Jesus Christ. This by itself need not be a contradiction of the ultimacy of Christ for *human* salvation. Nor should his attempt at metaphysical speculation seeking to relate the revelation in Jesus Christ to the unrevealable mysteries of God's being be considered in itself a compromise of the Christian faith. Indeed, many philosophical theologians within the history of Christian orthodoxy have made such affirmations and attempts, illuminating the Christian faith. But when Mozoomdar seeks a double salvation, one through the mediation of Jesus Christ, and the other a supplementary one through that part of the Divine Spirit which is beyond the revelation in Christ and without Christ's mediation, it amounts to a denial of the Christian faith that Christ reveals the ultimate truth of God in his relation to man's salvation, that he is the only mediator between God and man. As a result we find that he seeks to combine two spiritual experiences together –

one mediated through Christ and the other unmediated. There is also a conflict of two loves – between love as spiritual union and love as doing the will of God on earth. The following meditations from *Heartbeats* indicate the dual spirituality which he sought to reconcile in his doctrine of the Spirit: On 'the dual love', Mozoomdar says:

> Two strangely opposite desires consume me: the one is to be lost in the blessed consciousness of God; the other is to love, serve and be one with the sons of men. ... Amidst the conflict of these two desires I have achieved nothing to perfection. Yet it seems to me, backwards and forwards, I must go till the end....[54]

And on 'the double anchor':

> ... Yea my soul has cast a double anchor in the sea. I am securely fastened to the depths of God on the one hand and to the depths of inspired humanity on the other. God is my first anchor, his Son the other anchor. The love, faith, undoubted relationship, I bear to both form the iron cable, unbreakable, everlasting. If I am about to drag the one, the other keeps me. I am steady, unmoveable, I am deeply anchored.[55]

At this point, Jesus Christ ceases to be the sole source, centre and criterion of religion, spiritual experience, humanity and human salvation. Christo-centrism, which Mozoomdar affirms at many places, seems to have been displaced.

Thirdly, Mozoomdar is very right in his criticism of the Christian Church for not giving a proper place to the Holy Spirit in its doctrine, life and experience. Keshub's idea of the New Dispensation of the Spirit is developed a great deal by Mozoomdar who has also defined more clearly the necessity of checking the inspiration of the Spirit in individual conscience with the Scripture and the Church. He has also rightly emphasized the generation of the Son not only from God the Father but also through the Holy Spirit. Nevertheless, it must be pointed out that for him the reverse, namely that the Spirit proceeds through the Son, is not valid. Behind this is Mozoomdar's conviction that 'the Christian and Hindu doctrines of the Spirit form a many-sided synthesis' and that the two religions signify 'the poles' between which the self-manifestations of the Spirit are to be interpreted and experienced. The two poles are in his mind related to two revelations of the Spirit independent of each other and supplementing each other. At this point clearly the Holy Spirit ceases to be the Spirit proceeding through the Son. Mozoomdar's Spirit becomes an incoherent mixture of Spirits. Indeed Mozoomdar rejects the co-eternity of Christ with God and the Spirit, and reduces the Trinity to a Spirit-monism. This may be a valid protest against a great deal of the Christ-unitarianism of Christian theology, but it is not adequate to preserve the doctrine of Christ as the one Mediator of salvation for men.

NOTES

1 P. C. Mozoomdar, *The Oriental Christ*, Boston, 1883, p. 16.
2 *Ib.*, p. 16.
3 *Ib.*, p. 17.
4 *Ib.*, p. 42.
5 *Ib.*, p. 46.
6 *Ib.*, pp. 40f.
7 *Ib.*, pp. 41f.
8 *Ib.*, p. 41.
9 *Ib.*, p. 89.
10 *The Spirit of God*, Boston, 1894, p. 9.
11 *Ib.*, p. 10.
12 *Ib.*, pp. 28f.
13 *Ib.*, pp. 39–41.
14 *Ib.*, pp. 50f.
15 *Ib.*, pp. 49f.
16 *Ib.*, pp. 26f.
17 *Ib.*, p. 16.
18 *Ib.*, p. 56.
19 *Ib.*, pp. 60f.
20 *Ib.*, p. 62.
21 *Ib.*, pp. 63–5.
22 *Ib.*, p. 57.
23 *Ib.*, p. 261.
24 *The Oriental Christ*, p. 311.
25 *The Spirit of God*, p. 323.
26 *The Oriental Christ*, pp. 89f.
27 *Ib.*, p. 95.
28 *Ib.*, pp. 95f.
29 *The Spirit of God*, pp. 239f.
30 *Ib.*, pp. 240–2.
31 *Ib.*, pp. 243f.
32 *Ib.*, pp. 245f.
33 *Ib.*, pp. 246f.
34 *Ib.*, pp. 247–9.
35 *Ib.*, pp. 252f.
36 *Ib.*, p. 253.
37 *Ib.*, pp. 257f.
38 *Ib.*, p. 62.
39 *Ib.*, p. 259.
40 *Ib.*, p. 250.
41 *Ib.*, p. 261.
42 *Ib.*, p. 250f.
43 *Ib.*, p. 53.
44 *Ib.*, p. 19.
45 *Ib.*, pp. 21f.
46 *The Oriental Christ*, pp. 91f.
47 *Ib.*, p. 93.
48 *Heartbeats*, Boston, 1894, p. 177.
49 *The Oriental Christ*, p. 91.
50 *The Spirit of God*, pp. 68f.
51 *Ib.*, pp. 71f.
52 *Ib.*, pp. 301–4.
53 *Ib.*, p. 308.
54 *Heartbeats*, p. 6.
55 *Ib.*, pp. 135f.

CHAPTER FIVE

Brahmobandhav Upadhyaya: Christ as *Chit*

Romain Rolland in *Prophets of the New India* writes:

We may well ask with Max Muller whether the logical outcome of his [Keshub Chunder Sen's] theism was not to be found in Christianity; this is exactly what Keshub's friends and enemies felt immediately after his death.

Romain Rolland explains this reference in a footnote which it is necessary to quote here:

Max Muller in 1900 asked Pratap Chander Mozoomdar, who had taken Keshub's place at the head of the Brahmo Samaj, and who shared the 'Christocentric' ideas of his master, why the Brahmo did not frankly adopt the name Christian and did not organise itself as a national Church of Christ. The idea found a response in P. C. Mozoomdar himself and a group of his young disciples. One of them, Brahmobandhav Upadhyaya, deserves special study, for he has left a great memory. He passed from the Church of the New Dispensation to the Anglican and eventually to the Roman Catholic Communion. Another is Manilal C. Parekh, a biographer of Keshub, also a convert to Christianity. Both are convinced that if Keshub had lived several years he would have entered the Roman Church. Manilal C. Parekh says 'that he was a Protestant in principle and a Catholic in practice. . . . Christian in spirit, inclining to Montanism' [faith in the supremacy of the Holy Spirit]. For myself, I believe that Keshub was one of those who would have remained at the threshold of the half open door. But it was fatal that his successor opened the door wide.[1]

It is not our purpose to debate whether Max Muller or Romain Rolland was right about Keshub. But our study of the meaning of Christ in the context of Brahmoism will not be complete without looking at the theology of those who have found in Brahmoism their bridge to an indigenous form of Christianity. We have already seen a good deal of Parekh's theology in his critical evaluation of the theologies of Rammohan Roy and Keshub Chunder Sen on the one hand and in his opposition to the Western-oriented Christian orthodoxy on the other. It may be proper therefore to review the main elements of the theology of Brahmobandhav.

Bhawani Charan Banerji was a 'classmate of Vivekananda and a friend both of Ramakrishna Paramahamsa and of Keshub Chunder Sen'. He was one of the 'most brilliant members of the Brahmo Samaj', but he took 'one step more' which he advised P. C. Mozoomdar also to take. In 1891 he was baptized in the Anglican Church and, later the same year joined the Roman Catholic Church. He took the name Brahmobandhav (Sanskrit for Theophilus). In 1894 he put on the saffron robe and became a Catholic sanyasi. He edited an apologetic weekly journal *Sophia*. When it ceased publication he started another periodical, *The Twentieth Century*. Later in life his interest turned from religion to politics and he edited a daily paper *Sandhya* which became 'the leading nationalist vernacular paper of his time'.[2] The theological approach of Brahmobandhav is motivated by his concern for an indigenous expression of Christian faith and life. It finds expression in his efforts for:

(a) an integration of the social structure of India into the Christian way of life;
(b) the establishment of an Indian Christian monastic order;
(c) the employment of Vedanta for the expression of Christian theology; and
(d) the recognition of the Vedas as the Indian Old Testament.[3]

The theological implications of the integration of the caste system into the Christian way of life will be examined later. We shall be primarily concerned here with his use of Vedas and Vedanta in interpreting Christ against the Indian background. C. F. Andrews, writing in 1912, says that the writings of Upadhyaya were 'the most striking instances' he had come across up to that time, of the use of Hindu terminology by Christians for the expression of Christian truth. It was Upadhyaya's conviction that Vedantic thought could do the same service for Christian faith in India as scholastic philosophy once did.[4]

It seems it was Brahmobandhav who made current the use of the name *Satchitananda* for the Christian idea of Trinity within the Christian Church. He must have got it from Keshub Chunder Sen. Among the Hindu reformers of the nineteenth century who were attracted to Christ and Christian truths, both Keshub Chunder Sen (1838–84) and Mahadev Govind Ranade (1842–1906) had found in *Satchitananda*

an analogy of these component parts of the Sanskrit name of God to the Christian Trinity: *Sat* corresponding to the absolute existence of the Father, *Chit* to the Logos, and *Ananda* to the Holy Comforter.[5]

It is not necessary for us to enquire whether Keshub had any indebtedness to Ranade or *vice versa*. But it is evident that this analogy existed and came to fuller use in the theological formulation of Upadhyaya.

C. F. Andrews quotes his 'Hymn of Adoration' and 'Hymn of the Incarnation', as typical of his efforts to apprehend the Trinity and Christ in terms of the categories of *Satchitananda*. As they are hymns they do not have the quality of a theological system, but it is clear that he was seeking to apprehend the Christian truth from within the Indian heritage.

In the 'Hymn of Adoration' he addresses the Trinity as 'Being (*sat*) Intelligence (*chit*) Bliss (*ananda*)'. The Hymn of Adoration runs as follows:

> I adore,
> Being, Intelligence, Bliss
> The highest goal,
> Despised by the worldly, desired by the holy saints.
>
> I adore,
> The Supreme, Primeval, Highest
> Full, indivisible,
> Transcendent, yet immanent.
>
> I adore,
> The One with inner relations
> Holy, self-contained,
> Self-conscious, incomprehensible.

I adore,
The Father, Highest Lord, Unbegotten,
The rootless Principle of the Tree of Existence,
Who creates through Intelligence.

I adore,
The Son, uncreate, Eternal Word, Supreme
The Image of the Father, whose form is intelligence
Giver of highest Release.

I adore,
The Spirit proceeding from Being and Intelligence,
The Blessed Creator, intense Bliss, the Sanctifier,
Swift in movement, speaking through the Word,
The Giver of Life.[6]

With the Brahmo emphasis on the Vedas, it was natural that 'in the first years after his conversion, Brahmobandhav tried to find the "natural" foundation for the "supernatural" religion of Christ in the religion of the Vedas'.[7] Like K. M. Banerjll himself, he elaborated in his *Sophia* articles his 'Vedic-Christian theology'. He dwelt on the parallels between the Old Testament and the Vedas, and 'the sublime idea of the One True God' present in India's original religion.[8] He wrote:

Whatever may be the theology of the Vedas they are, from cover to cover, surcharged with the idea of a Supreme Being, who knows all things, who is a personal God, who is father, friend, nay even brother to His worshippers, who rewards the virtuous, punishes the wicked, who controls the destinies of man, . . . who watches over the welfare of His creatures, temporal as well as spiritual.[9]

He saw in the doctrines of transmigration and pantheism the great fall from original Hinduism. While he accepted as his own 'the primitive theistic truths taught in the sastras', he said he was totally opposed to

the doctrines that God is all and all is God, that God is subject to endless cycles of emanation or evolution, that God is not the creator, but only the moulder, that man passes through a series of births and deaths to expiate his sins and to attain perfection.[10]

From this standpoint, Brahmobandhav opposed the Arya Samaj, with its belief in transmigration, and opposed what he stigmatized as 'the grotesque theories of Mrs Besant and the diabolic errors of Vivekananda'.¹¹ As Brahmobandhav envisaged it, the 'conversion of India' involved 'a threefold task':

first to eradicate from the minds of the Indian people the erroneous and mischievous doctrines (pantheism and transmigration); secondly to lay the basis of Theism by help of the Vedas; and thirdly to build Christianity on that foundation.¹²

Calling Hinduism back to Vedic theism would be

to form, as it were, a natural platform upon which the Hindu taking their stand may have a view of the glorious, supernatural edifice of the Catholic religion of Christ.¹³

The primitive [Hinduism] and the new [Christianity] are linked together as root and trunk, base and structure, as outline and filling.¹⁴

Kaj Baago says that the year 1898 marks 'a decisive turning-point' for Brahmobandhav, from Vedism to Vedanta. This is however questionable in this exaggerated form because even *The Twentieth Century* deals with Vedic Theism.¹⁵ The evidence seems to suggest that perhaps he never gave up the view that the Vedas represented Indian monotheism parallel to the Old Testament and able to be connected with the Old Testament, and help India come to the New. It remains true however that he seeks from now on to interpet Christ in terms of the Vedanta in a qualified form. Manilal Parekh says that the synthesis he sought to create was 'between the Vedanta of Sankara and the teaching of the Catholic Church'.¹⁶ This agrees with Baago's conclusion, but Baago himself has pointed out that he rejected the traditional interpretation of *Sankara*, especially the concept of *Maya*, and the relation between *Brahma* and *Maya*. This in some sense supports Russell Chandran when he follows F. Heiler in saying that it was Brahmobandhav's conviction that 'if the Thomist system could make use of Aristotelian philosophy to interpret Christian faith, it would be equally if not more, appropriate to use an Indian system of philosophy which came much nearer to Christian understanding of truth than Aristotle's system, namely Visistadvaita philosophy of Ramanuja', and that Ramanuja's philosophy was 'peculiarly adapted as the expression of the Christian faith'.¹⁷

Probably Brahmobandhav did not commit himself to any of these systems but only used their categories, with a consciousness of the inadequacy of all of them. For he once argued the use of Vedantic philosophy in explaining the Christian faith and added:

> The association of Vedantic philosophy should not be opposed because it contains certain errors. Were not Plato and Aristotle also guilty of monumental errors?[18]

The periodical *Twentieth Century* of 1901 is the main source of Upadhyaya's thought in this new period. In it he gives 'A Brief Outline of Christianity'.[19] He says that the 'end of man' is 'to know God as He is: to behold Him, face to face; to be like Him; to be united with Him'. While man may know God as 'the First Cause (*salamba*) related to a chain of effects', man's destiny is 'according to the teaching of Christ and His apostles, to know Him intuitively without any medium, as being a life above and beyond the cosmos' – i.e. as 'the Absolute Being (*niralamba*)'. This vision is 'not attainable unless our nature be elevated and sanctified by grace', by the supernatural, which is 'not anti-natural but co-natural', perfecting nature.

Christianity teaches that God has himself revealed to man the nature of his inner life, how he lives within the unlimited horizon of the infinite without condescending to be a cause, and that the contents of that revelation can be acknowledged in faith, and assimilated in hope and love only by those who have been elevated and sanctified by grace. It also teaches that by practice of virtues (*sadahanam*) in accordance with the light of Divine revelation, man is fitted in the long run to behold the very essence of God abiding in the bliss of correspondence of self with Self.

Man had this Grace originally but he lost it. Therefore

> the pre-eminently practical feature of Christianity consists in its mission of restoration. God . . . has provided a means through which he can recover his original grace. And when it is restored to man, the end is not reached at once. Man has to fight against the downward bias (*sanskara*) imposed upon his nature by his *karma* (deed). . . . Christianity provides . . . help [in this fight] through visible and tangible instruments of grace.

The doctrine of the Holy Trinity reveals to us the inner life of God; it makes us perceive by the light of faith how the one, undivided essence subsists under three interior relations, how he begets his own self-image in thought and reposes on it with infinite delight.

The mystery of the restoration to grace is taught in the doctrine of the Atonement. It teaches how God did condescend to be united to humanity in suffering that men may be reconciled to him in joy. This act of divine condescension, this *at-one-ment* of divinity and humanity, this sweet mingling of the joy of holiness with the sorrow of compassion, is the central doctrine of the Christian religion, because without this exhibition of mercy man would be deprived of his glorious end.

We are also taught by Christianity that Christ has founded a Holy, Catholic Church which has been commissioned by Him to communicate His Mind in its inviolable integrity to all the nations of the world and administer the sacraments which are infallible channels of grace.

In a contribution to the previous number, entitled 'The Incarnate Logos',[20] B. Upadhyaya explains the 'True Being of God and Jesus Christ' thus: The finite ego requires 'an element outside the ego' to enable self-consciousness.

But in the act of Divine self-knowledge there can possibly be no foreign intervention because the Infinite is the All and includes all. What then is the note which distinguishes the subject-God from the object-God? Revelation teaches ... that the differentiating note in Divine knowledge is the response of intelligence. God begets in thought His infinite self-image and reposes on it with infinite delight while the begotten self acknowledges responsively His eternal thought-generation. ... The Infinite, Eternal God who recognises His own Self reproduced in Thought is the Father; and the same God who is the Begotten Image of Divinity, who acknowledges the Father in Reason, is the Logos, the Son. ... The eternal, intellectual act of Divine generation and the correspondence which binds the Father and his Logos-Image in the Spirit of Love completes the life of God and makes it self-sufficient. Revelation has given us a fore-glimpse of the inner life of God and has declared how His knowledge and love are fully satisfied by the colloquy of God with God in Spirit'.

We Christians believe that the Logos, the Eternal image of the Father, became incarnate, that is united Himself to a human nature, created and so adapted as to be wedded to Divinity. ...

I shall try to make [the doctrine of incarnation] explicit in a way familiar to the Hindu mind:

According to the Vedanta, human nature is composed of five sheaths or divisions (*kosha*). They are (1) physical (*annamaya*), which grows by assimilation; (2) vital (*pranamaya*); (3) mental (*manomaya*), through which are perceived relations of things; (4) intellectual (*vijnanmaya*), through which is apprehended the origin of being; and (5) spiritual (*anandamaya*), through which is felt the delight of the Supreme Reality. These five sheaths are presided over by a personality (*ahampratyayai*) which knows itself. This self-knowing individual (*jiva-chaitanya*) is but a reflected spark of the Supreme Reason (*kutastha-chaitanya*), Who abides in every man as the prime source of life and light. The time-incarnate Divinity is also composed of five sheaths; but it is presided over by the Person of the Logos Himself and not by any created personality (*aham*). The five sheaths and the individual agent, enlivened and illumined by Divine Reason, who resides in a special manner in the temple of humanity, make up man. But in the God-man, the five sheaths are acted upon direct by the Logos-God and not through the medium of any individuality. The Incarnation was thus accomplished by uniting humanity with Divinity in the person of the Logos. This incarnate God in man we call Jesus Christ. He took flesh from the womb of a spotless, immaculate Virgin for the formation of His body. As the first man (*adipurusha*) was produced by Divine *samkalpa* (will), so was the body of Jesus Christ, whom we hold to be the *adipurusha* of the spiritual world, formed by the power of the Spirit of God and not by the usual process of procreation. Jesus Christ is God by the necessity of His being, but He became man of His own free choice. It was compassion for us which made Him our Brother, like us in sorrow and suffering, but without sin. Jesus Christ is perfectly Divine and perfectly human. He is the incarnate Logos.

In another article he sets forth 'Christ's Claims to Attention'.[21]

The first . . . is His position as the Teacher Universal: He commissioned His apostles to teach *all* nations to observe *all* things whatsoever He had commanded them, and promised to be with them *all* days, even to the consummation of the world.

The second consists in 'His unfolding the mystery of God's inner life'. The possibility of the creature's knowledge of the Absolute who is 'above the plane of created existence (*maya*)' remains a problem. But

Jesus Christ has declared that God is *self-related* by means of *internal* distinctions that do not cast even a shadow of division upon the unity of His Substance.

Thus God is 'self-sufficient' and His 'knowledge and love are satisfied within the term of Infinity without coming into any contact with the finite', and the vision of such a God is 'bliss beatific'.

Jesus Christ claims to have laid open the mystery of Divine life that man may apprehend it in faith and walk by its light to the final goal of beholding God as He is, living in communion of self-relation within Himself.

The third claim is 'His Divinity'. Here Upadhyaya gives his interpretation of atonement of sin in more detail. Sin he defines as 'the bondage of *karma*' which cannot be undone by *karma*; it is alienation from God.

By choosing the finite (*anatma*) as our goal, we incur spiritual death and darken our understanding (*viveka*). . . . Sin leads to bondage and darkness from which there can be no escape notwithstanding the hardest struggle on our part.

And no punishment is adequate to compensate for the violation of 'the majesty and sanctity of law', the justice and order of God.

The only way, then, to salvation is to be one with a God who compassionates us by superimposing upon Himself sorrow and suffering for our transgressions. To be grieved with Him, to be humiliated with Him, is to be sanctified. Our guilty suffering has no value in the sight of infinite justice. But when it is joined to the Divine suffering caused by our sins, it acquires potency and efficacy. To compassionate a compassionating God, and thus to make His infinite humiliation one's own, is the only way to avail oneself of the adequate satisfaction of Divine justice. Jesus Christ claims to be the incarnate Divinity suffering in His union with human nature. He invites *all* to believe in Him and to partake of His sorrow by being one with Him in faith, hope and love.

Upadhyaya called himself a 'Hindu Catholic'. Speaking of Indian Catholics he wrote:

By birth we are Hindus and shall remain Hindu till death. But as *dvija* (twice-born) by virtue of our sacramental rebirth, we are Catholics, we are members of the indefinable communion embracing all ages and claims.

In 'custom and manners, in observing caste and social distinctions', also in 'thought and thinking' Indian Catholics are Hindus. Do they 'believe in Hinduism'? 'Hinduism has no definite creed', and the test of being a Hindu is not 'in religious opinions'.

Yet we have drunk of the Spirit of Hinduism. We think with the Vedantists that there is one eternal Essence from which proceedeth all things. We believe with the Vaishnavas in the necessity of incarnation and in the doctrine that man cannot be saved without grace. We agree in spirit with Hindu law-givers in regard to their teaching that sacramental rites (*sankaras*) are vehicles of sanctification. With wondering reverence, do we look upon their idea of establishing a sacred hierarchy vested with the highest authority in religion and social matters. In short, we are Hindus as far as our physical and mental constitution is concerned, but in regard to our immortal souls we are Catholics. We are Hindu-Catholics.[22]

Here we see a good deal of the influence of Keshub on Upadhyaya. In fact he is reported to have shared his plan of 'converting India through Hinduism' with Animananda, the sanyasi colleague of Upadhyaya.

Looking at his outline of Christianity, it looks very much like the Roman Catholic system in its entirety – with the emphases on the vision of God's essence, on the distinction between nature and supernatural grace, on redemption as restoration and on the infallible instruments of grace. And his Christology is not dissimilar to some of the theories of incarnation used in the debates on Christ among the fathers. It has a certain close similarity to the interpretation of the incarnate Christ as anthropos-logos. Possibly it does not distinguish clearly between the eternal Logos and the incarnate Logos, and therefore lacks the basis of concrete human individuality of Jesus Christ. But the position is not outside the Christological framework of traditional Christianity. Therefore it is hard to know why the Church discouraged him; perhaps his boldness in identifying himself with Hinduism and using Hindu categories of thought was too novel for the Church to tolerate.

And in the wake of Indian nationalism in Bengal, he joined the political movement, because, as Zacharias indicates,

He was gradually coming to the conclusion that before India could become Catholic, she must be politically free and that otherwise it would be impossible to extirpate the bane of Europeanism which he found so disastrously rampant in all the Christian missions of the period.[23]

It seems that opposition to the domination of European theology was part of his general opposition to Europeanism, and that his nationalism had in it a vital concern for indigenous Christianity.

Dr Heiler describes Brahmobandhav as the Indian Clement of Alexandria, because he regarded Vedanta as 'Tutor unto Christ'. And in many ways, in the Christian Church, he was a leader for

Indian Christian theology, as well as for the expression of Christian participation in Indian nationalism. At both these levels, his ideas were 'emphatically rejected' by the Church of his time and the life and death of 'this great Catholic patriot was a tragedy'.[24] But 'his general attitude to Hinduism as containing a *praeparatio evangelica*' (and, we may add, to nationalism as a legitimate expression of faith) 'received different levels of recognition in later Christian writers'.[25]

Apart from the tragedy of rejection by the Church, Brahmobandhav had also certain serious limitations in his attempts at developing an Indian Christian theology. He was so much a Thomist in the deepest levels of his philosophical and theological thinking, that he could think of an indigenous expression of the faith only within a Thomistic framework through a Thomistic evaluation and transformation of Indian philosophy and religion. Like the Judaism of the early Church which wanted everybody to come to Christ through acceptance of Judaism, Brahmobandhav sought to press Indian thought into the Thomist mould, in the process of adapting it to Christianity. This has been the bane of Catholic attempts at indigenous theology, whether the conversion to Thomism aimed at was Sankara's or Ramajuja's philosophy and religion. It is clear that it is only in the very recent past that men like Raymond Panikkar and Klaus Klostermaier have given up this kind of processing of Indian thought through the Thomist mould.

Indeed the emphasis on the vision of God as the end of man weakens the emphasis on the will of God and ethics. His complete acceptance of the caste-system (which we shall evaluate later) shows where this has led him. The characterization of the relation between Hinduism and Christianity as a relation between natural and supernatural religion, disables him from seeing the extent both of the perversions of idolatry and the potency of redeeming grace operating at depth in Hinduism, and also leads him to misunderstand revelation as a supernatural extra to nature instead of as the encounter of Christ with the totality of man and human life. With all these shortcomings Upadhyaya remains a pioneer in Indian Christianity.

NOTES

1 *Prophets of the New India*, Eng. trans., British edition, London, 1930, p. 96; American edition, New York, 1930, p. 112.
2 H. C. E. Zacharias, *Renascent India*, London, 1933, pp. 25, 27.
3 J. R. Chandran, unpublished thesis on *Christian Apologetics in relation to Vivekananda in the light of Origen, Contra Celsum*, Appendix C, p. 216.
4 C. F. Andrews, *The Renaissance in India: its Missionary Aspect*, London, 1912, Appendix VIII, p. 289.
5 G. A. Mankar, *Life and Works of the late Mr Justice M. G. Ranade*, Bombay, 1902, vol. I, p. 195 (quoted by Zacharias, *op. cit.*, p. 45).
6 Andrews, *op. cit.*, p. 290.
7 K. Baago, unpublished MS on Brahmobandhav.
8 *Sophia*, Calcutta, March 1894, p. 11. (This and other quotations from *Sophia* are taken from Baago's MS.)
9 *Sophia*, March 1896, p. 7.
10 'The Hindu Revival', *Sophia*, June 1894, pp. 1ff.
11 Quoted by Zacharias, *op. cit.*, p. 27.
12 Baago on 'The Conversion of India – An Appeal', *Sophia*, October 1894, pp. 15ff.
13 *Sophia*, January 1895, pp. 6ff.
14 'Clothes of Catholic Faith', *Sophia*, August 1898, p. 122.
15 *The Twentieth Century* I 5, Calcutta May 1901, pp. 117ff.
16 M. C. Parekh, *Christian Proselytism in India: a Great and Growing Menace*, Rajkot, 1943, p. 71.
17 Chandran, *op. cit.*, p. 320.
18 Quoted by Baago.
19 *The Twentieth Century* I 2, February 1901, pp. 32f.
20 *Ib.*, I 1, January 1901, pp. 6–8.
21 *Ib.*, I 5, May 1901, pp. 115–17.
22 This and the preceding paragraph quoted by Baago.
23 Zacharias, *op. cit.*, p. 27.
24 *Ib.*, p. 28.
25 Chandran, *op. cit.*, p. 320.

CHAPTER SIX

Vivekananda: Christ as *Jivanmukta*

Brahmo approaches to Jesus Christ were attempts to understand him within the framework of Hindu theism, and its struggle ontologically to comprehend the absolute divine personality and the relative human persons. The framework itself was determined by the impact of the idea that the Person of Christ reveals the ultimate within the bounds of human history.

With the emergence of the Ramakrishna movement and the Arya Samaj to dominance on the Indian religious scene, Brahmo theism with its Christwardness gives place to an affirmation of the more traditional core and forms of Hinduism.

In the Ramakrishna movement under the leadership of Swami Vivekananda, Vedantic Advaitism came to the forefront as the leading system of religious thought in India. And Jesus Christ, the Christian religion, and the relation between religions began to be interpreted in the context of the experience of mystic oneness with the ultimate and the supporting advaitic metaphysics. The motivation and rationale for service to society also were sought in the same mystic vision. Following Vivekananda, Radhakrishnan has built his Advaita system of philosophy and religion with a view both to define its relevance for contemporary life in India and to interpret the ethics and religion of Christianity itself within its framework. In this chapter we shall examine the manner in which the renascent Advaita Vedanta of Vivekananda grapples with the meaning of the ethical and religious truths of Christ and Christianity; and to indicate the way which Christians in India have sought to define the theology of their own faith in relation to the spirituality and theology of the Ramakrishna movement.

I. SRI RAMAKRISHNA

The central emphasis in Sri Ramakrishna was God-realization or *anubhava*. And under his different Gurus, he went through various spiritual disciplines – *tantra sadhana* through which he saw the Divine Mother in all things, and realized himself as *siva-sakti*; *bhakti sadhana* or loving devotion through which he enjoyed communion with the Bhagavan; *advaita sadhana*, the experience of *nirvikalpa samadhi* transcending all consciousness of plurality and ego and realizing the One without a second, leading to *bhavamukha* in which he alternated between seeing Brahma alone as real and seeing all as forms of Brahman.[1] Ramakrishna also went through the Islamic and Christian *sadhanas*, that is, seeking the religious experience of the other religions. It is evident that he 'approached Christianity also as a *sadhana*, as one aspect of *bhaktimarga*'.[2] He did not learn of Christ from a Christian. It was Jadu Mallick, a Hindu who had chosen Jesus as *Ishta deva*, who read the Bible to him. Clearly Ramakrishna never encountered the *kerygma* of the Church, and there is no record that he talked with Keshub about Jesus Christ. The story of Ramakrishna's experience of Jesus is related thus: While 'intently watching' the painting of the Madonna and child,

he became gradually overwhelmed with divine emotion and breaking through the barriers of creed and religion, he entered a new realm of ecstasy. Christ possessed his soul. For three days, he did not set foot in the Kali temple. On the fourth day, in the afternoon as he was walking on the Panchavati, he saw coming towards him a person with beautiful large eyes, serene countenance, and fair skin. As the two faced each other, a voice sang out in the depths of Sri Ramakrishna's soul: 'Behold the Christ, who shed his heart's blood for the redemption of the world, who suffered a sea of anguish for love of men. ... It is he, the Master Yogi, who is in eternal union with God. It is Jesus, Love Incarnate.' The Son of Man embraced the Divine Mother and merged in him. Sri Ramakrishna realised his identity with Christ, as he had already realised his identity with Kali, Rama, Hanuman, Radha, Krishna, Brahman and Mohammed. The Master went into *samadhi* and communed with the Brahman with attributes.[3]

Swami Nikhilananda comments:

Thus he experienced the truth that Christianity too was a path leading to God-consciousness. Till the last moment of his life, he believed that Christ was an incarnation of God. But Christ for him was not the only incarnation; there were others – Buddha, for instance, and Krishna.[4]

Ramakrishna held that all religions are different paths to the same goal, essentially the same under different forms and names. The following saying of his is often quoted:

A lake has several ghats. At one the Hindus take water in pitchers and call it *jal*; at another the Musalmans take water in leather bags and call it *pani*. At a third, the Christians call it *water*. Can we imagine that it is not *jal*, but only *pani* or *water*? How ridiculous? The substance is one under different names, and everyone is seeking the same substance; only climate, temperament and name create differences.[5]

Vivekananda and the whole Ramakrishna Mission believe that Ramakrishna not only recognized the validity of all Hindu *sadhanas*, and the religious experiences of other religions, but also considered the experience of *nirvikalpa samadhi* as the ultimate and apex of spirituality towards which all other experiences lead and must lead. And further:

The three great systems of thought known as Dualism, Qualified non-Dualism and Absolute non-Dualism – Dvaita, Visistadvaita and Advaita – he perceived to represent three stages in man's progress toward the Ultimate Reality.[6]

Whether Ramakrishna really taught the Advaita vision as the ultimate experience of God-realization and whether he arranged the three dominant systems of Hindu metaphysics Dvaita, Visistadvaita and Advaita into a ladder of progress are disputed.[7] But this is a debate which is not quite relevant to our discussion, except to cast doubt whether the Ramakrishna Mission has the authority of Ramakrishna himself for rejecting the equality of religious experiences and for arranging the experiences and the metaphysical systems of thought behind them in the form of a ladder with Advaita as the end and goal.

P. C. Mozoomdar has said:

He (Sri Ramakrishna) is the worshipper of no particular Hindu god: He is not a Saivite, he is not a Shakta, he is not a Vaishnava, he is not a

Vedantist. Yet he is all these. He worships Shiva, he worships Kali, he worships Rama, he worships Krishna, and is a confirmed advocate of Vedantic doctrines. ... He is an idolator, yet is a faithful and most devoted mediator of the perfections of the one formless infinite Deity whom he terms Akhanda Sachidananda (Indivisible Existence-Knowledge-Bliss). To him each of these deities is a force, an incarnated principle tending to reveal the supreme relation of the soul to that eternal and formless Being who is unchangeable in His blessedness and light of wisdom. ... These incarnations, he says, are but the forces (Shakti) and dispensations (Lila) of the eternally wise and blessed Akhanda Sachidananda who can never be changed or formulated, who is one endless and everlasting ocean of light, truth and joy.[8]

And most probably Ramakrishna did not care very much for the metaphysical framework of his *anubhava*, and P. C. Mozoomdar may be right when he says,

Ramakrishna was not in the least a Vedantist except that every Hindu unconsciously imbibes from the atmosphere around some amount of Vedantism, which is the philosophical backbone of every national cult. He did not know a word of Sanskrit, and it is doubtful whether he knew enough Bengali. His spiritual wisdom was the result of genius and practical observation.[9]

The impact of Ramakrishna on Brahmoism in general and on Keshub's theology in particular is of interest to us. There has been a great deal of controversy about the influence of Ramakrishna on Keshub in which Max Muller, Romain Rolland, P. C. Mozoomdar and the Ramakrishna sanyasis entered. Without doubt, certain phases in 'the later spiritual development of Keshub Chunder Sen'[10] could be explained only by the influence Ramakrishna had on him. We shall refer to this as much as it clarifies Ramakrishna's approach to certain aspects of Brahmo theology which the Brahmos held under the impact of their theological orientation to Christ. The following ideas reveal Ramakrishna's influence on Brahmoism:

1. We have already looked at Keshub's idea of the harmony of religion, and the three strands of thought regarding the relation between religions it contains. The central strand is the idea of the Christ-centred harmony in which he prophesied:

Surely the future Church of this country will be the result of purer elements of the leading creeds of the day, harmonized, developed and shaped under the influence of Christianity.[11]

In this idea there is only the recognition that all religions have elements of truth to be preserved, and untruth to be rejected, under the discriminating revelation of Christ. Ramakrishna's idea was to 'allow everyone to follow his own bent – whatever it might be – sincerely and wholeheartedly, without interference'. This idea must have been instrumental in Keshub's recognition of the religious value of Hindu polytheism, idol-worship and pantheism which he had earlier condemned very strongly. Mozoomdar has admitted that by associating with Sri Ramakrishna the Brahmos learned to 'realize better the Divine attributes as scattered over the 330 millions of deities of mythological India, the gods of the Puranas'.[12] But Keshub did it within the framework of his monotheism, though it was later 'exploited in favour of popular idolatry'.[13]

2. Further, Ramakrishna's idea of religion was essentially an individual man's experience of God in the inwardness of his spirit; and it was based on renunciation of the world. Brahmoism had a great emphasis in its religion on knowing the will and purpose of God for family, society and the material world. Ramakrishna never understood how Maharshi Debendranath Tagore 'at the same time enjoyed the world and led a religious life' and how a jnanin could have 'many children, all young' and reconcile himself to the world.[14] While he allowed the householder to follow the path of his duties, his own conviction was:

To lead a religious life in the world is to stay in a room with only a feeble ray of light. Those who are used to the open air cannot live in the prison.[15]

He was sure that the householder could never live the full spiritual life.[16] 'Renunciation of *Kamini-Kanchana* (woman and gold) is essential.'[17] The Brahmo concept was of 'a social and domestic religion'; it looked upon women as 'associates and helpers in all our spiritual struggles and social progress' and therefore emphasized the need of giving 'education and social liberty to woman'. Pandit Shivanath Shastri says that Ramakrishna vehemently rejected this idea.[18]

Even preoccupation with activities of social service and social reform was a hindrance to God-realization. He was critical of

Keshub because he was 'so preoccupied with social reform', 'so busy with the abolition of the caste-system, widow remarriage, intercaste marriage, women's education and such social activities'.[19] This business prevented Keshub from the vision of God. Indeed Ramakrishna did not conceive of '*sakti* manifesting himself in collective units', and of 'social groups as seeking values and pursuing goals' and realizing God. It was possible for individuals; and social groups – the family, society and the state – 'formed the background against which the individual pursues his goal'. And therefore the Brahmo idea of the Church as the Fellowship of the Spirit was ruled out.[20]

3. Ramakrishna rejected the Brahmo and Christian idea of the fact of the sinfulness of man and his need of salvation, and criticized their obsession with the feeling of sin. He said:

That's the one trouble with you Brahmos. With you it is always sin and sin! That's the Christian view, isn't it? Once a man gave me a Bible. A part of it was read to me, and it was full of that one thing – sin and sin! One must have such faith that one can say, I have uttered the name of God; I have repeated the name of Rama or Hari. How can I be a sinner? One must have faith in the glory of God's name.[21]

In his opinion, the man who constantly says he is bound, only becomes bound. 'He who says day and night, I am a sinner, I am a sinner, verily becomes a sinner.'[22] Devdas in her study says:

Though his explanation of sin as the dilemma of ego-involvement is deeply significant, in his discussion with his disciples he makes the desires of the senses the roots of sin.[23]

Therefore evil is sin, not in the contradiction of the spirit, but in the relation of spirit to the sense, between *vidya maya* and *avidya maya*. Thus there is no situation for man which is spiritually tragic.

4. The Brahmo believed in monotheism – God as One Personal Absolute, 'God with form but without attributes'. They kept clear of the two extremes of the monism of the Impersonal Absolute and the polytheism of Divine Incarnations and manifest gods. Ramakrishna's religion being concerned with individual religious experiences, and recognizing the validity of all experiences at their level as leading ultimately to the goal of realization, was not committed to any one conception of God. In fact the Brahmo idea of God sounded 'very dry' to Sri Ramakrishna. In his view:

For the purpose of meditation, some persons find it helpful to concentrate on a certain aspect of the Godhead in a particular 'form'; others prefer meditation of the formless Absolute. The *sadhaka* should choose the type of meditation that is helpful to him, and at all costs dogmatism is to be avoided.²⁴

It is evident from what has been said that Sri Ramakrishna represents a movement away from some of the important theological elements which Brahmo Samaj accepted under the impact of Christ and Christianity.

2. SWAMI VIVEKANANDA

Swami Vivekananda developed Sri Ramakrishna's ideas of spiritual realization into a total philosophy, and made it the basis of the Ramakrishna Order, Mission and Movement. We shall look at those aspects of the philosophy which grapple with the person of Jesus Christ and the religion of Christianity.

A. *Vedanta as the only Universal Religion*

The Introduction to *The Complete Works of the Swami Vivekananda*, says:

It must never be forgotten that it was the Swami Vivekananda, who while proclaiming the sovereignty of the Advaita philosophy as including that experience in which all is one without a second, also added to Hinduism the doctrine that Dvaita, Visishtadvaita and Advaita are but three phases or stages in the single development, of which the last-named constitutes the goal.²⁵

On the basis of the validity of all spiritual experiences, and their comprehension within the Advaita experience of self-realization the Swami clarifies how the Universal Religion of Vedanta and the theory of Ishta can provide the framework for inter-religious understanding and unity.

Speaking on 'the claims put forward' by Christians that 'Christianity is the only universal religion', he argues that it is 'the Vedanta, and the Vedanta alone, that can become the universal religion of man', as it alone is based on the solid rock of an eternal impersonal principle in contrast to the shifting sands of the historicity of a personality. Excepting the Vedanta, he explains, all other religions have their theories, teachings, doctrines and ethics 'built round the life of a personal founder from whom they get their sanction, their authority and their power'; and everything depends upon 'the historicity of the founder's life'. He adds:

If there is one blow dealt to the historicity of that life, as has been the case in modern times with the lives of almost all the so-called founders of religion – we know that half the details of such lives is not now seriously believed in, and that the other half is seriously doubted – if this becomes the case, if that rock of historicity, as they pretend to call it, is shaken and shattered, the whole building tumbles down broken absolutely, never to regain its lost status.

In contrast the religion of Vedanta 'rests upon principles':

Just as our God is an Impersonal and yet a Personal God, so is our religion a most intensely impersonal one, a religion based upon principles; and yet it has an infinite scope for the play of persons, for what religion gives you more Incarnations, more prophets and seers, and still waits for infinitely more? ... It is in vain we try to gather all the peoples of the world around a single personality. It is difficult to make them gather together even round eternal and universal principles. If it ever becomes possible to bring the largest portion of humanity to one way of thinking in regard to religion, mark you, it must be always through principles and not through persons. Yet, as I have said, our religion has ample scope for the authority and influence of persons. There is that wonderful theory of Ishta, which gives you the fullest and the freest possible choice among the great religious personalities.[26]

The theory of Ishtam says that there is a variety of spiritual sadhanas and religious paths, each one valid in its own level and for its devotee, and none should be disturbed in pursuing what suits his own spiritual temperament. The Swami defines Ishtam thus:

Your way is very good for you, but not for me. My way is good for me, but not for you. My way is called in Sanskrit my Ishtam. Mind you, we have no quarrel with any religion in the world. We have each our Ishtam.[27]

It is such an important doctrine in the Swami's approach to the relation between religions and the relation of all religions to the universal religion of Vedanta, that he has spelt it out in detail at many places. He explains that it means that though 'the absolute truth is only one', the Advaita reality and realization at the spiritual

Vivekananda: Christ as 'Jivanmukta'

centre, 'in relative perception, truth always appears various'. Therefore contradictions between religions need not be condemned as opposed to truth or to unity.

We ought to remember that both of us may be true, though apparently contradictory. There may be millions of radii converging towards the same centre in the sun. The further they are from the centre, the greater is the distance between any two. But as they all meet at the centre, all difference vanishes. There is such a centre, which is the absolute goal of mankind. It is God. We are the radii. The distances between the radii are the constitutional limitations through which alone we can catch the vision of God.[28]

The theory of Ishtam is not against a movement of spiritual growth or even mutual inter-religious aid in it. There is growth, not through a rejection of one's own Ishtam, but through a process of assimilation of new truths in it.

The Christian is not to become a Hindu or Buddhist, nor a Hindu or a Buddhist to become a Christian. But each must assimilate the spirit of the others and yet perceive his individuality and grow according to his own law of growth [i.e. within the Ishtam].[29]

Others can certainly help to 'take away the obstacles', and place the ideals they know before you, but you have to 'see by your own constitution what you like best, and which is most fitted to you. Take up that one which suits you best and persevere in it. This is your Ishtam, your special ideal'.[30]

One implication of this approach is that there can be no 'congregational religion'. Real religion is an individual's 'own concern'; a man's Ishtam is a private affair between a man and God. Being sacred, it should be kept secret and not 'made public'.

Let the churches preach doctrines, theories, philosophies to their hearts' content, but when it comes to worship, the real practical part of religion, it should be as Jesus says, 'When thou prayest, enter into thy closet, and when thou hast shut thy door, pray to thy Father which is in secret.'[31]

Along this path lies not merely a spiritual growth to the ultimate Advaitic spiritual realization, which is the end, i.e. fulfilment and finish, of all *sadhanas* and religions, but it also paves the way for inter-religious fellowship in the unity of the spiritual seeking and movement towards the ultimate goal.

We Hindus do not tolerate, we invite ourselves with every religion, praying in the mosque of the Mohammedan, worshipping before the fire of the Zoroastrian, and kneeling to the cross of the Christian. We know that all religions alike, from the lowest fetischism to the highest absolutism, are but so many attempts of the human soul to grasp and realise the Infinite. So we gather all these flowers, and binding them together with the cord of love, make them into a wonderful bouquet of worship.[32]

B. *Christ and Christianity Interpreted*

Swami Vivekananda seeks to interpret Jesus Christ in terms of the principles of the Vedanta which he has enunciated. Indeed, Vivekananda believes that Jesus Christ and the New Testament cannot be properly understood and interpreted except within the framework of the Vedanta. In accordance with his basic conviction that principle and not personality is the essence of religion, what Vivekananda does is to take out Jesus Christ from the religious framework which exaggerates historicity and personality and convert him into a manifestation of the eternal spiritual principle of the Vedanta. Indeed Christ to Vivekananda is a Vedantin. Here of course the Swami's clue is the 'ideal existence' manifested in Sri Ramakrishna. The Swami once contrasted Keshub Chunder Sen and Sri Ramakrishna:

[Sri Ramakrishna] never recognised any sin or misery in the world, no evil to fight against, [while Keshub] was a great ethical reformer, leader and founder of the Brahmo-Samaj.

The power is with the silent ones, who only live and love and then withdraw their personality. They never say 'me' and 'mine'; they are only blessed in being instruments. Such men are the makers of Christs, and Buddhas, ever living, fully identified with God, ideal existences, asking nothing, and not consciously doing anything. They are the real movers, the *Jivanmuktas*, absolutely selfless, the little personality entirely blown away, ambition non-existent. They are all principles, no personality.[33]

As a character Vivekananda sees Buddha as 'the greatest the world has ever seen; next to him the Christ'; but it is foolish to interpret these characters as other than the manifestations of the spiritual principle of Buddhahood or Christhood, to which every man is destined.

Jesus had our nature; he became the Christ; so can we and so *must* we.

Christ and Buddha were the names of a state to be attained. Jesus and Gautama were the persons to manifest it.[34]

Evidently Jesus and Gautama are unimportant except as instruments of the manifestation of the Buddhahood and Christhood. So when Christ is recognized, Jesus withdraws. The real problem with traditional Christianity is that it cannot separate the personality of Jesus from the universal principle of Christhood he has manifested. And he asks:

What is the origin of this superstition, this ignorance? The disciple thinks that the Lord can manifest Himself only once. There lies the whole mistake. God manifests Himself to you in man. But throughout Nature, what happens once must have happened before, and must happen in future. There is nothing in Nature, which is not bound by law, and that means that whatever happens once, must go on and must have been going on. . . . Let us therefore find God not only in Jesus of Nazareth but in all the great Ones that have preceded him, in all that came after him, and all that are yet to come. Our worship is unbounded and free. They are all manifestations of the same Infinite God.[35]

This recalls one of the sayings of Sri Ramakrishna:

It is one and the same Avatara that, having plunged into the ocean of life, rises up in one place and is known as Krishna, and diving again rises in another place and is known as Christ.[36]

In this approach, the historicity of Jesus and the personality are accidents, and should be held as the non-essential part of the Gospel of Christ. Speaking of Jesus Christ, he once said:

We are not here to discuss how much of the New Testament is true, we are not here to discuss how much of that life [of Jesus] is historical. It does not matter at all whether the New Testament was written within five hundred years of his birth; nor does it matter even how much of that life is true. But there is something behind it, something we want to imitate.[37]

Vivekananda connects the plurality of Divine incarnation and the history of our world, as held within the manifestation of the power of Maya and related to an endless cycle in which there shall be many worlds such as ours. And the purpose of the incarnation is to help man to be liberated from the whole Maya through knowledge of his true nature of identity with God. In his commentary on John 1.1,

'In the beginning was the Word, and the Word was with God' he says:

The Hindu calls this Maya, the manifestation of God because it is the power of God – the Absolute reflecting through the universe is what we call Nature. The Word has two manifestations, the general one of Nature, and the special one of the great Incarnations of God – Krishna, Buddha, Jesus and Ramakrishna. Christ the special manifestation of the Absolute is known and knowable. The Absolute cannot be known; we cannot know the Father, only the Son. We can only see the Absolute through the 'tint of humanity', through Christ.[38]

And about the goal:

In time to come Christs will be in numbers like bunches of grapes on a vine; then the play will be over and will pass out. As water in a kettle [begins] to boil [it] shows first one bubble, then another, then more and more until all is ebullition and passes out as steam. Buddha and Christ are the two biggest 'bubbles', the world has yet produced. Moses was a tiny bubble, greater and greater ones came. Sometime however, all will be bubbles and escape; but creation, ever anew, will bring new water to go through the process all over again.[39]

It is clear that even the purpose of the Divine Incarnations is to help the water become bubbles and escape, to help liberation from the total complex of the manifestations of Maya, including world history and personality through the Advaitic vision that God alone is.

Vivekananda affirms that Jesus Christ should be interpreted as a Divine incarnation in this sense. And he goes to the New Testament, especially St John's Gospel, to prove it. He makes three points interpreting the life and teachings of Jesus Christ in the context of the Advaitic framework.

1. Jesus Christ, according to the Swami, was a yogi, who realized himself as God in his spirit and showed others the path to the same spiritual realization as Messenger. The Swami says:

He [Christ] had no other occupation in life; no other thought except that one, that he was a Spirit. He was a disembodied, unfettered, unbound spirit. And not only so, but he, with his marvellous vision, had found that every man and woman, whether Jew or Greek, whether rich or poor, whether saint or sinner, was the embodiment of the same undying Spirit as himself. Therefore the one work his whole life showed, was calling upon them to realise their own spiritual nature. ... You are all sons of

God, Immortal spirit. 'Know' he declared, 'the Kingdom of Heaven is within you.' 'I and my Father are one.'[40]

Jesus renounced everything, most specially his ego-consciousness, so that 'to be unselfish, perfectly selfless, is salvation itself, for the man within dies, and God alone remains'. The pure in heart sees God, because 'it is only necessary to clear away the dust and the dirt, and then the Spirit shines immediately'. Giving up all to the poor and turning the other cheek and other principles of the Sermon on the Mount declare the ideal of renunciation, of unselfishness, of selflessness.[41]

Commenting on St John's reference to Jesus (1.29) Vivekananda says:

'Taketh away the sin of the world', means that Christ would show us the way to become perfect. God became Christ to show man his true nature, that we too are God.[42]

Vivekananda is vehement in rejecting the Christian idea of man as a sinner in need of grace. Vedanta admits *avidya* and 'error' but not sin suggesting a corruption of nature or violation of man's relation to God.

The greatest error is to call a man a weak and miserable sinner. Every time a person thinks in this mistaken manner, he rivets one more link in the chain of *avidya*, that binds him, adds one more layer to the 'self-hypnotism' that lies heavy over his mind.[43]

Sin denies the *atman* which is the transcendent self unaffected by the chain of empirical good or evil. Indeed what people call sin is only a 'low degree of manifestation',[44] and every man is moving towards *paravidya* (the ultimate knowledge), and, in this movement, sin has its relative place, as the 'struggle of the divine in us to throw off the animal'.[45]

2. Vivekananda rejects the ethical Christ for the mystic Christ. Indeed from Rammohan Roy through Keshub Chander Sen to Swami Vivekananda, there is a clear swing of the pendulum. As stated above, the Sermon of the Mount, for Vivekananda, is not primarily ethics, but an expression of the spirituality of self-renunciation. He rejects Unitarianism:

The Unitarian Christ is merely a moral man, ... [only] the Christ who is the incarnation of God, who has not forgotten His divinity, can help us [in our spiritual self-realization].

Rather than emphasize Jesus' ethical humanity, he would assert his divinity, of course in Vedantic rather than Trinitarian terms.[46]

If I as an Oriental have to worship Jesus of Nazareth there is only one way left for me, that is to worship him as God and nothing else.[47]

The Swami however may have found it difficult to dismiss the concern for moral goodness in the Old and New Testaments, and in the renaissance of Hinduism itself. In connection with his discourse on the meaning of Christ he deals with the relation between the struggle for goodness and the search for spiritual self-realization, the relation between Goodness and Truth. He declares that 'Good is near Truth, but is not yet the Truth', because Truth is beyond the dualism of good and evil. They 'are both chains and products of Maya' from which Advaitic vision liberates us. But the moral struggle could be a path towards spiritual liberation.

Evil is the iron chain, good is the gold one; both are chains. Be free and know once for all that there is no chain for you. Lay hold of the golden chain to loosen the hold of the iron one, then throw both away. The thorn of evil is in our flesh; take another thorn from the same bush and extract the first thorn, then throw away both and be free.[48]

While rejecting the idea of giving priority to moral goodness and social ethics, the Swami was concerned to build what he called Practical Vedanta. This he does through his ideas of *Karma Yoga* and *Jivanmukta*. *Karma Yoga* speaks of incessant work but without attachment; throwing overboard the idea of duty and of rewards and punishments.

Whatever you have to give to the world, do give by all means, but not as a duty ... Everything that you do under compulsion goes to build up attachment. Resign everything unto God.

When an old Bengal professor raised the objection, 'All that you say about charity, service and the good that is to be accomplished in the world belong after all to the realm of Maya,' Vivekananda replied: 'Does not even the idea of liberation (Mukhti) belong the realm of Maya? Does not the Vedanta teach us that the Atman is always free? Why then struggle for liberation?[49]

The Swami never ceased to emphasize that the Ramakrishna sanyasis had two goals, first to 'realize the truth' and the second to 'help the world'. The *Karma Yogi* is defined by the Swami in various ways, as one who 'thinking intensely' of the good and service of others, 'arrives at the vision of the Self which penetrates all living beings';[50] and as one who having reached 'the threshold of final liberation' retraces his steps and willingly renounces his own realization to help others.[51] And the *Jivanmukta* is the saint who having realized the state of *nirvikalpa samadhi* returns to the world;

he sees the Self in all beings and possessed of this knowledge he devotes himself to their service, so that thus he uses up all the *karma* that remains to be expended by the body.[52]

Nivanmukta has freedom in life. He has 'faith in all' and 'love for all' because he knows he 'is all' and is one with all.[53] *Karma Yoga* and *Jivanmukti* form the ethical basis for the Practical Vedanta of the Ramakrishna Mission's vast programme of loving service to society.

3. The Swami pictures the spirituality of Jesus as Advaitic, as the realization of his identity with the Brahman, and explains away the dualism in his teachings about a Personal God as a concession to the necessity of dealing with the uneducated masses and his disciples at their level thus proving the Swami's three stages of growth in spirituality. There are three ways of perceiving God.

All these three stages are taught by the Great Teacher in the New Testament. Note the Common Prayer he taught: 'Our Father which art in Heaven, hallowed be Thy name,' and so on; a simple prayer, a child's prayer, mark you, it is the 'Common Prayer' because it is intended for the uneducated masses. To a higher circle, those who had advanced a little more, he gave a more elevated teaching. 'I am in my Father, and ye in me, and I in you.' Do you remember that? And then, when the Jews asked him who he was, he declared that he and his Father were one; and the Jews thought that that was blasphemy. What did he mean by that? That has been also told by your old prophets: 'Ye are gods and all of you are children of the Most High.' Mark the same three stages; you will find that it is easier for you to begin with the first and end with the last.[54]

Thus through Dvaita and Visisadvaita Jesus leads men to his own realization of Advaita.

4. We have already seen that Vivekananda is preoccupied with the problem of metaphysical rather than of moral evil; that is, the problem of the Spirit getting involved in matter and plurality and its liberation from such involvement, and that Sin and Salvation themselves are understood in these terms. Since the moral problem is ignored, questions of Divine Justice and mercy and the problems of atonement and forgiveness of sin are irrelevant. So that while Vivekananda has a great deal to say about the teachings of Christ about men's relation to God, he has almost nothing to say regarding the Cross and Resurrection of Jesus. Indeed, his answer to a question about the crucifixion was:

Christ was God incarnate; they could not kill him. That which was crucified was only a semblance, a mirage.[55]

There is however, as Devdas points out a certain recognition of the idea of vicarious suffering whereby the *avatara* is able to take over the *karma* of others, 'because his own actions are spontaneously pure: he acts without attachment and therefore is not bound to the wheel of *samsara*.' The disciples of Ramakrishna realized it, says Swami Saradananda, because they got 'an indication of it in the life of Sri Ramakrishna' who explained his own bodily sufferings as vicarious. 'Even the Avatara cannot set aside the rigid working of Karmasamsara', he can rescue the devotee only by taking the inexorable effects of the devotee's *karma* on himself.[56]

3. SOME CHRISTIAN CRITIQUES

A. *C. F. Andrews on Vivekananda*

In 1912 C. F. Andrews, then in the early years of his missionary career in India, writing in *The Renaissance in India: Its Missionary Aspect*, gives a critique of Swami Vivekananda's theology.

The message which the Swami preached is on certain sides distinctly disappointing. One of the main tenets, namely, that all religions are essentially the same, is so palpably incorrect that it scarcely needs refuting. With regard to reformation of abuses, the teaching is even more unsatisfactory. It amounts to little more than an esoteric doctrine for the initiated.

But he is very appreciative of the doctrine of 'Practical Vedanta'.

A really important contribution however is made on the moral side in the interpretation given to the Upanishad doctrine of the identity of the self with Brahma. This is called by the name of Practical Vedanta. According to the school of Vivekananda, the identity of the soul with the Supreme is to be attained not by passive contemplation, but also by absorption in active selfless service.

This blending of Christian philanthropy with Vedantist philosophy has produced a strange exegesis of the New Testament. One member of the school has written an elaborate commentary on St John, containing the most extravagant interpretations. In Vivekananda's own works many passages of the Gospels are explained in a semi-gnostic, semi-Christian way.[57]

In a later passage he says:

It would be easy ... to show the utter illogicality of an 'impersonal yet personal God' and an 'impersonal yet personal religion'.

This, of course, was the line followed by Nehemiah Goreh. But Andrews does not recommend this line in Christian apologetics. He continues:

But a far nobler apologetic and a more positive argument may be constructed by working out afresh the full Christian doctrines of the Logos, which met and satisfied the same form of doubt and speculation in the first three centuries of the history of the Church. The Eternal Word revealed in creation, in nature, in human life, is the true answer to the demand that God's immanence should be completely acknowledged.[58]

Andrews looks back to the first formative years of Christian theology and sees in the challenge of Advaita Vedanta

the revival in a modern form and dress of objections which had to be faced by the early Church. Their recrudescence may prove to be a boon to the Church in correcting narrow and one-sided impressions of Christianity which have grown up in Christian lands.[59]

And he looks forward 'to a time when the great Aryan civilization of ancient India shall find its fullest and purest expression within the Church of Christ, the Son of Man'.[60]

Along with this positive approach to the relation between Indian Christianity and Vedanta, he had his criticism of Advaita Vedanta at three points, its idea of the essential oneness of all religions, its conception of the ultimate as impersonal and its lack of historical sense. Later in life, even when he ceased to value inter-religious dialogue at doctrinal level, he held to these convictions.

In a preface which he wrote for a volume of Swami Rama Tirtha's collected writings, Andrews wrote:

With the philosophy of the Advaita Vedanta I confess I have only a faint and distant sympathy. ... The West insists on the eternal quality of human personality and rebels against the thought of the loss of personal identity, as in the noble sorrow and faith of Tennyson's *In Memoriam*. I recognize the danger in this emphasis of self-assertion and selfish individualism; I recognize that it may need some balance and correction from the East; but the West will never accept as finally satisfying a philosophy which does not allow it to believe that love between human souls may be an eternal reality.[61]

But later, in a letter to Tagore in 1915, he accepts the correction from the East when he says:

I am sure now that Tennyson's craving for individual contact and recognition after death is morbid and wrong. True and simple love must break these bonds, before it is wholly rid of self.[62]

But, as his biographers point out, 'the pendulum soon swung back', seeking a definition of love and God which is personal but prepared to recognize a supra-personal dimension. They quote another letter of the same year:

In the future, after death, shall not the vast Ocean itself be a sounding of even deeper depths – no loss of consciousness, but an even larger life. . . . In the West violent passion has usurped love's place, and in India calm benevolence. It all goes back to our idea of God. What is the *Sat*? The paradox of motion and rest in one alone satisfies me.[63]

Discussing the Ramayana epic of Tulsi Das, he says:

In his Incarnation doctrine Tulsi Das differs fundamentally from the Christian position in two respects. In the first place, the story ... is entirely mythical. ... There is no 'Historic Faith', as Bishop Westcott would have called it ... Secondly, in Tulsi Das' poem, Rama has always, even in his babyhood, the consciousness of his own omnipotence. His human frailty is only a seeming, an illusion. His omnipotence can be appealed to whenever he will. ... There is ... an air of unreality clinging about it which gives a docetic colouring to the picture. The Incarnation story [of Rama] is in some ways parallel in its conception to those [of Jesus] given in the Apocryphal Gospels.[64]

This applies equally if not more to Vivekananda's ideas. Commenting on an article by Swami Aseshananda entitled 'The Hindu View of Christ', Andrews repeats his conviction of the necessity of a 'historical faith'. He quotes the Swami, who had written:

To the Hindus the historicity of Christ is not of much concern: for they always care more for the principle than for the personality. . . . Knowledge of historical veracity is not the last word and acme of true spirituality. . . . In this respect a suggestion given by Ramakrishna is highly significant. '*Whether*', he says, '*Christ or Krishna lived or not is immaterial*; the people from whose brain the Christ ideal, or Krishna ideal, has emanated did actually live as Christ or Krishna for the time being.' It requires a Christ to forge a Christ. Krishna may be a mythical figure, but the thinkers who contemplated such an idea and conjured up such an image were as great and noble as the Krishna they conceived.[65]

While appreciating the religion represented by the Swami, with its

sympathy for certain Christian ideals which is all to the good, [he regrets that] along with this there is an almost entire lack of appreciation of what may be called the 'historical sense'.[66]

Andrew's criticism of the doctrine of the equality of religions, is better dealt with in relation to Mahatma Gandhi's ideas, as he clarified it mostly in dialogue with Gandhiji.

Andrew's differences with Vivekananda arise from the difference in their interpretations of the words of Jesus 'I and my Father are one'. Vivekananda interprets it metaphysically, but Andrews morally.

B. *J. R. Chandran on Christian Apologetics*

There have been many systematic studies of Vedanta by several missionary theologians in the wake of the renaissance of Vedantism in India. The scope of our study does not permit us to examine them. Dr J. Russell Chandran has made a systematic study of Swami Vivekananda's views of Christ and Christianity and the formulation of principles of Christian apologetics in relation to them, in the light of the writings of Origen *Against Celsus*. The thesis remains unpublished. It will be useful for us to indicate some aspects of his evaluation of Vivekananda's views of Christ and Christianity.

Chandran examines the sources of the Swami's 'Gospel of Religious Harmony', through which he developed his message of 'unity within the vast ocean of all religious thought and all rivers past and present both western and eastern'.[67] The search for a unifying philosophy was a general tendency among the intellectuals of his day. The strongest influence on Vivekananda was Sri Ramakrishna's teachings on the basis of his *anubhava*. But Vivekananda found scriptural justification for it in the often repeated verse from the Rigveda which reads: 'That which exists is one, the sages call it by various names' (I 164-6). Vivekananda found in the *Gita* a more developed idea of harmony,[68] the climax of it in the verse: 'Even those who worship other gods, if full of faith in reality, worship Me, though not according to ordinance' (*Gita* IX 23). While recognizing that there were previous attempts at religious harmony, 'in India, in Alexandria, in China, in Tibet, and lastly in America',[69] he held that Sri Ramakrishna's teachings on it surpassed them all.

Whereas the Gita brought together only the Karma, Bhakti, Jnana and Yoga, Ramakrishna's gospel could reconcile every conceivable form of religion. Whereas Brahmo Samaj had to discard certain elements of each religion as chaff and worthless, his system was not compelled to reject any.[70]

He quotes the Swami: 'We reject none, neither theist, nor pantheist, monist, polytheist, agnostic nor atheist.'[71] Chandran points out that to the Swami, 'the fundamental question with which every religion is concerned is the cause of evil and disharmony in the universe' and adds in a footnote:

Vivekananda is not consistently concerned with moral evil. His primary emphasis lay on the metaphysical evil of the 'one' becoming involved in the 'many' and of the 'soul' immersed in the material world of *maya*.[72]

Evaluating the Swami's scheme of religious harmony, Chandran says, that in it 'non-Hindu religions possessed only a subordinate role not worthy of consideration'. He appreciates the attempt of the Swami to relate several Christian ideas, values and programmes to Vedantic thought, though it has brought about a lack of integration in the Vedantic system. For instance, in his definition of *maya*, 'ideas of illusion, ignorance, the power of self-limitation, paradox were held simultaneously without proper integration or correlation',[73] and the status of moral struggle for goodness and of social service in relation to the spiritual realization of oneness with God is not firm.[74] The Swami's 'greater interest in human welfare than in animal welfare . . . [is] more Christian than Vedantic';[75] and so is his introduction of 'the idea of love into the purpose of the Avatara'. But the main criticism of the Swami's system of religious harmony is that it is

virtually the abandonment of all principles of moral and religious discrimination. It is a potent acid meant to dissolve all religions into it, ignoring the differences as either temporary or unreal. It is a syncretism that denatures every religion that is brought into its arms and explains away all value judgments as purely subjective. . . . We cannot find any explanation for this faith except Vivekananda's ardent ambition to demonstrate that India had a unique principle of religious harmony.[76]

Chandran shows that 'Vivekananda's estimate of Christianity' is based on his reading of the biblical passages out of context and interpreting them in ways alien to the fundamentals of biblical religion. For example,

1. Though 'the Johannine language (in the Johannine Prologue) has been regarded by many as more akin to Indian thought than the biblical writings', Chandran finds 'little justification' for Vivekananda's exegesis of it in terms of *maya* and its manifestations, or for his suggestion that 'the Fourth Evangelist is only stating a common philosophical truth about the relation between God the Word and the Incarnations already known to Hinduism'. While there is no doubt the word *Logos* was 'intimately associated with the Greek metaphysical speculations', the Evangelist

is not so much interested in metaphysical speculation as in the religious affirmation of the Gospel. It is not the 'word' but 'the Word became flesh' which forms the core of his teaching. He is concerned not with a speculative deduction but with the proclamation of a fact.

There is also no 'real parallel' between the Word of the Prologue and the *maya* of Hinduism because the Word was 'eternally with God and was God, the very being of God', unlike *maya* which 'belongs ultimately not to the being of God, but to the world of unreality and illusion'. Again, in the Gospel the world was a creation and not a manifestation.

The distinction between the Word and the world for the Evangelist is that between creator and created, for Vivekananda merely a matter of different grades of immanence.[77]

Later Chandran again pursues 'the remarkable parallels' which exist between Indian thought and the Prologue of the Johannine Gospel. Ramanuja speaks of the Creator in the beginning sending 'the eternal word of the Veda' from which all creation originated.[78] Sankara taught that creation took place in correspondence with the 'Vedic words', which became manifest in the mind of the creator before creation.[79] The Sophia doctrine of the grammarians held that 'words and their sounds precede the creation of forms'. And Chandran recognizes the similarity of all this to the doctrine of the Logos in the Johannine Prologue. But he rejects the implications of it for Christian theology.

But fascinating linguistic similarities need not necessarily mean historical connection or identical ideas. What the Fourth Evangelist says in the Prologue has little connection with the Vedantic and linguistic speculations in India. The Logos in Hellenistic thought may have similarities with Indian speculations. But the Evangelist does not argue on the basis of Hellenistic speculations. The general tone of the Gospel indicates that he uses the word *logos* more or less as a synonym for the Hebrew idea of the *Memra* or *Torah*. The fact that the Hellenistic idea of the Logos does not appear in the rest of the Gospel should not be forgotten. Great care should be taken in biblical exegesis in India not to be misguided by false similarities, but to probe deeper into the thought of the writers and seek the original message.[80]

2. Vivekananda 'tries to derive from the Bible passages the doctrine of the mystical identification of the individual soul with the ultimate Brahman.'[81]

His principal text is 'I and my Father are one' which he repeatedly quotes.[82] Chandran grants that 'the idea of mystical union between man and God has a special emphasis in the Johannine writings'. E. F. Scott is quoted as saying:

The doctrine of a mystical union, in which the higher life flows uninterruptedly from Christ to the believer, contains the central and characteristic thought of the Fourth Gospel.[83]

But the mystic union of the Gospel is communion of the human person with a personal God. Vivekananda however approaches the text

with the assumption derived from metaphysics that ultimately there is no distinction between the Self which was in Jesus and the other individual selves, and that whatever is predicted about Jesus is applicable to each individual self. The New Testament on the other hand starts with the conception that Jesus had a unique relationship with the Father. When the Fourth Evangelist says, 'I and my Father are one,' he is not expounding the nature of the relationship between the Son and the Father, but affirming that 'Jesus is the object of faith and the organ of revelation and salvation, and that the honour which is paid to him is honour paid to the Father.'[84]

The Swami's use of other biblical texts to prove the biblical support for the Advaitic philosophy and spirituality, or pre-existence and transmigration of souls, or the Hindu idea of renunciation, is equally out of context. Regarding renunciation, in support of which he uses verses from St Matthew,[85] Chandran says:

There is certainly in the teaching of Jesus a demand for self-renunciation. Selfish attachment to the world is condemned. But in the *Karma-Yoga* the individual is bidden to withdraw completely from any active interest in the world. Whereas in *Karma-Yoga* there is no vision of an ultimate purpose in the particular action, the teaching of Jesus regards self-renunciation as an intensified interest in the world based on God's loving will. Asceticism by itself is no Christian virtue. It is seen to have value only in the light of God's redemptive purpose.[86]

Chandran takes up some of 'the specific areas of conflict between Vivekananda's thought and Christian doctrine'.

First, the relation between God, the world and man. On the basis of his Vedanta,

Vivekananda cannot conceive the possibility of a Personal God, bringing the world into existence *ex nihilo*.[87]

Vivekananda is right in saying that no Indian sect believes in creation *ex nihilo* and that *srshti*, the Sanskrit word used for creation, in fact means 'the projection of that which already existed'.[88] The general Upanishadic idea is that 'creation is an emanation from *sat* or being'. Even for Ramanuja, who believed in a personal God, *srshti* is only

the self-differentiation of the absolute into the plurality of the universe of *namarupa*. In the light of the theory of evolution and involution of cycles, the beginning of the world can only mean the beginning of a cycle and not the whole cosmos.[89]

The corollary of the Vedanta idea of *srshti* is that 'man is essentially divine and that his soul is uncreated and eternal', as the 'substance of God Himself'. Therefore all ideas of 'imperfection and sinfulness are hallucinations'; and what man needs is 'not divine forgiveness and reconciliation but a kind of dehypnosis'.[90] Eventually evil for him is 'bondage to the illusion of space-time-causation'.[91] On one occasion Vivekananda said that the problem of good and evil was an unsolved enigma for Hinduism.[92] There was a great deal of incoherence in his views on evil. But laying 'more emphasis on the metaphysical aspect than on the moral', Chandran says, 'Vivekananda fails to grasp the seriousness of evil and the meaning of sin'.[93]

Vivekananda considered the doctrine of 'special election' to be an example of the narrow-mindedness and exclusiveness characteristic of all dualistic types of religion.[94] Chandran illustrates this attitude by his statement:

It is blasphemy to think that if Jesus had never been born humanity would not have been saved.[95]

He was evidently arguing for the ultimacy of the Advaita and the Hindu theory of many avatars. Chandran thinks that the historic personality of Jesus Christ, his Cross, the Miracles and the Sermon on the Mount 'seem to have challenged [Vivekananda], but he tries to explain them away as not vital to the understanding of Christ'.[96] The docetic interpretation of the Cross 'arises from his axiom that God cannot suffer in reality'.[97]

In the light of all this Chandran comes to the conclusion that 'there is a fundamental conflict' between the Hebraic-Christian and the Hindu and Greek apprehensions of religious reality, which cannot be bridged. This is expressed in the differences between the understanding of 'man as creature and the object of God's love, and as sinner who cannot be redeemed except through God's grace', and history as 'a real and purposive unity in the hands of God' on the one hand, and on the other the view of 'the essential divinity of the soul and the interpretation of history in terms of meaningless repetition of cycles'. This does not lead Chandran to assert that the complexes of the different religions and philosophical traditions should remain mutually exclusive at all levels. But it does raise for the Christian Church the nature of the relation between them. In examining this question, Chandran goes to a study of Origen's Christian Apologetics, to see how he related Christianity to Greek metaphysics of which he was an admirer.

Origen, says Chandran, regarded Greek philosophy not only as a 'tutor unto Christ' but also as providing the basic premises for Christian theological formulation. But he gave priority to 'ecclesiastical Apostolic tradition' and accepted 'the whole Bible, the Old Testament as well as the New as the final authority to which even so valuable a tool as the Platonic philosophy must be carefully subordinated'. Indeed Origen's work was not even 'a synthesis between Christianity and Philosophy'; in his theology 'the hands may be the hands of Plato, but the voice is the voice of Jesus in His Church proclaiming a historical redemption based upon a once-for-all revelation in Christ'.[98] Chandran says that in 'the fundamental starting point' Origen and Kraemer agree, though the former proceeds to discover 'similarities and continuity,' while the latter emphasized 'the dissimiliarities and antitheses';[99] Chandran advocates that the Indian Church should follow Origen. Once the final authority of the Gospel according to the Scriptures is accepted, 'respect and positive appreciation of Hinduism, acceptance of parallels and use of illustrative material from Hindu sources should certainly form part of the Christian apologetic in India today'.[100]

In this context Chandran points to problems in discriminating between elements from Hinduism which can be used as tools for the expression of Christian faith and those which cannot. These problems arise from the fact that

whereas in religions like Hinduism we have the predominance of metaphysical principles over religion, Christianity is primarily a religion seeking a metaphysic subordinating the task of finding an adequate philosophy to the urgent need for moral regeneration and the primacy of ethical principles within itself.[101]

That is to say, for Christian religion morality has priority over philosophy. Generally speaking Brahmoism also had the same priority, and it struggled to 'reach a theistic synthesis separating higher Hinduism from the baser elements of idolatry as well as of absolute monism'.[102] Even this proved a hard struggle and the struggle has become harder after Vivekananda's neo-Hinduism has justified 'every phase in popular religion as relevant to a wider Advaitic scheme' which itself subordinates morality to metaphysics.

Origen's argument that 'true philosophy or true spirituality is the possession of moral excellence' has an important role to play in the Indian situation. It is 'an adequate answer' to Vivekananda's claim that 'the East is more spiritual than the West'. And the Christian apologist has the task

of exposing tendencies in non-Christian religions to minimize or eliminate the urgency of moral and spiritual demands on individuals as well as communities. Especially in the case of Vivekananda's teaching, it is necessary to show that the moral principles underlying his humanitarian ideals have no basis in his philosophical assumptions.[103]

Positively, the truth of the uniqueness of the Christian revelation and Christ and the falseness of the idea that all religions are the same, must also be exposed on the ground of 'the consistent and intimate relationship that exists between the core of the Gospel and the experience of moral regeneration'.[104]

In fact, the central importance of the 'personal' and the 'historical' dimensions of the faith lies in the affirmation of 'the sphere of morality' inherent in them.

The fundamental principle involved in the concept of the personal is a reciprocal relationship in terms of moral responses. The denial of personality consists mainly in a denial of the sphere of morality.[105]

So also with history. Where there is a religious sense of historical purpose the 'moral conflicts' of contemporary society acquire religious significance. And Christian theology in India should relate its arguments 'for regarding the personal as higher than the impersonal'[106] 'and for not leaving the historical background of the Word of God in favour of metaphysical postulates' to the moral problems of 'concrete situations of contemporary life rather than to metaphysical problems'.[107]

In other words, the [Christian] Apologist is called to show the challenging relevance of the Gospel to the present moral conflicts affecting individuals as well as groups in the social, economic and political relationships.[108]

The Christian message must be communicated through those elements of Hinduism which express an awareness of the moral purposes and issues in the world. Chandran adds:

With sufficient caution the Gita doctrine of the Avatara as a voluntary act of the deity in order to destroy evil from the world may be interpreted as a rudimentary recognition by the Hindu of the reality of moral issues in the world. More important is the modern movement for social reform within Hinduism which, rightly valued, might lead to a reconsideration of its ultimate significance.[109]

In this setting, Christian theology has the task of grappling with the truth and meaning behind the Advaitic assertion of the Impersonal Ultimate, and the ultimacy of the mystic experience of Brahman-atman identity. There is need to clarify further the Christian approach to the supra-personal nature of God through the Trinity. Chandran says:

The Christian doctrine of the Trinity which speaks not only of God as at one level of His life (Three Persons) akin to but immeasurably greater than ourselves, also reminds us of the unity of substance, in which God overpasses all that we know of Him and recedes from our gaze into rich vistas of being which we can neither fathom nor plumb. It is therefore incorrect to speak of Christians as believing in a personal God; the central doctrine of their creed asserts belief in 'personality plus' – a supra-personal God.[110]

With respect to mysticism, Vivekananda and Vedic Hinduism generally regard it not only as 'the common factor in all religions', but also as 'the goal to which religion is directed' Western theologians differ in their view regarding 'the place of mysticism within a genuine Christian response'. Many give it 'an integral place in Christian experience' while others 'deny the possibility of any mystical experience with God'. Even those who do give it a place in Christian experience, would point out that in Christianity it is not a criterion or norm of spirituality, that the Church should not specialize in it so narrowly as to isolate it from the evangelical experience of conversion and sanctification or the catholic type of piety centred in the sacraments, which it fosters in ordinarily endowed and simple people, that it should avoid the danger of depending on human experience rather than on divine grace, that it should make the person more human in his awareness of his individuality and of his relation with the tragedies of the world, and lastly, that it should aid the fullness of the Christian life which consists in an ever-widening community-consciousness.[111]

Chandran's concluding word is one of caution:

An apologetic Christianity undercutting the faith to a bare minimum of those approximations to Hinduism which the Hindu may be induced to accept, could never be adequate for the Christ who as Saviour, calls all to the bar of His judgment that He may show mercy to all.[112]

c. *Bishop Appasamy's Doctrine of Immanence and Mysticism*

Bishop Appasamy has not published any systematic study of the thought of Sri Ramakrishna and Swami Vivekananda, from the standpoint of his Christian theology. But his writings deal directly with Advaita Vedanta in its contemporary phase, and at many points deal with the issues raised by the Neo-Vedanta of the Ramakrishna Movement. In formulating his theological approach to these issues, we shall confine ourselves largely to two of his writings, the book *What is Moksha?* and the pamphlet *My Theological Quest*.[113]

Appasamy advocates Indian Christianity speaking of Christ to the Hindus

from the inside, feeling with their intense feelings, longing with them their deepest longings, thinking with them through their most baffling problems, following with them their highest ideals, doing all these in that measure and to that degree which our loyalty to Christ permits.[114]

And in the context of such an approach his response to any Hindu doctrine or practice is to ask

what it means, what it purposes to achieve, and whether our Christian doctrines should not be thought out again in relation to this idea.[115]

And along this line, he feels that Indian Christianity will lay much emphasis on mystic experience in its attempt to relate itself to

Indian thought and become a living force in the country.[116] He has reiterated it in his more recent writings:

When Christianity comes to its own in India, its mystical aspects will receive a new emphasis and a fresh vigour. Probably there will be new ways of stating the old mystical truths and they will be apprehended with a genuine vitality.[117]

In his thought, loyalty to Christ becomes the principle by which to discriminate between the various types of Hindu mysticism and for defining the content of the doctrine and experience of mysticism. So he can say:

The Mahavakya of the Christian religion is not 'I and my Father are one' but 'Abide in Me and I in you'.[118]

And in his books he has explained at length why. And herein we get his points of contact with the complex of the Advaita ideas and Advaitic interpretation of Christ and Christianity represented by Sri Ramakrishna and Swami Vivekananda coupled with his own emphasis on the Christian differentia in the light of the Johannine Gospel.

Appasamy takes up the verse 'I and my Father are one'. He admits that it 'looks very much like the well-known formula, "I am the Supreme Soul" and has been so interpreted by Neo-Hindu thinkers'. But he says that it must be taken in association with the other verse of Jesus, 'My Father is Greater Than I'. And here he criticizes two Neo-Advaitic interpretations. The first is that 'probably Jesus was living on two levels, one a level of unity and the other, a level of dependence'. And his answer is that the awareness of unity and that of dependence were integral to each other in Jesus and were woven together in the texture of his whole life. The oneness was experienced 'continually' and the sense of dependence was there 'all the time'. And Appasamy says, 'there was not a single occasion when he claimed for himself equality with the Divine'. The second assumption is that 'probably Jesus had two kinds of teaching', one to the 'multitude' and the other to the 'inner circle'. Appasamy answers:

The distinction between the two kinds of teaching given by Jesus has absolutely no ground in the Gospels. If there was anything which was characteristic of Jesus as a religious teacher, more than any other, it was that he was utterly lavish in the way in which he placed his utterances before the humblest of men.

All this points to the view that the oneness which he possessed signified 'a completeness of harmony between him and God in thought and purpose'.[119]

In defining the 'nature of fellowship' between man and God, he goes to two verses of the Prologue of John's Gospel (1.124). There he finds a combination of the metaphysical and the moral dimensions of the fellowship.

> Bhaktas are already children of God; this relationship may be described as metaphysical but the relationship does not become perfect until a moral relationship is added on to it, until they receive Him and by receiving Him obtain the right to become the children of God.[120]

The fellowship is both of 'nature' and of 'will'.

Appasamy points out that the Christian Church throughout its history has had mystics in it, even mystics who used 'extravagant language about the union of the soul with God', which seemed to 'obliterate the difference between man and God'. This raised no questions regarding their orthodoxy. They were regarded as seeking to express in words the intensity of their rapture in God. But in judging the orthodoxy of mystics, the test of the Church was 'impeccability: Do the devotees interpret that identity as rendering the soul permanently incapable of sin?' If the mystic drives his experience of identity to 'the logical conclusion that God alone exists and that as God is incapable of sin he too is incapable of sin, he becomes a heretic'. And Appasamy adds: 'This test is an excellent one and badly needed in India.'[121] Elsewhere he says:

> Hindu thinkers have canvassed the question: 'Can a *Jivanmukta* sin? Do his acts affect him . . . ?' We should not allow ourselves to live as we please in the pious belief that whatever we do is God's work. Such an idea of the indwelling Christ is entirely contrary to the deepest Christian teaching.[122]

Appasamy seems to say that it is at the point of man's denial of his sinfulness and his need for redemption from God that mysticism becomes a denial of the core of the Christian gospel.

Appasamy affirms on the basis of the Gospel of John that God has personal and impersonal aspects. He points out that there are various attempts throughout the Gospel to represent the Person in terms which are impersonal, for instance, the door, the vine, the Logos, the truth, the way etc.[123] The Evangelist begins with the meditation on the 'historic Jesus', but then occasions arise when

the outline of a definite historical personality seemed to melt away, giving place to spacious conceptions of Him as Truth and Love and Light. In thus equating Jesus with the great qualities he was not by any means minimizing the value of the Incarnation or the importance of personality. He was only giving expression to the profound feeling that a large enough conception of God requires us to postulate some such formula, transcending even the generally satisfying and, as far as we are concerned, the best available concept of personality.[124]

Appasamy recognized the danger of 'a cold barren intellectualism' when God is thought of as 'the Absolute beyond all categories of knowledge'; but 'the intimate personal way' has its danger of conceiving God as 'a magnified human being'.[125] We must not suppose that the historic Jesus exhausts God:

The Incarnation is but a working hypothesis helping and guiding men to reach a knowledge of the Divine and does not exhaust all the infinite grandeur of God.[126]

Appasamy recognizes as valuable the harmony of the personal and impersonal aspects of Reality, in Sankara's Advaita; but the Christian finds it difficult to accept it, because Sankara does it by dividing men into 'two classes – those who are capable of apprehending the Absolute and those who are not' which is against the 'genius of Christianity' and its teaching about 'complete equality'. It still remains true to say:

Beyond Christ is the great and mysterious God, great and mysterious in His love and goodness as well as in his power and might. We may not measure or fathom or comprehend Him fully.[127]

The Christian rejection of the separation of men into two classes arises out of the Christian idea of the corporate character of the experience of God as contrasted with the exclusive individual orientation of the Hindu devotee. Christianity insists that '*bhakti* is the path of love, not merely of love of God, though that is its supreme passion, but also of love to man',[128] for 'only in love for man is love for God perfected and fulfilled'.[129] Thus arises the double Christian emphasis – the centrality of the fellowship of the *bhaktas* and the concern for the transformation of social relations. Christianity believes in the fellowship of devotees because 'no experience of God can be complete unless its wealth and meaning are brought within the reach not merely of the highly spiritual but of the lowliest and meanest'.[130] In the Gospel of John (15.4–5; 17.20–3), God, Christ, and the *bhaktas* are knit together in a fellowship which is 'profoundly organic' in character. Christianity also demands concern for 'life, rich, full and abounding',[131] in the human ties of family and society. In fact:

Worship is to life what the centre is to a circle. It occupies but a small part though it is the most vital and important part. ... The manifold threads of human life combine together to form a mighty cord to draw us near to God.[132]

Appasamy's belief, based on his emphasis on *bhakti*-mysticism, is that

As it develops, Christianity in India will stress the doctrine of Immanence, but ... it will also, in loyalty to its inner spirit and its age-long tradition, point out that God is immanent in different objects in different fashions and in different degrees, and ... that God's presence in the human heart is determined by spiritual and moral conditions.[133]

He expands his Christian doctrine of immanence, showing both its points of contact with Hindu ideas of immanence and points of departure from them. His starting point is the Johannine idea of the Word, the Eternal Mind animating the whole world, and its unique incarnation in Jesus. This implies three doctrines, first, the presence of God, his being and purpose in the whole universe; second, the different degrees and progressive measure in which God is present in the world of nature, generally in mankind, in moral personality and supremely in Jesus in whom 'the Force or Energy that is immanent in the universe, guiding it in the moment of creation and continuing to guide it ever since, became flesh and dwelt among men';[134] and third, the obligation laid on every man to come to Jesus and decide to accept him. Appasamy recognizes that the idea of immanence, of the God indwelling in the universe, has often obliterated spiritual and moral distinctions. The supposition that 'His presence is of the same type and degree everywhere' has cut at the root of morality.

The belief that God is in the rogue and in debaucher also, though it appeals to even such an earnest religious man as Ramakrishna, seems counter to a great deal of human experience unless the limitations of such a belief are fully borne in mind.[135]

Appasamy recognizes that 'God is Lord of all, righteous and wicked alike'. He is 'already in us', but this should not prevent us from pointing out the moral aspect that 'we ought to abide in God'.[136]

The fact that God illumines the world does not make all men good or noble. Man has his important share in accepting or rejecting this light.[137]

4. AN EVALUATION

While Brahmoism as a movement of reform in Hinduism had absorbed a great many of the Christian notions about religion it had very shallow roots in the fundamental metaphysical framework of Hinduism. Nehemiah Goreh was certainly right in asserting that this metaphysical framework was Advaita Vedanta, which could be translated Absolute Monism, with its acosmic illusionism on the one hand and pantheism on the other; and, as he predicted, Brahmoism withered, without roots either in fundamental Hinduism or in the Christian revelation. But what he did not predict did happen, namely the redefinition of Advaita Vedanta, with its assertion of its mystic centre, but with a capacity to absorb into its framework the value of moral struggle and social service. Indeed it is possible to look at Vivekananda's religion as an attempt to synthesize Advaita Vedanta with Christian philanthropy as C. F. Andrews put it. Thus Hinduism, on its own fundamentals, is renewing itself to be relevant to the moral and social problem of contemporary India. Instead of looking at the Ramakrishna Movement under Vivekananda solely as the beginning of a sort of counter-reformation, we should see it as a movement which is also the instrument of bringing fundamental Hinduism to the point of grappling with the truths and values of human life represented by Christianity. Certainly, at a certain level, many of its aspects are a counter-reformation, but could we not take it also as a Christward movement of Hinduism at a greater spiritual depth than was possible through Brahmoism? The main point about Vivekananda is not that he rejects the core of the Christian faith and the spiritual ultimacy of personality and history, but that he is redefining the core of Advaitic faith to make room for personality and history, and make Hinduism relevant to the human issues raised in contemporary India through the impact of Western culture and Christianity. It was perhaps this insight that led K. T. Paul in 1928 to speak of the Ramakrishna Movement as

> the most living, as it is the most characteristic expression of Indian nationalism. Truly centred on the Brahma Sutras, the source to which Hindu culture has turned afresh in every generation, faithful also to the interpretation of Sankara, as the ultimate analysis of the Great Hypothesis that is possible to human reason, the Ramakrishna Order has still taken a clear step forward in enriching the content of *Karma-Yoga* by reading into it, in addition to selfless Dharma, unselfish service in the most human sense of the term, what indeed we cherish as the distinctive message of Jesus Christ. This is a process of evolution precisely as it should be. That it is taking place so normally, without any fuss or even notice from any one, is significant of the intrinsic merit of both systems of thought. That Hindu thought is herein immeasurably enriched is a great fact; that Christian thought has yet to find its enrichment in this most wonderful happening, still so unknown to it, is also a fact.[138]

H. C. E. Zacharias, the Catholic member of the Servants of India Society, thought this appraisal 'somewhat exaggerated'.[139] Nevertheless K. T. Paul's insight is significant in any Christian interpretation of the Movement and any fruitful formulation of a Christian approach to it. Of course, this only enhances the need of helping the Movement to move further forward in the direction of Practical Vedanta without slipping back into the amoralism of monism.

Scholars have criticized Vivekananda for taking the texts of the Bible out of context and interpreting them in a theological framework alien to the Bible. This criticism would be valid if Vivekananda claimed that he were clarifying the mind of the biblical authors in his interpretation. He makes no such claim. He is not making an objective scientific study of the phenomenology of Christianity. He has a theology of religion which sees the mystic vision and experience as the goal and end of all religious experiences, and what he does is to interpret the truths of the religion of the Bible in the light of his faith in the ultimate truth of the Advaita religion. This is not unlike the attempt of the Christian, who believes Jesus Christ to be the source and goal of all religion, interpreting the spiritual strivings and findings in the other religions in terms of their ultimate fulfilment in Christ. Bishop Appasamy can be understood only in this light. There is a Christian theological interpretation of Hinduism just as Vivekananda represents an Advaitic interpretation of Christianity. And so long as it is differentiated from a study of what a religion means to its devotees, a religion which claims to be all-inclusive has the necessity to show that its claim to all-inclusiveness is not contradicted by other religions which encounter it. If Christians can speak of an unknown Christ of Hinduism, Hindus can speak of an unknown Vedanta in Christianity.

Vivekananda by his militancy has shown clearly that there is an either/or choice to be made between the mystic and the prophetic apprehensions of the ultimate reality. The choice may settle the question as to which of these is ultimate and which relative. Biblical religion stands or falls by the ultimacy of the prophetic core of faith in the living God of Abraham, Isaac and Jacob, the Father of our Lord Jesus Christ, in the God who acts in history through creation, judgment and redemption to achieve his purpose for mankind. But this affirmation by itself does not solve the question of the relation of the Christian religion to mysticism, metaphysics and morality and their relative places in the Christian scheme. This has remained a live issue of Christian theology all through the ages and Indian Christianity has to grapple with it in the face of the challenge of Vivekananda's system. Clearly the Indian Church cannot take a purely negative or indifferent attitude to mysticism and metaphysics to emphasize the centrality of the realm of morality. This approach will only bring about greater isolation of morality from spirituality and metaphysics. Our concern should be that spirituality and metaphysics serve moral regeneration of life. Therefore the Church should be concerned with defining the positive meaning of mysticism and metaphysics within the context of the Christian faith and of its concern for spiritual and moral purposes in society and history. Herein lies the significance of Appasamy's insights as a starting point. Probably Indian Christianity has to take more seriously than he has done the prophetic tradition of the Old Testament in the interpretation of Christ.

There is however a very important point which both Andrews and Chandran have emphasized, namely that relevance to the moral regeneration of individual and corporate life in contemporary India is a most important rational criterion of truth in religion, spirituality and metaphysics. The pressure of contemporary India also is on all religions to recognize this criterion as a valid one. It is therefore within the context of a common concern for the moral regeneration of human society in which is present the pressure of a living God and his Christ on India, that the Christian apologist can undertake a fruitful intellectual dialogue on the adequacy or otherwise of the spiritual foundation of Vivekananda's Practical Vedanta to provide the motivation and dynamic for moral effort and social transformation, and on the comparative truth of the personal and Advaitic interpretations and evaluations of reality.

Indeed Vivekananda is aware of the need to provide, in his own Advaitic system of ethics, adequate motivation and dynamic to programmes of service and even of radical change in society. And his doctrines of *Karma Yoga* and *Jivanmukti* do provide a basis for human solidarity purposive action and selfless service. And at this point Vivekananda contends that his system of ethics is not different from personalist systems, only he puts things within a more philosophic framework. He says:

There is no limit to this getting out of selfishness. All the great systems of ethics preach absolute unselfishness. Supposing this absolute unselfishness can be reached by a man, what becomes of him? He is no more the little Mr So-and-So; he has acquired infinite expansion. ... The personalist, when he hears this idea philosophically put, gets frightened. At the same time, if he preaches morality, he after all teaches the very same idea himself.[140]

Certainly this equation of Advaitic renunciation of *jivatva* (selflessness) with the personalist renunciation of *ahamkara* (unselfishness) has proved true in the practice of the Ramakrishna movement. But the question of their differentiation is philosophically and theologically not unimportant and in the long run not irrelevant to the practice itself, especially if we are seeking to realize the dignity of the human person and the fellowship of persons as the fundamental values of our society. It is certainly relevant to the task of understanding and communicating the Gospel of Jesus Christ and his New Creation in the context of the Indian renaissance.

We shall look at some of the problems of Christian apologetics and Christian-Hindu dialogue as we encounter the Hindu apologetics of S. Radhakrishnan.

Vivekananda's concept of the endless cycles of *parinama* (evolution) and *pralaya* (involution) in which *prakriti* (nature) itself is seen as having no goal, in the sense of *telos* or *eschaton* in which or towards which it moves, is basic to his whole theological system. *Prakriti* provides the background for *jiva*, but there is no eternally significant relation between the essential human person, the self and the social and cosmic process. And Vivekananda seeks to synthesize *parinama* with the scientific theory of natural evolution from the lower to the higher, but all such evolution takes place between two moments of involution; therefore the cyclic picture remains. The idea of an ultimate spiritual purpose for social history and the cosmic process becomes difficult if not impossible for the Swami. In fact, the doctrine of many incarnations goes with that of the many cycles. No doubt the cyclic concept has a great deal of validity. Nature repeats its day and night and the seasons. The wheel of birth, growth and death is characteristic of individuals and civilizations and perhaps of worlds. The Christian understanding of historical and cosmic process need not deny the reality of the cycles of nature and life. But it stands or falls with the doctrine of the ultimate divine purpose of that process. The Christian view of history need not be crudely linear because it conceives of the fulfilment of the goal of history as having happened not at the end but in the middle of the movement so that it is possible to conceive this purpose either as the Beyond (Transcendence) or the End (Eschatology) in real relation with the empirical self and the process in which it is involved, cutting across its cycles and bringing into being spiritually purposeful persons realizing themselves in an ultimately meaningful history. It is only within some such framework of understanding that we can speak intelligently of a unique revelation of the divine purpose for the world. The germ of such an understanding is present in the protest of Swami Vivekananda against 'the Pharisees and Sadducees in Hinduism, hypocrites, who invent all sorts of engines of tyranny in the shape of doctrines of *Paramarthika* and *Vyavaharika*'[141] and in his struggles to bridge the discontinuity between *paramarthika* and *vyavaharika* levels of reality as a basis for his concern for man's dignity and for justice for men in society, and for historical action to realize it.

NOTES

1. Nalini Devdas, *Sri Ramakrishna*, Bangalore, 1965, pp. 7–24.
2. *Ib.*, p. 26.
3. *The Gospel of Ramakrishna*, New York, 1942, introduction, p. 34 (cited as *Gospel*).
4. *Ib.*, p. 34.   5. *Ib.*, p. 35.   6. *Ib.*, p. 39.
7. Cf. Devdas, *op. cit.*, pp. 56–64 and 104–13.
8. P. C. Mozoomdar, writing in the *Theistic Quarterly Review*, quoted in *The Life of Ramakrishna*, Advaita Ashram, Calcutta, 7th impression, 1955, p. 276 (cited as *Life*).
9. Quoted by Max Muller, *Ramakrishna: his Life and Sayings* (Collected Works, Vol. 15), London, 1900, p. 62.
10. Muller, *op. cit.*, p. 66.
11. Romain Rolland, *Prophets of the New India*, Part I, Life of Ramakrishna, New York, 1930, publisher's note, pp. 291f.
12. *Life*, pp. 274, 277.
13. Rolland, *op. cit.*, p. 144 (British ed., London, 1930, p. 122).
14. *Ib.*, p. 135 (115).   15. *Ib.*, pp. 174f. (146).
16. *Life*, pp. 283–7.   17. Rolland, *op. cit.*, p. 185 (154).
18. *Life*, p. 279.   19. *Gospel*, p. 653.
20. Devdas, *op. cit.*, pp. 89f.   21. *Gospel*, p. 511.
22. Devdas, *op. cit.*, p. 62.   23. *Ib.*, p. 82.
24. *Ib.*, p. 32.
25. *The Complete Works of the Swami Vivekananda*, 5th ed., Almora, 1931, vol. I, p. xiii.
26. *Ib.*, III, pp. 182–4.   27. *Ib.*, III, p. 131.
28. *Ib.*, IV., pp. 51f.   29. *Ib.*, I, p. 22.
30. *Ib.*, IV, pp. 52f.   31. *Ib.*, IV, p. 54.
32. *Ib.*, IV, p. 331.   33. *Ib.*, VII, p. 14.
34. *Ib.*, VII, pp. 20, 27.   35. *Ib.*, IV, pp. 147f.
36. Muller, *op. cit.*, p. 109 (Saying no. 52).
37. Vivekananda, *Works* IV, p. 142.   38. *Ib.*, VII, p. 1.
39. *Ib.* VII, pp. 5f.   40. *Ib.* IV, pp. 141f.
41. *Ib.* IV, pp. 145f.   42. *Ib.*, VII, p. 2.
43. Devdas, *Swami Vivekananda*, pp. 161f.   44. Vivekananda, *Works* II, p. 298.
45. Devdas, *Sri Ramakrishna*, p. 163, quoting 'Discourses on Jnana Yoga'.
46. Vivekananda, *Works* VII, p. 2.   47. *Ib.* IV, p. 143.
48. *Ib.* VII, pp. 2f.   49. Rolland, *op. cit.*, pp. 478–82 (388–90).
50. *Ib.*, p. 560 (451).   51. *Ib.*, p. 484 (391)
52. *Ib.*, p. 561 (451).   53. *Ib.*, pp. 363f. (454).
54. Vivekananda, *Works* IV, p. 144.   55. *Ib.*, I, p. 326.
56. Devdas, *Sri Ramakrishna*, pp. 98f.
57. C. F. Andrews, *The Renaissance in India: its Missionary Aspect*, London, 1912, p. 129.
58. *Ib.*, pp. 160f.   59. *Ib.*, p. 168.   60. *Ib.*, p. 258.
61. B. Chaturvedi and M. Sykes, *Charles Freer Andrews: a Narrative*, London, 1949, p. 65.
62. *Ib.*, p. 111.   63. *Ib.*, p. 111.
64. Andrews, *op. cit.*, p. 99.
65. C. F. Andrews, ' "The Hindu View of Christ" ', *International Review of Missions* 28, 1939, pp. 259–64; quotation from pp. 259f.; Andrews' italics.
66. *Ib.*, p. 259.
67. J. R. Chandran, unpublished thesis on *Christian Apologetics in relation to Vivekananda in the light of Origen, Contra Celsum*, pp. 136–40, referring to Rolland, *op. cit.*, Book II, Part I, chs. III–IV (British ed., pp. 437ff., 457ff.).

68 Vivekananda, *Works* IV, pp. 102ff. 69 *Ib* II, p. 382.
70 Chandran, *op. cit.*, pp. 140f.
71 *Works* IV, p. 103. 72 *Ib.* II, pp. 130, 168, 180, 182, etc.
73 Chandran, *op. cit.*, p. 152. 74 *Ib.*, p. 157.
75 *Ib.*, p. 161, referring to Vivekananda, *Works* VI, pp. 404f.
76 Chadran, p. 162. 77 *Ib.*, pp. 176f.
78 *The Vedanta Sutras* III (Sacred Books of the East, ed. Max Muller, vol. XLVIII), Oxford, 1904, p. 332.
79 *The Vedanta Sutras* I, *Ib.*, vol. XXXIV, 1890, p. 204.
80 Chandran, *op. cit.*, pp. 212f. 81 *Ib.*, p. 177.
82 Vivekananda, *Works* I, p. 321; II, pp. 142f.; IV, pp. 142, 144.
83 E. F. Scott, *The Fourth Gospel*, Edinburgh, 1908, p. 289.
84 Chandran, p. 179, quoting Edwyn Hoskyns, *The Fourth Gospel*, 2nd ed., London, 1947, p. 453 (on John 10.30).
85 Matt. 6.10, 24; 8.20; 10.39; 13.44; 19.21.
86 Chandran, pp. 181f. 87 *Ib.*, p. 196.
88 *Works* II, pp. 245f; III, p. 123; V, p. 237.
89 Chandran, pp. 196f. 90 *Ib.*, p. 200.
91 Cf. Vivekananda, *Works* II, p. 196. 92 *Ib.* II, p. 113.
93 Chandran, p. 203. 94 *Works* II, pp. 108, 142.
95 *Ib.* VII, p. 76. 96 *Ib.* I, p. 326.
97 Chandran, p. 207. 98 *Ib.*, pp. 321–4.
99 Henrik Kraemer, *The Christian Message in a Non-Christian World*, London, 1938 (in preparation for the Tambaram Conference).
100 Chandran, pp. 324f. 101 *Ib.*, pp. 327.
102 *Ib.*, p. 325. 103 *Ib.*, p. 329.
104 *Ib.*, p. 338. 105 *Ib.*, p. 339.
106 *Ib.*, p. 359. 107 *Ib.*, pp. 346f.
108 *Ib.*, p. 347. 109 *Ib.*, p. 347.
110 *Ib.*, p. 340, referring to C. C. J. Webb, *God and Personality*, London, 1918, pp. 61–88, 241–75.
111 Chandran, pp. 340–4. 112 *Ib.*, p. 348.
113 A. J. Appasamy, *What is Moksha?*, Madras, 1931 (cited as *Moksha*); *My Theological Quest*, Bangalore, 1964 (cited as *Quest*).
114 *Moksha*, p. 9. 115 *Ib.*, p. 20.
116 Appasamy, *Christianity as Bhakti Marga*, Madras, 1926, London, 1927, p. 1.
117 *Quest*, p. 31. 118 *Ib.*, p. 28.
119 *Moksha*, pp. 56–9. 120 *Ib.*, p. 70.
121 *Ib.*, pp. 95f. 122 *Ib.*, p. 161.
123 *Ib.*, p. 98. 124 *Ib.*, pp. 105f.
125 *Ib.*, p. 110. 126 *Ib.*, p. 112.
127 *Ib.*, p. 114. 128 *Ib.*, p. 117.
129 *Ib.*, p. 141. 130 *Ib.*, p. 129.
131 *Ib.*, p. 156. 132 *Ib.*, pp. 134f.
133 *Quest*, p. 32. 134 *Moksha*, p. 169.
135 *Ib.*, p. 177. 136 *Ib.*, pp. 175f.
137 *Ib.*, p. 179.
138 K. T. Paul, *The British Connection with India*, London, 1928, pp. 50f.
139 H. C. E. Zacharias, *Renascent India*, London, 1933, p. 25.
140 Vivekananda, *Works* I, p. 107. 141 *Ib.* V, p. 13.

CHAPTER SEVEN

Radhakrishnan: The Mystic Christ

In an autobiographical essay[1] Dr S. Radhakrishnan has spoken of the national pride which Vivekananda awoke in him with regard to Hinduism, and of the hurt to it inflicted by the attitude of his missionary teachers towards Hinduism. The whole edifice of Radhakrishnan's thought has in it his own search for truth in the context of the impact of Christianity on Hinduism in which his spirit and mind were involved from the time of his student days. Therefore Radhakrishnan's writings have the character of Hindu apologetics in which he seeks to redefine Hinduism for the intellectuals of modern India, from the standpoint of Advaita Vedanta bringing out its adequacy for contemporary life and interpreting and evaluating Christ and Christianity within its context. It is, as C. E. M. Joad has said, 'a counter-attack from the East'. The aim of this chapter is to outline the general framework of his thought and his views on Christ and Christianity and to indicate the issues they raise for Christian theology, as expressed by some Indian Christian thinkers.

Radhakrishnan has written a great deal. For our brief survey we shall confine ourselves mainly to his *Eastern Religions and Western Thought*[2] and to some parts of *The Philosophy of Sarvepalli Radhakrishnan*.[3] Radhakrishnan is primarily a philosopher. But our concern is with him as Hindu theologian. Indeed, in him philosophy and theology are integrally related.

1. THE FRAMEWORK

Radhakrishnan's starting point is that spiritual salvation is essentially *jnana* of *Brahman*, realization of the Absolute. He distinguishes the religions of the world into two classes, one Semitic, which 'emphasizes the object', and the other which 'insists on experience'. Hinduism and Buddhism belong to the second class.

For them religion is salvation. It is more a transforming experience than a notion of God ... Belief and conduct, rites and ceremonies, authorities and dogma are assigned a place subordinate to the art of conscious self-discovery and contact with the divine.[4]

The Divine is Brahman (Sanskrit for Absolute) which is 'the principle of search as well as the object sought, the animating ideal and its fulfilment'; men are 'saved not by creeds but by gnosis, *jnana* or spiritual wisdom'.[5] Man is both an empirical self and a transcendent self; and

the fundamental truths of a spiritual religion are that our real self is the Supreme Being, which it is our business to discover and consciously become, and this being is one in all.[6]

Inherent in it is 'the soul's experience of the essential unity with the whole being'.[7]

The religion of *jnana* has also its understanding of the relation of Brahman to the empirical world, for the Absolute can be viewed 'as it is in itself', and also 'as it is in relation to the world'. From the former viewpoint, 'the Absolute is said to have nothing of empiric being about it. It is perfection itself',[8] 'perfectly self-sufficient beyond all distinctions of the world'.[9] From the latter viewpoint, that is,

from the cosmic end, ... the Absolute is envisaged as *Isvara* or personal God, who guides and directs the process by His Providence.[10]

The Absolute is both these at once. The relation between Brahman, *Isvara* and the world is explained:

The dualism of God and matter, and good and evil, eternity and time, is not ultimate as with some Gnostics and Manicheans. It is subordinate to a fundamental monism. In the view of the Upanishads, the Absolute is not the creator of the world. . . . Creation of the world cannot be deduced ... from the Absolute (Brahman) which is perfectly self-sufficient beyond all distinctions of the world; but the world implies movement in God (*Isvara*) and its relation is not accidental or unnecessary.[11]

The world of multiplicity is *maya*, not in the sense that it is illusory or unreal, but in the sense that its creation is an 'ultimate mystery' and that the world is 'less real' than the Absolute-God. 'The manifold universe is not an illusion; it is being though of a lower order'.[12] It is relative reality and has only a derived meaning.[13] Divine *lila*, again, is not intended to suggest that the universe is a meaningless show made in jest. The world is created by God out of the abundance of His joy.[14]

And spirituality involves a realization both of 'the comparative unreality of everything else including the finite individual'[15] and of the degrees of reality inherent in the world as 'activities of the Spirit.'[16] This idea of a ladder of reality is basic to Radhakrishnan's framework of thought. He says:

Matter (*anna*), life (*prana*), consciousness (*manas*), intelligence (*vijnana*), and bliss (*ananda*) constitute a ladder of increasing reality which passes from the negative pole of pure nonentity to the positive pole of God's absolute being.[17]

The cosmic process is an evolution towards 'the spiritual orders of existence'.[18] Hence:

The view of the Upanishads does not destroy the sense of reality and importance of the historical process. History is not a meaningless repetition but a creative process determined by the free act of the individuals. The spiritual world is more real than the material world, and we can remake the earth in its likeness if we truly believe and practise the life of the Spirit.[19]

The world is 'to be enjoyed by man, but in a spirit of detachment,[20] and because 'the germ of divinity lies within each of us', all have 'the possibility of salvation',[21] that is of being 'free from *maya*', 'from bondage to the unreal values which are dominating us'[22] through the contemplation of the mystery of the divinity in us, identical with the Absolute. And 'the liberated individual works for the welfare of the world'[23] and continues to be 'a centre of action so long as the cosmic process lasts'.[24]

When ... the cosmic purpose is fulfilled, pure undisturbed truth of eternity burns up the world, ... and ... existence lapses into Absolute Being. ... There will be other world orders in an endless series, for God is infinite possibility. We do not equate God with this evolutionary process.[25]

2. THE MEANING OF CHRIST

Radhakrishnan uses this framework of Neo-Advaita Vedantism, with its ladder of reality oriented to mystic experience as the ultimate criterion and goal of spirituality, to interpret Christ and the truths of Christianity. Indeed in his view, this is fully justified, because 'while retaining the Jewish beliefs in a living God and passion for righteousness', Christianity has from the very beginning 'absorbed Greek thought' which is related intimately to the Hindu.

The Christian view represents a blend of the Greek and the Jewish conceptions of the historical.[26]

He seeks to show that Jesus himself is best understood as

a mystic who believes in the inner light, . . . ignores ritual and is indifferent to legalistic piety.[27]

The attempts to interpret Jesus purely in terms of the Jewish religious conceptions are a failure, for the conceptions of what Schweitzer and Heiler call 'the prophetic and world-affirming religions'

have more in common with neo-pagan faiths than with the self-denying, self-forgetful genius of Christianity whose symbol is the Cross.[28]

On 'the secret of the Cross', Radhakrishnan says:

The abandonment of the ego is the identification with a fuller life and consciousness. The soul is raised to a sense of its universality. . . . In Gethsemane, Christ as an individual felt that the cup should pass away. That was His personal desire. The secret of the Cross is the crucifixion of the ego and the yielding to the will of God. 'Thy will be done.'[29]

'Resurrection' and 'the Kingdom of God' and 'eternal life' represent the goals of man in the Christian scheme, which, in their truly spiritual reality, are best seen in terms of Hindu faith.

The resurrection is not the rise of the dead from their tombs, but the passage from the death of self-absorption to the life of unselfish love, the transition from the darkness of selfish individualism to the light of universal spirit, from falsehood to truth, from slavery to the world to the liberty of the eternal.[30]

The Kingdom is God within us, and we need not wait for its attainment till some undated future or look for an apocalyptic display in the sky.[31]

The Kingdom of God is *Brahmaloka*, the Kingdom of the Spirit, 'the transfiguration of the cosmos, the revolutionary change in men's consciousness, a new relationship among them, an assimilation to God'.[32]

Eternal life is one in which the universal spirit is all in all.[33]

The Logos and the incarnate Logos of the first chapter of the Fourth Gospel also find their place in the Neo-Advaitic scheme of Radhakrishnan.

If we start from the cosmic end, it is true to say 'in the beginning was the Logos', the personal creator God.[34] . . . Dualism . . . is subordinate to a fundamental monism.

The life of Jesus is not 'a mere event in history'.

As we have to live on earth, the spectacle of an incarnate God has great religious value, but a sharply defined anthropomorphism makes for narrowness and intolerance and takes us sometimes to absurd lengths.[35]

This last is a warning against making the 'historical person' of Jesus essential to the spiritual valuation of his Christhood; and in the 'Fragments of a Confession' he repeats it:

Christ is born in the depths of spirit: we say that he passes through life, dies on the Cross and rises again. Those are not so much historical events which occurred once upon a time as universal processes of spiritual life, which are being continually accomplished in the souls of men. Those who are familiar with the way in which the Krsna story is interpreted will feel inclined to regard Christhood as an attainment of the soul, a state of inward glorious illumination in which the divine wisdom has become the heritage of the soul.[36]

3. AN INTERPRETATIVE HISTORY OF CHRISTIANITY

Radhakrishnan's conviction that the life and message of Jesus are brought out best in his Advaita framework is reinforced by the results of historical research which have shown that Hinduism may have played a significant part in the shaping of the spirit of Jesus and the course of Christian history from early times. Of course Jesus was a

Jew, but the sources of his religion and ideas were not solely Jewish. And on that basis, he gives his own survey of the Gospel of Jesus, the formation of the primitive tradition and later Church history. This historical survey is a very important part of Radhakrishnan's Hindu apologetics.

Radhakrishnan relies on Prof. R. Otto's book *The Kingdom of God and the Son of Man*, in which he showed that the 'idea of the Son of God who was also a Son of Man' was not Jewish but Aryan. He quotes Otto as saying:

> The figure of a being who had to do with the world and who was subordinate to the primary, ineffable, remote and aboriginal deity is of high antiquity among the Aryans, ... the phrase 'This Son of Man' points back in some way [through Enoch] to influences of the Aryan East.

Radhakrishnan says:

> The predicates which are attributed to Enoch's God are those which are found in the Upanishads. ... It is the ancient Hindu tradition which Enoch illustrates and Jesus continues.[37]

And in this light, even the Synoptic Gospels point to 'two currents, the Jewish and the Mystic' which remained unreconciled in Jesus:

> From the synoptic Gospels it is clear that the two currents, the Jewish and the Mystic, the materialistic and the spiritual, were not perfectly reconciled in Jesus' mind – while the Messianic conception of the Kingdom belongs to the Palestinian tradition, the mystic concept is the development of the Indian idea. In Jesus' mind universalism and passivism conflict with the exclusiveness and militarism of His Jewish ancestors.[38]

Radhakrishnan sees 'the new current of other-worldliness' alien to the Jewish background emerging in John the Baptist, Jesus and Paul.[39] But it is mixed up with Jewish concepts. As a Jew Jesus believed in 'a corporeal resurrection', but in the mystic approach,

> Victory over death is the awakening of the spirit from the slumber that makes it capable of higher vision. Resurrection is not the revivification of a corpse.[40]

And the emphasis on the bodily resurrection of Jesus and the whole Christology and the doctrine of the Church based on the bodily resurrection came into Christianity as an answer to the frustration of the spirit of the early Christians; when they found that the prediction of Jesus' coming again 'as the exalted Son of God' in the Kingdom failed,

the eschatological claim became prominent. The conviction of the exaltation of God through death was the basis of the possibility that Peter and the rest believed after Jesus' death that they saw Him in spiritual vision as living with God. It does not seem to be a question of an empty grave or bodily resurrection. The simple story of the life and activity of Jesus was transformed with an epiphany of a heavenly being who had descended to earth and concealed Himself in robes of flesh. The picture of Jesus of the later Christology blurred the contours of the spiritual God. The Risen Lord takes the place of God and the Church replaces His Kingdom.[41]

And he explains the formation of the Gospel tradition, which resulted in the writing of the four Gospels:

Christianity began humbly among a band of disciples who knew and remembered the earthly life of Jesus, the ministry of a revolutionary prophet who announced the speedy coming of the Kingdom and demanded repentance. ... The historical facts were soon covered over by the accretions of imagination. Incidents of Jesus' life assumed the form of legends and it is not improbable that in the work the evangelists were unconsciously influenced by the cult of the Buddha.[42]

Primitive Christianity took form and developed in the Middle East in a climate of religious thought which had a dominant element of mysticism in it. Jewish Platonism, Gnosticism, and Neo-Platonism expressed the idea of mysticism in combination with various other elements. Philo's system was a 'mystic rendering of historical Judaism'.[43]

To Philo the anthropomorphism of the Pentateuch is only an accommodation. The free spiritual worship of the Eternal is the goal for which the worship of the personal God is a preparation.[44]

In fact according to Radhakrishnan, except for his monotheism, contempt for image worship and assertion of the superiority of the Mosaic revelation, 'all the other elements of his system are those found in Hindu thought'. He quotes Milman's *History of Christianity* in support of the idea that the influence must have come from a permanent Western settlement in the deserts of Egypt of 'the genuine Indian mysticism'.

Many of the chief features of gnosticism are also common to the Upanishads and the mystic tradition of Greece.[45]

And where Christianity emerged, Gnosticism 'became fused with Christian ideas'. Gnostics supplied a philosophy to Christianity, and were the 'theologians of the first century'. He quotes Harnack:

The Gnostic systems represent the acute secularising or hellenising of Christianity with the rejection of the Old Testament, while the Catholic system on the other hand represents a gradual process of the same kind with the conservation of the Old Testament.[46]

Radhakrishnan's conclusion is:

To the careful student, the close similarity between the teaching of the Upanishads and early Buddhism and Gnostic theories will be obvious.[47]

Christianity developed in the same world and breathed the same air as Alexandrian Judaism, Gnosticism and Neo-Platonism.

And even New Testament Christianity shows marks of the influence of the climate.

For Paul, Jesus is only the Lord and not God. . . . The insistence on the Neo-platonic idea of the Logos is so great as to reduce the human life of Jesus to a mere illusive appearance. If the name of Jesus is employed, it is only in a symbolic way, for St Paul says how 'all our fathers drank of the spiritual rock Christ', and Christ can be formed in each of us. He certainly warns us against over-estimating the historical instead of looking upon it as the symbol of metaphysical truth. . . . The foundation of St Paul's Christianity is a vision, not an external revelation. . . . In St Paul, Jesus becomes the centre of a cult where baptism and the commemoration of the Last Supper take the place of the sacraments of the mysteries.[48]

Of course, he has 'a different group of ideas from those of the mystery religions'

Paul knew Jesus to be a historical person who as the result of boundless devotion to the good of his fellows suffered a shameful death in loyalty to His Father's purpose. He looks upon this as the bringing near to man of the redeeming love of God.

Paul however, has a mystic understanding of Christ:

The life, death and resurrection of Christ are illustrations of a universal principle . . . Again we have the well-known doctrine of the phenomenality of the world (*maya*) in the saying: 'The things that are seen are temporal but the things that are not seen are eternal'. . . . In the spirit of true mysticism, he criticises ceremonial religion ... The Platonic words, fellowship, participation and presence are all in St Paul. 'I live not but Christ lives in me' ... In Romans 1 the invisible things are understood through the things that are made. The logos is the Absolute from the cosmic end, and so when the cosmic process is consummated, then all evil is subdued to good, time will end, and the Logos 'will deliver up the Kingdom to God, even the Father', 'that God may be all in all'. The distinction of perfected souls will be retained until this culmination is reached, when the world is taken over into God the Absolute.[49]

The discourses of St John are full of 'mystic elements'.

From the 'Father the Absolute One' arises the Son the Divine reason. Though He was with Him from the beginning, He is less than the Absolute: 'My Father is greater than I.'

Radhakrishnan sees 'an insistence on the unity of the whole' throughout St John's discourses: for example, in the prayer 'As Thou, Father art in Me, and I in Thee, so may they be in us'.[50]

And coming to the Church Fathers, Radhakrishnan notices a continuing battle between the dogmatic and spiritual approaches to Christianity.

The strife between Arius and Athanasius still continues in the hearts of men. Athanasius weaned the Church from her traditions of tolerance and scholarship, of Clement and Origen. Nicene orthodoxy gained victory over Hellenistic and heretical systems. Those who had a natural bent for speculative doubt exercised their scepticism on Christian dogmas.[51]

This dogmatism has to be broken if Christianity is to 'regain universality'; and every attempt in that direction will bring Christianity 'nearer the religions of India'. And he expresses his hope:

Perhaps Christianity, which arose out of an Eastern background and early in its career got wedded to Graeco-Roman culture, may find her rebirth today in the heritage of India.[52]

4. UNIVERSAL RELIGION

Radhakrishnan more or less consistently maintained a clear doctrine of the relation between religions, based on his idea that all historical religions are different forms of the true religion of the spirit at various stages of the march to the same mountain top of spiritual realization. Since Vedanta sees the formless one in all the different forms of religion it is 'not a religion but religion itself in its most universal and deepest significance'.[53]

Radhakrishnan has a whole chapter in *Eastern Religions and Western Thought* on the theme of 'The Meeting of Religions' in which he expands the doctrine of the essential oneness of all religions. Radhakrishnan finds this approach to the essential oneness of all religions a unique character of Eastern Religions, especially Hinduism.

In the supreme vision which Arjuna has [in the *Bhagavadgita*], he sees the different deities within the boundless form of the Supreme. The Puranas continue the tradition.[54]

This has found expression in a policy of religious toleration throughout Indian history, illustrated by such communities as the Christians of the Mar Thoma Church, the Jews in Kerala and the Parsees in Western India. Even to the Muslims and Christians who 'came as conquerors' the same toleration was shown.

As a result of this tolerant attitude, Hinduism has become itself a mosaic of almost all the types and stages of religious aspiration and endeavour, ... interpreting the different historical forms as modes, emanations or aspects of the Supreme.

The Hindu attitude is not the outcome of scepticism which despairs of ever reaching any stable truth. . . . It is not a mere concession to human imperfection.[55]

It is based on 'a definite philosophy' which sees direct realization of the Supreme in mystic experience as the ultimate goal of the religion of the spirit.

Creeds and dogmas, words and symbols, have only an instrumental value. ... The formless blaze of spiritual life cannot be expressed in human words. [To the mystic,] authority is no longer binding, and ritual is no longer support. [He] is indifferent to all questions of history.

The Christian mystic transcends the person of Jesus.

A temporal and finite symbolism cannot be regarded as unique, definitive and absolute.[56]

Formulae are useful to 'express the mysterious', but none of them has 'absolute value'.⁵⁷ Toleration can be based only on the idea that 'the different creeds are the historical formulations of the formless truth'.⁵⁸

In striking contrast to this

Christian religion inherited the Semitic creed of the 'jealous God' in the view of Christ as the 'only begotten Son of God', and so could not brook any rival near the throne.⁵⁹

And this has led to intoleration and religious persecution in the history of Christianity. Radhakrishnan speaks of three attitudes to other religions among the Christian theologians today. The first follows the line that 'the other religions are in fact untouchable'.⁶⁰ This is quite opposed to the attitude of the Church fathers, Clement, Origen and Augustine.

The second view discerns divine elements in other religions ... but contends that Christianity is the peak of the development of religion. It is the crown and completion of the religion of humanity, the standard by which others are judged. Other religions ... are merely preparations for the Christian religion, which is unique.⁶¹

But in Radhakrishnan's view, truth and salvation for the future lies with the third attitude, 'the Hindu one' which 'an increasing number of Christians' are adopting, and which looks forward to 'a world society with a universal religion of which the historical faiths are but branches', all religions 'assisting each other to find their own souls and grow to their full stature'. He concludes the lecture thus:

We are slowly realizing that believers with different opinions and convictions are necessary to each other to work out the larger synthesis which alone can give the spiritual basis to a world brought together into intimate oneness by man's mechanical ingenuity.⁶²

In his 'Fragments of a Confession' Radhakrishnan shares his mature views on the same theme. He once again affirms the universality of the tradition of direct experience of God.

In all lands, in all ages and in all creeds, the seers describe their experiences with an impressive unanimity.⁶³

Radhakrishnan: The Mystic Christ

This is the Religion of the Spirit around which a fellowship of religions becomes possible. He says:

> The world is seeking not so much a fusion of religions as a fellowship of religions, based on the realisation of the fundamental character of man's religious experience. . . . The different religious traditions clothe the one Reality in various images and their visions could embrace and fertilise each other so as to give mankind a many-sided perfection, the spiritual radiance of Hinduism, the faithful obedience of Judaism, the life of beauty of Greek Paganism, the noble compassion of Buddhism, the vision of divine love of Christianity and the spirit of resignation to the sovereign Lord of Islam. All these represent different aspects of the inward spiritual life, projections on the intellectual plane of the ineffable experiences of the human spirit.[64]

In fact in Radhakrishnan's view,

> It is misleading to speak of different religions. We have different religious traditions which . . . are versions in a series, part of the historical and relative world in which we live and move.[65]

The 'unchanging substance' of all religions is the evolution of man to the spiritual illumination in which the soul realizes itself. This is

> the eternal religion behind all religions, this *sanatana dharma*, the timeless tradition; . . . it is our duty to get back to this central core of religion. . . . Our historical religions will have to transform themselves into the universal faith or they will fade away.[66]

5. CHRISTIAN EVALUATIONS

The thought of Radhakrishnan has been critically evaluated from philosophical and theological points of view by many Christian thinkers. It is not our purpose to survey them all. We shall confine ourselves to a few of the evaluations, mostly by Indians.

A. *Religious Protest Against the 'Absolute': P. Chenchiah*

Probably the most fundamental criticism has come from Justice P. Chenchiah, in the course of his comments on a consultation with Dr Hendrik Kraemer in Madras in 1951. He opposes the very idea of the Absolute which is common to Kraemer and Radhakrishnan. He says:

There is a humorous side to this Barthian-Advaitic, Kraemer-Radhakrishnan duel. Both believe in the Absolute. Both discard relativism, one as sin and the other as *maya*. I am a relativist and don't believe in the absolute, whatever it may mean. I have a right to pick a bone with these. Why these blood brothers quarrel I don't know. I consider the absolute a construct of the mind. The absolute is metaphysical while the relative is historic.[67]

Chenchiah's is a religious protest which is not argued out philosophically. But it is clear that for him the Absolute is 'a construct of the mind', which weakens the 'historic' reality. In fact even in his review of Kraemer's *Christian Message in a Non-Christian World* he was fiercely opposed to Kraemer's idea of the Absolute and the implication it has for the doctrine of the Incarnation. In biblical Realism, Incarnation is

the advent of an incognito God [Who] touches the world as the tangent touches the circle – touching without touching, [and] does not enter into it, taking his place in the creation, but only tears the texture of history and creates a void.[68]

In the philosophy of India, 'the philosophic absolute and the religious absolute are the same' and the personal can never be comprehended in it. Therefore the absolute of both Kraemer's theology and Indian religion are incapable of giving reality to God the Emmanuel and Jesus the New Creation in history. And therefore Chenchiah says, he does not 'keep company with absolutists' but considers himself a relativist.

Relativism may renounce the 'absolute' God but does not for that reason forgo God altogether. The finite God is still God, yea even so our Lord Jesus Christ ... Who is to judge between the theologian's Absolute and man's human God.[69]

The religious insight behind this protest is of extreme importance. It is the demand of man for a God who becomes man and continues to remain man with man. Chenchiah thinks that the Absolutists, whether Christian or Hindu, are unable to conceive such an incarnation. He says:

In Indian Christian theology, Jesus belongs to man and even though he may sojourn in Heaven, he will return to earth, for here lies his home. A type of Christian theology approximates his function to that of the Hindu avatar. The Son became Jesus to offer his life on the Cross as propitiation and went to his home in Heaven after his mission was fulfilled. In that case, incarnation will be an adventure, an interlude in the Eternal Son's life, leaving no permanent deposit on earth or in heaven. He assumed the body for a purpose and when it was over he resumed his former status. Our conception of the Son of Man radically differs from this.[70]

Chenchiah, in fact, reverses Radhakrishnan's order and sees the process of human history as the ultimate, and the Absolute as the construction of the human mind.

Chenchiah's approach through the primacy of the Incarnation rather than the Absolute, he claims to be Upanishadic. In this connection Chenchiah's comment on Carl Keller's Christology in terms of Advaita philosophy[71] is of special interest. Chenchiah begins his comment by saying that the Indian interpretation of Christ is not primarily for intellligible communication to the Hindu, but for 'apprehending Jesus' through the spiritual eye of Hinduism.

Hinduism is our spiritual eye; but for its existence the Hindu convert could have passed by Christ. The Hindu heritage constitutes God's provision of an eye to the Hindu to see Christ.... Indian Christian theology stands on three pillars – Hindu heritage, *pratyaksa* experience of Christ, and for that purpose the guidance of the Holy Spirit. The contribution of the Jew and the Greek have already been made through St Peter and St John; the Indian Christian contribution remains to be made.[72]

Chenchiah maintains however that 'the typical Hindu religious experience' is that of the Upanishads but not that of Advaita. The experience that has entered into the make-up of the religious Hindu mind is not based on the assertion that Brahman alone exists and that the many are unreal, 'but that separation is unreal'.

The many can become one; what *maya* should lose is not itself but its sense of discreteness. 'I and my Father are one' is Upanishadic, but not necessarily Advaitic. The Upanishadic experience of becoming one will yield richer fruit, when applied to the interpretation of the relation of God to Jesus, than the Advaitic postulate 'One only exists'. Whether Jesus and God are initially one or two, in incarnation they have become one. Christians may be many, but in Christ they have become one; that is reincarnation.[73]

Chenchiah repeats that Barthians and Sankarites have a common predicament in apprehending 'Christ after the flesh – as if there were any other Christ; the resurrected and ascended Lord had a body and carried it to heaven'.[74] And for the apprehension of the historical Christ, we need not restrict ourselves to Sankara's Advaita as Keller had done but move to other schools of the Vedanta. No doubt 'modern Advaitins' are most helpful in interpreting Christ to the modern Hindu. But for himself, he would interpret Christ more in terms of Vallabha's *Suddadvaita* and Aurobindo's ideology. As for Vallabha:

> *Suddadvaita* pursues the *idam* line of thought to incarnation, in which it finds a culmination ... he stands for the primacy of the *avatar*, the absolute supreme reality of Krishna. The metaphysical was somehow absorbed into the physical.[75]

As for Aurobindo he 'comes nearest to St Paul's Second-Adam Christology'. And he hopes that with the help of Vallabha and Aurobindo Indian Christian theology can bring out the significance of Jesus' description of himself as the Son of Man. To Chenchiah, Keller's statement that the divine assumption of human nature cannot obtain absolute reality, does not ring true

> to apostolic teaching and conviction. The resurrection and ascension does not prove his point; for if we take them with the undeniable conviction of the second advent of Christ, Christ retaining His body all through, the reverse seems to be the case: they show the conviction of the absoluteness and ultimacy of the Incarnation.[76]

Chenchiah realizes however that ours is 'the exploratory period' and therefore we should have the picture of Christ in terms of all the *darsanas*.

> We shall have five or six interpretations ... then we can judge which of them comes nearest to Jesus.[77]

B. *The Struggle to Provide a Spiritual Basis for the New India: P. D. Devanandan*

Devanandan has left in his many articles his evaluation of the New Hinduism of which Radhakrishnan is the chief representative. He sees 'reform in social practices [entailing] a restatement of corresponding underlying religious beliefs'; and illustrates it by reference to Radhakrishnan's restatement of the concept of *karma* to signify not fatalism but continuity and man's freedom and capacity, 'if he wills', to improve on his past record and change the direction of the current.[78] And he recognizes Radhakrishnan's positive affirmation of human personality, purposive human history and the goal of human community on the basis of Neo-Advaita Vedantism and its understanding of *maya*. He says that Radhakrishnan

has no difficulty in accepting the wealth of meaning-content that modern western thinkers put into such terms as personality and community and ... sees no difficulties in reconciling them with the basic affirmations of Vedanta. What is more, he [Radhakrishnan] would go further and maintain that these modern concepts are in fact derived from the Vedanta view of life.[79]

Radhakrishnan has emphasized in his *Religion and Society*

a recognition of spiritual realities not by abstention from the world but bringing to its life, its business (*artha*) and its pleasure (*kama*), the controlling power of spiritual faith. Life is one and in it there is no distinction of sacred and secular. *Bhakti* and *mukti* are not opposed. *Dharma*, *artha*, and *kama* go together.[80]

Devanandan notes that generally in the Neo-Vedanta there is

a shift ... from speculation about the nature of the Absolute to a new understanding about the nature of man. ... The determinative doctrine in the evaluation of the Hindu outlook on life is no longer derived from its classical theology, but is being built upon a new anthropology. This anthropology is perhaps still in the making.[81]

But he raises the question whether Neo-Hinduism has succeeded in reconciling the new anthropology with the classical theology. And he answers:

The stumbling block [to success in this aim] continues to be the supreme difficulty of putting meaning-content into the term 'personal' as applied to God and His relationship with man, especially in view of the 'new' significance given in contemporary Hindu society to the concept of the *human* 'person' in relation to other persons. The other difficulty arises when the point is made that beyond all the activism, openly admitted as theologically valid, there is the 'actionlessness' of mystic *advaitam* (non-duality) of the finite self and the Infinite Self, still upheld as the one desirable end of all religious pilgrimage ... Finally, whatever the 'emphasis' (or the de-emphasis), adherence to the *Vedanta* view of Reality makes almost impossible belief in a doctrine of creation, especially such as would do justice to the reality of God's purposive work in world-life as directed towards an End and to the 'creative' activity of the human person as capable of co-operating with (or retarding) the fulfilment of the Divine purpose in creation. So far Hindu renascence has given no proof of its awareness of these theological issues.[82]

Devanandan finds that 'the dichotomy between secular and sacred' created by the 'traditional understanding of world-life as *samsara* and the highest religious good as *moksha* in the long course of Hindu religious history' remains unsolved 'despite the easy claims of Dr Radhakrishnan'.[83] He does not however make clear whether in his thinking it remains unsolved specially in Radhakrishnan's system of thought itself. But he affirms that the revelation in Jesus Christ of 'a God that is redemptively at work in the world for man's good',[84] the understanding of 'man as a sinful creature' and 'the theology of the purposive will of a personal God' are relevant to the problems which Hinduism faces in effecting 'a synthesis'[85] between the traditional world-view and the humanism of contemporary India.

Devanandan deals with Radhakrishnan's idea of *Sanatana dharma*, and its claim to represent religious universality. But he does it to clarify that it is grounded on certain basic assumptions, which have the character of a fundamental creed. This creed is no doubt different from the creed which defines the nature of the universality of Christianity. Devanandan's attempt is to show that Vedanta and Christianity are both based on different fundamental assumptions of the nature of ultimate reality which are at their core mutually exclusive. There is no point in denying that, at this level, a choice between creeds is involved.

Sanatana dharma, the beginningless and endless faith of Hinduism, is claimed to be a religion for all times and all peoples. Within the Hindu system, it includes 'all types of religion – primitive animism, popular polytheism, pietistic theism, philosophic monism and even agnostic mysticism'. The 'fundamental creed of this Pan-Hinduism' had four basic assumptions:

1. Ultimate Reality is essentially unknowable.
2. No one theological formulation about the nature of ultimate Reality can claim absolute validity.

3. Since all religions are partially true, the sum total of partial truths will certainly be more than the partial truth affirmed by any one religion [thus giving validity to religious syncretism].

4. Hinduism recognizes the right of every Hindu to accept and practise whatever way of life he may find useful for his mode of thinking and his peculiar social circumstances.[86]

Following Vivekananda, Radhakrishnan has interpreted the foundations of Vedanta to provide the framework for a unity which extends itself to include non-Hindu religions also. It is maintained that Hinduism as *Sanatana dharma* can include 'the essential concepts of Christianity', in which case

Christianity and Hinduism are not alternatives which call for a choice between the one and the other. What is called for is a recognition of the fact that in reality Christianity is part of Hinduism.[87]

But the question is, can the Vedantic universalism comprehend the essential aspects of Christianity? Devanandan explains what an affirmative answer means for the Vedantin and how it does violence to what Christianity itself considers as its essentials. For instance, Christianity regards the historicity of Jesus Christ, interpreted as God's redemptive action in human history, as belonging to its essence. Vedanta requires that this essential aspect of the spiritual significance of 'Christianity as a historical phenomenon' be regarded as a non-essential when it is included in *Sanatana dharma*. Again, Hindu religious universalism sees Christian evangelism generally as a denial of its basic creed. Firstly, 'evangelistic work among the simple village folk and unsophisticated tribal groups' of India denies the principle that people at 'different stages of spiritual growth and maturity' should not be disturbed from following their respective religious paths, however crude, because to them they are 'intrinsically good, not merely relatively so'.[88] Further, religion for the Vedanta in the final analysis is 'a matter of spiritual experience' of each individual, and rules out 'the idea of a religious community of believers'. The idea of congregational worship is largely alien to Hinduism.

Popular Hinduism has provided many occasions for mass expression of religious faith in pilgrim centres, huge temples, and popular shrines. But such gathering of worshippers is more of the nature of a collection of individuals essentially unrelated to one another, rather than a community of people in close personal relation. ... The conception of the Church is a rock of offence to the Hindu. ...

The reason is obvious. Religious maturity in Hinduism is the result of individual achievement in self-discipline towards which others like-minded can only help by the inspiration of example or through wise counsel. The idea of a transforming community is alien to the Hindu genius because of its basic belief about the nature of God as the eternal *Brahman* and ... the nature of man as essentially that of *Brahman* itself.[89]

According to the Vedanta, spiritual maturity lies through 'enlightenment' which is the result of self-discipline and self-culture moving towards self-realization in mystical union with the Absolute. Here again it contrasts with the emphasis in Christianity on preaching which testifies to 'a trascendent constraint, a total demand made upon man to recognize the authority of the Word of God revealed in Christ Jesus', and insists on 'decision' and 'conversion'. It is not a demand that 'we should do something', or 'produce something out of ourselves, or achieve something out of our strength', but a demand that we should 'allow something to be done in us', 'allow another to work His will in us'.[90]

Devanandan clarifies to an audience oriented to Radhakrishnan's doctrine of the unity of all religions how the Christian sees universality in religion on premises different from those of the Vedanta. Christian universality, he says, is based on the uniqueness of Jesus Christ. The Christian faith is

that what God has done in Jesus Christ has been done for all men. So that the claim for uniqueness is only an affirmation of its universality. In other words, ... Christians believe that with the coming of Christ, God Almighty identified Himself for a while with man in all man's struggles for perfection and the realisation of his true nature. Such identification initiates a new era in creation. It marked the beginning of a redemptive movement which takes in humanity in its entirety, that is the whole community of mankind inclusive of all peoples, whatever their beliefs, language and race. So that, far from wanting to shut others from participation (which would be being exclusive) the Christian wants the world of men to share his faith in this all-inclusive cosmic process of new creation.[91]

On the 'relation between religions' Devanandan dismisses 'the dogma that every religion leads to the same goal and that there are no differences that matter where religious faith is concerned' as unacceptable to the Christian.

What people differ about is not in regard to the value of religions but with regard to their validity. *Samadarsana* is one thing and *sarvasamaya samarasa* is another thing altogether. In fact equal validity of all religions is an affirmation of faith, which especially theistic religions will find it difficult to accept as being contradictory to the affirmation of their faith.[92]

The idea of reconciling differences between religions 'by setting them in the larger framework of an evolving world religion' overlooks the fact that each historic religion is 'a historic totality'. Any one of the systems may be repatterned, but the idea of 'producing an altogether new pattern' by welding together pieces arbitrarily cut out of different systems does violence to the integrity of men and faiths. The only proper inter-religious relation is to admit frankly that

there are differences which we should all be willing to accept and give all men of faith full freedom of religious self-expression.[93]

Indeed Devanandan has striven hard to explain, in the interreligious dialogues which he organized, how Christianity and Vedanta differ at their very foundations on the nature of God and man, on spiritual realization and on the method of achieving it. Therefore the meaning of terms in the two religions should be understood with reference to their respective basic core of faith. Even when the same words are used they indicate different content. Devanandan sees how difficult this truth is for devout Hindus to grasp. And he refers to Radhakrishnan as an example:

Here for example are the words of Professor Radhakrishnan: 'It is the aim of religion to lift us from our momentary meaningless provincialism to the significance and status of the eternal, to transform the chaos and confusion of life to that pure and immortal essence which is its ideal possibility. ... The divinizing of the life of man in the individual and the race is the dream of the great religions. It is the *moksha* of the Hindus, the *nirvana* of the Buddhists, the Kingdom of Heaven of the Christians. It is for Plato the life of the untroubled perception of the pure Idea'. But such an easy equation of *moksha*, *nirvana*, the Kingdom of God and Plato's 'pure idea' is disclaimed by Christian faith because of the basic difference in its understanding of ultimate truth.[94]

And the basic core of Christianity is that God the Ultimate Reality is Personal and that 'in the Person of Jesus Christ God has made known His mind to the world for all men'.[95] He agrees with Karl Barth that we shall 'make an idol out of God' if we do not conceive the Divine as 'personal in an incomprehensible way, in so far as the conception of his personality surpasses all our views of personality'. But God so conceived is 'supra-personal, not sub-personal, which is the dangerous implication in a view which lays too much stress on Ultimate Reality as impersonal'.[96] The significance of the historicity, the revelation, the realities of creation and New Creation, the hope of consummation and other truths of the Christian Faith form one complex with the fundamental apprehension of God as personal.

c. *Philosophical Criticism of the Doctrine of the Equality of Religions:*
D. G. Moses

D. G. Moses in his study *Religious Truth and the Relation between Religions*[97] examines the assumptions of Radhakrishnan's idea of 'a Parliament of Religions' as expressed in his lecture 'Meeting of Religions'.[98] Radhakrishnan has summarized the Upanishadic approach to *Sanatana dharma* as follows:

The oneness of the Supreme is insisted on but variety of description is permitted. The light of absolute truth is said to be refracted as it passes through the distorting medium of human nature. In the boundless being of Brahman are all the living powers that men have worshipped as gods, not as if they were standing side by side in space, but each a facet mirroring the whole. The different deities are symbols of the fathomless.[99]

As Moses points out:

Knowledge of any reality is knowledge of it as it really is when it appears to us ... so to talk of the human mind as distorting the reality it knows is to cut the ground [from] under our feet.[100]

Further, he argues that while God is all-inclusive and 'everything is an expression of God', all-inclusiveness cannot be 'the supreme characteristic' of God and 'not everything is an equal expression of God'.

Brahman or Reality is not only an all-inclusive whole; that expresses only one of its characteristics. It must have some identical nature; while it includes all determination, it must do so because it has its own determinate quality. ... Different powers, expressing the one identical nature of

Reality in diverse ways, could be regarded as facets of the whole. But how can contradictory powers, some regarded as benevolent and some as malevolent, mirror the same reality? ... Even Bradley's Absolute is not merely an all-inclusive whole; it includes all the appearances, but in concord. To do this the appearances need to be reconstructed and in some cases to be changed out of recognition. Bradley's philosophy is a warning that mere all-inclusiveness, in the sense of an uncritical inclusion of every power of nature, is not and cannot be the mark of the Absolute.

And if the Supreme is not merely boundless Being ... but a definite Reality, then only those ways that are consistent with his nature and property will be valid as ways leading to him.[101]

Moses analyses Radhakrishnan's arguments to show that within his own system the doctrine of the equality of religions cannot be maintained. Radhakrishnan defines religion as personal realization and gives only an instrumental value to creeds and dogmas. Moses points out that if they have an instrumental function to fulfil, then it is important to judge which are 'adequate instruments' and which not, and it becomes a criterion of discrimination among creeds and dogmas. Ideas of God are important because they have an intimate connection with the experience of God. Even in mystic experience, there is a credal counterpart. Rudolf Otto has shown how the mysticism of a theist differs from that of the pantheist, and implies

belief in one all-embracing tremendous Reality behind the multiplicity of things and in the possibility that this Supreme Reality can be apprehended by direct contact or immediate experience.[102]

Again Radhakrishnan considers all religious conceptions as 'only symbols; or signs of an enduring reality which is higher than man's conception or picture of it'. While Moses agrees with the danger of identifying human knowledge of God with the reality of God, he sees the 'pit of agnosticism' awaiting the man who over-emphasizes the symbolic character of that knowledge. Even if the symbolic nature of man's ideas of God is granted, it remains true that 'some symbols may be more capable of representing the Supreme Reality' than others; and it should be our effort to get symbols which correspond to the reality as precisely as possible.[103] Radhakrishnan states:

A temporal and finite form of symbolism cannot be regarded as unique, definitive and absolute.[104]

Moses replies:

If finite forms of symbolism cannot be estimated in terms of their truth-value and arranged in terms of their adequacy, it means ... that we cannot distinguish between truth and falsehood, or between the more true and the less true; this again is a trend in the direction of agnosticism.[105]

Moses admits with Radhakrishnan that God is beyond the reach of man and has more in him than we know. But he adds:

[This is] not because he is a characterless Being but because he has so many characteristics, is so full of reality that it is never possible for the finite mind to come to the last word about him.[106]

Moses flatly contradicts Radhakrishnan's thesis that in the pursuit of truth

the doctrine we adopt and the philosophy we profess do not matter any more than the language we speak and the clothes we wear.

According to Moses they do matter for spiritual progress.[107] Radhakrishnan says:

For the peace of a religious soul it is not necessary that its insight be perfect, but its faith must be sure.

Moses rejoins:

Faith itself is a kind of insight. ... Any faith must have as necessary elements insight and understanding.[108]

On another topic, Radhakrishnan asserts:

No formula however comprehensive, has absolute value. It has to be accepted so long as it creates for those who use it a true path to spiritual life. Its value lies in its suggestive quality; its power to involve or express the mysterious.

Moses sees in the statement the admission of a standard for judging the value of a formula:

If this is admitted, it should be possible to estimate the different formulae which try to express the mysterious and arrange them according to an order of value.[109]

Moses accepts the principle:

Correct intellectual belief does not necessarily lead to expression of goodwill. But ... we cannot [conclude] that therefore theological affirmations are of no use at all. Without them the individual's life would be lacking in direction.¹¹⁰

Moses also thinks that the choice is never between 'a theory which has all the truth and the others which are wholly devoid of truth'.

Again Radhakrishnan is of the opinion that

Our obligation to our religion or nation is not generally a matter of will or choice but one of blind fate or herd infection.

Moses replies:

One cannot allow a most intimate and important matter like religion to be determined entirely by mass suggestion.¹¹¹

He will not accept 'the inner certitude and devotion of its followers' as the criterion of the truth of a faith; and even if one recognizes the values that have come from one's traditional faith

it would be disloyalty to one's faith not to be able to modify and change it where change and modification would mean a fuller faith.¹¹²

Commenting on the thesis of Radhakrishnan, that 'the different creeds are the historical formulation of the formless truth', Moses says;

The truth that can be known by man must have some form.... It is an over-statement to say that every historical view is a *perfect* expression of the Divine. Some are more successful than others [in expressing the Divine].

And conversion understood as change of faith, says Moses, need not always mean the complete rejection of one historical view for another.¹¹³

On the use of the term 'finality' which Radhakrishnan rejects in religion, Moses says:

If the term finality is understood in the sense of that which is *fundamental*, that which has to be included in whatever further progress is achieved, or, in other words, if finality is thought of in terms of that which is *elemental*, then it is possible to regard even a historical religion as final.... Thus it is not necessary to regard finality as excluding progress or as incompatible with the finitude of man.¹¹⁴

And as for exclusiveness in religion Moses distinguishes between a narrow and a wide one, and makes his case for the wide one. He says:

A wide exclusiveness is that which does not destroy but fulfils. It includes and is willing to take in all that is best and noblest in other faiths and in the very act of including them is able to transform them by its own unique nature. If it is exclusive it is only with the exclusion of Truth. This will not breed bigotry but promote humble sharing.[115]

And the conclusion of Moses is that Radhakrishnan's Parliament of Religions 'can only be based on a complete ignoring of the truth element in the different religions'.[116]

D. *Christology in Terms of Dynamic Monism: Surjit Singh*

Surjit Singh's *Preface to Personality* is a discussion of 'Christology in relation to Radhakrishnan's philosophy'. The chapter on 'God, the Absolute and the Christ' is specially relevant as a Christian critique of Radhakrishnan's philosophy and Christology, but also as a Christian attempt at using Radhakrishnan's more creative ideas for a new Christology.

To Radhakrishnan, God, the Absolute, and the unity of God and the Absolute correspond to three levels of religious experience – first, the experience of a personal reality supporting man in the world interpreted in terms of personal God; second, 'the sense of rest and fulfilment, of eternity and completeness', require the conception of the supreme as self-existent Absolute; and third, 'Man as an integral being experiences the Supreme Reality in its wholeness', pointing to the feeling of oneness between God and Absolute on the one hand, and to an awareness that God and cosmic process are actualizations of a possibility within the Absolute itself on the other.[117] Along this line, Radhakrishnan denies 'creation' and sees the world only as the mystery of the self-limitation of the Absolute. 'The Absolute is the self and its other.'[118] Radhakrishnan on this basis has been seeking to build 'a dynamic monism capable of accounting for a growing universe with its time and change.'[119] Abstract monism which destroys personal values and reduces individuality to illusion, and a radical pluralism which means chaos and relies on good luck for harmony of the world, are both defective attitudes of life.[120] And Radhakrishnan himself sums up the outline of his 'dynamic monism' thus:

The Absolute is not an abstract unit, but a concrete whole binding together the differences which are subordinate to it. The whole has existence through the parts and the parts are intelligible only through the whole. The values we find and enjoy while on the way to it are preserved and receive their full supplementation in it. They are not annihilated.[121]

There is also a corresponding relation of duality within non-duality between *jivatman* and *atman*. Surjit Singh points to Radhakrishnan's statement that 'the supreme self . . . though distinct from everything is implicated in everything'[122] and comments that Radhakrishnan is not at all clear as to the nature of this implication. But Radhakrishnan's conception of the liberated souls retaining their individuality till the universal liberation is achieved, points to the view that 'eternity is implicated in history in a positive manner'; only Radhakrishnan does not make the point clear and does not go far enough. And like other critics Surjit Singh detects in Radhakrishnan's writings on the inter-relations of God and the Absolute, *atman* and *jivatman*, and the saved and the unsaved, 'a definite hesitation, an indecision which makes him waver' between abstract monism and dynamic non-dualism. The real issues relate, first, to the 'nature and meaning of the relative existence of the world' and then to 'whether what is achieved here is or is not annihilated in the Absolute'. The crucial question is this: Is the final spiritual harmony envisaged at the end of the cosmic process, a differentiated or an undifferentiated one? does the Absolute reconcile or obliterate human values and individuality? Surjit Singh says:

In asking what relation the actualised possibility bears to the Absolute we have asked the same question in different words. This argues that if some determinate aspects of the Real are involved and grounded in the actual and so also by reciprocal implication the features of the actual are preserved in the Real a further characterisation of Ultimate Reality becomes necessary. Thus pluralism is not only true 'within limits', i.e. within the cosmic process, but is implicated in Ultimate Reality. This does not indeed make pluralism the final truth but it does make it an essential element in the picture of Reality as a whole. Similarly Ultimate Reality as a unity is involved in pluralism and by no means exhausted by it. In this context individuality as laying claim to absolutism would be denied. But in so far as it aligns itself with the patterns of ultimate Reality, it is affirmed and preserved.[123]

Surjit Singh says that Radhakrishnan in his earlier writings sees pluralism not only in the cosmic process but also being 'completed and supplemented and not rejected and absolished'[124] in the Absolute. Instead of going forward in that direction, Radhakrishnan often, according to Surjit Singh, goes backwards to an abstract monism itself.

Surjit Singh contrasts the idea of individuality characteristic of Radhakrishnan's abstract monism with the Christian view. Since the final goal for Radhakrishnan is 'impersonal universalism', he refrains from making any ultimate distinction either between individuality and personality, or between individualization, individuality and individualism. In his philosophy, 'the moment the individualistic distortion of the universal and all-pervasive self is destroyed, the individual is also destroyed'. In the Christian view however, there is a third conception of individuality as revealed in Jesus Christ. Surjit Singh says:

> In Jesus the Christ individuality or finiteness is also destroyed. Finiteness embodying and affirming man's desire to be infinite or absolute is overcome. The theme of the temptations is the incitation on the part of evil forces to persuade Jesus Christ to affirm himself in his historical individuality as the supreme. The whole life of Jesus the Christ, and particularly the Cross, bears witness to the phenomenon of the destruction of individuality as laying claim to absolutism. On the other hand by positive righteousness he made himself so transparent to the divine that no contradiction remained between divinity and humanity. The relation of perfect union was achieved. By making humanity transparent, by stripping it off from any possibility of its asserting itself in its own right, the humanity was not by any means absorbed in the divinity, but only became completely responsive. Therefore the God-Man is not only a reality in history but is also beyond it.[125]

And what the universe saved in Christ achieves is transparency to the Divine Presence:

> The saved universe is transparent to the presence of God. He penetrates it through and through. This pervasive presence of God does not, however eliminate distinctions. Individuals are not lost, they have become transparent, but remain distinct. There are no differences, but there are distinctions. Radhakrishnan himself says that pluralism is not rejected or abolished but supplemented and completed.[126]

Surjit Singh finds in Radhakrishnan's conception of the liberated souls who retain their individuality to work for the salvation of others, 'a foreshadowing of the ultimate state where the one and the many will be reconciled', and not obliterated.

Their individuality is so reconciled to the spirit that it does not involve them again in the karmic cycle.

In this connection he explains the significance of the Resurrection of Jesus Christ. It means

that the whole man is uplifted to the divine world. Salvation is for the total man. Just as the spirit is redeemed, so is the body. Radhakrishnan misunderstands, when he says: The physical resurrection is not the important thing but the resurrection of the Divine.[127]

Surjit Singh goes on to relate the philosophy of dynamic monism (suggested by Radhakrishnan but not worked out by him) more directly to an understanding of the Person of Jesus Christ. He notes that the very name Jesus Christ in itself 'represents the unity of two realms' and is symbolic of the spiritual experience of the disciples. The starting point for Surjit Singh's christological restatement is the idea of the resurrection of the body, in which

the soul, gaining the ground to continue, is not left discarnate. It is clothed with a garment. The idea behind the resurrection is that soul-body is the complete or whole man. The soul is not itself the reality of man.[128]

Since the idea derives its basis and meaning from the Resurrection of Jesus Christ, Surjit Singh deals with it as signifying a historical individuality which is spiritual:

In his case the resurrection is also the resurrection of the body. The body in general, representing historical individuality is not discarded. During his stay in history, historical individuality played an important part. The Resurrection does not mean the continuance of the self-same individuality; that could be maintained only at the expense of grave contradiction. The meaning of Resurrection is, however, that he was not disembodied. He had a form suited to his being and the spiritual environment. The form is called 'spiritual', 'glorified' or 'God-Given'. Whatever the name, the truth is that historical reality is not a shadow or phantom but is taken up into the consummation of things and is preserved in the essential structure of Reality.[129]

Thus in Jesus Christ God and man meet and the divine human centre of the God-Man comes into being. Here is humanity which is 'characteristically the creation of and in history', and representing every human individual and all historical existence. Surjit Singh says:

> If his humanity were discarded or absorbed it would mean that history had no meaning – that history was meaningless, was a grand illusion.

But the God-Man is 'an eternal fact', thereby bringing historical existence into the very structure of the Ultimate Reality.

> Jesus Christ the unity of God and man represents that the picture of ultimate reality is not only divine but divine-human. Temporal and historical existence has made a difference. This is not to argue that this picture exhausts the depths of the divine being but that is how Ultimate Reality would appear to us. The God-Man is the representation of Ultimate Reality as it concerns us and as we are related to it ... the God-Man is the norm of Ultimate Reality. In him the criterion appears.[130]

Surjit Singh deals with Radhakrishnan's idea of the Incarnation as expressed in his introductory essay to his volume on the *Bhagavadgita*. Here again he sees in Radhakrishnan an alternation between Monism, which can conceive of incarnation only in terms of an 'ascent' of man to divinity, and Theism, which points to 'a descent of the Divine into the human frame', that is between 'deification' and 'incarnation'. But even in the more theistic statements of incarnation, Radhakrishnan says:

> The assumption of human nature by the Divine Reality, like the creation of the world, does not take away from or add to the integrity of the Divine. Creation and incarnation both belong to the world of manifestation and not to the Absolute spirit.[131]

In relation to this, Surjit Singh raises the question:

> How can the divine reality create or assume human nature if there is no internal and eternal justification within it for doing so?

> If the self-sufficiency of the Divine Reality is a richness of being, it cannot be chaotic but is 'internally ordered by the Divine Wisdom'.

> Thus to say that the Divine Reality creates or assumes human nature, in other words, accepts external limitation to manifest itself, will be meaningless, unless it implies that there is in the Divine Reality a ground for doing so – that ground is indeed the self-limitation of God in his eternity. . . . The

difficulty with Radhakrishnan is that his view of the nature of the Divine and hence of creation is defective. We invite him to consider seriously the meaning of *creatio ex nihilo*.

Surjit Singh admits that Incarnation raises no special problems apart from Creation. It is necessary however to clarify how the divine incarnation into the human level, rather than the sub-human, is important for an adequate manifestation of God. It is the 'human incarnation' which raises a special problem. Surjit Singh adds:

When we say that only man can be the most adequate incarnation of God, we concede in principle that every human individual has the possibility of being the incarnation. But whereas Man is an abstraction, human individuals are not. They fall within certain historical traditions. Hence God can manifest himself most adequately in the most responsive human personality in the most adequate historical tradition.[132]

Surjit Singh then discusses the relation of the gospel of Jesus Christ to other religions. He thinks that the 'Christian doctrine of the Logos as the pedagogue' put forth by the Church Fathers could be a fruitful basis of defining this relation. It witnesses to the 'truth of the reciprocal implication of God and the world', and considers that 'all truth is integral'. 'In this qualitative structure of truth Jesus Christ is the criterion. He is the judgment and the fulfilment'.[133] Radhakrishnan himself 'seems to hint at a conception similar to the Logos doctrine, but does not develop it'.[134]

Indeed Radhakrishnan's proposal of inter-religious 'sharing', and his denunciation of Christianity as exclusive, indicate that his reaction to Christianity is 'gnostic'. Radhakrishnan's idea of 'sharing in the Absolute' means that Christ be made 'a member of the Hindu pantheon'. This is 'an invitation to death' by absorption. But Christianity should be prepared for 'a positive relationship' of sharing with Hinduism. As between Hebraic and Greek thought, 'this positive relationship keeps the points of agreement and difference in their proper perspective'. Surjit Singh grants that there is an element of exclusiveness in Christianity, based on the idea of uniqueness, which is 'tied with the conception of history, especially where history is taken seriously'. Hinduism has also its 'claims to exclusiveness', where it is presented as 'the ideal religion of the future' in which 'other religions can be given a place'.

•

Just as the claim to a unique revelation is turned into a voice of exclusiveness, so also the claim of Hinduism to universalism becomes its exclusiveness.[135]

E. Questioning the Doctrine of Mysticism: Lesslie Newbigin and Stanley Samartha

The foundation of Radhakrishnan's philosophy of religion is that mystic experience which is universally the same in form and content in all religions is the direct spiritual apprehension of reality; and that it is the ultimate goal of spiritual realization and therefore the ultimate criterion and clue to the interpretation of religion in the religions. This foundational creed of Radhakrishnan has been evaluated by different Christian thinkers from various angles.

We have already referred to the criticism of D. G. Moses that in point of fact, mystic experience does not have the same form or content in different religions; that differences in doctrine about the ultimate reality (naturalism, theism, pantheism, Absolutism, etc.) lead to differences in form and content of the mystic experiences.

Bishop Lesslie Newbigin does not doubt the reality of the mystic experience; but the philosophy which posits it as 'the clue to ultimate reality', he says, is not a logical deduction from the experience but a decision of faith. The mystic, he says, begins by abstracting himself from all apprehensions of phenomena and ends with a state of pure unitary awareness, undisturbed by any kind of multiplicity.

From the standpoint he has taken, all multiplicity has ceased to exist because he has deliberately shut it out of his attention. But to conclude that this experience is the clue to ultimate reality is not a logical deduction, but a leap of faith, for the whole question is: What is the relation of that ultimate reality to the multiplicity of phenomena? We face here, surely, an ultimate decision, which is in the last resort, a decision of faith.[136]

And Newbigin considers the doctrine, that mysticism is the clue to ultimate reality, as 'a flat denial of the central truth of biblical religion'. Stanley Samartha in his *Introduction to Radhakrishnan* comments on this 'glaring gap' between mystical and historic (prophetic) faiths. It represents a gap 'between the Hindu philosophers and most of the Christian theologians' and at present it is 'so wide that any hope of building a bridge seems to be doomed to failure from the very beginning'. And 'the difference is fundamental'.

Samartha seems to support Tillich's view that mysticism need not contradict but may possibly intensify prophetic religion, but he does not expand the point. However he raises the (to him) more significant question, whether mysticism can be a path to world community or a fellowship of faiths. Here he sees greater possibilities for a historic faith.

But there is one issue here which is of greater significance: namely the search for a basis for world community or even a fellowship of faiths. The claim that mystical experience, because it is universal, can provide this basis is difficult to accept because mystical experience, by its very nature, is individualistic. It may generate toleration and courtesy toward similar experiences of others; but can it lead to corporate expression? In contrast, a historic fact, because it has become meaningful to a group, a community or a nation, inevitably leads to corporate loyalty and efforts.[137]

As an illustration he points out that it is 'not Mahatma Gandhi's experience' which has served as the basis for the common loyalty of Indian people, it is 'the historic fact of his life and his work' which has drawn together people of different communities and has served to give the nation a common loyalty. He says:

Without minimizing the reality and importance of mystical experience, one has to express doubts about its possibility to provide the basis and inspiration to an ongoing community life.[138]

F. *A Theology of Christian Non-Dualism: Mark Sunder Rao*

Mark Sunder Rao in his pamphlet *Ananyatva: Realisation of Christian Non-Duality* has taken a more positive line towards mysticism. In fact his attempt is to go behind the many doctrines of *Advaita* to the vision behind it and to distinguish between non-duality and monism in its interpretation; and to show that the experience of mystic union and the doctrine of *perichoresis* (coinherence) underlying the doctrines of Trinity and Incarnation are not only parallel with the Hindu vision and doctrines, but also provide a framework for incorporating them within Indian Christianity.

Sunder Rao follows Professor P. N. Srinivasachari in distinguishing between *darsana* and *siddhanta*, between the normative and constant perception and its interpretation, which is never final and binding, but always developing. This, he says, is something like the distinction between *kerygma* (message) and *didache* (doctrine) in Christianity. And therefore, while Christians and Hindus may begin their dialogue at the level of *siddhanta-didache*, it should move on to the *darsana-kerygma* level. 'That is when the dialogue can reach the sharpest point.' And Sunder Rao then moves on to consider 'the essential revelation of the *kerygma* and Vedanta, bearing upon the aim of life of man as intended by the Creator'. This aim, the goal of existence, is presented by the Church Fathers as '*perichoresis* – coinherence of the divine and human' and as *sahaja sayujya* by Hindus.

Sunder Rao speaks of four main types of *siddhanta* in man's relation to God in Hinduism – the *Advaita*, which says that the self is not other than Brahman; *Visistadvaita*, with its doctrine that the self as an *amsa* of Brahman has 'a kind of difference as well as non-difference' from it; *Dvaita* positing Brahman as the only independent and the self as dependent; *Saiva siddhanta*, in which the self is a finite manifestation of the creative energy, *sakti*, of God, and is an integral part of the divine being. All these are doctrinal interpretations 'to portray the unity of the *atman* and *Brahman* and their union. What really matters is to grasp the fact of such a relationship as being intimate, integral and eternal'.[139] The doctrines are different but the experience is common, 'an involvement' which could be evoked by a term like *ananytva* (non-otherness, non-alterity or non-duality). It may also be noted that Hinduism conceives of the divine-human union at four levels – the ontological (transcendental), cosmological (cosmic), the empirical (anthropological) and the pneumatical (immanental) with emphases by different *acharyas* falling on one or the other of the first three dimensions.

'The Church Fathers also regarded man's union with the divine as the end and aim of life',[140] and in the history of Christian thought, several patterns of this union have been defined – '*unio mystica, theosis, perichoresis* and so on'. They speak in different terms of one Christian reality, viz. the divine-human union. The emphasis in Christian thinking, as contrasted with that in the Hindu thought, is on the pneumatic dimension. Sunder Rao gives the reason for this:

Inheriting their faith from Israel they believed in the solity and mystery of the Godhead Whose inner being is unreachable; it arose from the conviction that though the creation had issued from God's act and really had Him for its cause and ground of being, this fact did not, so to speak, guarantee the union of the human and the divine, as the empirical (fallen) life so amply illustrates.[141]

Therefore the Christian Fathers set aside the ontological, cosmological and anthropological levels and reached out to the fourth dimension:

that of Indwelling Holy Spirit, the revealer within the Incarnate Word, the Son who is the image of the Father.[142]

And it is this 'almost exclusive emphasis' on the pneumatic union which makes the Christian position 'unique' and distinguishes it from the Hindu. Though the Trinity and the Incarnation were the main themes of the Fathers, the Third Person of the Trinity, the Holy Spirit, provided the undertone; and it is thus that 'the "great divide" comes about' between the Hindu and Christian concepts about the divine-human union. The point is that the Fathers clearly distinguished between hypostatic union and mystic union. Hypostatic union is ontological, a union of substance, and mystic union is union of mutual indwelling through the Holy Spirit. *Sankara* could be interpreted as standing for the hypostatic union, though a deeper examination, Sunder Rao thinks, reveals a different position, because *Sankara* could be understood as non-dual rather than monistic. Non-duality is an intuition of oneness, unity, where there is an awareness which can be spelled out as 'There are two, but *they* are not two.' Sunder Rao says:

Sankara advaita seems to offer hypostatic union with one hand and mystic union with the other. That seems to be the meaning of the two *sattas*, realities – the *paramarthika* and *vyavaharika*. In conclusion, since this analysis precludes ontological union of the divine and the human, the way is open for a pneumatological union, *unio mystica, perichoresis*.[143]

Sunder Rao refers to another distinction between the Hindu and Christian understanding of the divine-human union. This is inherent in the 'societary character' of the thought process of the early Church Fathers as distinct from the 'individualistic' nature of the Hindu thought process. This again arises from the Hebrew emphasis on the 'ultimate purpose of God being the creation of a community at one with Him' which they took over into their thought. Of course, in Hinduism, there has been a tradition of *sarvamukti*.

But on the face of it, it is not as a community but seriatim that the total *mukti* takes place; it is a far cry from the believers being a Mystical Body of Christ, a corporate spiritual entity.[144]

Sunder Rao explains how the doctrines of the Trinity and the Incarnation in the early Christian Fathers 'throw light on Christian non-dualism, *ananytva*, which is our thesis'. The two poles of God's total transcendence and His total immanence were 'gripped and held together in all their thinking'. In clarifying the way in which the Father and the Son and the Holy Spirit 'are three and yet *they* are one', they made for greater understanding of the divine-human relationship that ensues:

It is a well-known fact to students of early Church history that the Church Fathers solved this problem by the use of the words *hypostasis, ousia* and *perichoresis* (roughly rendered Person, Substance and Co-inherence). They said, 'the Three coinhere in One Another without coalescing, each possessing a perfect hypostasis and yet maintaining one *ousia*'. The word they used for this coinherence is *perichoresis*. The Three are One and in that oneness they preserve their separate identity. . . . In this way, incidentally the Fathers fought off, if we may say so, rigid monism and pluralism and affirmed what may be called non-dualism, *ananyavada*: There are Three Persons; they are not three; they are One. This built-in concept of distinction in unity is the norm not only of relationship *in divinis* but of relationship divine and human.

The union of divine and human natures in the Incarnation is also interpreted in terms of *perichoresis*, the coinherence of the divine and the human through the penetration of the divine nature into the human first and then that of the human into the divine. But the human nature assumed by God in Incarnation is 'not the fallen humanity, but the one already penetrated by the divine, divinized' and therefore 'the Incarnation is a hypostatic union, at the ontological level'. This union is 'unrepeatable and unsharable', because the human nature of other human beings is a fallen one. They can aspire only to be taken into a mystic union as distinguished from the hypostatic union of the Incarnation:

Though there is this important distinction between the two forms of union there is still the common experience of *perichoresis*, mutuality, which cancels the ultimate dualism of the divine and the human on the one hand, and on the other creates a oneness of the two. The ensuing relationship can, it seems to me, be termed non-dual or *ananyatva*.

The doctrine of the Holy Spirit is 'still unexplored territory'. But the Fathers have always considered the *perichoresis* as the work of the Holy Spirit. Thus if the Trinity may be spoken of as embodying the 'trascendence, revelation and immanence' respectively of the Godhead, the Holy Spirit is the 'effectualization of the immanence of God in man and creation'.

The Holy Spirit is thus the real *Antaryamin*, Indweller. And if it is remembered that the accurate translation of the word *perichoresis* is indwelling, it may be taken that in the Holy Spirit there is both the promise and the guarantee of *ananyatva*, non-duality resulting from *perichoresis*.

Given also the societary nature of the work of the Indwelling Spirit, we come to the doctrine of the Church which is

at once a mystery and a manifestation. It is a mystical Body of Christ whose oneness with its Head is manifest and hidden; promised as well as fulfilled; here and now, but far and away, at the same time.

It is within the context of such a faith, that Chenchiah's idea of the yoga of the Holy Spirit, oriented to 'a new creation in Christ through the same Spirit' becomes relevant.[145]

Sunder Rao considers the meaning of Christian yoga as a path to the experience of Christian non-duality. In doing so he distinguishes between three types of relationships which the self establishes with other selves – the I-It relation in which the self utilizes others; the I-Thou relation in which the self enters into a relation of mutual recognition of independence and prudential independence; and the I-in-Thou-in-Me where the selves are in a relation of 'mutual indwelling, interpenetration, union, oneness'. In this third dimension, 'the egoity that features in the first two relationships vitiating them is overcome and transformed by love (*agape*)'.[146] In *agape*, he says, there is a sense of otherness, but it is 'more like the self's own otherness, than anything else'. And in the spiritual interrelationship with which we are dealing here, we could say that 'the "otherness" and "outsideness" yields to otherlessness and interiority'. If this *ananyatva* is the core of spiritual interrelationship, 'a yoga or discipline is appropriate only in so far as it promotes this relationship'. And Sunder Rao presents the yoga presented by Christ in John 15.1-10 as *poorna yoga*:

I am the real vine. . . . Dwell in me, as I in you. . . . I am the vine, you are the branches. He who dwells in me as I dwell in him bears much fruit. . . . If you dwell in me, and my word dwells in you, ask what you will and you shall have it. . . .

Purushartha, the supreme goal of the experience of Christian non-duality, Sunder Rao says, seeks to 'draw out the height, depth, length and breadth, the infinite possibilities', of the *perichoresis* experience.[147] One supreme value realized is:

The separative egoity has yielded to communion and community in which the self, motivated by *agape*, sees the other as the self's other. But the *purna* (plenary) experience of *mukti* [the salvation of individuals one by one as in Hindu *sarva mukti* but also fulfilment of the destiny of the world] takes place when there is a new heaven and a new earth, when the historical existence of man and the rest of the world are taken up into the supernal. No part of the existing world falls outside the scope of the divine salvation.

6. COMMENT

After this survey of Radhakrishnan's view of Christ and Christianity and of several Christian evaluations of it, it remains for us to conclude with a brief comment. It is evident that Christian theologians have raised many crucial theological issues which Indian Christianity has to pursue. We may touch on a few of them.

First, Radhakrishnan's theology of humanism. Radhakrishnan in his 'Reply to Critics' has said that he has tried to restate *maya* so as to 'save the world and give it a real meaning'.[149] John Arapura in his study of Radhakrishnan's philosophy of Integral Experience has concluded that Radhakrishnan has brought into the Advaitic system of Indian thought the reality of purposive history. Here is what he says:

Radhakrishman's philosophy of integral experience involves a significant revision of the traditional Advaita. The questions that the Advaita has always been called upon to answer are: Is the drama of human life a meaningless story, an illusion, a mere 'tale told by an idiot, full of sound and fury, signifying nothing', or is it significant history? Are the struggles and travails of man of no avail or do human achievements have eternal value? Is the destiny of conscious life a mere return to where it came from or is it a consummation, a fulfilment that adds a new dimension to being? Is history such that it would make no difference if it had not been? Radhakrishnan answers all these questions positively and tries to do so as far as possible within the framework of Vedanta. This is no small achievement.[150]

There is no doubt that Radhakrishnan has grappled with the problem of building into the structure of Advaita 'a new humanism' which he saw arising in India; and thereby giving it a proper spiritual basis in India. P. T. Raju takes the view that 'humanism... is the core of Radhakrishnan's philosophy'. And in fact it is through the Neo-Hinduism of Radhakrishnan, Tagore, Gandhi and others that 'humanism is more and more consciously being recognized and entering the life and thought of India'.[151]

This is something to be heartily welcomed by the Christian Church in India, as the new humanism has within it the ferment of Christ and the abundant life promised to man in Christ. The question still remains whether Radhakrishnan has really succeeded in this task of giving ultimate reality to the personal God who is 'the Absolute humanized' and ultimate spiritual significance to 'the human world and its values'. Radhakrishnan has affirmed them, but the nature of 'the positive movement from the human to the spiritual', and the possibility of human values being protected in the spiritual, need further working out. Many thinkers including his own close students like Raju see contradictions, vagueness or incompleteness in his philosophical system at this point.[152]

Devanandan is certainly right in his observation that the Christian Church must get alongside Neo-Hinduism in the task of bridging the gulf that still exists between the classical theology and the new anthropology. But how does the Christian Church do it? Two lines are clearly indicated. So far as we can see, the final inability of Radhakrishnan's philosophy to come to terms with the new humanism within its classical conception of the Spirit is most evident in the way in which it deals with Christ and Christianity and in his attempts to separate the Christian religion from its original and essential foundation in the realm of the personal and the historical. And therefore Indian Christianity can best make its contribution to the development of the indigenous foundations of the new humanism in India by its insisting on its own fundamental prophetic core. But this is to be done not in isolation from but in dialogue with the Neo-Hindu philosophy and theology; that is, by restating the fundamentals of Christian faith positively within their terms which at the same time restructures the truths in Neo-Hinduism on Christian foundations. This is the cultural significance of all attempts at indigenous Indian Christian theology.

Second, the challenge of Radhakrishnan's Advaita Vedanta interpretation of Christ and Christianity raises two important questions. First, it asks how we can affirm that the primary concern of the Christian religion is with the historical existence of man and the purpose of God for it; and not with the metaphysical essence of the Divine or human self; that Christian theology is an explication of the truth that God so loved the world that He has given himself to men in Jesus Christ to save men from false purposes and renew the world. For this, Indian Christian theology has to give priority to the biblical message and to the task of interpreting it in terms of its meaning for individual and collective human existence.

In this latter, the Christian Churches will have much more in common with India's secular humanists and their ideologies than with the metaphysically oriented religions and philosophies. But this does not justify indifference to Indian metaphysics, which indifference, as we have said before, will only prevent the Christian message and social ethics from taking cultural roots. Therefore the second question is, how Christian theology can utilize the metaphysics of non-otherness of the Absolute, God, incarnations, men and nature, to affirm the reality of distinctions – of becoming as distinct from being, of a distinct human nature and its otherness from the Divine in its finiteness and freedom, and of the two natures in the unity of Jesus Christ which makes him other than all men as the mediator between God and man and the fulfilment of the purpose of becoming. In emphasizing this metaphysics of otherness, it becomes necessary to explain what place the Christian scheme gives to mysticism as an experience of non-otherness and to the doctrines of indwelling spirit expressed as the mystery of being within the becoming, in Christ and in all men.

The significance of the kerygmatic theology has always been emphasized by the Indian Church. The Indian Church has also

developed a great many theological insights through its concern for
the outcastes and poor of India's society, though the churches have
yet to formulate a theology of society as an essential part of their
theological enterprise. But the challenge of the Neo-Vedanta at the
philosophical level has hardly been met. The elements of a new
theology which meets this need are present in the writings of the
several theologians whose responses to Neo-Vedanta we briefly
surveyed. Some of them have sought to walk along the Neo-Advaitism
of Radhakrishnan and use its more dynamic elements to express the
Christian message, convey the experience of the indwelling Christ
and open the path for a new Christology and Christian philosophy
relevant to the Indian situation. The paths opened up by Surjit
Singh and Mark Sunder Rao seem especially significant for dialogue
within the framework of Advaita Vedanta. Only as the Indian
theologians get more grounding in the history of early Christian
thought and Indian metaphysics at the same time, will it be possible
to go further along this direction.

Third is Radhakrishnan's idea of the relation between religions.
D. G. Moses has exposed the rational fallacies in the philosophy of
the equality of religions. But one wonders whether Radhakrishnan's
position is that of equality. Perhaps it is one strand of his thought.
But the more pronounced aspect of Radhakrishnan's thought seems
to be that of determining the relative place of every religious experience within a comprehensive but graded system with the
religion of mysticism of identity as the apex. He says:

The worshippers of the Absolute are the highest in rank, second to them
are the worshippers of the personal God; then come the worshippers of
incarnation like Rama, Krishna, Buddha; below them are those who
worship ancestors, deities and sages; and lowest of all the worshippers of
the petty forces and spirits.[153]

Here, of course, Christianity is given a place at the middle level in
the hierarchy; and Radhakrishnan calls Christianity dogmatic and
intolerant because Christianity refuses to take this place and to be
transformed in this light. But structurally speaking this idea of inter-
religious relation on the basis of elevating Advaitic mysticism to be
the crown of Christianity, is not different from that based on elevating Jesus Christ and the fellowship in Christ to be the crown of

Hinduism, which is the position of the second of Radhakrishnan's three categories of Christian theologians who discern positive truths in other religions but would want to transform them in the light of their fulfilment in Christ. The difference lies in the choice regarding what constitutes the crown of religion. And ultimately this decision, as Newbigin has shown, is not based on logic, it is a decision of faith. At this level, there is an either/or choice. It is essential that both Hindus and Christians recognize the similarity of the foundational dogmas and the *a priori* nature of the choice between them. Once this theological aspect is clear and the element of mutual exclusiveness at the core in both positions is accepted, then there could be greater understanding, co-existence and co-operation between the two religions, involving a greater interpenetration of each other at the levels of what Devanandan calls cultus, ethics and culture, leading to the development of even a common ethics, philosophy, and culture informed by both religions built through inter-faith encounter and dialogue.

NOTES

1 'My Search for Truth', in *Religion in Transition*, ed. Vergilius Ferm, London, 1937, p. 15.
2 *Eastern Religions and Western Thought*, London, 1939 (cited as *Eastern Religions*).
3 *The Philosophy of Sarvepalli Radhakrishnan*, ed. Paul A. Schilpp, New York, 1952 (cited as Schilpp).
4 *Eastern Religions*, p. 21.
5 *Ib.*, pp. 22, 24.
6 *Ib.*, p. 32.
7 *Ib.*, p. 32.
8 *Ib.*, p. 92.
9 *Ib.*, p. 127.
10 *Ib.*, p. 92.
11 *Ib.*, pp. 126f.
12 *Ib.*, p. 30.
13 Schilpp, p. 800.
14 *Eastern Religions*, p. 93.
15 *Ib.*, p. 128.
16 Schilpp, p. 30.
17 *Eastern Religions*, p. 130.
18 Schilpp, p. 27.
19 *Eastern Religions*, pp. 128f.
20 *Ib.*, p. 131.
21 *Ib.*, p. 137.
22 *Ib.*, p. 47.
23 *Ib.*, p. 100.
24 Schilpp, p. 43.
25 *Ib.*, p. 46.
26 *Eastern Religions*, pp. 8f.
27 Schilpp, p. 807.
28 *Eastern Religions*, p. 66.
29 *Ib.*, p. 97.
30 *Ib.*, p. 47.
31 *Ib.*, p. 54.
32 Schilpp, p. 45.
33 *Eastern Religions*, p. 97.
34 *Ib.*, p. 126.
35 *Ib.*, p. 59.
36 Schilpp, p. 79.
37 *Eastern Religions*, pp. 160–2, citing R. Otto, *The Kingdom of God and the Son of Man*, Eng. trans., London, 1938, p. 187.
38 *Eastern Religions*, pp. 169, 171.
39 *Ib.*, p. 173.
40 *Ib.*, pp. 175f.
41 *Ib.*, p. 176.
42 *Ib.*, pp. 186f.
43 *Ib.*, p. 196.

44 *Ib.*, p. 193.
45 *Ib.*, pp. 197f., citing H. H. Milman, *History of Christianity*, London, ed. of 1867, vol. II, p. 41.
46 *Eastern Religions*, p. 200.
47 *Ib.*, p. 207.
48 *Ib.*, pp. 220f.
49 *Ib.*, pp. 222–4.
50 *Ib.*, pp. 225f.
51 *Ib.*, p. 275.
52 *Ib.*, pp. 304f.
53 Schilpp, p. 371.
54 *Eastern Religions*, p. 310.
55 *Ib.*, pp. 313–16.
56 *Ib.*, pp. 317f.
57 *Ib.*, p. 320.
58 *Ib.*, p. 327.
59 *Ib.*, p. 324.
60 *Ib.*, pp. 341f.
61 *Ib.*, pp. 344.
62 *Ib.*, pp. 347f.
63 Schilpp. p. 62.
64 *Ib.*, pp. 75f.
65 *Ib.*, p. 77.
66 *Ib.*, pp. 80f.
67 *Theology of Chenchiah*, Bangalore, 1967, p. 177.
68 In the symposium *Rethinking Christianity in India*, Madras 1938, reprinted in *Theology of Chenchiah*, p. 94.
69 *Ib.*, pp. 88f.
70 *Ib.*, p. 79.
71 Carl Keller, 'The Vedanta Philosophy and the Message of Christ', *Indian Journal of Theology*, March 1955.
72 P. Chenchiah, 'The Vedanta Philosophy and the Message of Christ', *ib.*, October 1955, p. 18.
73 *Ib.*, p. 20.
74 *Ib.*, p. 21.
75 *Ib.*, p. 22.
76 *Ib.*, pp. 22f.
77 *Ib.*, p. 23.
78 P. D. Devanandan. *Christian Concern in Hinduism*, Bangalore, 1961, p. 4.
79 *Preparation for Dialogue*, Bangalore, 1964, p. 35.
80 S. Radhakrishnan, *Religion and Society*, London, 1947, pp. 105f.
81 *Christian Concern in Hinduism*, p. 112.
82 *Ib.*, p. 80.
83 *Preparation for Dialogue*, p. 72.
84 *Christian Concern in Hinduism*, p. 92.
85 *Preparation for Dialogue*, pp. 36, 38.
86 *Ib.*, pp. 40f.
87 *Christian Concern in Hinduism*, p. 98.
88 *Ib.*, pp. 98f.
89 *Ib.*, pp. 101f.
90 *Ib.*, pp. 103f.
91 *Preparation for Dialogue*, pp. 137f.
92 *Ib.*, pp. 139f.
93 *Ib.*, p. 140.
94 *Ib.*, pp. 167f., citing S. Radhakrishnan, *An Idealist View of Life* (Hibbert Lectures, 1929), London, 1932, p. 123.
95 *Ib.*, p. 169.
96 *Ib.*, p. 166.
97 D. G. Moses, *Professor Radhakrishnan and a Parliament of Religions* (Claim, Content and Context of Christian Evangelism in India, 2), Madras, 1950, reprinted in *Religious Truth and the Relation between Religions*, Madras, 1950, Part II, Ch. I, pp. 99ff., from which it is cited.
98 *Eastern Religions* (see n. 2 above), pp. 306–48.
99 *Ib.*, p. 308.
100 Moses, *op. cit.*, p. 99.
101 *Ib.*, pp. 100, 102.
102 *Ib.*, p. 105.
103 *Ib.*, pp. 106f.
104 *Ib.*, p. 107.
105 *Ib.*, pp. 107f.
106 *Ib.*, p. 108.
107 *Ib.*, p. 109.
108 *Ib.*, p. 109.
109 *Ib.*, p. 110.
110 *Ib.*, pp. 110f.
111 *Ib.*, p. 112.
112 *Ib.*, p. 113.
113 *Ib.*, pp. 114f.
114 *Ib.*, pp. 116f.
115 *Ib.*, p. 118.
116 *Ib.*, p. 121.
117 Surjit Singh, *Preface to Personality*, Madras, 1952, pp. 96f., 101, citing S. Radhakrishnan, *An Idealist View of Life*, p. 342.
118 *An Idealist View . . .*, p. 109.

119 S. Radhakrishnan, *The Reign of Religion in Contemporary Philosophy*, London, 1920, p. 411.
120 *Ib.*, p. 410.
121 *Ib.*, p. 443.
122 *Eastern Religions*, p. 27.
123 *Preface to Personality*, pp. 105–7.
124 *The Reign of Religion . . .*, p. 445.
125 *Preface to Personality*, pp. 109f.
126 *Ib.*, p. 112.
127 *Ib.*, p. 122.
128 *Ib.*, p. 112.
129 *Ib.*, pp. 112f.
130 *Ib.*, p. 113.
131 *Ib.*, p. 120, citing S. Radhakrishnan, *The Bhagavadgita* [Introductory essay, Sanskrit text and English translation], London, 1948, pp. 32f.
132 *Preface to Personality*, p. 121.
133 *Ib.* p. 114.
134 *Ib.*, p. 118. citing *The Reign of Religion . . .*, p. 444.
135 *Preface to Personality*, pp. 116f.
136 Lesslie Newbigin, *A Faith for this One World?*, London, 1961, p. 39.
137 S. Samartha, *Introduction to Radhakrishnan*, New York and New Delhi, 1964, pp. 99f.
138 *Ib.*, p. 100.
139 Mark Sunder Rao, *Ananyatva: Realisation of Christian Non-Duality*, Bangalore, 1964, pp. 16f.
140 *Ib.*, p. 19.
141 *Ib.*, p. 20.
142 *Ib.*, p. 21.
143 *Ib.*, p. 22.
144 *Ib.*, pp. 22ff.
145 *Ib.*, pp. 26f.
146 *Ib.*, p. 30.
147 *Ib.*, p. 36.
148 *Ib.*, pp. 38–40.
149 Schilpp. p. 800.
150 J. Arapura, *Radhakrishnan and Integral Experience*, New Delhi, 1966, p. 204.
151 Schilpp, p. 520.
152 *Ib.*, pp. 519–25.
153 S. Radhakrishnan, *A Hindu View of Life*, London, 1927, p. 32 (quoted in Schilpp, p. 388).

CHAPTER EIGHT

Mahatma Gandhi:
Jesus the Supreme Satyagrahi

1. THE FRAMEWORK OF GANDHISM

Mahatma Gandhi was not a systematic philosopher or religious thinker. He was primarily a man of political and social action, inspired by a religious interpretation of human existence. Though we should not look to him for a fully developed creed, he had a theological framework for apprehending and responding to the realities of life. A full analysis of the elements of this framework is outside the scope of this study of Gandhiji's interpretation of Jesus and Christianity. But as the credal framework illumines the fundamentals of his Neo-Hinduism and its approach to the Christian faith, a brief survey of it is appropriate.

Writing in his Autobiography, he declares his philosophy of life as follows:

> My uniform experiment has convinced me that there is no other God than Truth. And the only means for the realization of Truth is Ahimsa – a perfect vision of Truth can only follow a complete realization of Ahimsa. To see the universal and all-pervading Spirit of Truth face to face one must be able to love the meanest of creation as oneself. And a man who aspires after that cannot afford to keep out of any field of life.[1]

Along with *satya* (Truth) and *ahimsa* (Non-violence) is the third principle of *swadeshi* (Service of immediate neighbourhood). This trio may be considered as the fundamentals of Gandhi's philosophy and creed.

Gandhiji is 'devoted to none but Truth' and owes 'no discipline to anybody but Truth'; and is never tired of affirming that he prefers to speak of Truth as God, rather than of God as Truth. To the question of a Christian student how one gets 'inspiration from this general idea', he answers:

That means to say you want a God who has form. Truth is too impersonal for you? Well, idolatry is embedded in human nature. But you may if you like worship God as Truth, if not Truth as God. God is Truth, but God is many other things also. That is why I prefer to say Truth is God. But you need not go into what may sound like mystic lore; you may simply worship what you find to be the Truth, for Truth is known only relatively. Only remember that Truth is not one of the many qualities that we name. It is the living embodiment of God, it is the only life, and I identify Truth with the fullest life, and that is how it becomes a concrete thing. God is His whole creation, the whole existence, and service of all that exists – Truth – is service of God.[2]

Elsewhere he has expanded his doctrine of Truth being God and his relation to the world in other words. He says:

I do not regard God as a person. Truth for me is God, and God's law and God are not different things or facts, in the sense that an earthly King and his law are different. Because God is an idea, Law Himself. . . . Not a blade of grass grows or moves without His will.

Man's freedom is 'less than that of a passenger on a crowded deck'. Nevertheless Gandhi appreciates that freedom as he has 'imbibed through and through the central teaching of the Gita, that man is the maker of his destiny in the sense that he has the freedom of choice as to the manner in which he uses that freedom'. But man does not control results, and when he thinks he does, 'he comes to grief'.[3]

C. F. Andrews and Stanley Jones have commented on Gandhiji's concept of God and have affirmed that it is not as impersonal as it appears on the surface. Andrews says:

I have never felt that there was any real difference between us with regard to this ultimate belief [in God]. Here we were on common ground. In this sense, Mr Gandhi is a theist and so am I; to both of us this belief in God is as certain and immediate as our own personal existence.[4]

Stanley Jones refers to his oft-repeated 'Truth is God' and comments:

Here he seems to rule out a personal God and make Him identical with an impersonal Law. And yet that isn't quite accurate, for he calls God 'Law Himself'. . . . An impersonal Law doesn't speak to you in this personal manner [as Gandhi's inner voice seems to do] and you don't want to see a Law 'face to face'. So this Law is more than impersonal Law – it partakes of the qualities of the Personal.[5]

In Gandhiji's thought *satya* is always coupled with *ahimsa*. Sometimes they are almost two sides of the same *dharma*. The Scriptures he says, have given us 'two immortal maxims'.

One of these is: *Ahimsa* is the Supreme Law or *dharma*. The other is: There is no other Law or *dharma* than Truth. These two provide us the key to all lawful *artha* and *kama*.[6]

But very often in his writings '*Ahimsa* is the means and Truth is the end'.[7] The ideal of Gandhi's Ashram was that of 'seeking Truth through the exclusive means of *Ahimsa*'.[8] It was Gandhi's conviction that *ahimsa* is 'the law of life' and 'the progressive recognition of the law and its application in practice' is the fundamental distinctiveness of man from the beast.[9] And the history of man is the story of steady progress from cannibalism towards greater and greater realization of *ahimsa*; and further progress towards *ahimsa* is the destiny of man:

If we believe that mankind has steadily progressed towards *ahimsa*, it follows that it has to progress towards it still further. . . . No one can remain without the eternal cycle unless it be God Himself.[10]

Ahimsa is the essence of being human;

Though we have the human form, without the attainment of the virtue of non-violence we still share the qualities of our remote, reputed ancestors – the urangutang.[11]

This does not mean that our practice of true *ahimsa* should be confined to mankind. '*Ahimsa* includes the whole creation, and not only human'.[12]

It is important at this point to recognize that Gandhiji interpreted the doctrine of *Ahimsa* and its implications in categories of Hindu religion. To say that *ahimsa* is the essence of being human is linked in his mind with the belief that the essence of man is his *atman* (soul) not the body, and he sees a never-ending opposition between the *ahimsa* of *atman* and the *himsa* of the body.

Man's nature then is not *himsa* but *ahimsa*, for he can speak from his experience in his innermost conviction that he is not the body but *atman* and that he may use the body only with a view to expressing the *atman*, only with a view to self-realization.[13]

The equation of body with *himsa* is carried further when Gandhi says:

Man cannot be wholly free from violence so long as he lives a bodily life and continues to be a social being.[14]

We may achieve a measure of *ahimsa* through detachment. Full realization of *ahimsa* comes only with the liberation of the soul from the body. Seeing the inevitability of some violence in the very process of living, Gandhi asks 'Should we commit suicide?' The answer is No:

Even that is no solution if we believe as we do that so long as the spirit is attached to the flesh, on every destruction of the body it weaves for itself another. The body will cease to be, only when we give up all attachment to it. This freedom from all attachment is the realization of God as Truth. Such realization cannot be attained in a hurry. The body does not belong to us. While it lasts, we must use it as a trust handed over to our charge. Treating in this way the things of the flesh, we may one day expect to become free from the burden of the body.[15]

And elsewhere he affirms the identity of *ahimsa* with 'uttermost selflessness' which, he says, 'means complete freedom from regard to one's body'. The sages have seen that

if man desired to realize himself, i.e. Truth, he could do so only by being completely detached from the body, i.e. by making all other beings feel safe from him. That is the way of *ahimsa*.[16]

From this arises the characterization of *ahimsa* as soul-force expressing itself in *satyagraha* or resistance to evil through voluntary suffering as contrasted with *himsa* as body-force, inflicting suffering on others.

The third of Gandhiji's credal trio is *swadehsi* (patriotism). It has been defined by Gandhiji thus:

Swadeshi is that spirit within us which restricts us to the use and service of our immediate surroundings to the exclusion of the more remote.[17]

There is an economics of *swadeshi* (economically self-sufficient villages), a sociology of *swadeshi* (*varnasrama dharma*) and a politics of *swadeshi* (nationalism based on *gram panchatyat*); and the *swadeshi* principle in religion means:

I must restrict myself to my ancestral religion – that is the use of my immediate surroundings in religion. If I find it defective I should serve it by purging it of its defects.[18]

Gandhiji has sought the roots of *swadeshi* in the *Gita* doctrine of *swadharma*.

Our present existence is a discipline which has to be lived within certain rules suited to this spiritual stage. We cannot choose at this stage, for instance, our own parents, or our own birth place, or our own ancestry. Why then should we claim as individuals the right during this present brief life-period to break through all the conventions wherein we were placed at birth by God Himself? The Gita has very wisely said that the performance of one's religious duty is preferable to the carrying out of the religious duty of others. This religious duty, which is called by the untranslatable word 'Dharma', appears to me to include the environment wherein we were placed at birth by God.[19]

Andrews explains that Gandhiji perhaps never

looks forward ... to a single World Religion and a single World State, but rather to separate units working out their individual destiny in cordial, harmonised, friendly relations.

The boundaries and the unsurpassable barriers between them are for him 'divinely ordained'.

To Gandhi their due observance appears essential in this present stage of human existence. Holding strongly a belief in reincarnation he seems to have no anxiety about reaching any further stage of unification in this present cycle of existence.[20]

And Andrews comments that *swadeshi* with Gandhi is not crude nationalism, but 'something more elemental, it goes back to the Varnasrama Dharma itself, the Religion of Caste'.[21]

With this background of the general framework of his interpretation of God, man and society, let us look at Gandhiji's understanding of the life and message of Jesus, his evaluation of Christianity, and his view of the relation between religions. In surveying Gandhi's thought on these questions we shall use mainly *Mahatma Gandhi's Ideas* by C. F. Andrews, *The Message of Jesus Christ* and *Christian Missions*, all of which are collections of Gandhi's writings made with care by friends or disciples of Gandhiji and in some cases with the blessing of Gandhiji himself.[22]

2. THE MESSAGE AND PERSON OF JESUS

Of the Sermon on the Mount Gandhi says:

The message of Jesus, as I understand it, is contained in His Sermon on the Mount. The Spirit of the Sermon on the Mount competes almost on equal terms with the *Bhagavadgita* for the domination of my heart. It is that Sermon which has endeared Jesus to me.[23]

While in England, Gandhi undertook the reading of the Bible. Though he found he 'could not possibly read through the Old Testament',

the New Testament produced a different impression, especially the Sermon on the Mount, which went straight to my heart. I compared it with the *Gita* ... My young mind tried to unify the teaching of the *Gita*, the Light of Asia, and the Sermon on the Mount. That renunciation was the highest form of religion appealed to me.[24]

He has acknowledged that it was the beginning of his real awakening to 'the rightness and value of passive resistance'. When he read the Sermon on the Mount, especially such passages as 'Resist not evil', he says, 'I was simply overjoyed and found my own opinion confirmed where I least expected it. The *Bhagavadgita* deepened the impression, and Tolstoy's *The Kingdom of God is Within You* gave it permanent form'.[25] In fact 'the independent thinking, profound morality and the truthfulness' of Tolstoy's book with its interpretation of the Sermon in terms of passive resistance 'overwhelmed' Gandhi, as it opened him to 'the infinite possibilities of universal love'. Even when Gandhi began to see the *Bhagavadgita* as a more spiritually scientific formulation of 'the Law of Love, the Law of Abandon as I would call it' contained in the Sermon on the Mount, he could still say:

The New Testament gave me comfort and boundless joy as it came after the repulsion that parts of the Old had given me. Today, supposing I was deprived of the *Gita* and forgot all its contents but had a copy of the Sermon, I should derive the same joy from it as I do from the *Gita*.[26]

It is evident from all his many writings that Jesus inspired Gandhi as the author of the teaching of 'non-resistance to evil'. Of all the things he has read from the New Testament, Gandhi says 'what remained with me for ever was that Jesus came almost to give a new law'.[27]

What is the relevance of the life and crucifixion of Jesus to his message of the Sermon? For Gandhiji the person is a representative of the principle. He says:

If Jesus represents not a person but the principle of non-violence India has accepted its protecting power.[28]

As he saw it, 'the Sermon the Mount was the whole of Christianity for him who wanted to live a Christian life'. No doubt, the personality of Jesus is important, but only as 'a beautiful example' illustrating the principle. He says:

The gentle figure of Christ, so patient, so kind, so loving, so full of forgiveness that he taught his followers not to retaliate when abused or struck but to turn the other cheek – it was a beautiful example, I thought, of the perfect man.[29]

He accepted Jesus as 'a martyr, an embodiment of sacrifice', and the Cross as 'a great example to the world'.[30] And he confesses:

Though I cannot claim to be a Christian in the sectarian sense, the example of Jesus' suffering is a factor in the composition of my underlying faith in non-violence, which rules all my actions, worldly and temporal. Jesus lived and died in vain, if he did not teach us to regulate the whole of life by the eternal Law of Love.[31]

He bowed his head in reverence 'before the living image at the Vatican, of Christ crucified'.[32] Nevertheless the historical person of Jesus is ultimately irrelevant to his teaching of the eternal law. On this point he has had no doubts:

I may say that I have never been interested in a historical Jesus. I should not care if it was proved by someone that the man called Jesus never lived, and that what was narrated in the Gospels was a figment of the writer's imagination. For the Sermon on the Mount would still be true to me.[33]

To those who live the Sermon, the birth, death and continued presence of Christ are not historical but ever-recurring eternal events in the moral life of every individual or corporate self engaged in sacrificial love. As such they are not news that can be transmitted by mouth, but a reality which can be communicated through the life of the heart. The following quotation is very significant in this connection:

As long as it remains a hunger still unsatisfied, as long as Christ is not yet born, we have to look forward to him. When real peace is established, we will not need demonstration, but it will be echoed in our life, not only in individual life but in corporate life. Then we shall say Christ is born. Then we will not think of a particular day in the year as that of the birth of Christ but as an ever-recurring event which can be enacted in every life – . . . You may certainly experience peace in the midst of strife, but that happens only when to remove strife you destroy your whole life, you crucify yourself. And so, as the miraculous birth is an eternal event, so is the Cross an eternal event in this stormy life. . . . Living Christ means a living Cross, without it life is a living death.³⁴

Elsewhere he has said:

God did not bear the Cross only nineteen hundred years ago, but He bears it today, and He dies and is resurrected from day to day. It would be poor comfort to the world, if it had to depend upon a historical God who died two thousand years ago. Do not then preach the God of history but show Him as He lives today through you.³⁵

Gandhiji, in affirming the primacy of the Principle over the Person, indicates his conviction that the fulfilment of the moral law of *ahimsa* was an attainment of moral striving and that doctrines of divine atonement and justification in the final analysis probably cut the nerve of moral effort by becoming excuses for sin. He had encounters with some Christians like the member of the Plymouth Brethren in England who argued that because 'Jesus suffered and atoned for all the sins of mankind' Christians could do anything immoral without a qualm of conscience, and who 'knowingly committed transgressions' and was 'undisturbed by the thought of them'. Gandhi did not 'seek redemption from the consequences of sin'; he sought to 'be redeemed from sin itself or rather from the very thought of sin' and till he 'attained that end' he was 'content to be restless'.³⁶ 'Asking for forgiveness' meant for him that 'we should not sin again'; and granting forgiveness 'means that we would have the power to resist all temptation'. He adds:

'Jesus was incapable of sin from birth', Gladstone said, 'but we could be such by constant striving' . . . There could be no [divine] forgiveness like the forgiveness that a criminal prays for and gets from an earthly king. It was a question of a change of heart brought about by contrition, of ceaseless striving for purification.³⁷

And as a result his reason and his heart rejected the idea of divine atonement and forgiveness through Jesus Christ. Though 'metaphysically there might be some truth in it', his reason was not ready 'to believe literally that Jesus by his death and by his blood redeemed the sins of the world'; and his heart refused to accept 'that there was anything like a mysterious or miraculous virtue in Jesus' death on the Cross'.[38] The most he could concede was that 'Jesus atoned for the sins of those who accepted his teaching by being an infallible example to them'.[39] Gandhi's conversation on Christianity with Kali Charan Banerjee also revolved round the theme of sin and atonement. In reply to Banerjee's affirmation that 'the only way' of absolution and deliverance from sin was 'surrender unto Jesus', Gandhiji 'put forward the *Bhaktimarga* [the path of devotion] of the *Bhagavadgita*, but to no avail'. He adds:

Even Banerji could not convince me. This was my final deliberate striving to realize Christianity as it was presented to me.[40]

Similarly Gandhi found that the idea of Divine Grace through Christ offering men freedom from law was a source of moral licence. He cites the instance of Indian Christians taking to beef-eating and intoxicating drinks and justifying themselves on the ground of their Christian faith. He says:

Whenever I have gently argued with them, they have quoted the celebrated verse, 'Call nothing unclean', as if it referred to eating and gave a licence to indulgence.[41]

Against this background any idea of a unique place for the Person or work of Jesus Christ in the moral and spiritual progress of mankind is ruled out. Gandhi is prepared to consider Jesus Christ as one of the many teachers and prophets of mankind, and even as one of the many names and incarnations of God, but without giving his divine nature, his atoning deed or his mediation between God and mankind any uniqueness. Recalling his encounters with orthodox Christian doctrines of the Person and work of Christ Gandhi says:

It was more than I could believe that Jesus was the only incarnate Son of God and that only he who believed in him would have everlasting life. If God could have sons, all of us were his sons. If Jesus was like God, or God himself, then all men were like God and could be God Himself.[44]

Gandhi grants that 'Jesus came as near to perfection as possible'. But no one limited by the bonds of flesh can attain perfection until after the dissolution of the body.

Therefore God alone is absolutely perfect. When he descends to earth, He of his own accord limits himself. Jesus died on the Cross because he was limited by the flesh. I do not need either the prophecies or the miracles to establish Jesus' greatness as a teacher. Nothing can be more miraculous than the three years of his ministry.[43]

He does not however see any 'fundamental distinction' between him and other great teachers to justify his being considered the only-begotten Son of God,[44] though under the Hindu practice of *ishta* each of us may choose our own different only-begotten son of God in a special sense.[45] Gandhiji of course realizes that certain parts of the New Testament do emphasize the unique place of the person and work of Jesus Christ as the only-begotten Son of God. And at this point, his advice is:

It becomes perhaps necessary to reread the message of the Bible in terms of what is happening around us. . . . Many things in the Bible will have to be reinterpreted in the light of discoveries, not of modern science, but in the spiritual world in the shape of direct experiences common to all faiths. The fundamental verses of St John do require to be reread and reinterpreted.[46]

As for St Paul's epistles, Gandhi thinks 'they are a graft on Christ's teaching, his [Paul's] own gloss apart from Christ's own experience'.[47]

3. RELIGION AND RELIGIONS

A. *Equality of Religions*

Equality of religions is one of Gandhi's cardinal beliefs. It is based first on the unfathomable and unknowable character of the One God who is over us all; secondly, on the never-ending forms of divine revelation and human religious responses to them, thirdly on the centrality of the law of non-violence enjoined by all the religions, fourthly, on the existence of errors and imperfections in all religions and, fifthly, on the conviction that all religions are in evolution towards fuller realization of Truth.

Speaking about the creed of Islam on the unity of God, Gandhi says that 'the God who is one is unfathomable, unknowable and unknown to the vast majority of mankind'; therefore both his revelations and man's worship of him are varied.

He is formless and indivisible, He is incarnate, has no father, mother or child, and yet he allows Himself to be worshipped as father, mother, wife and child. He allows Himself even to be worshipped as stick and stone, although He is none of those things.[48]

Gandhi believes that revelation is not the monopoly of any one nation or tribe, but that all the 'clean Scriptures' are revealed; and what is required is 'mutual respect and toleration of the devotees of the different religions'. He adds:

We want to reach not the dead level but unity in diversity. Any attempt to root out traditions, effects of heredity, climate and other surroundings is not only bound to fail but is a sacrilege. The soul of religion is one, but it is encased in a multitude of forms. The latter will persist to the end of time. Wise men will ignore the outward crust and see the same soul living under a variety of crusts.[49]

It is Gandhi's conviction:

If a man reaches the heart of his own religion he has reached the heart of the others too. There is only one God but there are many paths to Him. . . . [They all] converge to the same point. . . . In reality there are as many religions as there are individuals.[50]

So Gandhi pays 'equal homage to Jesus, Mohammed, Krishna, Buddha, Zoroaster and others that may be named'. But this is not a matter for argument but his 'deep and sacred conviction'.[51]

Gandhi believes that 'all religions are true but imperfect'. After a study of the major religions he came to the conclusion that all of them were right, 'but everyone of them imperfect, imperfect naturally and necessarily', as they have been interpreted by men and presented through human agency and 'bear the impress of the imperfections and frailties of human beings'.[52] All religions need moral correction and regeneration.

The truth that is common in all religions and makes them true is their ethical teaching and practice; they therefore have to be evaluated morally. Gandhi says that, from his youth upward, he 'learned the art of estimating the value of Scriptures on the basis of their ethical reality'. He accepts no Scripture and no revelation in itself as having any authority over him. He exercises 'his own judgment about every Scripture including the *Gita*' on the basis of his own conscience and reason. Since nothing in the Scriptures of any religion comes from God directly, everything has to be discriminated: 'I cannot surrender my reason while I subscribe to divine revelation.'[53] One's own heart and reason are the seat of religious authority. And he explains how he discriminates truth from error in each religion:

I have no difficulty in hitting upon the truth because I go by certain fundamental maxims. Truth is superior to everything, and I reject what conflicts with it. Similarly that which is in conflict with non-violence should be rejected. And on matters which can be reasoned out, that which conflicts with reason must be rejected.[54]

But asked whether he would on this basis evaluate religious prophets as having different degrees of divinity and whether Jesus would be judged 'most divine' he replies:

No, for the simple reason, that we have no data. Historically, we have more data about Mohammed than anyone else, because he was more recent in time. For Jesus, there is less data, and still less for Buddha, Rama, Krishna. . . . To say that Jesus was ninety per cent. divine, and Mohammed fifty per cent. and Krishna ten per cent., is to arrogate to oneself a function which really does not belong to man. [It is] impossible to compare [religions], . . . But the deduction from it is that they are equal . . . essentially all religions are equal.

We must consider all prophets, even Moses and Jesus, to be equal. 'It is a horizontal plane.'[55] Gandhi said to the Pole, Kozenski, that he considered that 'religion is one' with several branches (religions) which are 'all equal'. When Kozenski agreed that 'no religion lacks inspiration but all have not the same truth, because all have not the same light', Gandhi suggested to him 'a better position':

Accept all religions as equal, for all have the same root and same laws of growth. . . . Religions are always growing.[56]

Gandhi sees the relation between Religion and religions as similar to that between the Universal Soul and its bodies:

The Soul is one, but the bodies which she animates are many. We cannot reduce the number of bodies; yet we recognise the unity of the Soul.

'The one true and perfect Religion' becomes many as it 'passes through the human medium.' It is Gandhi's conviction that 'the principal faiths of the world' are all based on 'common fundamentals'.[57]

B. Swadeshi *in Religion*

We have already referred to Gandhi's principle of *swadeshi* and some of its implications. In religion it means that men should adhere to the religion into which they have been born, seek to purify it by correcting its defects, assimilate into it the truths of other religions, and build a fellowship of religions, helping one another in the pursuit of Truth.

The first reason for being a Hindu for Gandhi is that he was born in a Hindu family.[58] And a Hindu refuses to leave its fold because he considers it the best for him, 'as my wife to me is the most beautiful woman in the world', as 'others may feel the same about their own religion'.[59] Elsewhere he has said that a man adheres to his religion 'not necessarily because he considers it to be best' from an objective point of view but because he can 'complement it by introducing reforms'.[60] Thus Gandhi maintains that 'India's great faiths are all sufficient for her'. But in the process of self-purification of every religion, 'friendly contact among the followers of the great religions of the world' can help a great deal. 'Through such friendly contact it will be possible for us to rid our respective faiths of shortcomings and excrescences.'[61] Indeed, it will help every religion not only to purify itself, but also to understand itself better by the illumination of truths from others,[62] and what is more, to grow into fuller truth by the assimilation of the valuable features of other religions without losing its self-identity. Dr Cochrane, an American clergyman, asked Gandhi whether his religion was 'a synthesis of all religions'. His reply was:

Yes, if you will. But I would call that synthesis Hinduism, and to you the synthesis will be Christianity.[63]

One of Gandhi's best expositions of his doctrinal basis of equality and fellowship of religions runs as follows:

Ahimsa teaches us to entertain the same respect for the religious faiths of others as we accord to our own, thus admitting the imperfections of the latter. This admission will be readily made by a seeker of Truth, who follows the Law of Love. If we had attained the full vision of Truth, we would no longer be mere seekers, but would have become one with God, for Truth is God. But being only seekers, we prosecute our quest and are conscious of our imperfections. And if we are imperfect ourselves, religion as conceived by us must also be imperfect.

We have not realized religion in its perfection, even as we have not realized God. The religion of our conception, being thus imperfect, is always subject to a process of evolution and reinterpretation. Progress towards Truth, towards God, is possible only because of such evolution. And if all paths outlined by men are imperfect, the question of comparative merit does not arise. All faiths constitute a revelation of Truth, but all are imperfect and liable to error. Reverence for other faiths need not blind us to their faults. We must be keenly alive to the defects of our own faith also, yet not leave it on that account, but try to overcome those defects. Looking at all religions with an equal eye, we would not only not hesitate, but would think it our duty to blend into our faith every acceptable feature of other faiths.[64]

It is evident that this approach rules out conversion in the sense of change of religion. Gandhi tells the 'International Fellowship':

So we can only pray, if we are Hindus, not that a Christian should become a Hindu, or if we are Mussalmans, not that a Hindu or a Christian should become a Mussalman; nor should we even secretly pray that any one should be converted; but our inmost prayer should be that a Hindu should be a better Hindu, a Muslim a better Muslim, and a Christian a better Christian. This is the fundamental truth of fellowship. . . . Cases of real honest conversion are quite possible. If some people for their inward satisfaction and growth, change their religion, let them do so.[65]

But generally Gandhi does not allow even such exceptions. Mirabai was convinced that Hinduism was more true and more congenial to her spiritual growth than Christianity, but Gandhi wanted her to remain a Christian and assimilate the spirituality of Hinduism within its framework,[66] even as he himself remained a Hindu and had assimilated the spirit of Christ. He says:

I am against conversion, whether it is known as *shuddhi* by Hindus, *tabligh* by Mussalmans or proselytising by Christians.[67]

C. *Communication of Things of the Spirit*

In the conversation which Gandhi had with Dr John R. Mott, Gandhi explained his idea of the nature of communcation in the realm of spiritual and religious truths. He said:

> The highest truth needs no communicating for it is by its very nature self-propelling. It radiates its influence silently as the rose its fragrance without the intervention of a medium.[68]

Gandhiji has repeated times without number this analogy of the rose that transmits its own scent without movement and the communication of spiritual truth through life only; and the idea has been repeated many times more. It is central to his whole approach to the deeper spiritual truths. He does not believe in 'people telling others of their faith', for 'faith does not admit of telling; it has to be lived and then it becomes self-propagating'.[69] Humility is lacking when religion is communicated through speech. And in any case 'language is a limitation of the truth which can be only represented by life'. In an interview with a Christian, Gandhi explains it thus:

> Spiritual life has greater potency than Marconi waves. Where there is no medium between me and my Lord and I simply become a willing vessel for His influences to flow into it, then I overflow as the water of the Ganges at its source. There is no desire to speak where one lives the truth. Truth is most economical of words. There is thus no truer or other evangelism than life.[70]

Gandhi admits that 'if a person were to ask the source of such a life', there is place for speaking. 'Then you will draw him to you. You will not need to go for him.' He cites Aurobindo as an example in spiritual communication.

4. A REINTERPRETATION OF CHRISTIANITY

Gandhi rejects orthodox Christianity and calls for a new reinterpretation of its essence and form in India. Orthodox Christianity challenged Gandhiji to give up Hinduism and embrace Christianity; and he was prepared to do so 'should I feel the call'. He admits that he was 'tremendously attracted', and felt 'great leanings' towards Christianity and for a time wavered between Christianity and

Hinduism. But in the end, he 'saw no reason' for changing his religion. He came to the conclusion:

> To be a good Hindu also meant that I would be a good Christian. There was no need for me to join your crowd to be a believer in the beauty of the teaching of Jesus or try to follow his example.[71]

Indeed, Gandhi claims to have assimilated the spirit of Christ within the framework of his Hindu beliefs and would have no hesitation in claiming to be a Christian, provided he had to 'face only the Sermon on the Mount and my own interpretation of it'.[72] Thus in rejecting 'Orthodox Christianity'[73] Gandhiji gives his reinterpretation of it and seeks to persuade the Christian missions and the Churches in India to accept that as essential Christianity.

There are several aspects of the Gandhian reinterpretation of Christianity. We may deal in particular with three of the more important ones.

First and foremost is Gandhi's idea of a universalized Christianity arising from his understanding of Christ as the symbol of the eternal law of *ahimsa* (non-violence), expressed in the Sermon on the Mount. Christianity therefore is essentially a new life and not a religion,[74] and wherever the way of love is practised, Christianity is present. Not Christology but ethics as the means to Truth constitute fundamental Christianity, and it is the same in all religions. According to Gandhi, it is possible to say that 'where there is boundless love and no idea of retaliation whatsoever it is Christianity that lives'. At this point Christianity 'surmounts all boundaries and book-teaching'.[75] Gandhi admits that there is 'enough in the Bible to authorize us to invite people to a better way of life', but does not see that it involved invitation to a new religious community, the Church. He adds:

> If you interpret your texts in the way you seem to do, you straight away condemn a large part of humanity unless it believes as you do. If Jesus came to earth again he would disown many things that are being done in the name of Christianity. It is not he who says, Lord Lord, that is a Christian, but he that doeth the will of the Lord, that is a true Christian. And cannot he who has not heard the name of Christ Jesus do the will of the Lord?[76]

Gandhi is sure that 'many men who have never heard the name of Jesus Christ or have even rejected the official interpretation of

Christianity, will be owned by him'. Therefore Christians must learn that 'God and Christianity can be found also in institutions that do not call themselves Christian'.[77] It is Gandhi's belief that it was 'when it had the backing of a Roman Emperor' that the Church distorted Christianity into 'an imperialistic faith' and incorporated it into a system alien to it, 'based on might'. And he adds: 'India's contribution to the world is to show this fallacy.'[78] Gandhiji cannot conceive of Jesus approving of the organized religion of modern Christianity. He says:

If Indian Christians will simply cling to the Sermon on the Mount, which was delivered not merely to the peaceful disciples but a growing world, they would not go wrong, and they would find no religion is false. Co-operation with forces of Good and non-co-operation with forces of Evil are the two things we need for a good and pure life, whether it is called Hindu, Muslim or Christian.[79]

Secondly, Indian Christianity must dissociate itself from Western civilization, which is based on violence and materialism. European Christianity is allied with it and 'measures moral progress by their material possessions'.[80]

Thirdly, Gandhi seeks to persuade the Christian missions in India to recognize that the call 'Go ye into all the world' has been 'somewhat narrowly interpreted and the spirit of it is missed' and that they will 'serve the spirit of Christianity better by dropping the goal of proselytizing while continuing their philanthropic work'.[81] In his opinion, the philanthropic work of the Missions has been perverted by the proselytization motive.

Gandhiji seems to have many other aspects of conversion to Christianity also in mind, when he opposes it. He says that often it has meant the rejection of the *swadeshi* spirit in culture and politics, though he recognizes that a change is coming over Indian Christians in this regard.[82] He often refers to the less than religious motivation present in the missionary work among the unsophisticated Harijans of India, especially in the mass movement of conversion; and he is concerned that the disabilities of the Harijans are being exploited to tear them away from their roots in the ancestral religious community and social structure, even while Hinduism is awake to the necessity of reform. But all these many reasons reflect Gandhi's spiritual principle of *swadeshi* and its implications in religion, politics and culture.

Two Christian Statements

On this question there have been several dialogues between Gandhiji and Christians which reveal the issues at debate. We may refer to two statements by Christian leaders in India clarifying the enlightened orthodox Indian Christian view regarding conversion as change of religion. The first statement, prepared by Christians of the Madras International Fellowship, was transmitted to Gandhiji by A. A. Paul. It puts the Christian position in a series of propositions thus:

1. Conversion is a change of heart from sin to God. It is the work of God. Sin is separation from God.
2. The Christian believes that Jesus is the fulfilment of God's revelation to mankind, that he is our Saviour from sin, that he alone can bring the sinner to God and thus enable him to live.
3. The Christian to whom God has become a living reality and power through Christ regards it as his privilege and duty to speak about Jesus and to proclaim the free offer which he came on earth to make.
4. If any man's heart is moved by the hearing of this message so as to repent and wish to live a new life as a disciple of Jesus, the Christian regards it as right to admit him to the company of his professed believers which is called the Christian Church.
5. The Christian shall do all in his power to sound the sincerity of conviction in all such cases and shall point out, as he can, the consequences of such a step, stressing the duty a man owes to his family.
6. The Christian shall do everything in his power to prevent any motives of self-seeking on his part and of material consideration on the part of the convert.
7. Inasmuch as Jesus came to give full life, and that as a matter of history conversion has often meant an enhancing of personality, the Christian shall not be accused of using material inducements if conversion results in social uplift of the convert – it always being understood that such shall never be used as a means to an end.
8. The Christian is right in accepting as his duty the care of the sincere convert, body, soul and mind.
9. It shall not be brought against the Christian that he is using material inducements, when certain facts in Hindu social theory, out of his control, are in themselves an inducement to the Harijan. (See points 5 and 6.)

This statement itself arose in the climate of the challenges which Gandhiji presented to the Christian missions and churches to rethink the Christian mission especially in relation to conversion and proselytization. Gandhi published the statement in *Harijan*[83] and commented extensively. He points out that these propositions 'can be applied only in individual contacts, never to the mass of mankind'. He asks: 'If conversion is the work of God (No. 1) why should that work be taken away from him?' Even if man may be 'a humble instrument' of God, how can he judge men's hearts? The second and third propositions deal with the mysteries of the Christian religion which are a tradition handed down and accepted by common people without themselves testing their truth. This may be right for people within the Christian tradition. 'But surely it is a dangerous thing to present it to those who have been brought up to a different belief', which for aught we know, may be as true as the other. It is 'highly likely' that each belief may be good enough for the one who holds it. The other five propositions deal with principles to safeguard the integrity of the method and 'seem to be almost impossible of application in practice'. He adds: 'The start being wrong, all that follows must be necessarily so.' And as regards the last proposition, 'it takes one's breath away, for it makes clear that the other eight are to be applied in all their fullness to the poor Harijans', when the very first theological proposition of sin, salvation and union with God are so puzzling to 'some of the most intellectual and philosophical persons even in the present generation'. Are all preachers of the Gospel 'sure of their union with God'? If not, 'who will test the Harijan's knowledge of these deep things?' And he concludes by a restatement of his position, against 'conversion from one faith to another'. He adds:

It is a conviction daily growing upon me that the great and rich Christian missions will render true service to India, if they can persuade themselves to confine their activities to humanitarian service without the ulterior motive of converting India or at least the unsophisticated villagers to Christianity and destroying the social superstructure, which notwithstanding its many defects has stood now from time immemorial the onslaught upon it from within and from without.[84]

The second statement is a Manifesto issued by fourteen Indian Christians[85] of high standing on 'the missionary work among Harijans'. The group consisted largely of members of the Christian

Asrams in India who were leading the movement towards indigenous Christianity in India, and those concerned with the movement known as 'Rethinking Christianity in India', all of whom had come under the *swadeshi* spirit of Gandhi. The Manifesto was entitled: 'Our Duty to the Depressed and Backward Classes.'

The Manifesto begins by saying that 'as Indian Christians interested in the welfare of the country and the future of Christianity in the land', they are expressing their convictions on 'the propaganda that is being carried on in this country and the West' regarding opportunities of missionary work among the Depressed and Backward Classes in India. They do so to clear misunderstandings among the non-Christians. They then in Section I give their analysis of the situation. The general unrest in India included 'a note of religious quest', though secular nationalism has pushed 'religious values' to the background.

An arresting feature of the national upheaval is the spirit of revolt manifested by the leaders of the Depressed and Backward Classes against the lot that was assigned to their people in the social, economic and religious fabric of Hindu society for centuries, and the large measure of sympathy with which their demand for drastic remedies to meet their desperate situation is being met by Hindu reformers.

Today the Hindu incentive to do justice to the Depressed Classes comes more from 'nationalistic and humanitarian than through religious considerations' – the fear that with communal franchise their conversion to Christianity would be 'a loss to the nation'. And from the Christian standpoint, the fact that the Hindu community caters for the development of the Harijans eliminates 'worldly motives' from religious conversion. And the present situation is described thus:

In view of the political complications that have got so inextricably mixed with the uprising of the Depressed and Backward Classes and their desire for a fuller life, the redoubled enthusiasm of Muslims and Christian leaders to commend their religion to the acceptance of those people has naturally aroused the suspicion and resentment of Hindus.

In the face of this situation,

The Christian with a true missionary motive has the opportunity to conserve all that is conducive to national unity and depth of spirituality.

Then follows the second section dealing with 'convictions and conclusions'. The writers sympathize with the struggle of Depressed Classes and rejoice in the increasing success of the Hindu reformers. It will bring these classes 'immediate benefits on a large scale which the Church will not be able to give to the whole community'. Therefore they are 'unable to share the hope that the present upheaval is going to result in an influx of the Depressed and Backward Classes into the Christian Church in the phenomenal measure in which, it is said it is going to happen'. And the Church should heartily welcome the Hindu movements of reform:

[They are] bound to have a wholesome effect on the entire social structure of India, including the Indian Church, by solving the problem of caste prejudices in the home of their origin.

They point out that 'an aggressive evangelistic programme' in the present context will be misunderstood as exploitation of the difficulties of Hinduism and undermine common action towards social justice.

'Mass conversions' have in the past been motivated by the desire for uplift; they have in fact contributed to the uplift of the Backward Classes and they have also opened the eyes of the privileged classes of Hindu to the lot of the underprivileged. The signatories however recognize another aspect:

Mass conversions have generally lowered Christian standards so badly as to have left the Indian Church a legacy of deplorable caste prejudices and jealousies, on account of which its progress, solidarity and its proclaimed witness to the oneness of all humanity in Christ Jesus suffer not a little even to this day.

And then comes what Gandhi considers the most controversial paragraph on the missionary obligation and right of the Church.

We recognize that in an atmosphere free from the heat and dust of the present upheaval and apart from all political considerations, Christianity will continue to exercise the attraction which it has always had to the poor of the land and others in whom a hunger for the things of the spirit has been awakened. Men and women, individually and in family or village groups, will continue to seek the fellowship of the Christian Church. That is the real movement of the Spirit of God. And no power on earth can stem that tide. It will be the duty of the Christian Church in

India to receive such seekers after truth as it is in Jesus Christ and provide for them instruction and spiritual nurture. The Church will cling to its right to receive such people into itself from whatever religious group they may come. It will cling to the further right to go about in these days of irreligion and materialism to awaken spiritual hunger in all.

They hope that India will grant to all people religious freedom including the right of propagation so that the Church may continue to do its unique service to the moral regeneration of the country. The Church has an evangelistic obligation not only to the downtrodden but to all sections of the people; and the Church has also the function of leavening the whole national life. These aspects of the 'larger evangelism' should not be jeopardized by insisting now on mass conversions.

[It would be] unwise at this juncture to alienate the sympathy and spoil the openmindedness of the Hindus to the Gospel by any ill-considered attempts at external results of a questionable value.

Gandhiji published it in the *Harijan* with a critical comment, characterizing it as 'An Unfortunate Document' which, though designed to allay the fears of Hindus, had not done so but 'leaves a bad taste in the mouth'. He criticized the purpose of the Manifesto, which was not to 'condemn unequivocally the method of converting the illiterate and the ignorant' but to 'assert the right of preaching the Gospel to the millions of Harijans'. He quotes what he calls 'the key of the Manifesto' viz. Paragraph 7, and gives two comments: first, that whether Harijans or others, 'men and women do not seek the fellowship of the Christian Church'. The Harijans do not have any 'real spiritual hunger' which is waiting to be satisfied. The little they have 'they satisfy by visits to the temples, however crude that may be'. And it is not any 'special spiritual merit' of the missionary, but his 'material goods' which attract the Harijans. Secondly the Manifesto has turned the 'duty' of the Church into a 'right'; 'conceived as a right it may easily become an imposition on unwilling parties' and he asks the signatories to recognize that 'in the spiritual sphere, there is no such thing as a right'.[86]

5. SOME CHRISTIAN RESPONSES

We have surveyed the theological side of the many-sided personality of Mahatma Gandhi. Since Gandhi's thoughts on Christianity have often been formulated in conversations with Christians, a few of the comments on Gandhian theology by Christians have already been mentioned. But we may briefly touch on a few more.

A. *Christians of the Inner Gandhi Circle; S. K. George and C. F. Andrews*

There were some foreign missionaries like C. F. Andrews, Verrier Elwin and Ralph Richard Keithahn, and also some Indian Christians like Rajkumari Amrit Kaur, S. K. George, Aryanayagam, Bharatan Kumarappa and J. C. Kumarappa, who joined the Gandhian movement, formed part of the inner Gandhi circle, and have shared in large measure the basic Gandhian ideas of Christ and Christianity. Common to them all, is the centrality of non-violence for Christian life. The title of J. C. Kumarappa's book, *The Practice and Precepts of Jesus*,[87] is indicative. But they have been concerned with different aspects of the Gandhian movement and their ideas of the relation between Christian theology and the ethics of non-violence varied from person to person, and not all conformed to the Gandhian system, if we can speak of one. We shall in this study confine ourselves to a brief survey of the thought of S. K. George and C. F. Andrews on the Gandhian view of Christ and Christianity.

S. K. George's book *Gandhi's Challenge to Christianity* is significant because as his dedication points out, it was Mahatma Gandhi 'who made Jesus and his image real to me'. He speaks as an Indian Christian theologian who has heard and responded to the challenge of Gandhi not only to his life, but also to his theology. In his Preface to the first edition, he rightly affirms:

The real Christ of India, stricken for the transgressions of her people, standing in with them against oppression and injustice, smitten of God and afflicted, of his travail bringing life and light to the nation, is yet to find embodiment in the Indian Church.

The Indian Church can embody Christ to India only as it 'takes upon itself the sufferings of its people'.

For redemptive suffering love is the central principle in Christianity, and the manifestation of it in practice, and not the preaching of any dogma, is what is needed, is what will convince India of the truth and power of Christianity.[88]

And therefore 'Gandhi's Satyagraha is Christianity in action'. Under foreign leadership the Church failed to fall behind Gandhi in the non-violent movement for national liberation, and thus 'lost one of its greatest opportunities'.

Not to recognise in him the greatest ally of essential Christianity in India, the greatest worker for the Kingdom of God in the world today, is to betray gross inability to discern the working of God's spirit.[89]

In an autobiographical sketch George points out how Gandhi's 'non-co-operation' movement of 1919–21 'made real to his youthful mind the idealism and the passion of Jesus of Nazareth', and how, in the Bishop's College, Calcutta, he was confirmed in his conviction that 'the central thing in Christianity is Christ's message of the Kingdom and that the way to its realization is that of the Cross'. And he saw Gandhi as living out the principle of the Cross. And in the Civil Disobedience Movement of 1930–32 he felt it his Christian duty

to appeal to all Indian Christians to join in and to act as custodians of non-violence as became a community which claimed to believe in the supreme instance of triumphant *satyagraha* the world has seen viz., the Cross of Jesus of Nazareth.

He lost not only his job in the Theological College but also his affiliation with the Church. And his later life has been lived in this conviction:

An undogmatic Christianity, true to the spiritual insight of Jesus of Nazareth, will yet discover and establish its links with liberal elements in all other religions, and will especially find its rightful place in that larger fellowship of faiths that is yet to be. Of this fellowship Hinduism, with its genuine catholicity, is an earnest as well as a foretaste, though the coming fellowship will be far more vital and effective than the incoherent mass of present-day Hinduism.... India with her genius for comprehension ought to lead the way in that synthesis of religions and cultures that is clearly demanded by the times.[90]

George sees Indian Christianity realizing itself and saving itself by 'losing itself in the larger life of India and of the world to be, in the universal church of humanity that is yet to arise', of which Hinduism is a foretaste.

George speaks of the 'fact of Gandhi' as the challenge of a spiritual reality, not dissimilar to the 'fact of Christ'. George's belief that 'the way of suffering love, supremely illustrated in the Cross of Jesus of Nazareth, and now reduced to a science of mass-action by Mahatma Gandhi', has solved the great problem of man, namely 'how Love can realise Justice and yet remain Love'.[91] George explains this equation between Satyagraha and the way of the Cross still further: 'The Cross of Christ is the supreme, perfect historic example' of the victory of love over evil. But Christianity has made it a creed and dogma to secure a heaven, and the Cross had to be brought back as 'a working principle of life'. This is what has been done by Gandhi 'in whom the central principle of the Cross has again incarnated itself'. Christianity with 'the Cross for its centre' knows that it was pang-born and that Christian values 'can only be conserved and enshrined in the heart of a world it seeks to save by the willing endurance of pain'. Gandhi recalls Christianity to this great truth.[92]

Regarding Gandhi's critique of Christian missions, George says:

What an awakened Hinduism resents is not so much the methods of Christian missions – methods are but an expression of the faith – but the content of the message itself.[93]

He calls Kraemer's 'biblical realism' with its total rejection of mysticism and with its 'supra-rational doctrine of a unique revelation' fighting its way till it batters down all opposition and establishes world dominion, like the Nazi Fuehrer, 'a bleak and barren creed'. George seeks instead a reconciliation between the Hindu world view and Christian thought, and looks forward to Christianity finding its rightful place in the catholicity of Hinduism. He says:

It (Hinduism) has certainly a place for Jesus among the many leaders and teachers it reverences as revealers of God to man, nay as incarnations of God in his aspect as the Lover and Redeemer of man. Its conception of a Favourite God, *Ishta Devata*, would sanction even an exclusive worship of him to those who find in such adoration the way to God-realisation. But it would definitely place him in its own setting among the diverse modes and ways in which the Unfathomable and the Eternal manifests itself to mortal minds. Who can say that this is not the setting in which he will find his permanent place in the religious heritage of the race, at any rate in India.[94]

Indeed, Christianity in such a setting has a special contribution to make to the evolution of Hinduism itself, through its emphasis 'upon ethics, upon the moral holiness of God and His demand of such holiness from man, upon morality as the way to union with God'. In this Christianity will find itself 'at one with the new flowering of Hinduism in Mahatma Gandhi and will contribute towards its fruition and perpetuation'. It is George's belief that Christianity can never replace Hinduism in India, and that the attempt should not be made.

Any new light, any new emphasis that another religion may bring must be added to the ancient faith, rather than seek to blot out the ancient light.

And he visualizes Christianity in India as

a small shrine adjoining the central Hindu temple existing side by side with, never seeking to displace, the giant structure of Hinduism; but keeping the light of its own ethical knowledge of God bright and clear, that it may not be overlooked, whatever else the worshipper may find inside the great temple to satisfy the myriad needs of his whole self, which perhaps only a religion that has entered into the marrow of the life and culture of a people can wholly satisfy.[95]

George has been working to promote inter-religious co-operation on this basis first through the All-Kerala Inter-religious Student Fellowship and later through the Fellowship of the Friends of Truth, both of which accept Gandhi's idea of the relation between Religion and religions. For mutual respect between religions to be real, they consider that 'it is absolutely necessary that no member of the fellowship should claim for his religion any exclusive and final possession of truth' or should 'desire to persuade' any within the Fellowship to his own religious belief and practice.[96]

We shall consider the theology of C. F. Andrews in greater detail in the next chapter, where we deal with Christian interpretations of the National Awakening. It will suffice here to point out that he accepted Gandhi's emphasis on ethics as expressing the essence of Christianity more than any dogma. He always felt that Christ was the experience of a 'spiritual consciousness' and was suspicious of all intellectual definitions of it in metaphysical formulae. Speaking of the early spiritual experience which brought him to Christ, Andrews writes:

There was no need for me to formulate this in a creed. It was a spiritual consciousness that had come to me, not an intellectual definition, and whenever I have gone aside from that spiritual basis in order to define in metaphysical terms what I believe, it has seemed to me to bring weakness instead of strength, uncertainty instead of truth.[97]

And he rebelled against exclusivism of dogmas absolutized as the essence of Christian faith, as he did at Christmas 1912 when he heard the Indian Choir boys chanting the Athanasian Creed with the words:

Which Faith except everyone do keep whole and undefiled, without doubt he shall perish everlastingly.[98]

This led to his resignation from the priesthood. Later, reflecting on his experience of the presence of Christ in the 'burning passion of Gandhi's sacrifice for the weak and the oppressed', he wrote:

To be a Christian means not the expression of an outward creed but the living of an inward life.[99]

Nevertheless, 'Christ Jesus the Son of Man' was central to his religious and ethical life. He confessed that Jesus 'untrammelled by dogmas and doctrines' shone more in his heart than ever before.[100]

Nevertheless, the differences between Andrews and Gandhi are radical. They revolve round Gandhiji's equation of the essential self of man with the *atman* and the consequent rejection of the body and all matter as the source of all selfishness, From this arises Gandhi's negative attitude to sex, bodily pleasures, body-force and material luxuries, machines and Western civilization. From this also, arises Gandhi's incapacity to see the sources of evil present in spiritual self-righteousness. And in all Andrews' writings and in his many encounters with Gandhi, this is the central issue, which is debated. It is for this reason that Andrews finds himself as having greater spiritual affinity with the side of Rabindranath Tagore, in the Tagore-Gandhi controversies. In the development of Christian theology in relation to Gandhism in general, and Gandhi's interpretation of Christ and Christianity in particular, Andrew's critique of Gandhism at this level is extremely significant.

Gandhi has said,

Marriage is a 'fall' even as birth is a fall. Salvation is freedom from birth and hence from death also.

Andrews, quoting this, says that he cannot leave Gandhi's description of marriage as a 'fall' without comment, and continues:

Tagore, in a famous letter, refers to this side of Gandhi's ascetic disposition as akin to Buddhism rather than to the Upanishad teaching of early Hinduism.[101]

About the vows of the members of Gandhi's Sabarmathi Ashram, Andrews says:

Personally I had felt from the first that the vow of life-long celibacy had imposed a slur on marriage; and therefore I had objected to this vow being included along with that of Truthfulness and Ahimsa. ... This vow of celibacy for the whole Ashram appeared to sever one of the vital roots of the Hindu religion, and for this reason, I wrote to him urging its withdrawal.[102]

In the course of an interview which Andrews arranged between G. Ramachandran (then a student at Visvabharati) and Gandhi, Ramachandran asked whether Gandhi was 'against the institution of marriage'. Gandhi replies:

The aim of human life is deliverance. As a Hindu I believe that *moksa* or deliverance is freedom from birth, by breaking the bonds of the flesh, by becoming one with God. Now, marriage is a hindrance in the attainment of this supreme object in as much as it only tightens the bonds of the flesh. Celibacy is a great help, in as much as it enables one to lead a life of full surrender to God.

When Ramachandran pointed out that Andrews did not like this 'emphasis on celibacy', Gandhi replied:

Yes I know. That is the legacy of his Protestantism. Protestantism did many good things; but one of its few evils was that it ridiculed celibacy.[103]

According to Andrews,

Mahatma is one with the medieval saints in a passionate belief in celibacy as practically the only way to realize the beatific vision of God.[104]

Gandhi makes clear that his attitude to machinery also springs from this approach to the body as at best 'a necessary evil' to be delivered from. While his immediate concern is to make the machinery the servant rather than the master of man, he adds:

Ideally however I would rule out all machinery, even as I would reject this very body which is not helpful to salvation, and seek the absolute liberation of the soul. From that point of view, I would reject all machinery; but machines will remain because like the body they are inevitable. The body itself, as I told you, is the purest piece of mechanism, but if it is a hindrance to the highest flights of the soul, it has to be rejected.[105]

Gandhi's revolt against modern technological civilization is a necessary consequence of this approach. It is probably patterned after Tolstoy, whom Gandhi is 'prepared to follow to the extreme point in practice'. Gandhi 'rejects the city life with all its mechanical contrivances and artificial ways of living as essentially immoral'. He characterizes the cities of India as 'the real plague-spots of modern India'.

India's salvation consists in unlearning what she has learned during the past fifty years. The railways, telegraphs, hospitals, lawyers, doctors and such like have all to go, and the so-called upper classes have to learn to live consciously, religiously and deliberately the simple peasant life, knowing it to be a life giving true happiness.[106]

Andrews has commented on the theological roots of Gandhian asceticism. He says:

With Gandhi, the negative aspect of sin, as something which has to be rooted out by an almost violent self-discipline, is like the shadow of the Cross, always apparent, brooding as it were over his thoughts. For the human body, with its lusts and sins, is to Gandhi an evil, not a good. Only by complete severance from this human body can perfect deliverance be found.[107]

The deification of the spirit of man is a corollary of this idea of the body as evil. Therefore the soul, soul-force, and the expression of the soul-force in passive resistance or non-violence, *satyagraha*, are inherently good. And both Tagore and Andrews criticize Gandhi for his lack of discernment of the tendencies of self-seeking and the fanaticism of self-righteousness which hide themselves behind the pursuit of truth and non-violence. And at various points they have protested to certain of Gandhi's programmes of *satyagraha* pointing out the danger of soul-force being used to promote selfishness and self-righteousness. In one of the most eloquent protests, the poet writes:

Power in all its form is irrational; it is like the horse that drags the carriage blindfolded. The moral element in it is only represented in the man who drives the horse. Passive resistance is a force which is not necessarily moral in itself; it can be used against truth as well as for it. The danger inherent in all force grows stronger when it is likely to gain success, for then it becomes temptation.

I pray most fervently that nothing which tends to weaken our spiritual freedom may intrude into our marching line; that martyrdom for the cause of truth may never degenerate into fanaticism for mere verbal forms, descending into the self-deception that hides itself behind sacred names.[108]

C. F. Andrews himself made a similar protest against the spirit of self-righteousness and of aggressive nationalism which Gandhi was waking up by his programme of the burning of foreign cloth. Andrews wrote:

I know that your burning of foreign cloth is with the idea of helping the poor, but I feel that you have done wrong. There is a subtle appeal to racial feeling in that word foreign, which day by day appears to need checking and not fomenting. The picture of your lighting that great pile of beautiful and delicate fabrics shocked me intensely. We seem to be losing sight of the great world outside to which we belong and concentrating selfishly on India; and this must, I fear, lead back to the old bad selfish nationalism.
... I was supremely happy when you were dealing giant blows at the fundamental moral evils – drunkeness, drug-taking, untouchability, race arrogance, etc. – and when you were, with such wonderful and beautiful tenderness dealing with the hideous vice of prostitution. But ... destroying in the fire the noble handiwork of one's fellow men and women, of one's brothers and sisters abroad, saying it would be 'defiling' to use it – I cannot tell you how different all this appears to me! Do you know I almost fear now to wear the *khaddar* that you have given me, lest I should appear to be judging other people, as a Pharisee would, saying, 'I am holier than thou'. I never felt like this before.[109]

For Gandhi deliverance lay in a movement from the body to the soul. Therefore, his was a scheme of man redeeming himself through a movement of asceticism within one's own self. But Tagore and Andrews saw lurking in this ascetic movement an element of self-deception and self-righteousness. In fact, this awareness of a self that transcends the soul and utilizes soul-force for its own ends, brings a new dimension of sin and salvation which Gandhism seems unaware of. Andrews was aware of sin in the soul and it was for this reason that his religion was, more than ethical principles, 'the experience of a transforming Friendship'[110] with Jesus the Great Companion who brought salvation.

It is evident also that C. F. Andrews does not identify Gandhi's doctrine of *ahimsa* and its expression in his ideology and technique of *satyagraha* in their entirety with the way of *agape*, the way of the Cross of Jesus Christ, as S. K. George has done. Nevertheless, he sees many aspects of it as a translation of the way of the Cross and as making intelligible the deeper meaning of vicarious and redemptive suffering. Speaking of his experience of being with Gandhi at his historic fast in Delhi, Andrews writes:

Instinctively my gaze turned back to the frail, wasted tortured spirit on the terrace by my side, bearing the sins and sorrows of his people. With a rush of emotion, there came to memory the passage from the Book of Lamentations – 'Is it nothing to you, all ye that pass by? Behold and see, if there is any sorrow like unto my sorrow?' And in that hour of vision, I knew more deeply, in my own personal life, the meaning of the Cross.[111]

On the question of missionary motive and religious conversion also, C. F. Andrews was influenced by Gandhi, but without ever accepting Gandhi's position. Andrews writes in 1932:

I have longed above all else to make known what Christ Himself has made known to me ... rather through sharing with one another the joy of a religious experience than by imposing on anyone a religious dogma. ... Is not the ultimate thing needed for sharing any precious truth with another person just this – to keep the inner light in one's own soul so pure that the truth shines through with its own radiance? No truth worth knowing can ever be taught; it can only be lived.[112]

This is very much in the line of Gandhi's comparison of the aroma of spiritual truth to the scent of the rose. But there is on record a dialogue between Andrews and Gandhi on conversion which took place in 1936, when Andrews says to Gandhi that, though he has discarded long ago the position that there is no salvation except through Christ, on the question of conversion, he cannot 'go the whole length' with Gandhi. He is against mass conversions of the unsophisticated Harijans; and he does not accept the position that a believing Christian, however bad his life, is better than a Hindu. Then he adds:

But I do say that if a person really needs a change of faith, I should not stand in his way. . . .

If someone earnestly says that he will become a good Christian, I should say, you may become one, though you know that I have in my own life strongly dissuaded ardent enthusiasts who came to me. I said to them, 'Certainly, not on my account will you do anything of the kind.' But human nature does require a concrete faith.

And Gandhi asks Andrews to choose between the position of 'mutual toleration' and that of 'the equality of religions'.[113] His biographers clearly state that the question of conversion was 'one on which Andrews and Gandhi did not see eye to eye'. He would be against conversion from 'any other motive than that of genuine religious experience and conviction'. But when these existed, 'he would not and did not deny' people their right to change their religion; 'and men who had learned of Christ from him did from time to time, with his knowledge and support, seek baptism in the Christian Church'. And they refer to a letter written to Gandhi in 1937 which defines his position clearly, in which he says:

Your . . . formula, 'All religions are equal [does] not . . . correspond with history or with my own life experience. Your declaration that a man should always remain in the faith in which he was born appeared to be not in accordance with such a dynamic subject as religion.

Of course, if conversion meant a denial of any living truth in one's own religion, then we must have nothing to do with it. But it is rather the discovery of a new and glorious truth for which one would sacrifice one's whole life. It does mean also, very often, passing from one fellowship to another, and this should never be done lightly. But if the new fellowship embodies the glorious new truth in such a way as to make it more living and cogent than the old outworn truth, then I should say to the individual, 'Go forward.'

Conversion does not imply for Andrews the denial of any religious truth in the faith one leaves. And missionary motivation is inherent in the Christian's personal experience of Christ.

Christ is for me the unique way whereby I have come to God and have found God, and I cannot help telling others about it whenever I can do so without any compulsion or undue influence. I honour Paul the apostle when he says, 'Necessity is laid upon me. Woe is me if I preach not the Gospel!' I feel that the message which Christ came into the world to proclaim is the most complete and the most inspiring that was ever given to men. That is why I am a Christian. At the same time I fully expect my friend Abdul Gaffar Khan to make known the message of the Prophet, which is to him a living truth which he cannot keep to himself.

Andrews does not think that such propagation would always lead to 'fighting as to whose "Gospel" is superior'. Christians, Hindus and Muslims must recognize the 'clear-cut distinctions' between their religions even as they see 'a precious element of goodness which we can all hold in common'. According to Andrews, along this path, we can have 'peace in religion without any compromise, syncretism or toning down of vital distinctions'.[114]

B. *E. Stanley Jones' Interpretation*

C. F. Andrews belonged to the inner circle of Gandhi's friends. Therefore his evaluation of Gandhi's theology and views of Christianity have special importance for the Indian people, especially those who have been part of the Gandhian movement in one form or another. But there were Christian evangelists who sought to understand and interpret Gandhi sympathetically from within the orthodoxy of the Christian Church, on the basis of their own personal relation with Gandhi and Gandhism. Of such E. Stanley Jones was foremost. In the introduction to his book on Gandhi he speaks of the thirty years of being at the nerve centre of the controversy between Gandhiji and the missionary on the question of conversion. But Gandhi has won him to 'a whole-hearted affection'. He says:

I am still an evangelist. I bow to Mahatma Gandhi, but I kneel at the feet of Christ and give him my full and final allegiance. And yet a little man, who fought a system in the framework of which I stand, has taught me more of the Spirit of Christ than perhaps any other man in East and West.[115]

He was a Hindu by allegiance and a Christian by affinity.... [Christianity should] not try to claim him when he himself would probably repudiate that claim. He was a Hindu and belonged to Hinduism, but nevertheless when you strip away all controversies between East and West and religion and religion, we cannot help but recognize affinities he had with the faith in Christ.... The Mahatma was a natural Christian rather than an orthodox one. And yet how shall I defend that distinction? I don't. I leave it undefended. But it is the nearest statement of the facts I know.[116]

Jones has no difficulty in characterizing the death by assassination of Gandhi as 'the greatest tragedy since the Son of God died on a cross'.

He marched into the soul of humanity in the most triumphal march that any man ever made since the death and resurrection of the Son of God.[117]

Never did a death more fittingly crown a life, save only one – the Son of God.[118]

Jones says:

The Mahatma was influenced and moulded by Christian principles, particularly the Sermon on the Mount....[119]

In the practice of those principles he discovered and lived by the person of Christ, however dimly and unconsciously....[120] But he never seemed to get to Christ as a Person.

Jones once wrote him a letter about this very question. The letter represents a sincere evangelical Christian position with respect to Gandhi and may be quoted. He says:

I thought you had grasped the centre of the Christian faith, but I am afraid I must change my mind. I think you have grasped certain principles of the Christian faith which have moulded you and have helped make you great – you have grasped the principles but you have missed the Person. ... May I suggest that you penetrate through the principles to the Person and then come back and tell us what you have found. I don't say this as a mere Christian propagandist. I say this because we need you and need the illustration you could give us if you really grasped the centre – the Person.

Gandhi's reply includes these words:

I cannot grasp the position by the intellect; the heart must be touched. Saul became Paul, not by an intellectual effort but by something touching his heart. All I can say is that my heart is absolutely open ... I want to ... see God face to face. But there I stop.[121]

And Jones comments that it is in having received such a heart-revelation of the Person of Christ that

the ordinary sincere devotee of Christ goes beyond the Mahatma....

Christ brings a certainty and joy and release from past and present sin which makes him bubble with gratitude, and which makes him want to share Christ with everybody.

Lacking this, Mahatma never understood the passion for evangelization, and considered it as an expression of lack of humility. Jones adds:

From the Mahatma's standpoint he was right, for he looked on salvation as an attainment through disciplined effort. ... If one believes that ..., it is his own.

To speak of it would therefore be an expression of pride. But salvation is different for the Christian – it is a gift of Grace.

I could talk about that, for in doing so I was laying the tribute of my love and gratitude at the feet of Another. Not to talk about it would be indelicate and would lack humility, for it would thus be your own. ... It was at this place that the Christians and the Mahatma never got together, ... never understood each other.

And, probably with Gandhi's ideas about cheap forgiveness in mind, Jones adds:

I know that salvation by Grace seems too cheap and easy, but it is not cheap; for when you take the gift you belong for ever to the Giver.[122]

Jones admits that Christians should 'take very seriously the rose perfume emphasis [of Gandhi] as a corrective', but to rule out the evangelism of lips is 'onesided and unnatural'. Jesus lived the Gospel, but also commended it in words. 'It was all of a piece'.

According to Jones, when Gandhi spoke of equality of religions he made it clear that he was speaking only of 'the principal faiths of the world', or 'the great religions.'

But the moment he did that, he gave away his case, for he introduced a distinction. If this distinction holds at one level why shouldn't it hold all the way through? ... Are we to mentally abdicate when it comes to the deepest choices of life?

To the point that this would involve 'an unholy rivalry' among religions, Jones points out, that he does not conceive of the Gospel of Christ as a religion at all.

Religions are men's search for God. ... There are many religions; there is but one Gospel. . . . A religion was built around Jesus, . . . but the Gospel confronts that man-made and fallible system with the same demand and offer as it does other religions. . . . Our message is not the system, but the Saviour. He is the Gospel. The Gospel lies in His Person. He himself is the Good News.[123]

Jones speaks of Gandhi's opposition to mass conversion of the depressed classes. In this he sees religious reasons mixed with Gandhi's fear of the consequent weakening of the integrity of Indian society, culture and political nationalism. And he wants Christians to rid Indian nationalists of the fear of denationalization and superficial westernization through conversion. And he relates an interview in which he shows Gandhi himself accepting the right to conversion when these fears are taken away. Stanley Jones with two Indian Christian leaders, the Rev. S. Aldis and Principal D. G. Moses, met Gandhi at Wardha and said something like this to him:

Suppose a man should be inwardly convinced that Christ is the One to whom he should give his allegiance. He needn't change his dress or his name; he could stand in the stream of India's culture and life and interpret Christ in a framework of India's heritage. If you will allow such a man to stay in his home without disability as an open, baptised member of the Christian Church, then as far as some of us are concerned – and I think I represent the leading Indian Christians in this – we are willing to see the Christian community as a separate political entity fade out, leaving a moral and spiritual and social entity, the Christian Church, to contribute its power to India's uplift and redemption.

Jones reports that the Mahatma replied that not only he would keep his son 'a member of his home without penalty or disability' if he became a Christian under such conditions, but also that on that basis 'most of the objections to Christianity would fade out of the mind of India'. When the interview was published there was a retraction issued, 'with or without the Mahatma's knowledge and consent', but Jones concludes:

I am persuaded that this did represent the Mahatma's mind, for it was sincerely and straightforwardly said without hesitation.[124]

In all this, for Jones as an evangelist, 'Christ and His Kingdom is the issue'. He says to India:

Take Him direct. You don't have to take our interpretation of Christ, except as you find it helpful in forming your own. . . . Christ is Universal, but he uses local forms to express that universality. We expect you in India, out of your rich cultural and religious past, to bring to the interpretation of the Universal Christ something which will greatly enrich the total expression. Especially now that Mahatma Gandhi has lived and died we think you can interpret Christ in terms in which we are lacking in the West. It will take the sons of men to interpret the Son of Man.[125]

The last part of the above quotation comes out of Jones' conviction that Mahatma Gandhi has created a soil in India conducive to an Indian interpretation of Christ. No doubt Gandhi did not see the Cross as divine action for the atonement of the sins of mankind. But as Jones also says:

Never in human history has so much light been shed on the Cross, as has been through this one man and that man not even called a Christian. Had not our Christianity been vitiated by our identification with un-Christian attitudes and policies in public and private life, we would have seen at once the kinship between Gandhi's method and the Cross. Non-Christians saw it instinctively.[126]

He agrees with the *Indian Social Reformer* that Gandhi has 'turned India's face to Christ and the Cross'. In his opinion, Gandhi calls not only India but the whole world, including the Christian world, to the Cross.[127]

c. Paul D. Devanandan on Gandhi's Critique

Among the Indian Christian theologians Dr Paul D. Devanandan has dealt with Gandhi's views of Jesus Christ, Christianity and the Bible in several of his writings. Perhaps the most systematic is an article entitled 'Gandhi's Critique of Christianity', which is a review of the small collection of Gandhi's writings published under the title *What Jesus Means to Me*.[128] According to Devanandan, the pamphlet makes clear that 'the Mahatma encountered sincere and serious difficulty in understanding the Christian position'. He mentions several of Mahatma's difficulties.

The first was the close relation of Christianity with Western culture and the consequent denationalization of Indian Christians. Devanandan says that denationalization was 'more true of Indian Christians who belonged to his (Gandhi's) generation than ours'.

The charge continues even today, though usually without facts. The rethinking within the Church in India has led to a deliberate effort 'not only to dissociate Christianity from Western culture but also to indicate that the faith of the Christian transcends all cultures'. It may be that the charge persists because many Hindus think that being 'culturally an Indian' should mean, 'culturally a Hindu'. Devanandan says,

There is some such thing as Indian culture which has evolved in the process of these many centuries of our history as a result of a fusion of many strains of cultural heritage. The heritage should be distinguished from social practices and cultural values enforced by religious sanction which are apparently Hindu by belief and practice.[129]

The situation is complicated by the secularization of culture, which dissociates cultural institutions from all religions to further modernization of life, and breaks up all religious cultures to reintegrate them on a new basis. There is further the tendency of the majority religion to 'give a Hindu religious bias to our culture'. He says:

Plans for national integration should not impose upon these [religious] minorities the heavy price of sacrificing, much less denying, their religious convictions in order to accept cultural institutions and values which are distinctively Hindu.

With these qualifications of what is meant by being Indian, Devanandan asks Indian Christians to take to heart Gandhi's plea that 'conversion must not mean denationalization', but rather 'a life of greater dedication to one's own country'.[130]

On the question of proselytization and Christian evangelism, Devanandan notes the many reasons behind Gandhi's objection to the Christian enterprise in India. He suspected, first, that numerical expansion by the Christian Church would mean that a number of people were lost to the nation; they would become, as it were, tools of the Western colonial power; second, that the methods of the Christian evangelist were questionable; third, that conversion produces no 'real change of character in the inner life', and fourth, that it destroys the stability of the social superstructure. Devanandan says that 'for a very long time Christian evangelists themselves have been giving much thought to these very issues'. As for 'mass conversion', Devanandan points out that it came into being at the initiative not of missionary evangelists but of the unprivileged groups who felt they could not overcome their disabilities from within the larger social structure of caste in Hinduism, and 'wanted to become members of the Church as groups', as they could then 'carry over into their new life their characteristic traditional institutions, social organizations and group loyalties'. The evangelists knew well that group conversion was only 'the beginning of a process of change' requiring, for its culmination in a deep religious experience, 'adequate instruction and pastoral care' which perhaps were not always given. Nevertheless it remains true that many of the present Indian Christian leaders who are making no mean contribution to the nation are 'in most cases the third and fourth generation descendants of these very simple folk who at one time decided in groups to join the Church'. Further, the movement of mass conversion 'did in fact stab awake the social conscience of Hinduism'. Devanandan does not defend the method of group conversion, he is only pointing out historically that the decision of some groups to join the Church was not 'completely misguided and futile'.[131]

On the religious objection to Christian evangelism, Devanandan says that Christians should make clear that when they talk of 'propagation' of the Christian faith they are not thinking of 'a propaganda for the Christian religion'. In propaganda, questionable methods of persuasion and indifference to motives come in, and the intention itself is that of 'getting people to our side', which is wrong. But about the 'propagation of the Gospel' Devanandan affirms that it is 'the mission of every Christian believer', and he adds:

It is primarily to spread abroad the good news that God has initiated a movement in the history of mankind by Himself entering into this very world of want and violence, of disease and death, of human sin and wilfulness, in order that this whole realm of world-life may be transformed into a veritable new creation in which will be acknowledged the sovereignty of God. The Christian believes that in the Person and Work of Jesus Christ, God Himself has begun this process of renewing the whole creation.[132]

Propagation of the Gospel, therefore, is 'witness'. Witness is not drawing attention to the moral achievement of Christians. Witness is to what the Christian believes 'God has done and is doing, for the redemption of the world'. He continues:

Consequently the witness takes the form of a declaration of the good news, pointing to the communication of God Himself in the Person and Work of Christ, the Word made Flesh. It also takes the form of an invitation to everyone who accepts this good news to join the fellowship of those who are already persuaded in faith of the mighty acts of God in Christ Jesus.

Devanandan makes clear that this fellowship is not of the like-minded but of those who are bound by the 'common worship of God as revealed to them in Christ Jesus, conscious of an inner constraint' to proclaim the good news of God's sovereignty. The witness also takes the form of service, following the servant-Christ.

So the propagation of the Gospel, the fellowship in the Church and the ministry of service are all integral, though, to the outside observer, these three constituent elements of the Christian faith may appear to be separable and independent.[133]

On the relation between the Gospel and the religion of Christianity Devanandan makes a distinction and says:

Christianity is also one other of the many religions of mankind. But it is not as a religion that it claims the right to propagate its doctrine. Nor would it be true to say that it is as a religion among other religions that it claims to be revealed [or is preached].[134]

The Christian claims are made for the Gospel of Christ. But Devanandan goes on to point out that there is a clear distinction also between Religion and Ethics and that it is not possible to comprehend religion within ethics as Gandhi tends to do. He says:

Ethics, principles of conduct, based on standards of goodness, should not be confused with religion which concerns faith in ultimate human destiny and the eternal being of God.

No doubt, ethics is derived from religion. But it is wrong to make ethical teaching 'the standard of religion', or to compare the relation between Christianity and Hinduism by comparing 'the ethic of the Sermon on the Mount with the ethic of *nishakama karma* of the *Bhagavadgita*', and affirm that because they both have more or less the same appeal, the religions are essentially the same. This is precisely what Gandhi does. The Christian holds that

Christian ethical teaching is not to be confused with the faith of the

Christian. Therefore, the Sermon on the Mount is not the essence of the Christian faith. Nor is Jesus Christ merely an ethical teacher.... Jesus Christ, to Christian faith, is the self-disclosure of God as righteous and merciful, as just and forgiving, of God as love. Consequently the Christian faith makes central the person and work of Jesus Christ, and not the Sermon on the Mount. Its value and validity are derived. The grace of God in Jesus Christ is the enabling power which makes possible such ideal goodness as the Sermon on the Mount portrays. Its ethic of absolute love is made possible for mankind only when they have been totally transformed by the new creation in Christ.[135]

Devanandan adds that 'no Christian would deny' the presence of this enabling grace in Gandhi to the extent that he lived the Sermon on the Mount. 'To that extent Gandhi acknowledged Jesus Christ as Lord and sought to do the will of God in his life for his time', even if his faith was not that of a Christian.

Speaking of Gandhi's claiming to be 'a Christian, a Mussalman with my own interpretation of the Bible or the Koran', Devanandan admits that the study and interpretation of Scriptures other than one's own according to the spirit and standards of one's own faith is 'an enriching experience'. The Hindu has the right to interpret the Bible or the Koran from the point of view of Hindu faith, but

to maintain that, therefore, the interpretation of the Bible by the Christian or the Koran by the Muslim is distorted, inadequate and wrong would be doing violence to these men of other faiths. Such an evaluation fails to take account of the faith which conditions the approach of people to their own Scriptures.[136]

Gandhi finds difficulty in appreciating 'the true significance of the Christian Church', as he sees too many 'nominal Christians' in it. Devanandan points out that this is a problem of all religions, and the Church is constantly making efforts at renewal. Christians have never based their reason for Christian witness on their own perfection, 'but on the faith which they wish to communicate that there is a continual process of renewal of the merely human in our world, in which not only Christians but all people are involved'. That the Christian Church claims itself to be a closed community with some special privilege with God and with salvation exclusively theirs, is a misunderstanding. The Church is not a 'closed body'. He adds:

What the Christian believes about the Church is that it is essentially a fellowship of the Spirit within which there is a conscious, corporate effort to apprehend the will of God for man as declared in Jesus Christ. Therefore the emphasis in membership within the Church is placed on discipleship. . . . The invitation to join the Church, as the Christian understands it, is not extended by any human agency. It comes from God himself in the Person of Jesus Christ. . . . The Church is not only built by the Spirit of God working within it, but also by the Spirit of God working outside it.[137]

The rhythm of the life of the Church is in moving between the Church and the world; and Christians should avoid 'the danger of confusing the mere expansion of the Church with the extension of the Kingdom', though this extension requires the commitment of more and more people to the knowledge of Jesus Christ.

Should those who make this commitment to God in Christ accept baptism and join the fellowship of the local manifestation of the world-wide Church? It is not for Christians to judge the vocation for Christian witness of those who think that it is not for them. They are answerable to God, and not to Christians.

But such individual decision in response to individual experience does not however rule out the Christian claim that it is in the Fellowship of the Church that corporate witness to what God has done in Christ is made possible. That is where the rite of baptism becomes an act of public witness whereby the decision to belong in a community of the faithful is openly declared.

Christians cannot presume to judge devout souls like Gandhi 'who have deliberately decided against the claims of the Christian faith'. But they cannot be criticized for desiring 'that such extraordinary men of faith should also belong to the Church'.[138]

6. AN EVALUATION

There is universal recognition of the Christian significance of the fact of Gandhi and its challenge to Christianity in India. And because of his life and death, the meaning of suffering love has been deepened and its larger application to the struggles for political and social justice opened up for the whole world. Indeed, Martin Luther King and a great many others who are applying the technique of *satyagraha* for the humanization of structures of collective life cannot be understood apart from Gandhi. And Gandhi has made intelligible to India the idea of vicarious suffering, in a way which makes it impossible for India to return to the doctrine of Karma in its old individualistic form as the clue to the meaning of all suffering in the world. Dr A. G. Hogg has said that if there is to be a creed formulated by the Indian Church, it would be necessary to emphasize in it that Divine Justice requires unmerited suffering which is vicarious and able to bear the Karma of others.[139] And Gandhi has made such a creed possible not only for Indian Christianity but also for the Neo-Hinduism of India. And it is significant that Hogg himself in his Christmas sermon to the Meeting of the International Missionary Council at Tambaram in 1938[140] spoke of the incarnation of God as the transcendent *satyagraha* of God. This is a most telling expression to indicate the unique act of God in Jesus Christ, an expression made possible by Gandhi and the idea behind Gandhi's *satyagraha* itself.

Indeed the crucial issue in the theological debate between Christians and Gandhi is whether the historical Person of Jesus Christ is an essential part of the Christian kerygma, or whether his significance for the life of mankind was exhausted by being accepted and assimilated as the supreme symbol of the principle of redemptive love. On this issue hangs also the central question of the Christian missionary motivation. And at this point, even so close a Christian friend as C. F. Andrews had to differ radically from Gandhi. There is an either/or decision which is to be taken between the orthodox and Gandhian approaches to catholicity, one which bases itself ultimately on the principles of the Sermon on the Mount, and the other which bases itself on the Person of Christ as the divine deed of reconciliation between God and man and among men, to whichever living religions and secular faiths they belong.

It seems to us that Gandhi's identification of the soul with the pure essential self and the body as the source of all evil, makes him look on knowledge of moral principles and the spiritual effort to achieve them against the lust of the body as the path to salvation. And as such, it is a self-sufficient path. But in this approach Gandhi does not see the dimension of the self that transcends body and soul and is able to utilize moral idealism and spiritual efforts for the ends of self-interest and self-righteousness. And it is here that Gandhi cannot comprehend the Christian idea that the spirituality of the moral man seeking his own righteousness in works is the essence of sin and that not more moral principles but divine forgiveness is the only answer to it. Lacking the awareness of this dimension of sin and the need of divine forgiveness, Gandhi does not move through the principles to the Person. Probably the basic theological issue in the debate between Gandhism and Christianity lies precisely in the concept of human selfhood. The Christian message of the centrality of the divine act in the Person of Christ for reconciliation stands or falls with its view of the tragedy inherent in man's pursuit of a righteousness of the law, and of the need of divine initiative from beyond the tragedy. This does not mean that Christianity should set Christian principles and the Person of Christ in opposition to one another, but rather seek to move through the principles to the Person. Indeed one of the most important tasks of the Church is to reconstruct the Gandhian insights about the ethics of Christ within the framework of its doctrine of redemption in Christ.

This does not rule out the necessity for thinking through the question of the implications of conversion to Christ for the relation between Christianity and Hinduism, as religions. Does conversion to Christ mean conversion to Christianity as it is organized and expressed today? or could it find expression in a new form of Christianity indigenous to India? and could this indigenous form be considered as having a vital relation to Hinduism not only as the major cultural stream of India, but also as the major religion of the country? Gandhi's challenge to Christianity remains, not perhaps at the level of conformity to Gandhian theology as S. K. George sees it, but at the other level of exploring the fuller meaning of the ethics of the Sermon on the Mount for an Indian understanding of God's reconciliation of the world with himself in the Person of Jesus Christ, and of the idea of the Church as the witness to him among the religious communities and secular ideologies of India.

NOTES

1 Mahatma Gandhi, *My Experiments with Truth*, London, ed. of 1945, p. 404.
2 *Harijan*, 25 May 1935.   3 *Ib.*, 23 March 1940.
4 C. F. Andrews, *Mahatma Gandhi's Ideas*, London, 1929, p. 34.
5 E. Stanley Jones, *Mahatma Gandhi: an Interpretation*, London, 1948, p. 112.

6 Quoted in M. K. Gandhi, *The Law of Love*, ed. Anand T. Hirigorami, Bombay, 1962, p. 86.
7 *Ib.*, p. 27, quoting *Yervade Mandir* ch II.
8 Andrews, *op. cit.*, p. 134.
9 *Harijan*, 26 September 1936.
10 *Ib.*, 11 August 1940.
11 *Ib.*, 8 October 1938.
12 *Ib.*, 14 March 1936.
13 *Young India*, 24 June 1926.
14 *The Law of Love*, pp. 38, 35.
15 *Ib.*, p. 26.
16 *Young India*, 4 November 1926.
17 Andrews, *op. cit.*, p. 120.
18 *Ib.*, p. 120.
19 *Ib.*, p. 129.
20 *Ib.*, pp. 127f.
21 *Ib.*, p. 130.
22 M. K. Gandhi, *The Message of Jesus Christ*, Bombay (cited as *Message*); *Christian Missions*, Ahmedabad, 1940 (cited as *Missions*).
23 *Message*, cover page.
24 *Ib.*, p. 2.
25 *Ib.*, p. 3.
26 *Missions* p. 28.
27 *Ib.*, p. 35.
28 *Message*, p. 35.
29 *Ib.*, preface.
30 *Ib.*, p. 7.
31 *Ib.*, p. 79.
32 *Ib.*, p. 37.
33 *Ib.*, p. 35.
34 *Ib.*, pp. 36f.
35 *Ib.*, p. 21.
36 *Ib.*, p. 5.
37 *Ib.*, p. 27.
38 *Ib.*, p. 7.
39 *Ib.*, p. 46.
40 *Ib.*, p. 8.
41 *Ib.*, p. 1.
42 *Ib.*, pp. 6f.
43 *Ib.*, p. 140.
44 *Ib.*, pp. 12, 23.
45 *Ib.*, p. 40.
46 *Ib.*, pp. 19f.
47 *Ib.*, p. 30.
48 *Missions*, p. 32.
49 *Ib.*, pp. 33f.
50 *Ib.*, p. 13.
51 *Message*, p. 12.
52 *Ib.*, p. 9.
53 *Ib.*, pp. 46, 48.
54 *Ib.*, p. 53.
55 *Ib.*, pp. 54f.
56 *Missions*, pp. 166f.
57 *Message*, p. 51.
58 *Missions*, p. 36.
59 *Message*, p. 29.
60 Andrews, *op. cit.*, p. 121.
61 *Message*, p. 34.
62 *Missions*, p. 147.
63 *Ib.*, p. 174.
64 *Message*, pp. 50f.
65 *Ib.*, pp. 28f.
66 *Missions*, p. 196.
67 *Message*, p. 32.
68 *Ib.*, p. 32.
69 *Ib.*, p. 22.
70 *Ib.*, p. 44.
71 *Ib.*, pp. 6, 13, 16.
72 *Ib.*, p. 24.
73 *Ib.*, p. 9.
74 *Ib.*, p. 22.
75 *Ib.*, p. 36.
76 *Missions*, p. 159.
77 *Message*, pp. 10f.
78 *Ib.*, p. 48.
79 *Ib.*, p. 19.
80 *Ib.*, p. 16.
81 *Ib.*, p. 16.
82 *Ib.*, pp. 15, 21.
83 *Harijan*, 28 September 1935.
84 *Missions*, pp. 74–8.
85 K. K. Chandy, S. Gnanaprakasam, S. Jesudason, M. P. Job, G. Joseph, K. I. Mathai, A. A. Paul, S. E. Ranganathan, A. N. Sudarsinam, O. F. E. Zachariah, D. M. Devasahayam and G. Y. Martin.
86 *Harijan*, 3 April 1937, pp. 129–37.
87 J. C. Kumarappa, *The Practice and Precepts of Jesus*, Ahmedabad, 1945.
88 S. K. George, *Gandhi's Challenge to Christianity*, Ahmedabad, 1960, p. xiv.
89 *Ib.*, p. xv.
90 *Ib.*, pp. xvii f.
91 *Ib.*, p. 10.
92 *Ib.*, pp. 23, 29.
93 *Ib.*, p. 36.
94 *Ib.*, pp. 38–40.
95 *Ib.*, pp. 47–9.
96 *Ib.*, p. 81.
97 C. F. Andrews, *What I Owe to Christ*, London, 1932, pp. 103f.
98 B. Chaturvedi and M. Sykes, *Charles Freer Andrews: a Narrative*, London, 1949, p. 84.

99 *Ib.*, p. 102.
100 *Ib.*, p. 107.
101 *Mahatma Gandhi's Ideas*, pp. 37, 42.
102 *Ib.*, pp. 111f.
103 *Ib.*, pp. 337f.
104 *Ib.*, p. 344.
105 *Ib.*, pp. 341f.
106 *Ib.*, pp. 185–7.
107 *Ib.*, p. 343.
108 *Ib.*, pp. 252f.
109 Chaturvedi and Sykes, *op. cit.*, pp. 177f.
110 *Ib.*, p. 235.
111 Andrews, *Mahatma Gandhi's Ideas*, p. 314.
112 Chaturvedi and Sykes, *op. cit.*, p. 234.
113 *Christian Missions*, pp. 208–10.
114 Chaturvedi and Sykes, *op. cit.*, pp. 309f.
115 E. Stanley Jones, *Mahatma Gandhi: an Interpretation*, London, 1948, pp. 11f.
116 *Ib.*, pp. 76, 79.
117 *Ib.*, pp. 17, 23.
118 *Ib.*, p. 56.
119 *Ib.*, p. 80.
120 *Ib.*, p. 105.
121 *Ib.*, pp. 80f.
122 *Ib.*, p. 82.
123 *Ib.*, pp. 83–5.
124 *Ib.*, pp. 88f.
125 *Ib.*, p. 85.
126 *Ib.*, p. 137.
127 *Ib.*, pp. 194–205.
128 P. D. Devanandan, 'Gandhi's Critique of Christianity', *Preparation for Dialogue*, Bangalore, 1964, pp. 97–119, reviewing *What Jesus Means to Me*, Ahmedabad.
129 *Op. cit.*, pp. 98f.
130 *Ib.*, pp. 100f.
131 *Ib.*, pp. 101–3.
132 *Ib.*, p. 105.
133 *Ib.*, pp. 106f.
134 *Ib.*, pp. 107, 114.
135 *Ib.*, pp. 109f.
136 *Ib.*, p. 113.
137 *Ib.*, pp. 115–17.
138 *Ib.*, p. 118.
139 A. G. Hogg, *The Christian Message to the Hindu*, London, 1947, pp. 75f.
140 International Missionary Council, *Tambaram Series*, London, 1939; vol. 7, *Addresses and Other Records*, p. 136.

CHAPTER NINE

The Theology of National Renaissance

The impact of the West on Indian life and thought and the awakening of the Indian people to a new nationalism are two events of great historical significance very closely related – in some ways as cause and effect. The Christian missions corresponded with the period and spirit of Western imperial expansion in India; and they were fully involved in the Western cultural and spiritual penetration of India by becoming the main agency of Western education. It was the elite oriented to Western education who became the leaders of India's national awakening. It found expression in the organization of the National Congress and its aspirations for political freedom and national community. In this context the Christian missions and Churches were faced with a new reality, with implications for religion, society and politics.

Many missionary theologians have sought to interpret the Western impact and the national awakening in the light of the Christian faith. Of those who sought a theological interpretation of the Western impact on India, the educational missionaries, Alexander Duff, John Wilson and William Miller were foremost. And of the missionary interpreters of Indian nationalism in the first decades of the twentieth century probably the names of Farquhar, Bernard Lucas and C. F. Andrews stand at the top of the list. Some of the Indian Christian leaders shared deeply the spirit of the national awakening; and though they have not systematized the manner in which they related their Christian faith to nationalism, they have left behind fragments of their thinking on the question. We have already seen the fragments of thought of Brahmobandhav Upadhyaya. Others were laymen like S. K. Rudra, S. K. Datta, K. T. Paul and the Kumarappas and Christian ministers like Bishop Azariah. They have not attempted a systematic exposition of the theological foundations of a Christian nationalism and indigenous Christianity. But they were Christians responding positively to the national renaissance, in their lay and spiritual vocations, for avowedly Christian reasons. They have left fragments of their theological reasoning, in their efforts to explain the attitudes and actions to Christians and men of other faiths. The phrase 'Christian nationalism' was used by K. T. Paul in an address on the Christian approach not only to the political aspect of the national awakening but to the stirrings, social and spiritual as well as political, represented by nationalism. It is in this total sense that it is used here. Thus the theology of nationalism involves the theology of politics, society, culture and even religion.

I. THE IDEA OF DIVINE PROVIDENCE

From Rammohan Roy onwards up to Gopala Krishna Gokhale, there has been a long line of prophets and leaders of Indian nationalism, who have considered the British connection with India as having taken place under the design of Providence. H. C. E. Zacharias in his study of the Indian renaissance from Rammohan Roy to Mahatma Gandhi says that though Rammohan Roy might have preferred the political institutions of France to that of England, as a better expression of Democracy, 'at all events he considered British rule in India as due to a dispensation of Providence'.[1] The same thought occurs in the writings and speeches of many leaders of the Indian National Congress in the early period. Perhaps it finds its classical expression in the Preamble to the Constitution of the Servants of India Society, founded by Gokhale. It runs thus:

[The Society's] members frankly accept the British connection, as ordained, in the inscrutable dispensation of Providence, for India's good.[2]

Gokhale had continued to defend this article of faith even after the emergence of Tilak's more militant nationalism. In 1907, in a discussion about it, Gokhale reaffirmed his faith. Nevinson reports him as saying:

The dispensations of Providence were inscrutable but still he believed the British connection was ordained for India's good. Above all, it had instilled into the Indian nature a love of freedom and self-assertion against authority that Indians used to lack.³

The British connection is seen as providential in that it brought about an awakening of the spirit of 'freedom and self-assertion' in India. Evidently there was a great deal of substance in the criticism from the side of the extremists among nationalists that Gokhale's idea of Providence did work as a sort of historicism, involving a fatalistic surrender to the inevitabilities of history. It is possible that the traditional fatalism has played a part in the formation of the idea. But it was Pheroz Mehta who contended in one of his addresses to the Indian National Congress that the idea must be considered an 'active fatalism' which introduces an element of purpose in the interpretation of history. Ranade had given the best expression to it in a passage in which he speaks of the purpose of God at work in the history of the Indian people:

If the miraculous preservation of a few thousand Jews had a purpose, this more miraculous preservation of one fifth of the human race is not due to mere chance. We are under the severe discipline of a high purpose.

And the same purpose operates in the awakening to new virtues:

the love of municipal freedom, . . . the exercise of virtues necessary for civil life, . . . aptitudes of mechanical skill, . . . the love of science and research, . . . the love of daring and adventurous discovery, . . . the resolution to master difficulties, and . . . the chivalrous respect for womankind. . . . The Christian civilization which came to India from the West was the main instrument of renewal.⁴

Indeed, many missionaries had from the very beginning shared this idea of the providential character of British rule over India. It was crudely put by Alexander Duff, but became more refined and in C. F. Andrews; it became the basis of his active support of Indian nationalism. Duff was thinking primarily in terms of what British rule in India would mean for the Western mission of civilizing and evangelizing the world in his generation when he said:

And can it be, that Britain, the most central kingdom of the habitable world – in as much as of all existing capitals, its metropolis is that which would form the centre of the largest hemisphere tenanted by man – Britain the most highly favoured with the light and life of Revelation – Britain the most signally privileged with the ability and the will and the varied facilities for dispensing blessings among the nations: can it be without a reference to the grand designs of Providence and of grace that Britain, so circumstanced and endowed, has in a way so unparallelled, been led to assume the sovereignty of India? India, that occupies the same commanding position in relation to the densely peopled regions of Southern and Eastern Asia that Palestine does to the Old World; and Britain, to both Old and New? – India which – itself containing a *fifth* of the world's inhabitants – when once thrown open, may thus become a door of access to *two-fifths* more? – India which, when once lighted up by the lamp of salvation, may become a spiritual pharos, to illume more than half the population of the globe? No: it cannot be.[5]

Similar sentiments were later expressed by W. Miller also.[6] It was more or less the same idea of Providence which C. F. Andrews saw in British rule, but he was particularly aware of the part it played in the awakening of educated India, and in the emergence of the 'ideal of Indian nationality'. He says:

In the dry light of history it seems almost certain that the only method by which Western thought could enter India was that of conquest. Reform from within had become impossible and a strong external hand was needed to weld together again the broken fragments of a nation. ... Already educated India is tingling with new life. ... Thought and literature also are experiencing the beginning of a renaissance.[7]

Andrews did not find any 'direct and final antagonism between Indian nationalism and British raj'. Indian nationalism was the fruit of Western political and cultural impact made possible by the British raj. Andrews saw a continuity between the history of British raj and that of Indian nationalism, and interpreted the whole of that history, including nationalism, within the framework of divine Providence. It is this line which Indian Christian leaders followed.

It is hardly necessary to say that Andrews was an exception; the more common missionary line of thought was to see a direct and final antagonism between Indian nationalism and the British raj and to interpret Indian nationalism as set against the providential design of God in establishing the British raj. This was so because most of them defined Providence in more static than dynamic terms, and considered an ordered legal framework for Christian evangelism rather than scope for the creativeness of human freedom as the basic function of Providence. Indeed, later, the Metropolitan of

India, in a controversy with J. C. Kumarappa and S. K. George, considered British rule in India as part of the natural order and its law, to defy which was against the ordering of Providence.[8] This is always the danger when Providence is sought to be understood in terms of natural law or the order of creation rather than in the light of the Gospel of the New Creation in Christ. When Indian nationalism is seen within such a static framework of Providence, it too lacks the capacity for self-criticism and judgment and becomes national idolatry. But many of the Indian Christian leaders scrupulously avoided this danger by interpreting divine Providence within the dynamic framework of the divine acts of judgment and redemption as revealed in Jesus Christ.

K. T. Paul has given his approach to Indian nationalism in an address he delivered at a public meeting arranged on the occasion of the All-India Christian Conference in Cuttack in 1919. The question he faces frankly is 'whether Nationalism can be consistent with the Spirit of Christ' especially when nationalism has shown itself in the West to be aggressive and idolatrous and 'opposed to the Spirit of Christ'. He starts with the idea of the divine Providence in history and seeks a place for nations in general and the British Indian connection in particular, speaks of the potentiality of enhanced creativeness and destructiveness present in Indian nationalism which gives the Christian Church its mission in relation to nationalism. He expounds the status of nations and international relations within the design of Providence thus:

... The history of mankind cannot be read from a theological viewpoint without discerning the inscrutable wisdom of Infinite Providence. It was in His design that nations should emerge in the course of human evolution, should at a later stage so freely intermingle as to teach and help one another and to advance the race towards its goal of perfection. What wonder if in such an immensely complicated process drawn out over thousands of generations there should be failures and conflicts, even Armageddons and revolutions? ...

The possibility of failure is the one condition of virility in success. Such is God's own method of nature. The process is costly involving suffering which sometimes falls on the undeserved. We cannot enter into the metaphysics of that side issue. The main fact is that in the 'one increasing purpose' of God for mankind, Nationalism has a designed place of necessity.[9]

And on the specific question of the British connection with India which has stimulated a national renaissance at all levels in India, he says:

To the student of history, accustomed to discern in the great course of human events the loving touch of the God and Father of Jesus Christ, it is an inscrutable fact that, in the fullness of time, there came about the contact of India with Western culture, and not without significance the introduction of the contact entrusted to the peculiar people of Britain.

Here of course, he knows he is in line with the 'explicit creed of the Servants of India Society and of more than one political party in India. Isolation thus is inconsistent with faith.' Such an idea of the providential character of the British Indian relations and the emerging Indian nationalism makes the task of the Christian nationalist 'doubly onerous' because of its potentiality for good and evil.

He has to bring out of the stores of God things both old and new. The stores of God are in India and the West. The old he has to bring out of the former and the new from the latter. In both places there is much rubbish, which are not God's gifts but the deceptive creations of the Enemy, who is the beast in man. To select with faith in both places, to denouce with courage in regard to both traditions, to be single-minded over the purity of the ideals of Christ, that is the responsiblity of the Christian Nationalist.

In this process of selection and reinterpretation, 'there shall be severely excluded all elements which are not consonant with the Spirit of Christ'. In the light of such a 'searching criterion' the benefits of the meeting of Britain and India are not all onesided.

[Britain should] realize equally with India the full implications of the 'providential arrangement' of the ultimate contact ... There are forces embedded in Indian personality and treasures enshrined in Indian culture, which are waiting to be tapped by the seeker after better things.

There are in India 'certain valuations of things and events which are more approximate to the mind of Christ than what obtains in corresponding matters among nations who have borne the name of His religion'. This makes the Christian nationalist 'enthusiastic in his patriotism'.

For while he realizes that there is much within that is clearly inconsistent with the Spirit of Christ and that it must be rooted out, he rejoices to realize that the main fact remains that India has also been under the guidance of the Eternal Father of Mankind, has been disciplined in particular ways for His purpose of love, and that his clear joy and responsibility is to discern His present processes in her affairs and to direct his own life and service in consonance with them.[10]

H. C. E. Zacharias from a Catholic point of view also follows Gokhale:

With my great master Gokhale I . . . hold that India's linked destiny with Britain is ordained by Providence for India's good.[11]

He is using this idea as an argument against the militant nationalism which asked for *Purna Swaraj* in the sense of 'an India absolutely independent and therefore absolutely isolated'. Of course, *Purna Swaraj* has since been defined without meaning the absolute isolation Zachariah criticizes. It is evident however that the idea of Providence redefined within the framework of the Christian understanding of 'India's good' has been a criterion for a Christian critique of British and Indian political ideologies as they operated in India.

2. PRAEPARATIO EVANGELICA

What impelled the educational missionaries in building in India institutions of higher education on Western lines was the theological conviction that Western culture was a real preparation for the Gospel of Christ. Perhaps some of the noted British Civil Servants who supported the introduction of the system of English education for India were also guided by a similar conviction. William Miller of Madras Christian College has put this conviction as follows:

Let it be remembered . . . that from schools where Western thought and English literature are studied, whether those in the hands of the Government or the many others on a non-religious base, the exclusion of the Christian element cannot be complete. Very largely, especially when contrasted with the tendencies which prevail in Hinduism, European thought is Christian thought. . . . If Christian institutions . . . stood foremost, or among the foremost, especially if one of them should come to be accepted as the representative organ of Western thought, as the highest model of what a school of Western learning ought to be, there was hope that the whole new movement might be prepared by it to recognize the supply of all its spiritual wants in Him who, even when they know it not, is in some sense 'the desire of all nations'.[12]

This was because Miller saw the 'revelation of love' in Christ as 'the key to human history and the germ of all true progress', and it was therefore legitimate to consider the relation between the Scriptures and Western learning as between 'the spearhead' and the well-fitted handle'.

The Scriptures were to be the spearhead, all other knowledge the well-fitted handle. The Scriptures were to be the healing essence, all other knowledge the congenial medium through which it is conveyed.[13]

The idea of Western-oriented education as a *praeparatio evangelica* for India was first expressed, according to Miller, in a sermon preached by Dr Inglis in Edinburgh in 1818.[14] Duff, of course, was the pioneer in India. He has explained the idea of *praeparatio evangelica* in his own way. After quoting in detail examples of this idea from biblical and church history he asks:

Judging from these and other similar analogies, must we not naturally expect a process of *preparation* in a country like India? And what mightier engine of preparation can there be than an enlarged system of Christian education instituted to rear teachers and preachers? By it the abomination of idolatry must be consumed; and the subtleties of pantheism must be identified with the age of presumptuous ignorance. The minds of hundreds and thousands will be surcharged with the elements of change. Even when no direct conversion ensues, much of the spirit and influences of Christianity will cleave to the rightly educated youth, whatever may be their future situation in life.[15]

Note in Duff's statement the attitude to Hinduism inherent in his approach. He considered it as a vast system of evil, preventing people from seeing the truth of progress and the Gospel. And the object of education in Western learning was in Duff's own words 'the preparation of a mine' and the 'setting of a train' which would one day 'explode and tear up' Hinduism from the 'lowest depths'.[16] Lord Macaulay probably had the same negative approach to Hindu culture and religion, as is evident from his expectation to destroy Hindu idolatry within a generation, through Western education. It may not be correct to consider them as fully representing the ideas of all educational missionaries and Christian British administrators. But we are dealing with types of theological thinking regarding the status of Western culture and Hinduism *vis-à-vis* the Gospel.

The further religious history of India did not prove the theory of the educational missionaries that the Western learning would prepare the way for educated India to accept Jesus Christ. There were two trends which worked to make for greater resistance to the Gospel. The first was the trend toward materialism and rationalism among the Western educated. The second was the trend toward the resurgence of Hinduism with assimilation of Western culture, but with greater resistance against Christianity. The Lindsay Commission, reporting on Christian Higher Education in 1931, was to notice these trends; they observe:

The result [of Western learning] has not been that the light has shone over India in the manner in which apparently Dr Miller anticipated that it would.... The *praeparatio evangelica* which was effective for the Hinduism of 1830 and even of Dr Miller's time is not what is wanted for the Hinduism or indeed for the India of today. No one now can think of Western learning in itself as being the needed *praeparatio evangelica*.... What is the modern equivalent of that early *praeparatio evangelica*?[17]

But we have jumped to 1931. We must go back to the first decade of this century.

What the early educational missionaries had in mind as their goal was the total displacement of Hindu culture and religion and their substitution by Western culture and Christian religion. C. F. Andrews among the educational missionaries and Arthur Mayhew among the Christian-oriented educational administrators were typical of the sea change taking place in the theological climate by the early decades of the twentieth century. Adhering to the same interpretation of Western culture as a *praeparatio evangelica*, they advocated in the place of the policy of substitution of Hindu culture by Western, a policy of Christian assimilation. In his *Education of India* Mayhew's personal view is that 'moral progress in India depends on the general transformation of education by explicit recognition of the Spirit of Christ'; but he argues that it is only when the educated India is helped not to discard or compartmentalize his indigenous traditions, but to reinterpret them in the light of the scientific approach and values of Western culture, that the proper indigenous cultural foundations of new life will be laid. Andrews summarized Duff's principle thus:

Christianity is not a mere skeleton of abstract doctrines, but a living spirit clothed in flesh and blood. Christian civilisation is in one sense the embodiment of the Christian faith, and this Christian civilisation must be given to India, as well as the Christian message, if the message is to become intelligible. English education, which expresses that civilisation, is not a mere secular thing, but steeped in the Christian religion. . . . When English subjects are taken up by Hindus, they cease to be secular, for they contain Christian ideas. Even Western science, when taught with sympathy and understanding, may be to Hindus a true *praeparatio evangelica*.

Andrews adds a comment and a correction:

Theologically stated this truth which Duff grasped is part of the belief in Christ as the Eternal Word, the Light as well as the Life of men. On one side Duff's conception needed subsequent modification. He looked forward to the supplanting of one civilisation by another, the uprooting of the Indian civilisation and the substitution of the English. We have learnt since his day that the problem is one of assimilation, rather than of substitution. The mistake, as we shall see later, was a mistake of the early Victorian age, and was shared by Macaulay from a political point of view. Nevertheless, in spite of his limitations, Duff grasped the primary truth in a measure sufficient for his age, so as to give to events a right impetus and direction. It remains for our age to apply the further truth of Christian assimilation.

A little later he says:

To neglect the past of India is to fail to utilise the deepest springs of Indian national life. The idea of Anglicising over three hundred million people scattered in thousands of villages needs only to be stated to reveal its inherent impossibility.

More than these pragmatic considerations his fuller understanding of Christ as 'the Eternal Word, the Light as well as the Life of men', made him see the transcendence of Christ over all cultures and the presence of Christ as Judge and Redeemer in all cultures.

The . . . aim . . . is now [that] the wealth of English literature, science and culture . . . is . . . grafted on to the original stock; it is no longer taught in a kind of vacuum without reference to the background of Indian thought and experience.[18]

The movements of Hinduism assimilating Western values and Christian ideals within its own life and spirit, and of Christianity in India taking root in the indigenous culture and expressing Christian faith and devotion in the life-forms and thought-forms of Hinduism acquired a new significance for Andrews. He still considered the Western culture which has been informed by the Gospel for a long stretch of time to be a preparation for the Gospel. But it is to be discerned not in its attempt to supplant indigenous culture, but in producing the reform movements within Hinduism and Islam expressing positive response to the Christian values and truths embedded in Western culture. Thus not Western culture as such, but the national cultural awakening which its impact has produced is the preparation for the Gospel. He says:

The growth of new national life which is now appearing is due ultimately to the planting of the Christian seed in the rich and fertile soil of India more than a century ago. . . . It is possible of course to deny the Christian leaven which has been so manifestly working and call the great movements of the new spirit fortuitous or inexplicable; but no one could do this who has really grasped the full significance of the incarnation, and believes that Jesus is indeed the Son of Man. Movements of the human heart which are so deep and vast cannot be without supreme religious significance to the believer in Him who is the 'Light that lighteneth every man coming into the world'.[19]

It is possible to see the history of the impact of Western culture and India's positive response in the indigenous cultural awakening as one continuum. The radical break with Indian traditional culture and religions is not necessary because Christ the Eternal Word has been at work preparing for his coming in India. Andrews says again:

We may surely believe that the Eternal Word was the light of the Buddha and Tulsi Das in their measure, even as He was, in so much greater a degree, the light of the Hebrew Prophets; that Hinduism in its higher religious history was a true *praeparatio evangelica*, even though in its lower forms it has sometimes proved unspeakably degrading.[20]

Incidentally, Principal S. K. Rudra, who influenced Andrews' thinking a great deal, addressing a Convention of Religions, held in Allahabad in January 1911, on 'The Christian Idea of the Incarnation' spoke of the traditional Hindu speculations regarding the relation between the conditioned and the unconditioned being, and the traditional Hindu attempts at explaining the conditioned human existence. He added:

> To my Indian way of looking at things in the light of Christianity there could not have been a better *praeparatio evangelica*, a nobler preparation for the Gospel, than this thought of my country. I for my part, as a Christian, feel that I owe a boundless debt of gratitude to these giant ancient thinkers of India.[21]

Here Hinduism in its higher reaches is seen as in itself a preparation for the Gospel.

On the whole Indian Christian thinking follows more or less the pattern of interpreting the social and cultural awakening associated with Indian nationalism as springing from the seed of the Gospel latent within Western culture and visible in the Western missionary enterprise, and in turn preparing the soil of India for the Gospel of Christ. H. C. Zacharias, a Catholic member of the Servants of India Society, writing of Devadhar, Karve, Gokhale, Ranade and other leaders of social reform associated with renascent India, has said that it is impossible for a Catholic not to be

> profoundly touched by the deep religious fervour which shines through it all, and by the pathos of this groping, as in semi-darkness, after the Light which enlighteneth every man, but which to them remains 'the Unknown God'.

He sees in the self-revelations of the heart of the Hindu reformers

> the religious element, the hunger and thirst after righteousness, the willingness to suffer persecution for justice's sake, the doing of things in accordance with and on account of the designs of God, who loves mercy and truth and justice. . . . That religious element . . . exists even in those men who have deliberately shed all religious belief and who have become atheists: for this class is also met with among these Indian Reformers, some of whom are ardent Rationalists or, to use a technical term which is more accurate, Naturalists.[22]

Here we see not only renascent religion but also secularism brought within the social humanism characteristic of India's national

The Theology of National Renaissance

awakening, resulting from the Western-Christian impact. Zacharias goes further and sees them and later leaders of social and cultural awakening like Mahatma Gandhi, playing unwittingly a 'great role' in India's *praeparatio evangelica*.[23]

K. T. Paul also follows the same line of thought when he sees the Christian values of Western culture as having awakened India, through the National Movement, to Christ as the 'meaning of the inner history of Hindu culture'. Writing on the National Movement he says:

> The deeper one realises the meaning of the inner history of Hindu culture, the clearer is the conviction that the continuity of its history, in spite of the most potent adverse circumstances within and without, is because its content, as also its discipline, is derived from certain eternal verities of human life and relationship. It is this culture, so ancient, so strong in its tried strength, so distinctive, so true, and so precious as a heritage, that Western culture encountered with the spearhead of the British connection. And Western culture has done what nothing else was able to do! ... The intrinsic quality of her method of service and the essential reality of the best in her message were the supreme factors. In other words, where Western culture was at its best, that is at the standard of Christ, time and method being ancillary, she did penetrate. ... As a matter of fact, the penetration is deep and extensive; and the National Movement of India is the symptom of it. ... Thus India has been struggling to find fresh forms of expression for her soul in response to those of the impulses from the West which have been life-stirring. Here we are on sacred ground; and need much humility and reverence to discern the inwardness of the phenomena.[24]

Here is given the theological substance of Indian nationalism, namely the Christ in the Western culture awakening the Christ in the Indian culture and preparing India for the new life and the Gospel of Christ. K. T. Paul specifically points out as an illustration of his thesis the trial and conviction of Mahatma Gandhi:

> All India seemed to have become suddenly aware of the meaning of the Cross. ... [This was merely part of] a widespread process brought about by a tacit recognition of the values that are in the mind of Christ as the supreme criterion for all human conduct, public and private. It is no acceptance of Christianity, but strictly and literally a recognition of Jesus Christ as a direct untarnished expression of what is centrally real in man.

Through this process, every realm of Indian life is tested in the light of Christ's values; and 'this readjustment of values and the consequent rearrangement of action' is taking place even in the creed and cultus of Indian religions. The Indian National Movement is nothing less than 'a subtle process of national rehabilitation' in the light of 'Christ's values'.[25]

This implanting of 'ethical purpose' into the very core of the National Movement is an achievement of Mr Gandhi. . . . Mr Natarajan wrote in his *Indian Social Reformer* . . . that Mr Gandhi had in these years done more to bring Jesus Christ to India than all the missionaries had accomplished in three centuries. That was true, very true, when literally understood. But one has to reckon that Mr Gandhi himself and the entirety of the India which responded to him are the products of the National Movement, the comprehensive nature, causes and issues of which we have been trying to analyse, . . . to which . . . a thousand agencies and sufferings had contributed through a century and more. . . .

The inner meaning of what was happening was signified in a strange remark which an eminent Brahmin lawyer friend made to me at that time in the Madras Bar Library. He said, 'Christ is the only hope of Hinduism!' He did not say 'India', but 'Hinduism'. He meant it. He meant 'Hinduism to stay and go forward to further strength'.[26]

And, speaking of the prospect of India's response to the Christian message in this connection, Paul says that Indian nationalism calls for a more correct thinking about the distinction and interrelation between Christ, Christianity and Christian civilization for the disentangling of the message from religion and culture to enable it to become indigenous to the religion and culture of India and speak to the universally human.

[In the past] the religious message [was] vitiated by reason of the superior plane from which it presented as much as by its foreign flavour and concomitants. If in spite of this the Hindu has come to recognise Christ as of supreme excellence, it is because of his own heritage of spiritual experiences and religious discipline which enables him to discern what is true and great. Is it not evident that this 'recognition' of Christ is widely current among those who are outside the range of organised Christianity? And does not the Hindu make a clear distinction between Christ whom he reverences and 'Christianity', which he reserves for cold criticism, or again between 'Christianity', which he is willing to consider as one of the 'ways of life', and Western civilisation, which he loathes even when he adopts its conveniences? And in all this measure of accpetance, such as it is, is not the genuine sacrificial friendship of good men and women the one factor which above all else secures for truth its human values?[27]

3. THE GOSPEL AS A MESSAGE OF FELLOWSHIP

The Gospel of Jesus Christ is not a cult of individualistic spirituality, but is essentially a message of reconciliation of relationships, of righteousness, of right relations with God and with one another resulting in a new quality of fellowship. This has been basic to a Christian understanding of the nature of both Church and society shared by the advocates of Christian nationalism. In fact the 'Christian values' which have made their impact, through Western liberal humanism or through Christian religion, on Indian social life and its religious foundations are precisely the values associated with the idea of *koinonia* or fellowship in which men are reborn in Christ. Their approach to caste and race distinction in this connection is of paramount importance.

The Christian Church between the Portuguese period and our own day has taken different attitudes to the caste-structure. One may mention three of them. On the premise that the realm of religion is entirely separate from that of social structure and institution, the first approach leaves the whole caste-system unassailed and untouched. Advocates of this approach are to be found among foreign missionaries and Indian Christians of the Roman Catholic and evangelical persuasions, who consider Christianity primarily as a religious creed or cultus of a group or else the mystical or evangelical spiritual experience of the individual, to neither of whom the question of social structure presents itself as a problem of religion. Maintaining this religious indifference to caste structure, they are prepared to utilize caste-solidarities in order to propagate the Christian religion. Roberto de Nobili separates the spiritual law of Christ from the law of caste so as to present the religion of Christ to the high-caste Hindus. He was clearly impelled to do so by the vision of the universality of Christ and the necessity of bringing it to all races, cultus and castes. He said:

The holy spiritual law which I proclaim obliges no man to renounce his caste or to do anything incompatible with his caste-honour. This law which I proclaim has been preached in this very land by other men, Sannyasis and saints alike. Whoever maintains that this law is peculiar to the Pranguis or the Pariahs commits a great sin; for since God is Lord of all castes, His law must likewise be observed by all.[28]

Later the mass movements were based on utilizing group solidarity and structure to make converts to Christianity.

The second approach was the opposite of this, namely, to consider caste as an absolute religious and social evil of heathenism with which the Christian must radically break at the time of baptism. Of course, it was often based on an absolute identification of Christianity with Western culture and Western patterns of social behaviour; so that the convert broke with caste and entered the mission-compound society imitating Western manners and customs. This has been more or less the position of many of the Protestant missions since the nineteenth century. Richter, who on the whole accepts this position as the right one, has argued:

That the middle and higher classes of Sudras, from whom during the eighteenth century the principal influx of converts was received into the native Church, have withdrawn themselves more and more from contact with Christianity, and that the different Churches have sunk more and more to the level of Pariahs and Panchamas, is surely a consequence of the sharp opposition to caste which has prevailed since the beginning of the nineteenth century.[29]

There is a third approach which recognizes the fact of the toughness of the caste-structure, and the Christian goal of a casteless brotherhood, but is prepared to accommodate it to a certain extent in Church and society so as to give time for the ferment of the Christian fellowship to work within the caste-system, redeeming it of its evils and finally revolutionizing it more radically. Richter explains this position thus:

That the pagan caste spirit and the heathen devil of pride must be cast out is obvious; but it is very questionable whether this will really be best accomplished by tearing up social distinction by the roots and causing Brahmins, Sudras and Pariahs to meet on one level and to have intercourse one with another. . . . 'The supreme principle must be that . . . all which does not oppose the recreating energy of the gospel may remain. Above all, distinction of caste must never, especially at the Holy Sacrament, be allowed to exist within the Church. . . . Further, ordination may only be granted . . . to such as specifically promise never to allow themselves to be hindered in discharging the duties of their office through any caste differences, and also that they will especially cultivate fellowship at the Lord's Table with all Christian brethren in any case where the avoidance of such fellowship would seem to cast a slur upon their brotherly love.' – thus writes a decided friend of caste, Dr Graul, Director of the Leipzig Missionary Society. . . .[30]

There is no doubt that in this philosophy the gradualness of change has sometimes become so gradual as not to be very different from the first method of acceptance without change.

From the time of Rammohan Roy onwards, and in the heydays of Ranade and Gokhale, Gandhi and Nehru, Indian nationalism has been deeply exercised about the idea and expression of *community* in the context of the impact of Western liberalism and Christianity. They have been seeking first to fight the dominant evils of caste, its social tyranny over the individual reason and conscience, its too rigid adherence to inequality of status by birth and its immobile hierarchy, and later to fight the system itself in the name of national community; and above all they struck at the religious and spiritual roots of caste by their advocacy of radical religious reform of Hinduism. Probably no Hindu reform movement has been fully able to break with caste in practice. Such is the hold of caste on the Indian people. But many have broken with it in idea. As Sitanath Tattvabhushan has said of the persistence of caste attitudes in Brahmo Samaj,[31] it is necessary 'to mark the very broad difference [between] having caste distinctions in the very foundations of a society and having it, not in the foundations, but only in creeks and corners of the structure'. At certain periods in the history of Indian nationalism, especially under Balagangadhara Tilak, there has however been a reaction against the liberal and Christian social values as foreign and subversive of Indian religious culture and society, and nationalism has meant a total return to the traditional scheme of values. But Indian nationalism in general has not surrendered itself to such a spirit of traditionalism, though the desire to affirm continuity with past traditions has been part of the search for selfhood inherent in all nationalist ideologies.

Among the Indian Christian thinkers who have come under the influence of the New Dispensation of Keshub Chunder Sen,

Brahmobandhav Upadhyaya has advocated the integration of the caste-system into the Christian Church and the national society; and later Manilal Parekh has levelled the charge of being spiritual foreigners against Christians because they disturbed the traditional caste-system. Upadhyaya in an article 'Varna Asram or the Aryan Social Divisions'[32] criticizes Ranade for his social crusade against caste. He says:

The late-lamented Mr Ranade, in spite of his wonderful balance of judgment, favoured the reformed view more than the orthodox. In his inaugural address read before the last Social Conference held at Lahore, which is published elsewhere, not a very complimentary view has been taken of the Aryan social divisions and their growth . . . When we survey the two positions – the orthodox and the heterodox – we feel more inclined to side with the former than with the latter. The reformer's contention seems to us to be unscientific.

Any organic society requires a structure with 'marked divisions of classes and privileges'. Second,

Aryan society was during the Vedic period in its primitive vigour. The principles of differentiation . . . were working . . . till at last it was organized into one integral whole by the well-co-ordinated inter-relations of the four *varnas*.

Ranade's idea that caste is a later growth is a mistake which

arises from the current exaggerated notion of liberty and equality, which cannot tolerate the existence of a special class of men to be held before (*purohita* . . .) God as advocates of the welfare of humanity. This bias precludes them from noting the process of development which leads in every full-formed social organism to the formation of a sacerdotal hierarchy.

Thirdly, *varna asram* preserves the 'great principle of social differentiation according to vocation' which we can appreciate specially 'when all ancient landmarks are being swept away by the on-rush of competition'. It is in line with this whole approach that after becoming a Christian he should have done *prayatchita* for violation of caste and re-entered Hindu society. Against the identification of Christianity with modern Western society he was affirming the transcendence of Christian religion over society and its ability to relate itself to Indian society. But he converted the transcendence almost into a separation. His criticism of exaggerating liberty and equality to the extent of denying structure is well taken. But his defence of 'sacerdotal hierarchy' looks too much like Catholic special pleading for the society of medieval Christendom. His idea of vocation can be used more to criticize caste rather than to defend it. On the whole, Upadhyaya in spite of some good arguments in favour of a class structure of society does not make a strong case for caste, which determines status by birth. In fact, in trying to defend it, he empties Christianity of a good deal of its social ethical content.

Manilal Parekh does not come within the early period of Indian nationalism we are studying. Nevertheless, since he represents the same line of thought as Upadhyaya, in fact moving to a more radical separation between Christian spirituality and social ethic in the name of nationalism, his approach to caste may be dealt with at this point. We have already looked at the debate between him and Bishop Azariah on the significance of Keshub Chunder Sen's idea of the Hindu Church of Christ. Parekh's understanding of the Church and its relation to caste structure is expanded at length in his book *Christian Proselytism in India: a Great and Growing Menace*. His motives for writing the book are two: first, to warn the people of the danger of a 'national schism' through Christian proselytism similar to the one brought about by Islam, and second, to point out 'the distortion and perversion of the pure religion of Jesus'. Thus the book defends 'the interests of Hinduism and Indian nationalism at their highest and also those of the Kingdom of God as taught by Jesus'.[33]

Parekh shows Roberto de Nobili as 'a true missionary' because he did not disturb the caste-system in his presentation of the Gospel.

[This missionary policy] was fully in conformity with the teaching of Christ, his apostles and the Catholic Church. All these never meant the Christian religion to be a social or a political revolution, their aim being mainly to change the life of the individual from sinfulness to godliness.[34]

The 'spiritual' as contrasted with the social character of Christian salvation was expressed in the acceptance by the early Church of the system of slavery. The position of the slaves then was 'much worse than that of the Pariahs in India'; yet 'St Paul is clear on the matter and he speaks with the authority of the Holy Spirit within himself that the new doctrine, which means Christianity, did not teach social revolution'. And indeed Christianity has gone 'so far as not only to tolerate slavery for the last eighteen centuries and a half but even to buttress it with arguments drawn from the Scripture itself'. Parekh shows up the contradiction in the behaviour of American missionaries – when they were 'trying to destroy caste here, their own leaders and Bishops in their own land were upholding the system of slavery by all means in their power.' He comments: 'In this the latter may be right or wrong, a matter with which we are not concerned here.'[35] The comment is rather interesting in that it shows the total emptying of Christianity of social ethics. And Parekh later condemns the confusion created by enlarging the meaning of Christian fellowship to include not only a spiritual but also a social message. Out of this has arisen the necessity for Christians from high castes to join with outcastes not only in 'Christian fellowship but even socially'.[36]

On two points, no doubt, Parekh has a relatively strong case. First, while the Christian missions and missionaries were critical of Indian culture, they considered Christianity as identical with Europeanism in culture; Christianity has worked in India as 'the religion of the European, a kind of Europeanism which is out to destroy their [Indian] civilization and culture, race and religion. To them [Indians] to be a Christian under the circumstances is to be a traitor to their land, their culture and religion. It is a *paradharma*.' Second, while they were critical of caste structure and its inequalities and discriminations 'they remained as a group even more conservative in the regulation of relations between the British and the Indian than any body of religious or social diehards.'[37] Parekh finds fault with Western Protestant critics of caste-churches who 'conveniently forget that even they have separate churches for the white and the coloured people in America and Africa and to a large extent even in Asia itself'.

Deliberately and rejoicingly they compromise and make allowance with European culture, Western civilization and colonial imperialism, swallowing camel loads of these things, while they strain at a gnat of what they mistakenly think to be a compromise with the caste-system or Hinduism in any form.[38]

And he is also right in pointing out that the 'so-called Indian

Christian Churches' form a community among other Indian communities and 'not a Church' transcending them. All these are well put. But as with the early Church's acceptance of slavery, Parekh mentions compromises of missionaries and Indian Churches with Western culture, white racialism and religious communalism, not as showing a failure to understand properly the transcendence of the *agape* ethic or of the Church's being, but only to justify caste and Hindu denials of fellowship and to condemn their critics. Thus we see little of a social ethical content in his understanding of what he calls 'the pure religion of Jesus' and 'the Kingdom of God'. The advocates of Christian nationalism who criticized the discrimination of both caste and race and the compromises of the transcendence of the Church in relation both to Western and Indian cultures were more representative of a true idea of Christ and his Church in India.

C. F. Andrews, S. K. Datta, S. K. Rudra, K. T. Paul and Bishop Azariah reject outright the suggestion that

> an inward belief in Christ should be sufficient and such outward acts as those of Baptism and Holy Communion (wherein caste is visibly broken) should not be required [of Christians].[39]

We have already seen that Bishop Azariah also rejects it.

In *The Desire of India* S. K. Datta admits:

> The question how far the Church may tolerate the prejudices of the Hindu convert in his relation to other Christians belonging to the degraded sections of the Indian community is a perplexing one.

He speaks of the ecclesiastical recognition given to caste-distinctions in the Church by 'the missionaries of the old Danish-Halle Mission, such as Schwartz' and by Bishop Heber. He quotes Heber's report on the subject:

> With regard to the distinctions of caste as yet maintained by professing Christians, it appears they are manifested – (*a*) in desiring separate seats in Church; (*b*) in going up at different times to receive the holy communion; (*c*) in insisting on their children having different sides of the school; (*d*) in refusing to eat, drink or associate with those of a different caste.[40]

And Datta speaks of the strong stand against caste-distinction at the point of receiving the sacrament, taken by Bishop Wilson and of 'common meals' instituted by one missionary society. Some of the strong measures, he comments, were 'perhaps hasty and unwise' and he advocates instead of ecclesiastical discipline the provision of a suitable spiritual climate to fight against caste-prejudices which exist in the Church. But at one point he is quite uncompromising, namely against refusal to take the sacrament together. This paragraph is worth quoting.

In South India especially, considerable prejudice exists among Christians of the upper castes against free inter-marriage and even against eating with those of a lower caste. Similar prejudices are found even in Christian countries. For the renewal of those artificial barriers more dependence must be placed on the growth of a strong Christian sentiment than on the exercise of ecclesiastical discipline. On the other hand, the Church cannot tolerate caste distinction when the high caste Hindu refuses to partake of the sacrament with the Pariah.

But the Christian Church cannot stop there. It must press forward to enlarge the *koinonia* at the Holy Communion to the total life of the religious and social life of the Church. He says:

The danger of Christianity in India, as the present Bishop of Madras has pointed out, is 'not simply that it may perpetuate the divisions of Western Christendom but that it may add to them a hundred-fold by splitting up into an infinite number of caste churches. . . .' It will be fatal to the influence and power of Indian Christianity to have every Christian sect broken up into Brahman, Sudra and Pariah. This is the rock on which every spiritual movement in India has split.[41]

Datta however goes further to speak of the necessity that the Christian Church should work out the expression of *koinonia* in relation to India. Caste, no doubt, 'served in the past a useful purpose' as a dyke against disintegration and as a substitute for the Poor Law. But today if the 'community spirit is confined to the narrow limits of a single caste, nationality in the true sense becomes impossible'. And 'where Christianity joins issue with it is the denial which caste gives to the equality of man and to the worth of individual personality'. Nevertheless it may be possible to modify the system to make it exercise its 'enormous power' in the 'interests of morality' expressing the new social humanism.[42]

C. F. Andrews speaks of those who argue that caste 'should be treated as slavery was treated in the early Church and allowed to die a natural death within the Christian atmosphere'. To him caste is much worse than slavery.

> The analogy of slavery breaks down. . . . The slave could kneel side by side with the freeman and receive the sacrament; the caste man cannot do this while remaining in caste.

And it is his opinion that compromise with caste has been the cause of stagnation of the life and mission of the Church in India.

> The Christian Church in India, turning away from Christ, has attempted again and again to compromise with caste. The most ancient form of Christianity in India, the Syrian Church, has not been able to check its observance. The same was the case with the Jesuit missionaries of the sixteenth century. Two centuries later the early Lutheran missions allowed the same compromise to take place. Even in our own modern missions in South India caste has again and again reappeared among the converts. But wherever and whenever this has been allowed stagnation has resulted.[43]

> Caste-ridden Christianity has paralysed missionary effort. This has accounted for the unprogressive character of certain forms of Christianity [in South India].[44]

> The Church can only succeed if she refuses to harbour within her own fold those very racial and caste evils from which India is longing to be set free.[45]

She can help in the regeneration of Indian society only if she witnesses to the *koinonia* in terms of a 'a casteless brotherhood in Christ',[46] where, in St Paul's words, there cannot be Greek and Jew, circumcised and uncircumcised, barbarian, Scythian, slave, free man, but Christ is all, and in all.

In fact therein lies the social mission of the Church to the Indian nation. He says:

> Rabindranath Tagore has given us in his own words what India requires of us. 'Do we not need', he cries, 'an overwhelming influx of higher social ideals? Must we not have that greater vision of humanity which will impel us to shake off the fetters that shackle our individual life? . . .'
>
> If ever there was a claim upon the Church of Christ to come forward in the name of the Lord, it is to be found in words like these. Has she not to offer that 'influx of higher social ideals', that 'greater vision of humanity'? . . . No! She cannot succeed so long as she allows within her fold

those very racial and caste evils from which India is struggling to be free. . . .

The final victory of the Christian faith in India depends upon the spiritual power manifested in bringing about the union of the English and the Indian, as Christians; the union of the Brahmin and the Pariah, as Christians; the union of Hindu and the Musalman, as Christians; then and then only will the heart of India respond fully to the Christian message and a new Indian nation rise, enabled and strengthened to fulfil her great destiny in the world.[47]

This was written in 1910. As Chaturvedi and Sykes say, Andrews later moved further along on the question of the Christian meaning of the relation between different communities, and the phrase 'as Christians' may have changed in his mind to mean 'in Christ', but his concern for a fellowship transcending racial and caste distinctions, both in the Church and in the larger society, as an expression of witness to Christ, remained the same.

K. T. Paul as a lay leader has dealt with the Christian approach to the caste system and other aspects of traditional Indian society primarily in relation to India's struggle for a new society. His emphasis has been on social reconstruction. He has popularized the phrase 'rural reconstruction' in the YMCA and in India. He speaks of two distinguishing features of traditional *dharma* (or *Aram* as it is called in the South):

Dharma is duty and not right; it is enforced by the will of society and not by the authority of a central government. In both these particulars it differs radically from the conception of citizenship in the West. . . . The principle of *dharma* which conserved our culture through the centuries of chaos is a spiritual inheritance of infinite value.[48]

With all its faults it was a discipline of social responsibility. But much of what *dharma* secured, chiefly the social fabric, is now hopelessly broken by the impact of the Western influences. The most potent of these is of course democracy with its idea of individual rights and of individualism expressed 'not only in law and its courts but in every department of the civil administration'.[49]

Democracy is in line with those fundamental principles of human personality which religion and philosophy have been alike reinforcing in justification of history.[50]

[No one can deny] the infinite value of the self-knowledge, self-reverence and self-control implied in individual personality. The beast in man may lower it to arrogant conceit or beggarly selfishness; the spirit in man however does raise it, thank heaven, very often to most useful purposes in the economy of society.[51]

Other Western influences include education in the values of liberal and scientific humanism, embedded in 'Western science, history and literature' and the idea of 'political power co-extensive with the compelling dominance of its culture'. 'With the disorganization of our social fabric' under the Western impact we are summoned to reconstruct a 'new *dharma* of citizenship which will be a harmony of the two great ideals: *dharma* of India and citizenship of the Christian West'.

Such a practice and discipline of citizenship in this generation is indispensable for the future advance of India in its divinely-guided career and towards its God-appointed destiny.[52]

4. THE MEANING AND RELEVANCE OF JESUS CHRIST

The Christian nationalists explore the meaning and relevance of Jesus Christ in relation to the national awakening to new life.

S. K. Datta speaks of 'India's need of Christ'. India certainly needs 'to break down the tyranny of caste, prevent child-marriage, rescind the restriction against widow remarriage, purify the temples and ennoble the worship of the people'. But 'the reform needed is more radical' than these.

It is nothing less than to give India a new outlook upon the world and human life [through faith in] those great truths which alone can save and give hope to a nation – the righteousness of God and the moral order of the universe, the Fatherhood of God and His redeeming love for mankind, the eternal value of the human soul and hence of this life in which man is afforded his opportunity to develop character.... To mankind they were revealed in their fullness through the life and death of Christ. He alone has the power to make men and nations believe that these truths are eternal verities and to render it possible to build upon the individual and corporate life. Given an India with a hold on these fundamental truths revealed in Christ we may trust her to work them into her life and experience. Round them she will weave her imagination, her devotion and her love.⁵³

Herein lies the need of the Christian mission. British rule is working for the 'material prosperity' of India. But it is the responsibility of the Church

to give to India a message which she will understand and which will touch her heart. . . . This alone can give completeness to the work which Great Britain is carrying on in India today.⁵⁴

S. K. Rudra speaks of the great task of building up 'the one Indian nation out of all the diverse races and divisions'. Its difficulties are of an 'internal nature'. They are not removed by 'the mere wave of nationalism by itself'. Has secularism this power? If it is urged that

religion must be left severely alone in nation-building, that the path of progress lies in adopting reforms on secular lines and on a rationalist basis, and that in due time difficulties caused by mutually exclusive churches will vanish, it is sufficient to reply that the hope is remote and indefinite, that it can never move emotion, or colour the imagination, or be the working creed of a great cause.

In India, religion alone is able to move the masses. Therefore 'a great Indian Church is needed to form a great Indian nation'.

It is a religious movement and religious movement only which contains in itself the forces of nationality that India needs for its political emancipation. Only then can the aspiration of educated India be realised. If a great Indian Church can be formed, an Indian nation must necessarily follow.⁵⁵

Both the Hindu Church, with its twin evils of 'idolatry and caste', and Islam have proved in experience to be impotent as nation-building forces. The formation of a great Indian Church demands radical change in Hinduism and Islam. What power can change them? In a moving passage he answers: Christ. It is worth quoting in full.

To distracted India, with its whole head and heart sick there has come a message of hope, a message of no rigid hidebound system such as caste, of no regulation of a book such as Quran, but of a living Person who declares, 'I am He that liveth and was dead, and behold I am alive for ever more and have the keys of Hades and of Death.'

That living Person in the plenitude of His spiritual power embodies in Himself all the moral forces which go to create a vital and progressive organism – an organism which may find its goal in a united and independent Nation. He embodies them, not merely as being the teacher, but as being Himself the Living Motive Power behind them, the Power who gives new moral life to those who come to Him. For He is no mere prophet or moralist, who stands outside the life of His disciples, but the Lord of Life Himself, who has declared His own unconquerable power by His supreme sacrifice of love and by the moral glory of His risen life. . . . In Him, the Living Person, and not in any human philosophy or system, lies the key to India's future. For Christ stands out before all mankind for faith and belief in the one Invisible and Incomprehensible God, in whom He Himself dwells, and whom He has revealed as the Father, implying thereby the sonship of men to God, and their brotherhood with one another. This revelation is supremely ethical and moral. It is not couched in terms of metaphysical theology (though itself the summit of all theology) but in terms of human love which go to the very hearts of learned and unlearned alike, and apply to every side of human life. But even that is not all. Christ is also the source and fountain head of recreative moral strength for depressed humanity. He stands for ethical truths; He embodies them; He also gives power to fulfil them. . . . In Christ are inherent the principles of progress and of building up society into an organic whole. . . . If then Christ becomes the object of the contemplation and love of India, who can place any limit to the assimilation of His Life and Spirit. And if Christ's Spirit is assimilated who can estimate its individual social and political effects? . . . Thus to India would come at last in Christ the centre of unity which it so sorely needs. India's children would gain in Christ the full function of their new-formed national consciousness. A great Indian Church would become possible and therefore a great Indian Nation.[56]

In his address to a Convention of Religions held in Allahabad in 1911 he follows up further his understanding of 'The Christian Idea of the Incarnation'. In it he begins by defining the central question of religious faith namely

What is man's relation to the Invisible God? The relation of man to his fellowmen is included in that question, and is dependent on its answer.[57]

He affirms the quest of India for 'the Real, the Eternal and the Unchanging', and shares the Hindu's conviction (which is also that of the Jewish Scriptures and Greek philosophy) of the impossibility of finite man knowing

the nature of the Invisible whom we call God. It is impossible for the conditioned being to know with certainty in and through his own conditioned existence the essential character of the unconditioned God. The search along that line seems to me vain; and if I were not a Christian, I would certainly be a positivist or an agnostic.[58]

However, he applies the Indian concept of Brahma saguna to Logos and to Jesus Christ.

But once go further with Indian philosophy as a guide and allow that the Brahma Nirguna who cannot be known may become the Brahma Saguna who can be known, and then the Christian position of the Logos, the Incarnation of God, is a highly possible conception and the question of the historical fact would alone remain. The knowledge of the invisible God is only possible through Him who is the objective self-expression of the Unknown ... that knowledge, so the Scriptures state, comes through the Son, the Logos, the Revealer of the Father. The Invisible God, the Father, is expressed in and through the Son, the Visible Image of the Father.[59]

The Incarnation expresses the eternal unchanging reality whom we call the Father in ways that we who are human can understand, the philospher as well as the peasant.

Christ's consciousness of his Sonship and of his oneness with the Father, is a stupendous fact.

The witness of the Incarnation is the self-consciousness of Christ supported by His Works and Words, His life, death and resurrection.

[Man's destiny is realized] only by union with the Incarnate God in Christ ... through the actual participation in the life of Christ, by what St John calls 'Abiding in Him'.

And the results are social progress and human community at all levels:

Organized forces are thus set into operation making for solidarity, the Christ-life within the individual linking him to all humanity and creating organic forms, corporate bodies, inspired with a single spirit and life. The organic forms are charged with vital resistance to evil in every shape and are penetrated with living energies of goodness. In this way, an ever-increasing and widening social progress in all directions becomes the direct

The Theology of National Renaissance

issue of the union of the individual with God in Christ. When at last humanity has found its centre in Christ the Son a fully organized human society embracing all the world in one common brotherhood will be both possible and practicable. Mankind we believe is pressing forward to that consummation through innumerable obstacles. The one dynamic that human society needs therefore for its uplifting and unification is Christ the Incarnate God. Without a centre, humanity can never become one. We can conceive of no other ultimate centre but Christ the Incarnate God.[60]

Rudra affirms that his whole faith is 'bound up with the historic character of the Incarnation'. While the fire of modern criticism has cleared away many minor points, it has only brought out 'more and more distinctly' the picture of the 'supreme central figure of the historic Christ'.

It is history that vindicates the undying Majesty of Christ, the moral and spiritual character and activity revealed amid the strain and stress, the vissicitudes and natural circumstances of the daily life of the Son of Man. ... The Cross [is] the exhibition of the mystery and the majesty of the Eternal God, ... not in terms of power, not in terms such as 'the Unknowable', but ... in terms of deathless love, for God is love. Further, we Christians believe in the real and true resurrection of Christ from the dead, not in the revivification of the mortal body, but in the real and true resurrection from the dead of the endless life of Christ who is alive today and works today as he has ever done. ... Through communion with this Living Personal Christ, we have today the sure means of access to the Father, the Unchanging, Eternal Being, the quest of our great thinkers of old. ... Can the better mind of India refuse this power and repudiate the primal source of new life offered to it for its acceptance?[61]

The faith of Rudra in the resurrection of Christ saw it both as historical happening and as existential experience held together in faith. About this C. F. Andrews has written thus:

Faith in Christ was the very soul of his soul, the very heart of his heart, the very life of his life ... Again and again when I questioned him and asked him about this wonderful and beautiful faith, he would tell me that it came to him through a sense of the mystery of the resurrection of Christ from the dead; Christ was always to him the Risen Christ of mankind, the living Lord of life and death. It was this Risen Lord whom he himself followed. According to the words of the Apostle Paul, he could say, 'Ye are dead and your life is hid with Christ in God. If ye then be risen with Christ, seek those things which are above.'

The resurrection of Christ from the dead was therefore to Susil Rudra, not so much a simple historical truth (though he believed implicitly in the historical fact of the resurrection) but rather a living experience to be experienced anew every day with living power. He was in communion day by day, not with any fanciful picture of Christ, not with some mythological theory of Christ, but with One whom he truly felt to be living and risen from the dead, and the Lord of life and death. This then was the source of all the strength of his inner life. . . .[62]

C. F. Andrews in his early writings shows almost the same pattern of thought as that of S. K. Rudra, and quotes a great deal from him. Since India's national aspirations arose out of the transplanting of Christian thought in India, he was convinced that their fulfilment could come 'only on the acceptance and practice of the Christian faith'. He made a special study of the history of the Roman Empire, and it led him to see how Christianity 'far from being a denationalizing factor, might in fact inspire the higher patriotism and act as a purifying and unifying force'. As we have seen already, Christian faith to him 'could reconcile by transcending' the rival religious, caste and other groupings of India, by bringing them into the common life of the Christian Church. By 1910 his study of the movements of Hindu renaissance and his intercourse with men of other faiths led him to find the clue to the all-inclusiveness of Christ in the idea of the 'Son of Man', and he sees commitment to Christ as transcending the commitment to be a baptized member of the Church.

Because Christ is Son of Man, Christianity must be all-comprehensive, larger far than the Church of the baptized. The Christian experience must be one of an all-embracing sacrament, in which Christ is seen and revered in all men.[63]

This, however, did not prevent him from seeing the need of radical change in Hinduism in the light of Christ. Even as Judaism, 'Hinduism great and lofty as it is, must die and be reborn before it can live in Christ'.[64] Nor did it prevent him from warning against 'the growth of a roving unattached Christianity which does not recognize the primary Christian duty of Church membership at all'.[65] The 'challenge of Hinduism' in its renascent phase, he says, demands 'a deeper realization of our Lord's Work and Person' especially at four points:

Christ the Eternal Word, the Life and Light of millions who have not yet consciously known Him; Christ the Son of Man suffering in each indignity offered to the least of His brethren; Christ, the Giver of more abundant life to noble and aspiring souls; Christ the Divine Head of Humanity, in whom all the races of mankind are gathered into One – these are the great truths which we must express in act as well as creed, if we are to meet the Hindu challenge.[66]

It is interesting to consider the idea of the relation between creed and act held by Andrews and the Indian Christian nationalists we are studying. Suffice here to state that while they did not consider either creed or ethics as exhausting the content of faith, they all preferred acted ethics to creed as a better expression of the faith in Christ. This by no means meant they did not emphasize the necessity of understanding and expressing the centrality of Jesus Christ for man's relation to God and his fellow men in minimal intellectual terms. This is by the way.

The whole life and theology of Andrews was an exploration of the universality of Christ as the Eternal Word, the Son of Man, the Source of Life and the Divine Head of Humanity. Christ as the Eternal Word finds emphasis and formulation in his study of the missionary aspect of the renaissance of India.[67] In many ways, it is an attempt to discern Christ as the Eternal Word in the traditional and renascent religious movements of Hinduism and to distinguish him from errors and superstition. Thus he critically evaluates the religion of Buddha and Tulsi Das, Rammohan Roy, Keshub Chunder Sen and Justice Ranade, Swami Vivekananda and Ram Tirtha. His criterion is that the incarnation of God in Jesus Christ is historical and real, not mythical or docetic, and reveals a God personal, not impersonal. At the end of his critical evaluation of the more and less of the presence of the eternal Logos in the religious movements dealt with, he says:

We may surely believe that the Eternal Word was the Light of Buddha and Tulsi Das in their measure, even as He was, in so much greater a degree, the Light of the Hebrew prophets.[68]

Later he says:

There are multitudes who have never heard the name of Christ, and yet have this light within them, leading them to the Father. This is taught by Christ in the parable of Judgment, when those who did not know Him are welcomed by Him as His friends and helpers. It is also seen in Christ's own recorded words, 'Other sheep I have which are not of this fold: them also I must bring and they shall hear My voice, and there shall be one flock, one Shepherd.' This latent affinity with the Christian spirit – which Tertullian calls the *anima naturaliter Christiana* – is perhaps more deep and profound in India than in any other non-Christian country, for India has been the home of religion from the first dawn of civilisation. It is to this spirit that the missionary, on one most vital side of his teaching, makes his appeal. He claims, not that it should be denied, but rather that it should be recognised to the full. This does not imply that there is no need to set in the very forefront the teaching of repentance from past sin and conversion to a new life of righteousness. The Epistle to the Romans is as essential for the higher-caste Hindu as for the low-caste. But the doctrine of Christ as the Light of the World can never be subtracted from Christian theology without the danger of serious misstatement.[69]

His encounter with the fact of Tagore and Gandhi and his reflections on the meaning of that fact confirmed this approach. But it made him see Christ and his presence expressed less in creeds and more in a spirituality expressed in ethics. He wrote to Tagore in March 1914:

The ... consequence of this position would be that we might see in the world's higher religions a branching family tree.... It will mean a lonely pilgrimage for me, for it means giving up claims for the Christian position, which every one in the West whom I know and love could not conceive of doing.[70]

In another letter in 1915 he says:

I must expand the truth of Incarnation to the whole of human life, indwelt by God – His visible Image, His Logos ... The Atonement must be widened out far far beyond a single act of Christ, however representative.[71]

And he seems to struggle to absorb and assimilate in his Christian experience new dimensions of ultimate reality he has encountered in Hinduism through great Hindu personalities, namely, 'the paradox of motion and rest' in the idea of God, of the personal and impersonal in the infinitude of God, without giving up the centrality of the unique historical incarnation of the personal in the Divine in Jesus Christ. As his biographers put it, he did not follow his friend Stokes in giving up the name Christian when he gave up the traditional dogmas of Christianity.

The centre of his religious experience was an intrinsic personal devotion to a living human Christ; his prayers were intimate talks with a Great Companion, vividly, warmly present at his side, the Jesus of the Gospels.[72]

As he wrote in 1927:

Christ has become for me in my moral and spiritual experience the living tangible expression of God. With regard to the infinitude of God that lies beyond this, I seem able at this present stage of existence to know nothing that can be defined. But the human in Christ, that is also divine, I can really know; and when I see this divine beauty, truth and love in others also, it is natural for me to relate it to Christ.[73]

In his paper on the missionary motive presented to the Tambaram meeting of the International Missionary Council in 1938, he quotes St Peter's words regarding salvation, 'There is no other name ... [but the name of our Lord Jesus Christ] whereby we must be saved', and asks what that means 'in the light of the indubitable *experience* of the presence of the Spirit of God among men who are not Christians'. And he continues:

These very questionings drove me back to Christ Himself, and the result was revolutionary. The scales fell from my eyes, and I saw with a thrill of joy how all outer names and titles – all man-made distinctions – were superseded in the light of the one supreme test, love of God and love to man. This was the Gospel, the good tidings – a gospel from God worth bringing down from Heaven. This is the vision of Him which impels His followers to go out to distant lands across the sea. We go out, not merely to quicken those who are dead in trespasses but also to welcome with joy His radiant presence in those who have seen from afar His glory.[74]

Even with this expansion, which made creeds less important than ever before and the fellowship of Christ larger than Christianity, he never gave up his emphasis on the historical Jesus as the revelation of the Eternal Word present in all things and all men, and therefore as the ultimate criterion for discrimination and judgment in religion and ethics; while he accepted the Eastern correction of Western individualism, he never gave up the Christian idea of the 'eternal quality of human personality' and the 'eternal reality' of 'love between human souls'. And he never ceased to fight against the idea of the essential equality or sameness of all religions,[75] and to affirm the right of religious conversion. We have already discussed in greater detail the question of conversion, involving even a change of fellowship, when we considered the dialogues of Andrews with Gandhiji. Andrews also continued throughout his life to maintain his opposition to the monistic view of Vivekananda and the Ramakrishna Mission that history and historicity do not have significance for the higher reaches of religion and spirituality. This is evident in the article he contributed to the *International Review of Missions* of 1939 on ' "The Hindu View of Christ".' In his encounter with the Swami of the Ramakrishna Mission, which he recounts, he makes clear that his transcendence of creeds is on the basis of Jesus's parable of the Last Judgment in Matt. 25,

where the final judgment is given by the sole criterion of active love due to the least of those whom He calls His brethren. I pointed out that in this passage there is no mention of any outward profession of a creed. Those whom Christ counts as His own in the parable hardly know that they belong to Him at all. But they have done God's will. That is the one final test.

And Andrews ends the article thus:

Here then, in such utterances as these, we find the universal Christ who embraces all mankind. There is no note of exclusiveness ... all are one man in Christ Jesus.[76]

The centrality of 'active love', of *agape*, in his interpretation of Christ's divinity, has already been noted in various quotations from Andrews's statements. Christ is the 'divine humanity' which is the centre and goal of all human life and human history. Here comes his emphasis on Jesus Christ as the 'Son of Man suffering in each indignity offered to the least of His brethren'. Andrews has described to us the vision he once had of the coolie-Christ, a vision which led him to spend his life in the service of the Indian coolie.

One morning about noonday while I was thinking of these things, lying on a chair on the verandah, I saw in front of me the face of a man in a vision. I was not sleeping, my eyes were quite open. It was that poor runaway coolie I had seen in Natal. As I was looking, the face seemed to change in front of me and appeared as the face of Jesus Christ. He seemed to look into my face for a long time and then the vision faded away.[77]

This vision is very much in line with his Christology, and illuminates his spiritual secret and his theology of service to suffering humanity.

Andrew's interpretation of Christ as the source of a universal humanity transcending races, castes and nations comes from the same vision of the divine humanity of Christ. It is this that makes Christ the Divine Head of Humanity. And it is on this understanding of Christ that Andrews criticizes all group aggressiveness, whether in the racial imperialism of the whites, or the self-righteousness of Indian nationalism expressed in the burning of foreign cloth or the caste exclusiveness of the traditional society. As he wrote in the book of his maturity, *What I Owe to Christ*:

After thirty years of life spent in the East, certain great facts in my own religious thinking stand out in the foreground. By far the greatest of these is this ... that Christ has become not less central and universal; not less divine to me but more so, because more universally human. I can see him as the pattern of all that is best in Asia as well as in Europe.[78]

Perhaps Andrew's Christology is best expressed in the following quotation from the same book:

No one can know the Father as (Jesus) does or reveal him as Jesus can, because – that is his great secret – he and his Father are one. He is the Son of God, not in any narrow, abstract, metaphysical, sense, which has no moral meaning, but in a deep spiritual sense of oneness; one in mind, one in will, one in purpose, one in character itself. Herein is the character of God, is the profoundest religious change that Jesus offers to all human estimates and values. It is a change so deep, so original, so incredibly simple, that it makes the Christian faith a new religion indeed – not a compendium merely of what had gone before but startling in its originality, and in its outward results nothing less than a fresh beginning in human history.[79]

Here we see the ethical interpretation of Rammohan Roy and the spiritual one of Keshub Chunder Sen combined, without the theological errors of either. Of course, it could be argued that in defining Christ's transcendence over the creed and religion of Christianity, Andrews sometimes has made a too great separation of faith from Christian creed and cultus and has almost fallen into the ahistorical tendencies of certain Hindu spirituality, which he rejects. And sometimes his ethics without creed, of *agape* without the name of Christ, becomes almost a self-sufficient humanism or a syncretistic spirituality, both of which he would repudiate. There are heretical tendencies which any Christian theology of the frontier of national life in India must necessarily risk, to be living and relevant. There is however no doubt that Andrews has carried the idea of the Divine Humanity of Christ as the centre and goal of universal religious and social history, to a new stage of development.

K. T. Paul expresses the idea of Christ as the spiritual and moral goal of all humanity in lay language theologically less sophisticated than that of Andrews. He is not preoccupied, as Andrews is, with the relation of Christ to religions. His concern is more with the realm of the secular life of the awakened nation. And what he says is prophetic of the present ecumenical emphasis on the theological status of the lay members of the Church and their witness in the lay world. Speaking in 1930 to the Convocation of the Serampore College, he said:

The history of the next decade will depend on the integrity of those who claim to be fellow-workers with God in the coming of His Kingdom, an integrity expressed in active aggressive influence as widespread as possible, not merely through direct religious work, but through the multitudinous responsibilities which are called secular. For it has been observed everywhere that the human conscience in its higher levels invariably responds to the standards of Jesus. As a recent observer has said, 'If an authority is to be set up in "No man's land", it will be the corporate conscience of the Christian Church.' This conscience is the only adequate authority for a world in chaos. The building of this conscience is a challenge to every Christian and every Christian church.[80]

5. THE STRUCTURE OF THE CHURCH FOR SERVICE AND MISSION

It is significant that K. T. Paul ended his Serampore Convocation Sermon raising questions regarding the Church and its corporate mission to serve the nation by helping to form its public conscience. These are his searching questions:

What is the place of the Church of Christ in the currents of India's thought

The Theology of National Renaissance

and feeling and aspirations and action? Is it an effective factor in determining India's standards, in the evolution of its corporate conscience? What is the contribution of Christian citizenship to public opinion in India?[81]

S. K. Datta links the evangelization of India intimately with the demanding and relevant service which the Church will render the nation in its corporate struggle for renewal. He writes that it might come about not primarily by the doctrinal appeal of an indigenous theology, which is desirable, but 'by the slower and more exacting method of the growth of a Christian community efficient, well-equipped, a potent factor and the bond of unity in the corporate and national life of the people'.[82] Both Datta and Paul were deeply concerned with the structure of the Christian community in relation to the emerging national community and its political expressions, and it was largely owing to them 'that the leaders of the Indian Christian community throughout India took up their attitude' in opposition to communal representation for Indian Christians. It was an uphill battle both against the British Government, who 'imposed the communal system upon all minorities at the dictation of the Moslems' and at the insistence of Roman Catholics, and against Indian Christians, the majority of whom shared 'narrow views of communalism to which they had been unfortunately wedded'.[83] In 1930, in his address to the Round Table Conference, as a representative of the Indian Christian Association, K. T. Paul made clear that he stood for 'national as opposed to communal development' and was at one with 'all the national parties' in their quest for national freedom. In advocating a secular nationalism, he did not make religion a private personal affair unrelated to public life. In fact he said that Indian Christians derived their 'deepest and most powerful direction for our private and public life and relationships' from the Christian religion which 'has come from outside'. [But]

it should be realised that we have been in India for seventeen hundred years.... Nor do we feel isolated in point of culture and tradition. We drink from the same founts of literature, art and music, and in fact the most modern tendency of even our religious thought and expression is to relate them, in all loyalty to its past history and tradition, to the categories that are derived from what is characteristically Indian lore. And so, with the deliberate advantages that we have of understanding the best in the mind and spirit of Britain, our community in general and its youth in particular, are now in the midcurrents of the nationalist movement which is surging in the country.[84]

Therefore the attitude of the Christian community is 'one of trust and confidence'. Not that 'the fact of the minorities problem' can be ignored, but that it will be solved by a Constitution which will safeguard human rights, establish a strong central government able to maintain their rights in practice and keep the nation open to international contacts. And the Indian Christian community is 'anxious that no mistake should be made to weaken her (Indian) integrity as a united, indivisible entity which has stood for something distinctive in the world'.[85]

C. Rajagopalachariar hailed K. T. Paul as a 'pioneer in the building of a truly Indian Christianity' by having 'grafted Indian national aspirations and Indian self-respect to Christianity', and Radhakrishnan commended his refusal to tolerate 'the idea of forming a separate political entity called the "Indian Christian community".'[86] And Mahatma Gandhi said:

His Christianity ... not only did not interfere with his being a thorough nationalist; on the contrary, in his case it seemed to have deepened his nationalism.[87]

Christian nationalists were concerned with more than the political witness of the Church. They were concerned with redefining the total structure of the Church's life, theology and methods of work with a view to enable it to become relevant and effective in Christian evangelism and service in a nationally awakened India. The two ideas which were to become the clarion call for the next generation of Indian Christians were those of National Mission and Indigenous Church. They contain the idea of a Church in India with a new selfhood able to form and give spiritual and moral content to the new selfhood of the nation, and to declare the meaning of Christ and his salvation and his Church in terms of the indigenous life and aspirations of the people as awakened by nationalism. In this context the theological thinking (fragmentary as it might be) behind the formation of the National Missionary Society in 1905, the emergence of the Christian Asram Movement and the development of the Student Christian Movement in the later decades, and the movement for the unity of the Churches need to be studied carefully to promote further the Indian Christian understanding of the structure of the Church and its tasks in renascent India.

This may be the best place to speak of Narayana Vamana Tilak, the Christian poet of Maharashtra who was a pioneer in the search for an indigenous mission and Church. Tilak was primarily an evangelist, but he had great appreciation of the relevance of the Gospel of Christ to the struggle of the Indian nation for new life. Towards the close of his life, he wrote:

I believe that unless India follows Jesus Christ, all her efforts to improve her status will ultimately fail. I am exclusively and wholly a preacher of Jesus and Him Crucified. I repent to have wasted much of my life in trying to serve my country by taking part in all her different activities. Jesus was a patriot and worked to serve His country, and He tried to lay for its future structure the foundation of the Kingdom of God. Without that foundation, civilisation may prove a way to utter destruction, materially as in the case of Belgium, or morally as in the case of Germany.[88]

He made a distinction between Christ and Christianity, especially in its Western form which he knew, and wanted India to be evangelized through Indian apostles. In 1916 he wrote:

India needs Christ, not so much Christianity, and Christ she is to get in and through Indian apostles as God raises them. I am praying for this.

In fact, he saw himself as 'the elected Tukaram for Maharashtra, a Tukaram and a St Paul blended together'.[89] Indeed he visualized an Indian pattern of discipleship of Christ and of a Church of Christ transcending the community of the baptized. In 1917 he resigned from the Missionary Society to launch the movement of 'God's Durbar'. Its purpose was:

To form a brotherhood of the baptised and unbaptised disciples of Christ, by uniting them together in the bonds of love and service without in any way opposing or competing with Christian Missions, Churches and other Christian organisations; to esteem all as our brothers and sisters, since our Father God dwells in all hearts; to imitate 'the Son of Man', the Lord Jesus Christ as our Guru, who served men in utmost love though they nailed Him to the Cross; to manifest an eager desire to be considered the true brothers and sisters of that 'Son of God'; this brotherhood to become a real universal family, to be known as real friends of men and real patriots, through whom the world gains once more a vision of the Lord Jesus Christ, so that the Christ who was originally Oriental may become Oriental once again; that Christian love, Christian freedom, and Christian strength which enables men to rise above circumstances may be demonstrated to the world, that Christianity may gradually lose its foreign aspect and become entirely Indian and the character of this brotherhood shall be such as to create in our fellow-countrymen the kindly attitude which will lead them to glory in thinking of Christian people as their very own.[90]

Tilak desired to end the foreignness of Christianity and the popular suspicion of the Christian people as outside the national stream of life. And he helped the Christian people to 'study and love the older Marathi Literature, especially the devotional poetry of Dnyanashevar, Namdev and Tukaram on which he fed his own spirit'. He believed that he came to Christ 'over the bridge of Tukaram's verse' and considered the poetry and sayings of Marathi saints as a *praeparatio evangelica* and as 'our first Old Testament'. And Tilak's Marathi devotional lyrics and his adoption of *Kirtan* as a means of preaching and edification have given the Church and its mission indigenous roots in the Marathi culture as nothing else has done and enriched the life and mission of the Church in that region.[91]

S. K. Datta wrote in 1908:

The institutions of Western Christianity are alien to the genius of the [Indian] people. If it were possible to conduct a pious Hindu round a mission station with its extensive grounds, large hospital buildings and schools, and the mission house in the centre, he would not feel instinctively that this was a religious institution. . . . The ideal which he cherishes in his heart as the highest expression of the religious life is that of the philosopher and ascetic.

And he raises the question:

Can the Indian ideal of asceticism be reconciled with the teaching and spirit of Christianity?[92]

As for theology,

The Indian Church has failed on the whole to produce a distinctive theology capable of reaching the minds and hearts of the people. . . . Indian Christianity is as yet a Western product in the process of being grafted on to India. . . . New interpretations of Christian doctrine will scarcely be possible till the intellectual level of the Indian Church is raised.[93]

C. F. Andrews writes in a tone of regret:

Few Indian Christian thinkers have yet been able to apply the terms of Hindu philosophy to the expression of Christian doctrine in the way that Tertullian, Athanasius and Basil used the terminology of philosophic thought current in the later Roman Empire.[94]

In a pamphlet entitled *Indigenous Expressions of Christian Truth*, which as a young educational missionary he wrote for the SCM of India, he speaks of 'the Apostolic Church both Catholic and National' and advocates that the Indian Church should be open to all the sciences and philosophies of the age, an openness which the Eastern portion of the early Church in the Roman Empire practised in its time.

We find at Antioch, Alexandria, Edessa, great schools of Christian philosophy carried on by the most eminent scholars of the age. Origen's course of instruction at Alexandria has come down to us. It went through all the lower sciences, till it reached its crown and consummation in the Christian view of life. Such centres of Christian learning, where the best thoughts of the age were assimilated and appropriated for Christian use, served a threefold purpose. They made Christians themselves appreciate the glory of their own faith. They kept the Christian ideal vividly before the pagan world. They prevented the Christian faith from becoming out of touch with the science and philosophy of the age.[95]

And he was very critical of the curriculum of the Indian theological colleges which destroyed 'indigenous original Christian thought'.

His own proposal was that the whole accumulation of peculiarly Anglican and Western subjects should be swept away, and the students' attention centred on the Bible itself, the early formative period of Christian history and the relation between Christian doctrine and the living current of Hindu and Islamic thought among which Indian Christians passed their lives.[96]

Once let there be the real and unmistakable birth of the Christ-life in India, and we may say to the Indian Church concerning the treasures of Indian spiritual life, past, present and future, 'All things are yours, for you are Christ's'.[97]

S. K. Rudra, with the support of Andrews, claimed for the Indian

Church its 'Christian liberty' and opposed the imposition of the Thirty-nine Articles and the Athanasian Creed on the Indian Church of the Anglican communion in India.[98] Both Rudra and Andrews were convinced that in India,

The Christian ideal will find acceptance just in proportion to its embodiment of all that truly belongs to the heart of India.[99]

The Indian Church must find roots in the Indian national life, especially link itself with the new cultural renaissance taking place in India. For instance the word and symbol of 'Mother' has been applied to India in an appealing way.

The affection contained in that word must gather round the Church, if she is to be in very truth the nursing Mother of the Indian peoples. The Church which St Paul has called 'the mother of us all' ... [is a symbol] infinitely nobler and purer in character than that of Mother Ganges or Mother Kali, round which the reverence and devotion of millions of Hindus now centre. St Boniface cut down the sacred oaks which the Germans worshipped and built with these Christian churches. This action is a parable with regard to many transformations which must be made in India if Christianity is to reach the hearts of the people.[100]

The necessity of 'the naturalization of the Christian message amidst Indian conditions of life and thought' remained a permanent conviction with him. For this, Christian identification with the national aspirations, was crucial. But he saw that it should take place 'through the medium of art, music and poetry more than through the channels of controversy and hard reasoning'.[101] He himself had to resign his ministry in the fellowship of his Church, and remain so for a period, to make the Church realize the necessity of linking its life with the reality of the national renascence. But in 1920, at an All-India Students' Conference,

Andrews urged the young pioneers to work in the fullest possible way within the Christian fellowship of the Church. There was no longer any need, he felt, for the lonely and costly step that he himself had taken in 1914.[102]

The Churches themselves have begun to realize the need of dialogue with the new life in the nation.

This was in no small measure the result of leaders like K. T. Paul and Bishop Azariah, who stayed within the power-structure of their

Churches and promoted the movement among the Indian Churches to claim their Christian liberty, to stand loose with the creed, cultus and culture of Western denominational confessionalism and to reformulate them in relation to the cultural heritage of India's past, and the new urges of Indian nationalism. The movement of indigenization and unity had thus become officially recognized by the Churches themselves. For instance, it was through the efforts of K. T. Paul at the Assemblies of the South India United Church in 1910 and 1912, that action was taken to appoint a Committee of indigenous worship which 'prepared the Lyrical Order of Service in Tamil' which was widely used in the Church.[103] And the part played by Azariah and Paul in the process of bringing about the Church of South India is well known. And most of the Christian Asrams which were in the forefront of indigenization of Christianity and Christian national service in villages had been linked to the National Missionary Society led by Paul, Azariah and others.

NOTES

1 H. C. E. Zacharias, *Renascent India*, London, 1933, p. 19.
2 Quoted by Zacharias, *op. cit.*, p. 89.
3 Quoted by Zacharias, *ib.*, p. 154.
4 Quoted by C. F. Andrews, *The Renaissance in India: its Missionary Aspect*, London, 1912, pp. 138f.
5 Alexander Duff, *India and Indian Missions: including Sketches of the Gigantic System of Hinduism both in Theory and Practice*, Edinburgh, 1837, p. 26.
6 William Miller, *Indian Missions and How to View Them*, Edinburgh, 1878, p. 16.
7 C. F. Andrews, in an article in *The Hindustan Review*, Allahabad, January 1907 (reprinted as a pamphlet).
8 See J. C. Kumarappa, *The Religion of Jesus*, where the correspondence is printed.
9 Issued as a pamphlet, K. T. Paul, *Christian Nationalism*, 1921, pp. 3f.
10 *Ib.*, pp. 6–9.   11 Zacharias, *op. cit.*, p. 296.
12 W. Miller, quoted by McNiven and Wallace, *The Madras Christian College: a Short Account of its History and Influence*, Edinburgh, 1905, pp. 13f.
13 *Christian Higher Education in India* (Report of the Lindsay Commission), London, 1931, pp. 144f.
14 Cf. Miller's quotations from this sermon in his paper, *Educational Agencies in Missions*, pp. 7f.
15 Duff, *op. cit.*, pp. 346–9.
16 Duff, quoted by Lal Behari Day in *Indian Christians: Biographical and Critical Sketches*, Madras, p. 26.
17 *Christian Higher Education in India*, pp. 43, 145.
18 Andrews, *The Renaissance in India*, pp. 33–9.
19 *Ib.*, pp. 253f.   20 *Ib.*, p. 163.

21 S. K. Rudra, *The Christian Idea of the Incarnation* (a pamphlet), Madras and London, 1911, p. 5.
22 Zacharias, *op. cit.*, pp. 66f.   23 *Ib.*, p. 216.
24 K. T. Paul, *The British Connection with India*, London, 1928, pp. 38–40.
25 *Ib.*, pp. 51f.   26 *Ib.*, pp. 145–8.   27 *Ib.*, pp. 198f.
28 Roberto de Nobili, quoted by Julius Richter, *A History of Missions in India*, ET, Edinburgh and London, 1908, p. 63.
29 Richter, *op. cit.*, p. 260.   30 *Ib.*, pp. 259f.
31 Sitanath Tattvabhushan, *The Philosophy of Brahmoism* (lectures delivered 1906–7 and subsequently published), p. 324.
32 *The Twentieth Century* I 1, January 1901, pp. 8–12; quotation from pp. 8f.
33 M. C. Parekh, *Christian Proselytism in India: a Great and Growing Menace*, Rajkot, 1943, preface, p. vi.
34 *Ib.*, p. 59.   35 *Ib.*, pp. 181–3.
36 *Ib.*, p. 186.   37 *Ib.*, p. 167.
38 *Ib.*, pp. 6of., 66.
39 Parekh, *op. cit.*, p. 173, gives a striking statement of the position here rejected, namely that Christian spirituality should be concerned only with an individual's beliefs and/or inner spiritual experiences, when he quotes a complaint made by some upper-caste Christians of Tanjore to Macaulay, then Law Member of the Supreme Council, against the missionaries: 'These Missionaries, my Lord, loving only filthy lucre, bid us eat Lord's Supper with Pariahs as lives ugly, handling dead men, drinking arrack and toddy, sweeping the streets, mean fellows altogether, base persons, contrary to that which St Paul saith: I determined to know nothing among you save Jesus Christ and Him crucified.'
40 S. K. Datta, *The Desire of India*, London, 1908, p. 219.
41 *Ib.*, pp. 221–3.   42 *Ib.*, pp. 66–8.
43 Andrews, *The Renaissance in India*, pp. 181, 184.
44 *Ib.*, p. 245.   45 *Ib.*, pp. 188f.   46 *Ib.*, p. 244.
47 Andrews, *India in Transition*, Delhi, 1910, quoted by B. Chaturvedi and M. Sykes, *Charles Freer Andrews: a Narrative*, London, 1949, p. 63.
48 K. T. Paul, *Citizenship in Modern India* (originally an article in *Young Men of India*, January 1921), pp. 2, 13.
49 *Ib.*, pp. 3–5.
50 Paul, *The British Connection with India*, p. 73.
51 Paul, *Christian Nationalism*, pp. 3f.
52 *Ib.*, pp. 7, 10, 13.
53 Datta, *op. cit.*, pp. 108f.
54 *Ib.*, pp. 143f.
55 S. K. Rudra, *Christ and Modern India*, p. 6 (originally an article in *The Student Movement*, January 1910).
56 Rudra, *op. cit.*, quoted by Andrews, *The Renaissance in India*, pp. 248–51.
57 Rudra, *The Christian Idea of the Incarnation*, p. 2.
58 *Ib.*, p. 5.   59 *Ib.*, pp. 6f.
60 *Ib.*, pp. 10–12.   61 *Ib.*, pp. 13–16.
62 Andrews on Rudra in *Indian Christians*, pp. 334f.
63 Chaturvedi and Sykes, *op. cit.*, pp. 62–4.
64 *Ib.*, p. 73, quoting *The East and the West*, 1911.
65 *Ib.*, p. 64, quoting *The East and the West*, July 1912.
66 Andrews, *The Renaissance in India*, p. 174.
67 *Ib.*, p. 34.   68 *Ib.*, p. 163.   69 *Ib.*, pp. 179f.
70 Quoted by Chaturvedi and Sykes, p. 102.
71 *Ib.*, p. 111.   72 *Ib.*, pp. 111, 235.
73 'Why I am a Christian', article in a Japanese newspaper, 1927; quoted by Chaturvedi and Sykes, pp. 235f.

74 Chaturvedi and Sykes, pp. 310f.
75 See next note.
76 Andrews, ' "The Hindu View of Christ" '; *International Review of Missions* 28, 1939, pp. 259–64.
77 Quoted by Chaturvedi and Sykes, p. 112.
78 C. F. Andrews, *What I Owe to Christ*, London, 1932, pp. 152f.
79 *Ib.*, p. 218.
80 K. T. Paul, quoted by H. A. Popley, *K. T. Paul: Christian Leader*, Calcutta, 1938, p. 170.
81 *Ib.*, p. 171.
82 Datta, *op. cit.*, pp. 262f. 83 Popley, *op, cit.*, pp. 210–16.
84 Report of the Round Table Conference, 1930, pp. 137–40, quoted by Popley, p. 193.
85 Popley, p. 194.
86 Quoted by Popley, pp. 242f. 87 *Ib.*, p. 194.
88 In *Indian Christians*, p. 216. 89 *Ib.*, p. 309.
90 *Ib.*, pp. 312f. 91 *Ib.*, pp. 292–4.
92 Datta, *op. cit.*, pp. 213, 216. 93 *Ib.*, pp. 255f.
94 Andrews, *The Renaissance in India*, p. 289.
95 Andrews, *Indigenous Expressions of Christian Truth*, p. 11.
96 Chaturvedi and Sykes, *op. cit.*, p. 75.
97 *Ib.*, p. 73, quoting *The East and the West*, 1911.
98 Nicol Macnicol, *C. F. Andrews: Friend of India*, London, 1944, pp. 18f.
99 Andrews, *The Renaissance in India*, p. 257.
100 *Ib.*, p. 262. 101 *Ib.*, p. 220.
102 Chaturvedi and Sykes, *op. cit.*, p. 163.
103 Popley, *op. cit.*, pp. 47f.

CHAPTER TEN

Epilogue: Criteria of an Indian Christian Theology

We have concluded our survey of 'The Acknowledged Christ of the Indian Renaissance'. We have included in it critical evaluations of the theology of Hindus and Christians. Implicit in them there are theological assumptions to which the author is committed. It seems useful in this concluding chapter to make some of them more explicit. It may not be inappropriate in this connection also to explicate some of the guiding principles which the Church in India should keep in mind as it seeks to build an Indian Christian theology, which will help promote its dialogue with contemporary religious and secular India. What follows are the reflections of one who makes no claims to understand adequately the setting of the world-wide contemporary rethinking on theology or to have explored at depth the theological issues he is handling. But even non-experts, who see theology primarily as the tool of Christian witness in the world of religion and society, have their contribution to make to the evolution of an Indian Christian Theology.

I. THE NATURE AND FUNCTION OF THEOLOGY

A. *The Nature of Faith*

Before we go into the discussion of our subject proper, viz. the Theological Task in India Today, it is necessary to consider the nature and function of theology in Christianity.

The first question to ask is: what is the nature of faith? Faith is the response of man to God who encounters him. There are two aspects here: the divine initiative and the response of the human self. They are inseparable and even indistinguishable.

Wherever there is a decision of faith, there is awareness of the

Divine initiative as integral to it. As St Paul puts it, faith is taking hold of that for which 'Christ once took hold of me'.[1] To come to know God is to be known by God. 'Now that you have come to know God, or rather to be known by God . . .'[2] or, as the New English Bible puts it, 'But now that you do acknowledge God – or rather, now that he has acknowledged you . . .' Faith itself is the gift of God. St John is equally emphatic about the primacy of the Divine initiative. 'We love because he loved us first.' 'You did not choose me: I chose you.'[3] God is the great 'hound of heaven'. In fact, in all faith-response, there is the awareness or vision of a reality which is inescapable; and therefore the most active decision of faith becomes the most passive movement in which one ceases to run away from reality. 'The Lord God has spoken; who *can but* prophesy?'[4] or Luther: 'Here I stand, I *can do* no other.'

Faith is spiritual in the sense that response to God involves the total self and not merely a part. 'If one wants to speak . . . of a Biblical epistomology' says Hendrik Kraemer, 'then the "heart" is its organ.'[5] Here the heart should be understood not as the source of human emotions, but as the centre or core, as in 'the heart of the matter.' This is what is implied in contemporary emphasis on 'depth.' Though Bishop Robinson[6] uses the category of depth in its contrast to that of height, on the whole among modern theologians, philosophers of religion and psychoanalysts, 'depth is the dimension of the wholeness of man'.[7] It indicates a dialogue between God and man taking place at a level which is beyond that of 'pedestrian reason' involving the whole self. The 'primordial decision' against God which the natural man has made, thus placing himself in opposition to God as sinner, has happened, according to Kraemer, 'in the depth between God and man'. God's dialogue with man, and man's response, are conceived as taking place at the core of the human self, beyond or below the level of consciousness in the depth of man's spirit, a dialogue in which man responds positively or negatively, a response for which he is ultimately responsible. It is in this sense that every man, whether he acknowledges God mentally or not, has a dimension of self-awareness of the presence of the ultimate and of ultimate responsibility. And Christian faith also should be seen as a reality at this dimension of the engagement of the total man in acknowledging God as revealed in Jesus Christ.

B. *The Expressions of Faith*

The dialogue between God and man at depth, involving the total selfhood of man in faith-response, finds its expression in all the functions of the human selfhood. P. D. Devanandan used to say that every faith expresses itself in 'cultus, creed and culture'. *Cultus* includes the liturgy, the sacramental and other rites and festivals involving religious symbols and myths, and the community bound by them. Through them, we express our faith-response in worship and devotion and in our apprehension of God in imagery. Here we are dealing with the levels of feeling and imagination. *Culture* deals with the patterns of human existence, the ethics and ethos characteristic of a faith. This is the sphere of values and structures of personal and social behaviour, expressing the faith in human relations. *Creed* is faith in search of understanding. It formulates faith and its cultic and cultural manifestations in terms of intelligible concepts and beliefs. This is the proper sphere of theology. The true relation of creed to cultus and culture, and of faith to all its expressions, is a matter of enquiry.

From the point of view of the history of religion, it seems clear that cultus precedes creed. Peter Munz says:

The symbol picture ... composed of ... rites and myths ... must be prior to all religious thought. [Symbols] precede religious theories. ... The common view is that both ritual and myth are men's response to religious beliefs. We think of religious duties as flowing from the dogmatic truths we accept. We think that the primary datum is the belief in a religious theory and that all religious behaviour, all ritual and all myths, are derived from belief ... and that rites are actions which we expect, on the assumption that the belief is true, to yield to certain results. I propose to argue the reverse.[8]

Whether, for this reason, cultus has greater importance than creed in expressing the faith is a matter of debate. Today, the study of the human psyche in religious and secular life has brought out in a new way the greater power and appeal which images and myths have in the life of man and society. And the contemporary discussion on the place of religious symbolism in the expression and communication of religious faith indicates that probably we are moving in the direction of recognizing the supremacy of images over concepts in religion. It is however evident that conceptualization is necessary to criticize, correct and renew imagery to correspond with the realities of faith.

It is equally interesting to examine the relation of creed to culture, that is between beliefs and behaviour or, to use more sophisticated terms, between dogmatics and ethics. Ethics deals with willing and doing, with the response of faith to the moral responsibilities of individual and social existence in the world of men within the context of historical situations. It is faith expressing itself in love. The self in turning from itself in acknowledgement of the sovereignty of God in faith at the same time acknowledges and affirms the neighbour. Therefore in the New Testament 'faith working through love'[9] has both chronological and moral priority over faith expressing itself through right beliefs. In fact true existence is considered necessary for true knowledge. 'Whoever has the will to do the will of God shall know....'[10] John Macquarrie says:

> Faith has indeed its intellectual element, but this is thought of as derivative from action.... Revelation has to be lived in order to be apprehended.[11]

And D. T. Niles points out how in many lives ethics of faith may be found without the credal confession of faith, and goes on to affirm the necessity of the latter as the only secure base for the former.

> The working of the Spirit is often evident in people's lives before they confess 'Jesus as Lord'. Indeed it is because this is so that the Church's mission to proclaim Jesus as Lord becomes a pressing one. Only in Jesus is the fruit of the Spirit secure, to Him alone the glory of that fruit belongs, in His service it must be used.[12]

Of course the Epistles of St Paul do start with credal affirmations of the faith and are linked with the ethical part by 'therefore'. This only underlines the point made by Niles that Christian belief is necessary for continued Christian conduct.

The existentialist theologians have raised some fundamental questions about the nature of dogma in contemporary theology. Dogma is faith in search of understanding. But understanding of what? Is it to be oriented to understanding of the truth of God's being or God's purpose for human existence. John Macquarrie writes:

> On the one hand, there is the view of dogma as the expression of objective

supernatural truths; on the other there is the view of dogma as the more or less mythical expression of a way of life. The first view is maintained by official Catholic teaching and of course by much Protestant orthodoxy besides; the second view is put forward by Bultmann and by those more or less heterodox elements in the Catholic Church which emphasize willing and doing.[13]

The former would emphasize Christology for instance as pronouncements about the 'nature' of Jesus and the latter as giving expression to his 'significance' for man. In the one the temptation is to consider dogma as 'an imperfectible deposit of objective truth' and in the other, to reduce it 'entirely to statements about possibilities of human existence'. Macquarrie's conclusion of the discussion is as follows:

The approach to the problem of being is by way of existence, because man, as existent, is the entity which not only is but has some understanding of its own being; yet that understanding which he has of his being can be clarified only in the light of an understanding of being as a whole. . . . In the long run, the existential and ontological senses of dogma cannot be divorced.[14]

This evidently accepts the existentialist point of entry but affirms:

The body of Christian doctrine as a whole has a two-fold function – it sets forth a way of life, an authentic existence for man, and yet at the same time it sheds light on the problem of being as a whole. . . . The existentialist interpretation needs to be supplemented by an ontological interpretation.[15]

If this approach is valid as we believe it is, then we can never reduce theology to ethics or dispense with metaphysics in theology.

The relation of faith to its expressions in cultus, ethics and creed is dialectical. On the one hand, the Divine presence and man's response in the depth of the human spirit cannot be separated from its symbolic expressions. The symbols share and mediate the spiritual core of the Divine-human encounter of faith. Cultus, ethics and creed are the language through which the dialogue between God and man takes place, and therefore they should be adequate to fulfil the function. Here there can be no idea of 'pure spirituality'. Cultus, ethics and creed are necessary to faith, and are by no means nonessential. On the other hand, faith transcends them. They belong to the realm of the relative. There should not be any absolutization of the symbols themselves, though they have absolute significance as expression and realization of faith.

It is necessary to keep both these aspects of the relation of faith to theology in mind. As we saw earlier, D. G. Moses has joined issue with Dr Radhakrishnan's devaluation of the significance of 'creeds and dogmas' and his doctrine of the ultimate invalidity of all of them. Moses says:

> Symbols, being the ... instruments of thought, will never be identical with the supreme reality, which they try to symbolize, but it would be an unwarranted conclusion to infer from this that therefore all symbols are of the same symbolic value. Some symbols may be more capable of representing the supreme reality than other symbols. ... The overemphasis on the symbolic nature of our knowledge can have only one consequence; it can only lead to a final disbelief in the possibility of valid knowledge about the Supreme Reality.[16]

While avoiding the danger of agnosticism, Moses himself is conscious of 'the other pit of religious thinking, namely, anthropomorphism' which absolutizes creed and dogma and forgets their instrumental character. Paul Devanandan discusses the relation between faith and doctrine thus:

> Faith consists in a total commitment on the part of man, and doctrine involves an intellectual assent to formulated statements of belief. There is danger in attaching more importance to statements of belief than to the faith which they generate. ... True, we may not minimize the doctrine. But the insidious danger is in forgetting that doctrines are also, in a sense, symbolic. They stand for a reality which they do not always fully represent nor totally exhaust.[17]

c. *The Function of Theology*

Reasoning is a characteristically human activity. However, it cannot be isolated from the totality of the self and its responses and functions. It is conditioned by the responsible self, in fact it is self becoming aware of itself, to survey, criticize, evaluate and correct itself. In this sense while reason is a function of the self, it also transcends it. Similarly we may speak of theology as faith seeking rational understanding of the truth and meaning of its commitment. The divinehuman encounter of faith at spiritual depth comes to consciousness in theology, and makes possible its own critical evaluation so that a renewed commitment of faith and a correction of its expressions are continually made possible. The categories of rational understanding may be mythical, ontological or scientific. The importance for the life of faith lies in the 'reciprocal interplay between the two levels' of spiritual awareness at the unconscious depth and rational awareness in consciousness.[18]

The same relation of theology to faith exists in the life of the Church. Theology is the servant of the community of faith. It helps the Church to understand, evaluate and renew its nature and functions. The Church is a fellowship (*koinonia*) called to preaching (*kerygma*), teaching (*didache*) and service (*diakonia*); and theology clarifies the essential being of the Church and its essential mission and thus becomes a means of renewal of the Church.

2. THE CHANGELESS AND THE CHANGING ASPECTS OF THEOLOGY

In theology, we are dealing primarily with intellectual formulations of the Christian faith, which we may call Christian beliefs. Since reason takes hold of any reality through rational abstractions, theology is inevitably involved in 'concepts' and 'propositions'. But Christian theological concepts and propositions are 'true' only so far as they point to the realities of the Christian faith, namely, the revelation of God in Jesus Christ and the response of faith to it. Therefore Christian theology is concerned with 'propositions' about certain revelatory 'events', through which God encounters man and elicits his answer. The Scriptures and creeds are themselves not the revelation, but they are the record of it and are essential to safeguard and communicate it. As L. Hodgson says:

The Divine revelation is given in acts rather than words. ... The Bible comes to us in the form of propositions, because only by statements in the form of propositions could those whose eyes were opened bear record to future generations of what they saw. It is not the propositions as such which are the revelation. They bear record to the revelation, but as the ages go by they can only continue to indicate the revelation in so far as each generation of men's eyes are opened to see for themselves the significance of the revelatory acts of God to which they bear witness.[19]

We said that theological propositions point to 'events'. Here C. H. Dodd's distinction between a 'happening' and an 'event' is important.[20] A happening becomes a historical event only when it is remembered or recorded; and it is remembered or recorded only when it is significant to some men. Therefore a historical event is always a happening plus its significance for a community of men. In this sense theology is concerned with certain events, that is, some happenings in history interpreted by faith as the revelatory acts of God. And when theology speaks of the unchanging core of Dogma, it is thinking of the givenness of the fact of Jesus interpreted as the deed of God for man among men. It is the datum of all theological formulations.

It will be useful to see how the different trends of contemporary theological thought define 'the faith once for all delivered to the saints',[21] the unchanging core of the Christian dogma. The approaches may be classified under five groupings.

1. The approach characteristic of a good deal of orthodoxy (Roman Catholic, Protestant, or Eastern) upholds not only the event of Jesus Christ but also the philosophical concepts and theological propositions through which the Church across the centuries has sought to understand, explain and safeguard its truth and meaning, as belonging to the unchanging corpus of Christian dogma. The Encyclical *Humani Generis* of Pope Pius XII (1950) criticizes those who would sever the intrinsic connection between the divinely revealed truths and the traditional philosophy to which the Church has given authoritative approval. Here dogma is defined as 'a truth immediately revealed by God which has been proposed by the teaching authority of the Church to be believed as such'.[22] 'Beliefs' are considered as part of God's revelation to the Church and therefore unchangeable. Pope John XXIII however has made a distinction between 'the substance of the ancient doctrine, contained in the "deposit of faith"' and 'its formulation'.[23] E. L. Mascall, the Anglican theologian, follows this distinction between substance and formulation when he makes a clear distinction 'between any proposition which is asserted and the form of words in which it is made'.[24] He says:

That there is an unchanging nucleus of belief and practice to which the Christian is committed he is bound to hold; that any particular expression of it is absolutely permanent and immutable and complete he may well doubt.[25]

And he envisages the task of theology as putting into a new 'form of words' or giving new 'expressions' to the 'unchanging nucleus of belief' or 'propositions' contained in the 'deposit of faith'. Perhaps the continuing task, within the framework of this approach may be defined as one of 'translation'. However in its modern form, this approach does 'readily and joyfully insist' that 'India and China and Africa have contributions to make to the fuller understanding of the Christian faith', which 'Europe could never have made'.[26] The limited but large extent to which it can stretch the 'formulation' to assimilate new insights about the Christian faith from non-western cultures is clear in the following quotation from Mascall:

> There are three principles that we must unfailingly bear in mind. First we must be quite clear . . . about the distinction between the substance of the ancient doctrine and its formulation; there must be no compromise about the former, in loyalty to our Lord and in charity to his children. Secondly, while resisting all temptations to impose permanently upon others those formulations of the doctrine and its practical expressions that are the product of our own particular cultural setting, we must be ready and anxious to share with others the blessings which we have received in the course of our Christian history. And thirdly, we must encourage and assist new formulations and expressions which we could never have produced, but from which, when others have produced them, we may profit no less than they. For we are not concerned simply with the adaptation of the theoretical scheme to the requirements of a novel situation, but with the integration of fresh men and women and fresh cultures into the historic Body of Christ. And we must be quite clear that there are not a European Christianity, an Asian Christianity and an African Christianity; there is one Christianity, within which the European, Asian and African cultures may find fulfilment in their several modes of expression and may share with one another the gifts that God has given to each.[27]

2. The approach which has its inspiration from Karl Barth has been called by Hendrik Kraemer 'biblical realism'. It sees the apostolic preaching (*kerygma*) and the formulation of Christian faith as it has developed in the New Testament as embodying the fundamental unchanging core of any doctrinal formulation. Here the emphasis is on the Scripture as containing all the 'doctrines necessary for sal-

vation'. It therefore values the later developments of creeds and confessions only in so far as they are substantiated in the light of Scripture; and since the central emphasis is on the biblical categories within which the Christian faith has found expression, it does not think of the metaphysical categories within which Christological debates were carried on in the early Church as in themselves essential to theology or unchangeable in doctrinal formulations of the faith. This emphasis on 'biblical theology' can be contrasted with that on the Church's tradition of 'philosophical theology' in the first approach we have dealt with. There are various kinds of biblical theology. Leaving aside those who stand by a biblical literalism in theological formulations, there are others who consider philosophical reason as irrelevant to theology. They would not care to go beyond the explication of the faith in categories and words of biblical language, and would condemn Hellenistic categories of thought as deflecting the faith from the God of Abraham, Isaac and Jacob and Jesus Christ to the God of the philosophers. There are many others who value philosophical reason in the development of apologetic theology. But all theologians of the biblical school would emphasize the need to preserve the forms in which faith finds expression in the New Testament as the unchanging fundamental nucleus in any theological formulation.

C. H. Dodd's *Apostolic Preaching and its Developments*[28] has outlined the development of forms of the preaching of the Gospel in the New Testament. Many of the New Testament writings are here shown as containing formulae used in the confession of faith at the time of baptism. References to already established traditional formulae are abundant. For instance, St Paul speaks of such a tradition of the Gospel he has received and handed down without change. Writing to the Corinthians, he says:

First and foremost, I handed on to you the facts which had been imparted
  to me;
That Christ died for our sins, in accordance with the Scriptures;
That he was buried;
That he was raised to life on the third day, according to the Scriptures;
And that he appeared to Cephas, and afterwards to the Twelve.
Then he appeared to over one hundred of our brothers at once, most of
  whom are still alive, though some have died.
Then he appeared to James, and afterwards to all the apostles.[29]

We may note here that in this tradition, there is the centrality of a fact with its significance for man: 'that Christ died for our sins'. The historical fact of Jesus of Nazareth and his significance as God's saving act for men are held together and cannot be separated in the fundamental core of the Christian *kerygma*. And biblical realism would affirm that the fact and its interpretation are inherent in the Christ-event independently of man's acceptance or rejection and in this sense given. As Hoekendijk has said:

Professor Dodd has shown that the apostolic preaching, the *kerygma*, was strictly objective. For this history of God's great acts, there was apparently no point of contact in our life. We cannot use our own experiences to interpret or to clarify what God has done.[30]

This objective transcendent eschatological reality of the Christ-event can be understood and experienced only in the context of the Bible and in terms of biblical categories. This event defines the essential unchanging core of all Christian theology. It is only as we become 'fully at home in this strange new world of the Bible . . . that we can concretize and articulate the *shalom* in a different way in different situations'.[31] This articulation (which involves theology) 'in a different way in different situations' is made possible by the independence of the gospel-*kerygma* from all cultures, philosophies and religions including all forms of historical Christianity. In fact, the theological task in every age and every culture becomes more than a translation of the substance of established concepts and propositions, it is a creative act of mediating the judgment and redemption of the unchanging Word of God given in the Gospel to the world of culture, society and religion.

3. The school of demythologization represented by Bultmann affirms the centrality of the *kerygma* that God has acted in Jesus Christ for the redemption of man, but believes that its essential meaning should be separated from the out-of-date thought-forms of a biblical mythology (in contrast to biblical realism) and of classical Hellenistic theism (in contrast to orthodoxy) in which it is clothed and expressed in the language of the modern philosophy of existence to make it intelligible to twentieth-century man. Instead of the 'objective truth' of the fact or significance of Jesus Christ

apart from man, this emphasizes the 'subjective meaning' of Jesus Christ for human existence and the new self-understanding of man which faith-response to the proclamation of the Gospel brings. It accepts that the Gospel is *from* God, but its primary affirmation is the other aspect, namely that it is *for* man and his salvation. It affirms that the New Testament world view itself is primarily existential. Therefore it is considered proper to translate the history of God's saving act in Jesus Christ as the possibility for the man who hears the preaching of the Gospel to move from a false to an authentic human existence. In fact the two emphases are preaching and the responding faith – both of them in the contemporary present. But the preaching is of God's saving or justifying act in the Cross of Jesus Christ. In this sense, the objective happenedness of the Cross-event is affirmed, but the Resurrection of Jesus is given only subjective validity. In fact, Bultmann regards the Resurrection only as a symbol created by faith, expressing the significance of the Cross for the believer, having no objective reality other than as a psychical event in the minds of believers.

The Easter faith is the recognition by man of the power of the preaching of the crucified Jesus Christ to bring about a transformation of his human existence. Therefore the Church which is the community of the Easter faith, within which the Cross is preached and its meaning for present existence continuously recognized, is the objective Easter-event. In this sense the *kerygma*, the faith and its validity are held together and have as a fundamental basis the continuity of salvation-history. The history of God's saving act in Christ and the history of the community of faith the Church are the same.

Paul Tillich speaks of the scholars 'who understand the Resurrection as a symbolic interpretation of the Cross without any kind of objective reality'. His critical comment shows that he takes a position between biblical realism and demythologizing at this point. He says:

The New Testament lays tremendous significance on the objective side of the Resurrection . . . it was a combination of event and symbol . . . without the factual element, the Christ would not have participated in existence and consequently not have been the Christ. But the desire to isolate the factual from the symbolic element is, as has been shown before, not a primary interest of faith. The results of the research for the purely factual element can never be on the basis of faith or theology.

... The factual element is a necessary implication of the Resurrection (as it is of the symbol of the Cross). ... It is the certainty of one's own victory over the death of existential estrangement which creates the certainty of the Resurrection of the Christ as event and symbol.[32]

Bishop Robinson seems to take more or less the same position. For him too the question of the empty tomb is 'quite secondary' to the faith which affirms the resurrection on existential grounds. He says:

It becomes evident in discussion that most people simply equate 'the Resurrection' with 'the empty tomb'. But the empty tomb is to the Resurrection what the shell of the cocoon is to the butterfly. St Paul, whose whole gospel is centred in 'Jesus and the resurrection', never once explicitly mentions the empty tomb (though he refers in detail to the appearances). Belief in the Resurrection is the conviction (on which the whole apostolic Church was grounded) that Jesus is not just a historical memory but a living presence. How the disciples first came to the conviction, how physical or psychological were the appearances, or what precisely happened to the body, are secondary, though important, questions.[33]

There are others however who, like Ronald Gregor Smith, while affirming that the Resurrection is the symbol of the new life on which in faith we may enter, would go further and argue that if resurrection is an objective event it becomes a denial of the Gospel of God acting for man's salvation in the powerlessness of the Cross. He says:

But in that case the resurrection would be conceived as something much more than an act of despair in itself, as though God were forced to write off not only previous history, but also the history of Christ's life and death, by an action which bears no conceivable relation to history. ... [It] would turn Christianity into sheer incredibility. On my view any attempt to describe the resurrection as 'suprahistorical' or 'supernatural', as 'transhistorical' or 'metaphysical', as the 'second primal miracle' (as Künneth calls it) or as belonging to *Geschichte* but with only a 'narrow historical verge' (as Karl Barth says) – any such description partakes of the same inability to make sense. That is, such descriptions do not make sense adequate to the historical reality of the message concerning Christ as the eschatological event. ... God's only way of being, as historically available in the reality of faith, is the way of powerless self-giving.[34]

4. Next we consider the school of dekerygmatization. Bultmann and his school are standing firm on the givenness of the *kerygma* – the act

of God for human salvation in the life and death of the particular person Jesus of Nazareth. As we have seen, their concern for preaching the Gospel to contemporary man in demythologized contemporary language and thought-forms has led them to interpret the Resurrection as no more than a symbol created by faith about the meaningfulness of the Cross. But some advocates of theological existentialism would like to go further and interpret the Cross and Resurrection as both symbolic of the gift of renewal of all human existence, and not requiring the mediation of Jesus Christ or the context of preaching or the Church for its appropriation. Thus the Gospel of Christ is in essence the same as the philosophy of the ethic of 'existence founded on love' and the function of Jesus Christ is psychological – of bringing to human self-awareness of what is already immanent in human existence. According to Buri, says John Macquarrie,

> The business of theology is to explore the powerful symbols of the Christian faith so as to bring out their existential significance, that is to say, to show how they depict an existence founded on love. But although it works within its peculiar tradition, theology must frankly recognize that secular philosophies may arrive at pretty much the same results without reference to the Christian tradition.[35]

To risk a facile generalization, Buri's theistic humanism, Van Buren's secular humanism and Altizer's atheistic humanism may all be spoken of as arising from a universalization of the 'meaning' of human existence inherent in the 'symbol' of Jesus Christ, but without essentially requiring the particularity of the 'person' of Jesus Christ for its mediation. In them, 'existence in love' or Christian *agape* is the only unchanging core of the Gospel of Christ.

5. While this process of dekerygmatization moves along with secularization to the ultimacy and universality of an ethic, there is a parallel process of emptying the Gospel of the eschatological and mediatorial centrality of the historical Jesus which moves in the direction of identifying Christ with the universality and ultimacy of the philosophical vision and religious experience of self-realization, of mystic oneness of the human soul with the Divine. If theological existentialism empties objective history by a new definition of

history, this approach frankly accepts the spiritual unreality of the very dimension of the historical. Many of the Christian thinkers who emphasize mysticism as the religious experience *par excellence* or have come to appreciate the deeper aspects of the Eastern philosophy of non-duality and its spiritual vision, have a tendency to define the Gospel as the realization of the Eternal Christ in the inwardness of the human spirit, with the historical Jesus providing the symbol and means of this self-realization.

Where do we stand in this discussion about the unchanging and changing aspects of Christian theology. We may make the following comments:

The approach of orthodoxy is concerned to affirm the value of the tradition of theological formulation in the history of the Christian Church across the ages for any new theological reformulation in the contemporary present. This is valid. The creeds and the historical confessions and the teaching authority of the Church are safeguards against heresy in the reformulation of Christian faith. But it sometimes amounts to absolutization of the tradition and assumes that the Church already knows the full 'substance' of the Gospel, and that no new theological truth can emerge in the encounter of the Gospel with new cultures and situations. The truth is that theology is always the explication of the truth of the contemporary encounter between the Gospel and the situation. Therefore living theology is always in the situation, and cannot be abstracted from it. Of course, past theological tradition consists of abstractions from past situational theology; they are valuable guides but not absolute guides, because new situations call for appropriation of new aspects of the truth and meaning of the Gospel of Jesus Christ. Theological task is never therefore a task of translation but of new creativity.

Indeed biblical realism saw this distinction between Christ on the one hand and Christianity and Christian philosophy on the other; and it has been an attempt to disentangle the core of the Gospel (*kerygma*) from the theological and philosophical expressions of it in the past, so as to make it the criterion for new theological and philosophical formulations of the Christian truth in new situations. It achieved the disengagement in a return to the biblical categories and it was of immense value because it showed the transcendence of the Gospel over all ages and cultures and paved the path for a creative encounter of the *kerygma* with the contemporary age and the non-Western cultures. But it was itself confined to the biblical formula, and could never undertake the new creative re-engagement with new situations.

It is here that the demythologization of the Bible as a process of expressing the truth and meaning of the Gospel of Christ in terms of the world-view of the contemporary scientific age has behind it a very real evangelistic concern. From New Testament times the concern for evangelism has led the Church to be engaged in the process of demythologization of its message and its reinterpretation in new categories of thought and existence. To an age to which categories of classical and biblical theism such as the Absolute or the Transcendent are less intelligible than the ontologies of historical human existence, this is important. But in this process it has tended to define the 'historical' almost solely in terms of a philosophy of existentialism which has under-emphasized the objective 'happenedness' in the historical and also conceived human selfhood as a disembodied spirituality isolated from the objective structures of nature, society and history. Therefore its interpretation reduces the Resurrection event to a subjective experience, and the Gospel to a new cult of spirituality and pietism. In this connection the following words of Paul Devanandan are very relevant. He says:

At the threshold of this century, we talked of evangelism in terms of a Social Gospel. Though we erred in our understanding of its true nature, we have come to admit that God's redemptive work must radically affect human relations in society. Perhaps as we reach the middle of this century, we are coming to realise that the total sweep of the Good News envelopes God's entire creation. The ultimate end is a new heaven and a new earth, a new creation. How utterly impossible can it be for any fragment of mankind to be changed or even for all humanity to be transformed, unless the grossly material and purely animal content of world life is also transformed! Is that not why the fact of the Risen Lord forms the core of the Gospel we proclaim? It was so from the beginning of the apostolic ministry.[36]

But certainly there are more philosophies of existence than Heidegger's and theologians like Daniel Williams and Schubert Ogden consider the process philosophies of Whitehead and Hartshorne as more adequate for the reinterpretation of the Christian Gospel. Perhaps Karl Marx may also be brought in.

So far as the movement keeps the dialectical tension between objective truth (event) and subjective meaning (symbol) and is rooted in the crucified Christ as the saving act of God and emphasizes the contemporary presence of its saving power in faith, it may be recognized as a relatively valid theological reinterpretation of the Christian faith. No theology can do justice to the fullness of the Gospel; one-sidedness is inevitable in theology and does not become heretical provided it stays in dialogue with scriptural criteria and the continuum of the ongoing catholic theological tradition, and functions within the community of faith as the servant of the mission of the Church in the contemporary world. In fact, the theological task in any age and culture must be seen as a task involving the theologian walking the razor's edge between the biblical *kerygma* and the process of its demythologization with a view to remythologizing its truth and meaning for men in different climates of thought and cultural milieux, however partial the result may be.

In fact in an age when anthropology or true human existence is the basic concern of men, theology must concern itself with the battle for a true anthropology and philosophy of life and express itself in their terms. A Christian ethic presupposes Christian faith, and therefore a discussion of ethics at depth involves matters of faith-presuppositions, whether they are so articulated or not. Debate about the meaning of existence involves the reality of God *versus* idol. And men may respond to Jesus as the Christ at depth through their intellectual and moral acknowledgement of the validity of the understanding of existence as existence in *agape*, symbolized by Bonhoeffer's interpretation of Christ as the Man for Others. Indeed moral and cultural acknowledgement of the meaning of life as revealed in Jesus Christ may remain a valid expression of faith without making its other expression in explicit intellectual formulation of doctrine. So also there is a mystic experience of the unity of the Indwelling Christ, 'Abide in me and I in you', which is mediated through the Gospel of the divine act in Jesus and may remain a valid expression of faith even where there is no doctrinal acknowledgement of the mediating act. These are however different from an avowed and conscious affirmation of human self-sufficiency which seems inherent in theologies which speak of the realization of reconciled existence in *agape* or in non-duality, outside and without the necessity of the divine act of salvation in Jesus of Nazareth. Probably, it is a debate about the very meaning of salvation and implies no more than a protest against the restriction of salvation to conscious assent to a doctrine of Christ, and against the identification of salvation history with Church history; it may also be an attempt to discern the work of Christ and his work of salvation outside the Church. If it is so, it is most welcome. This however should be done without reducing the essence of the Gospel exclusively to an ethic of love or to a mystic experience. And it is possible if we acknowledge that God's saving act in Jesus Christ has objectively made a difference in the existential potentiality of all mankind, and also define the Christian mission within the framework of the discernment of the work of Christ and the ferment of the Kingdom in all histories. Schubert M. Ogden comes to the same point through a different line. He says:

The claim 'only in Jesus Christ' must be interpreted to mean, not that God acts to redeem only in the history of Jesus and in no other history, but that the only God who redeems any history – although he in fact redeems every history – is the God whose redemptive action is decisively represented in the word that Jesus speaks and is.[37]

D. T. Niles says:

The important thing to recognise is the fact that that which determines the Church's mission remains independent of it.... This means that those engaged in the mission must be prepared to encounter in their work the result of God's free initiative, the previousness of Jesus Christ in every situation, the all-embracing work of the Holy Spirit within which the mission of the Church is set.[38]

This is the *kerygma* of biblical realism restated in terms of a universalism to justify demythologization in every situation without losing its kerygmatic character. Probably this is the only form of universalism which can ultimately be called Christian.

The Role of Pre-understanding

What we have said above raises the question of the role of patterns of understanding which exist in a situation in expressing and communicating the truth and meaning of the Gospel in that situation.

The fact of Jesus of Nazareth and the core-faith which interprets him as God's act in relation to man are both given. This, as we have said, forms the Christ-event, the datum of the Christian faith. However, both Oscar Cullmann[39] and Reginald Fuller[40] have shown how the theological formulation of the truth and meaning of Jesus Christ takes different lines, depending upon the patterns of pre-Christian understanding held by the witness or the hearer. In fact, Fuller has separated three distinct strands of christological formulae in the New Testament corresponding to the apprehension of Christ by the Palestinian Jewish Christians, the Greek-speaking Jewish Christians of the *Diaspora* and the Hellenistic Christians. Macquarrie has this to say about the role of pre-understanding in Christian theology:

When confronted with anything, I understand it *as* something, and in so doing refer it to some area of experience of which I have a *prior* understanding. . . . It is worth recalling that the New Testament writers themselves in seeking to interpret the person of Jesus Christ, employed categories with which their readers would be already familiar. Christ is represented *as* the Son of Man, *as* the divine Logos. Confronted with something which they believed to be quite new or even unique, these writers nevertheless began the quest towards an understanding of the novelty by tying it in with concepts which they already had. Yet, this is not to say that they laid down in advance how the novelty must be understood. As the interpretation developed, the categories developed as well. 'Son of Man' took on a meaning of which the Jewish apocalytic writers never dreamed, and 'Logos' acquired a significance which it did not have in Hellenistic speculation. . . . The function of the pre-understanding is not normative but ancillary. It elicits the meaning of the text, and is indeed the necessary precondition for eliciting any meaning at all, but as the interpretation develops, the pre-understanding develops too. It would be normative only if it were rigid and immutable, and it is not so.[41]

Here the *ancillary function* and the necessary *development* of pre-understanding are both well stated. W. M. Roth in an article on 'An Approach to the New Testament Christology'[42] underlines the same point: He says that in answering the question, 'Who is Jesus?' the first Christians 'naturally employed categories and thought-forms which they knew, i.e. concepts alive in Jewish and non-Jewish philosophy, theology and especially eschatology'. The result was 'a great number of christological concepts'.

However no single title was in fact considered sufficient to 'comprehend the infinite fullness disclosed in Christ'. Furthermore, it must be understood that these titles gave not so much a categorisation of Jesus but were an attempt to explain 'his uniqueness'. In the process of working out christological approaches and answers, syncretistic and even mythical elements were pressed into service but subordinated to an understanding of Christ which received its basic structure not from them but through the Old Testament background and rootage of the early Church which believed itself to be the New Israel, thus emphasising both the continuity and the discontinuity as far as the people of the Old Covenant were concerned.

Roth underlines the idea that the 'basic structure' of New Testament Christology had 'Old Testament background and rootage' and that other aspects of the pre-understanding were subordinate to it. Though Old Testament categories had this predominance over others, even they were not normative in character.

The fathers of the Church after the New Testament period utilized the categories of Hellenistic thought to understand and communicate the Gospel of Jesus Christ. The struggle of the Fathers to speak of Christ in metaphysical language intelligible to the Greek world was a great theological adventure and set a pattern for the Church to follow in other ages and cultures. The Protestant Reformers and some biblical theologians of recent times have been critical of their use of non-biblical ideas in theology, because of their suspicion of metaphysical speculation and non-biblical mythologies. Where metaphysics is a matter of existential importance, it cannot be dismissed as an exercise in speculation; and faith must find ways of speaking of Jesus Christ and his salvation in metaphysical fashion. When metaphysical or mythical thought-patterns are used as normative rather than ancillary, as basic rather than subsidiary to the givenness of the Christian truth, there is danger. But this cannot be avoided by ignoring metaphysics and myths; in fact it is increased where a people's pre-understanding is left alone without bringing it under the service of the Christian Gospel. They will remain pre-Christian in their mind, and this will affect the whole person in due course. Their response to the Christian faith, being unrelated to their inner thought-patterns, will remain limited and immature. The answer to the danger therefore lies in learning to speak of Christ in terms of pre-understanding, and in that process to transform and develop those patterns themselves, bringing them into dialogue with the Gospel of Jesus Christ along with its biblical background.

Not only the nurture of Christian maturity but also the communication of the Gospel to those outside the Church require that we speak of Christ in their language, whether it is mythical, metaphysical or secular. Otherwise those who accept the Gospel or reject it will not do so understanding what they accept or reject.

Dr Merle Davis has illustrated from Madagascar the problem of communication in its relation to existing patterns of understanding:

> In Madagascar, after a generation of proclaiming Jesus as the Lamb of God who sits on the right of His throne and whose blood alone can save from sin, the old chief of a tribe which has resisted the Christian message revealed the reason for his people's indifference. 'We are a cattle-raising people; we despise sheep. Our clans asked the early missionaries whether there was a place on God's throne for a cow as well as a sheep and when they were told "no", they closed their hearts to the Christian Gospel'.[43]

It is no doubt true that the Gospel produces spiritual longings and thought-patterns, but it does so, not in a vacuum, but by challenging and transforming the existing longings and patterns. A. G. Hogg has argued the case for theology becoming relevant to the existing 'consciousness' while challenging it. He says:

> Dr Kraemer has recorded it as the general experience of missionaries in Africa that 'not the consciousness of sin brings men to Christ but the continued contact with Christ brings them to consciousness of sin'. I think it likely that most Indian missionaries would make report to a similar effect. Just because lost sheep are really lost, the Good Shepherd can find them only at the point where they actually are, not at the point where they ought to be. He finds the Indian sheep tangled in a helpless longing for serenity rather than sanctity, oppressed by enchainment to the wheel of birth and rebirth rather than the terrors of a guilty conscience. Finding them there, He gives them deliverance there. He wins their trust by meeting the need which they feel, being confident that as they follow Him, they will develop a consciousness of the needs they ought to feel.[44]

It is possible to argue that consciousness of sin is not the only consciousness to which the Gospel is relevant. Sin defined in its biblical Old Testament definition may have been the basic consciousness in relation to which Christian message was defined by the early Church. But sin as 'alienation from God' and as 'the wrong-

date and irrelevant to express it at another time. Many theologians of all traditions now argue that the development of pre-understanding and therefore of theology is integral to Christianity as a 'historical' religion.[46]

This underlines the tremendous significance for the future of theology of patterns of secular humanism which have become worldwide in our generation through the development of science and the impact of technology and ideas of social justice. It has been argued by many contemporary theologians that the process of secularization and the secular human patterns of understanding existence are in themselves the products of the ferment of the Gospel working on the mythical and metaphysical patterns and transforming them.[47] If this is true, as I believe it is, Bonhoeffer's idea of the Church speaking of God and Christ in a 'secular fashion' and the theologies of 'secular Christianity' have a new universality and relevance. We are only at the beginnings of building up a theology in dialogue with the secular mind of our time. Perhaps even here, perhaps here more than elsewhere, it is necessary to emphasize the ancillary (as contrasted with the normative) character of understanding in faith.

3. CRITERIA OF A LIVING THEOLOGY

We are in a position now to clarify to ourselves under four heads the principles of a 'living theology'. This phrase 'living theology' indicates a certain dynamic quality of good theology and it has been given validity by the leaders of Asian Churches who met in Kandy, Ceylon, in December 1965 under the auspices of the East Asia Christian Conference.[48]

1. A living theology is always 'situational' or 'contextual'. This is repeating a point which has been already made before. Dr J. R. Chandran seems to be very cautious in speaking of theology as by its very nature 'contextual'. Since no theology is derived from the situation alone, the caution is well taken. The presence of Christ in any situation has to be recognized and interpreted in the light of Jesus of Nazareth, that is, Christ incarnate in another situation. With this proviso, we can legitimately speak of theology as situational. Chandran says:

ness of existence', may have many forms, and if Jesus Christ is God's answer to man, it may not be right to start theology by totally rejecting spiritual questions raised outside the Old Testament categories as altogether irrelevant to the Gospel. Some of them may be. But others may not be, and may indeed bring to light new facets of the Christian truth. Challenging relevance to the existing patterns of understanding may therefore be a better way to maintain openness to new truths in Christ than the one that rejects all but the categories of sin and salvation in any one particular form for theological formulation.

Canon Streeter, in a comparative study of Gautama Buddha and Jesus Christ, has shown that the same moral insights may find themselves expressed in diverse doctrines depending upon the different world-views they are clothed with. He says:

The barrier which separates the Buddha from Christ is due, in the last resort, more to the intellectual theories which he inherited than to disagreement in the findings of his own very original moral insight. When the Buddha was most himself, then he was most like Christ.[45]

Arguing along the same line, could we affirm that the same ultimate truth of the Gospel of salvation in Christ will find different expressions within our various inherited intellectual theories. While inherited theories are important and need transformation in Christ, Streeter points to the possibility of Christ clothing himself with them even when they are inadequate.

Indeed, as has been shown by Reginald Fuller, the New Testament itself has more categories than salvation from sin and allied ideas for interpreting Jesus Christ. The New Testament churches found some spiritual longings which were then thought non-biblical to be very meaningful expressions of the divine-human encounter, and found their categories relevant to express and communicate the Christian Gospel. And it is not impossible for some new non-biblical categories to be very meaningful vehicles for the Gospel in certain contemporary situations. We cannot give finality to any theological formula or tradition. If patterns of understanding which the Gospel meets with develop in new forms through the impact of the Gospel, it is not impossible that even some of the formulations which were genuine expressions of the Gospel at one time may become out of date and irrelevant to express it at another time. Many theologians of all traditions now argue that the development of pre-understanding and therefore of theology is integral to Christianity as a 'historical' religion.[46]

This underlines the tremendous significance for the future of theology of patterns of secular humanism which have become worldwide in our generation through the development of science and the impact of technology and ideas of social justice. It has been argued by many contemporary theologians that the process of secularization and the secular human patterns of understanding existence are in themselves the products of the ferment of the Gospel working on the mythical and metaphysical patterns and transforming them.[47] If this is true, as I believe it is, Bonhoeffer's idea of the Church speaking of God and Christ in a 'secular fashion' and the theologies of 'secular Christianity' have a new universality and relevance. We are only at the beginnings of building up a theology in dialogue with the secular mind of our time. Perhaps even here, perhaps here more than elsewhere, it is necessary to emphasize the ancillary (as contrasted with the normative) character of understanding in faith.

3. CRITERIA OF A LIVING THEOLOGY

We are in a position now to clarify to ourselves under four heads the principles of a 'living theology'. This phrase 'living theology' indicates a certain dynamic quality of good theology and it has been given validity by the leaders of Asian Churches who met in Kandy, Ceylon, in December 1965 under the auspices of the East Asia Christian Conference.[48]

1. A living theology is always 'situational' or 'contextual'. This is repeating a point which has been already made before. Dr J. R. Chandran seems to be very cautious in speaking of theology as by its very nature 'contextual'. Since no theology is derived from the situation alone, the caution is well taken. The presence of Christ in any situation has to be recognized and interpreted in the light of Jesus of Nazareth, that is, Christ incarnate in another situation. With this proviso, we can legitimately speak of theology as situational. Chandran says:

Epilogue: Criteria of an Indian Christian Theology

If we understand it aright, the principle of a contextual theology will give to theology greater power and relevance than the theology which seeks to be of perennial significance. This principle is inherent in the missionary calling of the Church.[49]

As the EACC Consultation put it:

A living theology is born out of the meeting of a living Church and its world.[50]

It spells out two implications of this insight:

(*a*) The theological task in Asia today involves a new evaluation of the classical and confessional theological traditions the Asian Churches have inherited from the West. The Report emphasizes the need for the Asian Churches to relativize the historical confessional theologies and move forward to an act of confessing the faith in the specific contemporary situation they are in.

In the past we have been too inhibited by our fear of syncretism and too tied to inherited traditional and conceptual forms of confession to make such ventures. Such formulations have been guideposts and pointers to the truth, but we have often interpreted them, or had them interpreted for us, as the final word of truth, so that we have encamped around them, forgetting that even as people of other times and cultures made their own confession, we too must do the same in our time and culture. When we make absolute the written confessions of the Churches of another culture or age, we become incapable of discovering the new depths of truth God can reveal to us in Christ amidst Asian life. . . .[51]

The Asian Churches so far and in large measure have not taken their theological task seriously enough, for they have been largely content to accept the ready-made answers of Western theology or confessions.

(*b*) A deep involvement in the Asian situation is the condition of a new theological renewal.

Theology is a living thing, having to do with our existence as Christians and as Churches.

The Churches cannot stand on the side-lines as spectators, but must involve themselves in contemporary Asian existence in solidarity with the human and spiritual struggles of 'the world of the Asian renaissance and revolution'.

A living theology must speak to the actual questions men in Asia are asking in the midst of their dilemmas; their hopes, aspirations and achievements, their doubts, despair and suffering. It must also speak in relation to the answers that are being given by Asian religions and philosophies, both in their classical form and in new forms created by the impact on them of Western thought, secularism and science. Christian theology will fulfil its task in Asia only as the Asian Churches, as servants of God's Word and revelation in Jesus Christ, speak to the Asian situation and from involvement in it.

2. The content of living theology is the discernment of what God-in-Christ is doing in the situation and the interpretation of the truth and meaning of Jesus Christ in terms of the situation and its self-understanding. As the EACC document puts it:

We discern a special task of theology in relation to the Asian renaissance and revolution, because we believe God is working out His purpose in the movements of the secular world.

It speaks of God-in-Christ revealing more of His truth to us 'as we seek to understand His work among men in their several Asian cultures, their different religions and in their involvement in the contemporary Asian revolution'. Indeed, this belief in the creating, judging and saving work of God and his Christ in every situation and the underlying assumption that the dialogue between God and man in Christ through the work of the Holy Spirit is previous to the presence and words of the Christian are basic to the theological participation and dialogue of the Christian and the Church in the situation. The ferment of the Kingdom of Christ and of Salvation-history is not confined to the Church. The Church is to discern, witness to, respond to and (in relation to the theological task we are considering) interpret the dynamics of the Kingdom or salvation in every situation.

3. The stuff of living theology is the life and witness of the laity in the lay world and the fellowship of the Church's congregation responding in Christ to save the secular neighbourhood. This is in a sense a corollary from the nature of theology as situational. As J. C. Hoekendijk puts it:

Apostolate and laity belong essentially together ... The signs of God's *shalom* must, after all, be established in-the-situation. One cannot talk the *shalom* from the Church into the world; it wants to be *lived* in the world. That must take place on the spot, precisely because *shalom* involves a corrective intervention, a bringing about of wholeness. Well, the layman is the figure who really lives in-the-situation. We ministers live far too much in the tradition to be able to be really and completely in-the-situation.[52]

In fact, theology is a reflection on the meaning of the *shalom* (peace, wholeness) of the Gospel lived in the situation, by the congregation of the laity scattered in the work-a-day world. Some laymen are capable of fragmentarily articulating the meaning of this lived *shalom*; others are inarticulate. It is the professional theologian's responsibility properly to articulate it. He is trained to do it. But he must listen to the laymen to be able to do it.

[Theology] is the Word confronting the world. Therefore the life and activity of the layman seeking to hear and obey the Word of God in the day-to-day decisions of the secular job is the stuff of living theology. Outside the layman, theology is formal and dead. ... As an expert in the field of theological reflection, [the theologian] has the task of making explicit what the Christian layman, through his confrontation with the world, knows to be the contemporary Word of God, but which he cannot properly articulate in theological language.[53]

The life of the Christian congregation witnessing and serving the larger human community in a situation is also engaged in theological action; and it too forms the substance of theological reflection.

The articulation of theology at the level of a living situation is often partial, fragmentary and unsystematic. And the professional theologians and the systems of theology abstract out of it a body of theological insights or even a system of theology. The primary datum of theology is the theological action and fragmentary reflection of the *laos* of Christ in the situations. The theologian can do his theology only in dialogue with this theological datum. It seems that interaction between theologian and laity of God is what the EACC is seeking to express in the following:

For Asian Churches to be confessing Churches in the contemporary world of Asia means that they must extend their worship of God from the sanctuary to the secular world; their creeds and confessions from the liturgy to the life of the whole people of God; and their theology from the study or the seminary to the world of Asian thought, philosophy and religion – the world of Asian renaissance and revolution.

4. We need a new understanding of the meaning of orthodoxy (or catholicity)[54] and heresy with respect to Christian theology. As we have already indicated, even the best theological definitions of the faith are necessarily fragmentary, one-sided, situation-bound and inadequate to express the plenitude of God in Jesus Christ. This is evident to anyone who has studied carefully, for instance, the christological debates of the early centuries of the Christian era, or the discussions on the nature of the Christian faith in relation to human existence in our day. To see only partial aspects of the truth that is in Jesus Christ cannot be called heresy; and the man who defines Christ in the terms of his personal apprehension cannot be considered a heretic. Any theology developed in the frontier between Christian faith and the cultural and the social revolutions of our time will contain not only inadequacies but even blindness to some aspects of the Christian truth. In fact, all dynamic evangelistic or apologetic theology will have and will contain 'heresies' if we define heresy as one-sidedness or erroneous understanding of the faith. One-sidedness and error are characteristic of all living theology. Indeed in the past the 'heretic' (defined as one-sided) has often been a better Christian and invariably a better evangelist than others who held to the orthodox definitions of the faith. This was and is still so, because he is on a particular frontier in dialogue with the world of men there. There is something wrong in such a definition of orthodoxy and heresy.

What then constitutes orthodoxy and heresy in theology? Orthodoxy lies in the preparedness of the theologian and any theological community to stand within the historical community of 'the Great Tradition' and to affirm unity with the universal community of the faithful, namely, the Church; and the heretic is one who considers his theology so absolute as to be sectarian and separate himself from the continuity of the Great Tradition and the unity of the Church. Christian theology in the final analysis is a corporate activity of the Church as it expresses its life and fulfils its function; and therefore dialogue with the theological tradition, the universal deposit of faith handed down, and submission to the consensus of the Church within the situation in which theologizing is done, are the marks of orthodoxy. In fact, it is the theologian who separates himself from the community of theologians and the life and witness of the Church which is the stuff of living theology, who is a heretic; and it is the heretic alone who creates heresy. The 'heresies' within the community of Christian fellowship committed and witnessing to the core of faith and receiving its constant correction, are not truly heretical in character, since they are not sectarian. In this light, the question may be raised as to who is more heretically sectarian, the established Church which drives out the theology of the new frontiers in the name of a formalized secure theology considered absolute, or the theologian who separates himself from the fellowship of the Church in the name of the new truths of Christ he has seen. This is a moot question. The separation from the unchanging core of the faith and the absolutization of a relative theological definition can take place in the established churches with a historical institutional continuity, and what appear to be sectarian confessions may be more continuous with the apostolic testimony. Who is affirming or breaking the continuity and unity of the tradition of faith therefore remains a matter of debate. In recent times, the ecumenical movement towards the unity of the Churches has been based on acknowledgement by the different parts of the divided Church of their common involvement in and responsibility for the sin of division. This must be considered a movement from the spirit of heresy to the spirit of orthodoxy on the part of all. For heresy lies in absolutization of one-sided doctrinal positions leading to breaking away from continuity and unity of the corporate life of the community of the faithful, and orthodoxy is their relativization in the determination to be in dialogue within it.

The EACC, speaking about the new theological task in Asia, points out the necessity for the Churches to stand within the consensus of the Great Tradition while sitting loose to the confessional traditions.

The faith which the Asian Churches have to confess in the midst of these nations is that which the Church has always held and which is found in the Scriptures of the Old and New Testaments. This faith, continuously confirmed in the spiritual experience of the Church of Christ, is witnessed to and safeguarded by the creeds of the early Church. ... We have inherited the 'Great Tradition' from those who brought the Gospel to Asia, but we believe that Christ has more of His truth to reveal to us as we seek to understand His work among men in their several cultures, their different religions and in their involvement in the contemporary Asian revolution.⁵⁵

In this context, a comment on an Indian Theological Conference by P. Chenchiah may be relevant to indicate the kind of new meaning 'heresy' and 'heretic' are acquiring in theological discussions, within the charity of a fellowship committed to the Gospel of Christ. Chenchiah is reminiscing about the third Indian Theological Conference in Jabalpur, January 1950, where Emil Brunner was also present.

When this writer finished his speech on the reconstruction of Christology, Dr Brunner said, 'He [the writer] is bursting with dangerous Bergsonisms and he has heresies but is not a heretic; even if a heretic, he is to me a brother heretic.' Dr Brunner affirmed that the Virgin Birth was a heresy and it is time we made up our minds about it. The Catholic delegate in his turn characterized Dr Brunner's denial of the Virgin Birth a heresy, but applied the words of Dr Brunner to himself. 'You have heresies, but you are not a heretic; you are a brother to me.' When it came to the time of the speaker to reply, he said, if he has to go to jail for his heresy, he could not wish for better company than Dr Brunner! If the Church exhibited this Christian spirit to the heretic, how many blots on its fair name, how many charges of want of Christian spirit would have been avoided!⁵⁶

4. SOME RELEVANT INDIAN DISCUSSIONS

It may be relevant in this connection to refer to some of the Indian discussions on the nature of the theological task in India, and on the criteria of living theology.

The first significant organized corporate discussion begins with the first Indian Theological Conference in Poona in 1942 which produced the 'Poona Findings' on 'The Theological Task'. The 'Findings' make a distinction between *dogma* and *doctrine*. By dogma is meant:

> The absolute element – the central core – the Word of God. ... That given, permanent living core, which must determine the characteristic shape of any expression or application which is to be recognisably Christian.

Epilogue: Criteria of an Indian Christian Theology

Doctrine is defined as:

> The relative element – the expression, interpretation, application ... [which are necessary] on the one hand for building up Christians and on the other for presenting the Gospel to others.[57]

J. R. Chandran is 'not quite sure about the appropriateness of these terms for expressing the distinction which has to be made' between the unchanging and changing aspects of theology.[58] Leaving aside the question of terminology let us look at what the conference considered as constituting Dogma, the permanent absolute element which alone makes any theology Christian. The Poona Findings say:

> The characteristic differentia of Christian dogma is the fundamental assumption that God, the ground and source of all reality, has revealed Himself in an Act – in Jesus Christ our Lord – by which the world has been redeemed. Here our terms are provided primarily from the Bible. There are many terms accumulated from elsewhere during nineteen centuries, and more may yet be gathered in India, but Christian dogma, everywhere and always, stands or falls with the Bible. Here we must begin. We take the Bible as the permanent and final witness to the Being and Nature of God, and His relation with men, as disclosed by Him in His dealings with the people whose history is there recorded and interpreted.[59]

Here the Christ-event, the disclosure of God in Israel's history and the biblical categories and terms in which they were given form the permanent elements of Dogma in theology. In explaining Dogma further, Marcus Ward gives 'The Preaching of the Churches', 'the Creed' and 'Christian Experience' as 'Secondary Sources of Dogma'.

The reality revealed is not the mere bare fact, but the event plus the meaning which is given by the Biblical writers and which we in turn accept by faith. It is for this reason that I have thought it right to include the Preaching, Creed and Experience of the Christian Church as real, if secondary, sources of dogma.[60]

According to the Findings, it is necessary to fix Dogma first, and then go on to the explication of Doctrine, because 'we cannot attend to the second part until we are certain that there is no dispute about the essential content of the Gospel'. Doctrine is 'translation' (a word which Marcus Ward emphasizes and explains at length in his book) of the Dogma; here lies the relevance of Indianisation.

Here we would stress our opinion that the 'Indianisation' of Christianity refers only to such changes in external forms and terms as will make the unchanging gospel intelligible in India.[61]

In the explication of Doctrine, the Findings emphasize both the function of the Church, and the Church's discernment of the Indian situation and learning from the heritage of the Church.

All living Christian doctrine grows out of, reflects and cannot be understood apart from, the worshipping community. ... This involves clear discernment of our actual situation as Christians both within the Church and facing the needs and circumstances of India. Each age has its own problems; and in different ages men have arisen who have so handled the needs and forces of their own time as to create a living synthesis, which has not only satisfied contemporary requirements, but where conditions which produced it are no more, still remains a classic expression from which succeeding generations may learn. We shall do well to remember that such an inheritance is part of our actual situation. Although we have to consider the dogma in the setting of our world, yet we may seek guidance from those who, facing similar tasks in their own generations, have so carved out the work of an interpretation as to do justice to the real issues.

So the theological task calls for study:

(a) of the Bible;
(b) of the Patristic Age, for methods of interpreting Christian dogma in the context of a non-Christian environment;
(c) of Church History with a view to understanding our Christian heritage;
(d) of Indian non-Christian religious thought, with a view to understanding our non-Christian heritage and reinterpreting it in the light of Christ;
(e) of contemporary life and thought, particularly in India, with a view to indicating the relevance to our age of the Christian doctrine of man, the Christian interpretation of history, and of the Christian ideal of society.[62]

The Findings end by deprecating 'any tendency to seek quick results or to make premature synthesis'.

The approach is conservative in its emphasis at several points, but it indicated for the Indian Churches a fresh thinking-out of their theological task in India. Justice P. Chenchiah, looking back in 1950,

Epilogue: Criteria of an Indian Christian Theology

sees both conservative and revolutionary trends in the Poona Conference. He says:

At the first conference there was expressed the uneasy sense of intellectual bondage self-imposed to the theological systems of the West and a desire to declare freedom of thought not knowing how to do it or what to do with the freedom asserted. The sub-conscious feeling that Indian Christian theology, if true to itself, may mean parting company with the theology of the West, alarmed the traditionalist champions on one side and timorous intellectual would-be revolutionaries on the other. In a book stating the Christian doctrine published by Rev. Marcus Ward – a book much appreciated – a warning against breaking away from the traditional moorings was gently sounded.[63]

At the time of the publication of Marcus Ward's book, Chenchiah reviewed it and defined Jesus Christ as the only absolute in Christian theology and saw theology as appropriation of new truths of Him. He spoke of 'two views of the task of theology in India – one the broad and the other narrow'.

The broad view holds that the only fixed immutable absolute centre in Christianity is the fact of Christ, and places Christian experience and faith in the relative sphere and sets theology the task of renewing direct experience of Jesus. Believing that God's training to different nations in different ways enables them to see new features and appropriate new powers in Jesus, not hitherto appropriated by others, this view assigns for theology the function of building, with new experiences and power, new structures of faith. The other view working with three absolutes of unchangeable core, unalterable faith and essential deposit, allots to theology the limited function of translating the fixed faith into a variety of languages, seeking proper ideas and words to express the three absolutes. The province of theology shrinks and expands according as you believe there are three absolutes or one in Christianity.[64]

These 'two views' of the theological task in India have been present in other Indian theological conferences which followed Poona. In 1964 there was another Conference in Jabalpur on Indian Understandings of Jesus Christ. Besides surveying the Hindu and Indian Christian understandings of Jesus Christ, there was also a discussion on the implications of the modern studies of New Testament Christology and that of the early Church, for building an Indian Christology. The paper of W. M. Roth, which stimulated this discussion, shows less bondage to the categories of Scripture and traditions and gives larger scope for creative christological endeavours in India. He draws four principles from New Testament studies. First, 'the classical Trinitarian and Christological formulae' do not bind, but rather show '*how* the Church in certain historical situation had the courage to launch out into non-Christian categories of thought in order to set forth the uniqueness of Christ'. Second, the New Testament has

no standard christological system or synthesis; ... most christological titles could indeed be considered christological possibilities two thousand years ago as well as today.

Third, this wide range of possibilities 'does not set limits to present-day christological thinking but calls for a similar broad range of approach to Christology'.

The question 'Who is Jesus' cannot be answered by one or several standard formulae, to be held exclusively and perpetually valid, but in the actual confrontation of Christ with the world in preaching and teaching in each period and place.

And fourthly, since theology is 'the concern not of individuals but of the Church as a whole', the final criterion of validity for any theology is 'its endorsement through the Church in its discerning members'.[65]

Here, faithfulness to the Bible and the Fathers is defined in a new way. It is no mere *adherence* to a dogma with its given terms, giving the Indian Church only the task of translation to the situation in theology, but *continuity* with their living core and spirit, releasing the Indian Church to consider theology as a creative endeavour to bring out new facets of the truth and meaning of the Person of Jesus Christ and his salvation.

If the context of Indian Christian theology is the dialogue between Christ and India, the Indian Church should be prepared to look for theological insights both in the Church as she seeks to confess the faith among the peoples and cultures of India, and outside the Church among those who grapple with the truth and meaning of the Person of Christ. The Indian Church and the Indian nation have both their theological history and its evaluation is an obligation laid upon every new generation.

Epilogue: Criteria of an Indian Christian Theology

NOTES

1 Phil. 3.12 (New English Bible). 2 Gal. 4.9.
3 I John 4.19; John 15.16 (NEB). 4 Amos 3.8.
5 Hendrik Kraemer, *Religion and the Christian Faith*, London, 1956, p. 245.
6 J. A. T. Robinson, *Honest to God*, London, 1963, ch. 3.
7 R. H. L. Slater, *World Religions and World Community*, New York, 1963, esp. the chapter on ' "Depth Religion" and Western Dogmatism', pp. 177ff. (citation from p. 185).
8 Peter Munz, *Problems of Religious Knowledge*, London, 1959, p. 65, quoted by Slater, *op. cit.*, p. 195.
9 Gal. 5.6. 10 John 7.17 (NEB).
11 John Macquarrie, *The Scope of Demythologizing*, London, 1960, p. 115.
12 D. T. Niles, *Upon the Earth: the Mission of God and the Missionary Enterprise of the Churches*, London, 1962. pp. 86f.
13 Macquarrie, *op. cit.*, p. 119.
14 *Ib.*, pp. 115, 127. 15 *Ib.*, p. 128.
16 D. G. Moses, *Religious Truth and the Relation between Religions* (see ch. VII, n. 97), pp. 105–7.
17 P. D. Devanandan, *I Will Lift Up Mine Eyes*, Bangalore, 1963, p. 114.
18 H. H. Farmer, *Revelation and Religion* (Gifford Lectures), London, 1954, pp. 72f., quoted by Slater, *op. cit.*, pp. 189f.
19 L. Hodgson, *The Doctrine of the Trinity*, London, 1943, p. 35.
20 C. H. Dodd, *History and the Gospel*, London, 1938.
21 Jude 3.
22 Ludwig Ott, *Fundamentals of Catholic Dogma*, Eng. trans., Cork, 1957, pp. 4 ff., quoted by Macquarrie, *op. cit.*, p. 110.
23 'The substance of the ancient doctrine, contained in the "deposit of faith", is one thing, its formulation quite another.' Quoted by E. L. Mascall, *The Secularization of Christianity*, London, 1965, p. 1.
24 *Ib.*, p. 26. 25 *Ib.*, p. 2.
26 *Ib.*, p. 30. 27 *Ib.*, p. 32.
28 C. H. Dodd, *The Apostolic Preaching and its Developments*, London, 1936.
29 I Cor. 15.3 (NEB).
30 J. C. Hoekendijk, *The Church Inside Out*, Eng. trans., Philadelphia, 1966, p. 27; London, 1967, p. 25.
31 *Ib.*, p. 28 (26).
32 Paul Tillich, *Systematic Theology*, vol. II, London, 1957, pp. 153–5.
33 J. A. T. Robinson, *The Honest to God Debate*, London, 1963, p. 267 n.
34 Mascall, *op. cit.*, p. 100.
35 Macquarrie, *op. cit.*, p. 140.
36 Devanandan, op. cit., p. 128.
37 Schubert N. Ogden, *The Reality of God*, New York and London, 1967, p. 173.
38 Niles, *op. cit.*, p. 86.
39 O. Cullmann, *The Christology of the New Testament*, Eng. trans., rev. ed., London, 1963, pp. 315–28.
40 R. H. Fuller, *The Foundation of New Testament Christology*, New York and London, 1965, pp. 243–6.
41 Macquarrie, *op. cit.*, pp. 46f.
42 W. M. Roth, 'An Approach to the New Testament Christology', *Religion and Society*, XI 3, September 1964, pp. 56–60.
43 J. Merle Davis, 'Missionary Strategy and the Local Church', *International Review of Missions* 38, 1949, pp. 401–11; citation from p. 408; quoted by Hoekendijk, *op. cit.*, pp. 27f. (25f.).

44 A. G. Hogg, *The Christian Message to the Hindu*, London, 1947, p. 95, quoting Kraemer, *op. cit.*, p. 345.
45 B. H. Streeter, *The Buddha and the Christ*, London, 1932, p. 71.
46 See L. Dewart, *The Future of Belief*, New York, 1966.
47 Harvey Cox, *The Secular City*, New York and London, 1965; A. T. Van Leeuwen, *Christianity in World History*, Eng. trans. London, 1964.
48 *Confessional Families and the Church in Asia*: Report from a Consultation convened by the East Asia Christian Conference and held at Kandy, Ceylon, 6–8 December, 1965. See esp. 'Questions Relative to the Confessing Church in Asia and the Theological Task', pp. 19–23.
49 J. R. Chandran, 'The Theological Task in India', *Union Seminary Quarterly Review*, November 1964, p. 248.
50 *Op. cit.*, p. 21.   51 *Ib.*, p. 21.
52 Hoekendijk, *op. cit.*, p. 87 (85).
53 M. M. Thomas, 'Irrelevant Profession', *Student World*, 1951, p. 323.
54 The words 'orthodoxy' and 'catholicity' are interchangeable and are intended here to express the wholeness of the faith.
55 *Confessional Families and the Church in Asia*, pp. 20f.
56 P. Chenchiah, 'A Layman among Theologians', *The Guardian*, Madras, 16 February 1950.
57 Marcus Ward, who took a leading part in the formulation of the 'Findings', made them the basis of a book, *Our Theological Task*, London and Madras, 1946, Quotations from pp. 1 and 3.
58 Chandran, *art. cit.*, p. 225.
59 *Our Theological Task*, pp. 1f.   60 *Ib.*, p. 66.
61 *Ib.*, pp. 2f.   62 *Ib.*, pp. 2f.
63 P. Chenchiah, Editorial in *The Pilgrim IX* 2, June 1950.
64 Chenchiah in *The Guardian*, 1947, pp. 20f.
65 Roth, *art. cit.*, p. 60.

APPENDIX I

Short Biographical Notes

William ADAM was one of the Serampore missionaries; he became a Unitarian as a result of the influence of Raja Rammohan Roy. This led to the formation in 1821 of a Unitarian Mission in Calcutta under a committee of Indians and Europeans.

Charles Freer ANDREWS (1871–1940) came to India as an Anglican missionary in 1904 and taught in St Stephen's College, Delhi, under Principal S. K. Rudra for about eight years. Then he was attracted to Dr Rabindranath Tagore and worked in close association with him at Santiniketan. He also worked with Mahatma Gandhi both in South Africa and in India, and became the trusted friend of most of the Indian national leaders. He strove for the uplift of the Indian labourers in different parts of the world, and also sought to interpret India and its leaders to the West. His writings include: *The Relation of Christianity to the Conflict between Capital and Labour* (London, 1896); *The Renaissance in India: its Missionary Aspect* (London, 1912; Madras, 1913); *Christ and Labour* (London, 1923); *What I Owe to Christ* (London, 1932); *The Sermon on the Mount* (London, 1942). There is a good biography by B. Chaturvedi and M. Sykes, *Charles Freer Andrews: a Narrative* (London, 1949).

Aiyadurai Jesudasan APPASAMY, a Bishop of the Church of South India, was a pioneer in the cause of an indigenous Indian Christian theology, and a prominent member of the 'Rethinking Christianity' Group (see p. 334). His special study is in the fields of Western philosophy and of Indian religions, especially Hinduism. He has sought to interpret Christianity as *Bhaktimarga*. His numerous books include his well known biography, *Sundar Singh* (London, 1958); *Christianity as Bhaktimarga* (Madras, 1926; London, 1927),

Temple Bells (selected verses from Indian Bhakti poems, London, 1930); *What is Moksha?* (Madras, 1931); *An Indian Interpretation of Christianity* (Madras, 1924), and a Commentary on the Fourth Gospel.

John G. ARAPURA is a member of the Syrian Orthodox Church of India. After teaching philosophy and religions at Serampore College, West Bengal, and elsewhere, he is now on the staff of the Department of Religious Science at McMaster University, Ontario. His doctoral thesis for the University of Columbia on 'The Integral Philosophy of Dr S. Radhakrishnan' was published as *Radhakrishnan and Integral Experience* (New Delhi, 1966).

Vedanayakam Samuel AZARIAH (1874–1945) was one of the leading Christians of his day and a pioneer of ecumenism. He was one of the founding fathers of the National Missionary Society in 1905 and was for many years Chairman of the National Christian Council. He was the first Indian Anglican Bishop, and was Bishop of Dornakal in Andhra Pradesh. He took a leading part in the negotiations for Church Union which finally ended in the inauguration of the Church of South India in 1947. He wrote a series of studies on Christian Stewardship; his book *Christian Giving* (World Christian Books No. 2, London, 1954) has been translated into many languages. He contributed to journals on such subjects as 'The Christian Gospel and the Villages', 'The Necessity of Christian Unity for the Missionary Enterprise of the World', and 'The Expansion of Christianity'. See *Azariah of Dornakal* by Carol Graham (London, 1946).

Krishna Mohan BANERJEE (1813–1881) was the acknowledged leader of the Indian Christian community in Bengal and as such became the first president of the Bengal Christian Association, which was organized in the 1870's to establish a national church ministered to by Indians and supported by Indian money. He was a professor at the Bishop's College, Calcutta, and served as a member of the Senate of the University of Calcutta. His publications include translations of the Hindu Scriptures, *Dialogues on Hindu Philosophy* (Calcutta and London, 1861); *The Relation between Christianity and Hinduism* (Calcutta, 1881), and articles on the need to reform Hindu society.

J. Russell CHANDRAN is Principal of the United Theological College, Bangalore. His thesis on Vivekananda (see ch. VI note 66) was written at Mansfield College, Oxford, and awarded the degree of B.Litt. He has for some years been a Vice-Chairman of the World Council of Churches, and chaired some of the sessions of the Uppsala Assembly in 1968.

Pandippedi CHENCHIAH (1886–1959) was a lawyer by profession and rose to be Chief Justice of Pudokottai High Court. He was an ardent nationalist and with other members of the 'Rethinking Christianity' Group believed that Christianity and its mission must be thought of in a new way suited to the aspirations of the people of India. He was a prominent member of the Bangalore Continuation Conference which met regularly to rethink the nature and form Christianity should take in India. He contributed largely to *The Guardian*, to *Asrams Past and Present*, and to *Rethinking Christianity*. He was for a time editor of *The Pilgrim*, which was concerned with the relation of Christianity to other religions. He had close links with the Indian Christian Theological Association from its inception. A collection of his writings has been published under the title *Theology of Chenchiah* (Bangalore, 1967).

Lal Behari DAY (1824–1894) was a prominent Bengali Christian leader of his time. He was ordained in the Anglican Church. With K. M. Banerjee he gave leadership to the independent Bengal Christian Association, and envisaged a national church comprising all the existing churches and without the domination of Western missions. He also took a leading part in the controversy with Brahmoism. His book on Vedantism was written in Bengali but was also translated into English. He contributed to the series *Papers for Thoughtful Hindus* and was also the author of a number of tracts explaining Christian doctrines, and of a book entitled *Bengal Peasant Life* (London, 1874).

Surendra Kumar DATTA (1878–1942) was Principal of Foreman Christian College, Lahore. He had earlier worked as a travelling secretary of the SCM in Britain, and as Associate and General Secretary of the National Council of YMCAs of India. He was a member of the Legislative Assembly and participated in the Second Round Table Conference on the Indian Constitution. He followed K. T. Paul in orienting the Indian Christian community towards nationalism. He was the author of *The Desire of India* (London, 1908) and *Asiatic Asia* (London, 1932).

Paul D. DEVANANDAN (1901–1962) after studies at Madras University and in California, and association with the Christian nationalist K. T. Paul, gained his Ph.D. at Yale University. After working as Literature Secretary of the YMCA and as Professor of History of Religion at the United Theological College, Bangalore, he became Founder-Director of the Christian Institute for the Study of Religion and Society, Bangalore. His contribution to the Hindu-Christian dialogue is unique. His books include *The Concept of Maya* (London, 1950); *Christian Concern in Hinduism* (Bangalore, 1961), and a number of monographs on various subjects, especially on different facets of Neo-Hinduism.

Alexander DUFF (1806–1878) is considered the greatest of the four early educational missionaries sent by the Scottish Church, the others being John Wilson, William Miller and John Hislop. Dr Duff played a very large part in the development of higher education in India through the medium of English. Raja Rammohan Roy was associated with all his educational activities. The college in Calcutta which originally bore his name is now known as the Scottish Church College. A number of Bengalis were converted to Christianity through his influence. See *Alexander Duff* by William Paton (London, 1923).

John Nicol FARQUHAR (1861–1929) went to India under the London Missionary Society but then took charge of the Literature Department of the YMCA, and pioneered in publishing the *Heritage of India* series (London, 1915 ff., later Calcutta), which was sensitive to the national awakening and religious renascence of India. His own books *Modern Religious Movements in India* (New York and London, 1915) and *The Crown of Hinduism* (London, 1913) are classics on religious studies and the theology of the relationship between religions respectively. *Not to Destroy*, by Eric Sharpe (Lund, 1965), is largely a study of Farquhar's life and thought.

Mahatma GANDHI (Mohandas Karamchand Gandhi) (1869–1948) has been called the Father of the Indian nation. His contribution to the cause of Indians in South Africa and to the achievement of India's freedom is well known. He was an ardent advocate of the application of the principle of non-violence in political life. The *Sarvodaya* (welfare of all) Movement in India which follows Gandhiji seeks to achieve non-violent revolution in society through non-violent means.

S. K. GEORGE (1900–1960) was a Christian theologian who after teaching for a time in Bishop's College, Calcutta, was strongly attracted to Gandhi's interpretation of the Cross and of Christianity, and called on Christians in India to join his *satyagraha* movement for Indian independence. He therefore had to resign from Bishop's College, and afterwards engaged in the activities of the Inter-religious Student Fellowship. Later he was leader of the Fellowship of the Friends of Truth and edited a quarterly, *Gandhi Marg*. In addition to numerous articles in journals he wrote *The Life and Teachings of Jesus Christ*, and *Gandhi's Challenge to Christianity* (Ahmedabad, 1947).

Gopal Krishna GOKHALE (1866–1915), after teaching in Fergusson College, Poona, began his public life as an associate of Mahadev Govind Ranade, who made him a Secretary of Sarvajanik Sabha of Poona, at that time the chief political association of India. Gokhale also worked as Secretary of the Deccan Education Society, and was one of the important personalities of the Indian National Congress in its early days. Mahatma Gandhi considered him his political *guru*. In 1905 he founded the 'Servants of India Society', more of less on the pattern of the Society of Jesus. His work for the Indians in South Africa affected his health and contributed to his early death. See *Gopal Krishna Gokhale* by J. S. Hoyland (Calcutta, 1933).

Sastri Nehemiah GOREH (1825–1895) was a Brahman pundit of the Hindu sastras in Benares before he was converted to Christianity. He is one of three famous converts from Maharashastra, the others being Pandita Ramabai and the poet N. V. Tilak. He was a prolific writer in theology, and in refutation of Hindu theological systems, Brahmo theism and Roman Catholicism. He was a member of the Anglican Society of St John the Evangelist, and spent his latter years in the Society's House in Poona. See the *Life of Father Goreh* by C. E. Gardner (London, 1900).

Alfred George HOGG (1890–1954), an educational missionary from Scotland, spent his working life in Madras Christian College, as Professor of Philosophy and for some years also as Principal. The former President of India, Dr S. Radhakrishnan, was one of his students. His earlier writings include *The Christian Interpretation of Mediation*. His *Karma and Redemption* (Edinburgh, 1911; Madras, 1912) and *Christ's Message of the Kingdom* (2nd ed., London and Madras, 1910) were original contributions to theology. He took a prominent part in the debates on Christianity and other religions in the period after the Tambaram Conference, both in India and elsewhere. *The Christian Message to the Hindu* (London, 1947) was written after his retirement.

E. Stanley JONES, an American evangelist, has an Ashram in Sat Tal, at the foot of the Himalayas, and has concentrated his evangelistic work among the Hindu and Muslim intelligentsia through Round Table Conferences and public meetings. His *Christ of the Indian Road* (London, 1925) set the pattern for his evangelism. He has been a friend of many Indian national leaders, including Gandhi. Though now in retirement, he still visits India in alternate years.

Joseph Cornelius KUMARAPPA (1892–1960) was one of the few Indian Christians who completely identified himself with Gandhiji, particularly supporting his idea of village industries and promoting the Village Industries Associations. In addition to numerous articles he wrote *The Practice and Precepts of Jesus* (Ahmedabad, 1945) and *Christianity: its Economy and Way of Life* (Ahmedabad,

1945). His younger brother Bharatan was also associated with Gandhi and the *Sarvodaya* Movement.

Bernard LUCAS (1860–1920) came out to India under the London Missionary Society in 1886. After a period at Wardlaw High School, Bellary, he moved out into a wider sphere of missionary work. He was one of the founder-members of the United Theological College, Bangalore, and the South India United Church owed much to his enlightened leadership. He contributed to many journals such as *The Harvest Field* on a wide variety of subjects ranging from Church union and Indian leadership to a common script for the Indian languages. His many books include *Christ for India* (London, 1910) and *Our Task in India: shall we Proselytise Hindus or Evangelise India?* (London, 1914).

Joshua MARSHMAN (1768–1837), with William Carey and William Ward, was a pioneer missionary in Serampore; they played a major part in the history of the Baptist Church in Bengal, stressing missionary work as well as social reform. It was Dr Marshman who in 1820 entered into controversy with Raja Rammohan Roy after the publication of the latter's *Precepts of Jesus – the Guide to Peace and Happiness*. Marshman's contributions to the controversy were printed in one volume as *A Defence of the Deity and Atonement of Jesus Christ in Reply to Rammohun Roy of Calcutta* (London, 1822).

Sir Pherozeshah MEHTA (1845–1915) was a member of the Parsi community in Bombay, and one of the founders of the Indian National Congress, which under Gandhi's leadership won freedom for India. As a liberal nationalist, he was one of the leaders of the moderates in Congress.

William MILLER (1838–1923), an educational missionary like Alexander Duff, is remembered as the man behind Madras Christian College. As a member of the Madras Legislative Council he contributed in no small measure to the cause of higher education. In later life he was elected Moderator of the Church of Scotland.

David G. MOSES has recently retired after many years as Principal of Hislop College, Nagpur. He has been a President of the

World Council of Churches, and President of the National Christian Council of India. His special field of study is Indian Philosophy and Religions; his most important book is *Religious Truth and the Relation between Religions* (Madras, 1950).

Pratap Chander MOZOOMDAR (1840–1905) was a loyal follower of Keshub Chunder Sen and succeeded him in the leadership of the Brahmo Samaj. His best known books are *The Life and Teachings of Keshub Chunder Sen* (Calcutta, 1887) and *The Oriental Christ* (Boston, 1883).

J. E. Lesslie NEWBIGIN, now Bishop in Madras, was the first Bishop of the Church of South India in Madurai, and has also served as Secretary of the International Missionary Council. His theological writings include *The Household of God* (London, 1953); *A Faith for This One World?* (London, 1961); *Honest Religion for Secular Man* (London, 1966).

Daniel T. NILES is at present Moderator of the Methodist Church of Ceylon and Chairman of the East Asia Christian Conference. He is well known in the Ecumenical Movement as a preacher, Bible teacher, ecumenical theologian and organizer. His most important contribution to ecumenical theology was made during his years as Chairman of the World's Student Christian Federation and General Secretary of the EACC. Of his many books mention may be made of *Upon the Earth: the Mission of God and the Missionary Enterprise of the Churches* (London, 1962).

Roberto de NOBILI (1577–1656) was an Italian Jesuit missionary in Madura during the period of Portuguese domination in India. He was the first missionary in India to translate into missionary policy the idea that religion and culture are distinct, and should be distinguished both in Christianity and in Hinduism, and that therefore the Christian religion should adapt Hindu culture and social structure to make Christianity indigenous to India. See *A Pearl to India* by Vincent Cronin (London, 1959).

Raymond PANIKKAR is a Roman Catholic theologian and a student of Hinduism and of Indian Philosophy. He divides his time each year between Benares and the Centre for the Study of Religion in the University of Harvard. His book, *The Unknown Christ of Hinduism* (London, 1964) has gained wide acceptance among scholars.

Ramakrishna PARAMAHAMSA (1836–1886) whose original name was Gadadhar, was priest at the Kali temple at Dakshineswar. Under different *gurus* he went through several spiritual disciplines of self-realization and became the centre of a renascence of Hinduism on its own fundamentals. His chief disciple was Vivekananda, who later organized the Ramakrishna Mission and Mutt, a growing movement both in India and elsewhere.

Manilal C. PAREKH (1885–1967) was attracted by Keshub Chunder Sen and became a member of the Brahmo Samaj; through the Samaj he came nearer to Christ and was baptized, though he did not attach himself to any particular church. He wrote a number of books on the Brahmo Samaj, including *Brahma Samaj to Christianity* (Rajkot, 1929). After working closely for some time with Dr Stanley Jones, he was attracted to Gandhiji and became a nationalist; his book *Christian Proselytism in India: a Great and Growing Menace* (Rajkot, 1943) criticizes the methods adopted by missionaries in India. His other writings include *A Hindu's Portrait of Jesus* (Rajkot, 1953).

K. T. PAUL (1876–1931) was an Indian Christian leader of all-India stature. He was one of the founders of the National Missionary Society at Serampore in 1905 and became its Secretary. In 1913 his post as Secretary of the YMCA led him into the work of rural reconstruction. He became General Secretary of the National YMCA in 1916, and in this capacity travelled widely outside India. As President of the South India United Church he was involved in the movement for union which ultimately led to the Church of South India. He lectured and wrote pamphlets on such subjects as 'Christian Nationalism', 'Citzenship in Modern India', 'Can Christianity be Nationalized?' His two books are *The British Connection with India* (London, 1928) and *Christianity and Indian Nationhood*.

Sir Sarvepalli RADHAKRISHNAN has a high reputation as a philosopher and an able exponent of Advaita Vedanta and of its adequacy to provide the spiritual foundations of India's new humanism. He has occupied chairs of Philosophy and Religion in several universities including Oxford. He was India's Ambassador to Russia, and finally served as President of India. Some of his books on philosophy, the comparative study of religions and the Hindu Scriptures are mentioned in the notes to ch. VII.

Pandita RAMABAI (1858–1922) had a unique place in the history of social service in India. She was a Brahmin and a Sanskrit scholar who in early widowhood was converted to Christianity. She first concentrated on helping young widows, whose condition was then pathetic, but then in time of famine extended her work and sheltered thousands of children. She built Mukti Home in Kedgaon near Poona as a centre of spiritual and social service. She has been recognized as a national leader of women's emancipation in India. She also engaged in Bible translation and evangelism.

Mark Sunder RAO is a Brahmin convert to Christianity, and a student of Indian philosophy and Hindu religion. He has been editor of *The Guardian* and General Secretary of the National Missionary Society, and was till recently on the staff of the Christian Institute for the Study of Religion and Society, Bangalore. His small book *Ananyatva: Realization of Christian Non-duality* (Bangalore, 1964) is an attempt to relate Christianity and Advaita Vedanta.

Mahadev Govind RANADE (1842–1901), a judge of the High Court, was the founder of Prarthana Samaj in Bombay on the model of the Brahmo Samaj in Bengal. He looked upon the Indo-British contact as providential, but stood also for the freedom of India, and even earned the title 'Patriarch of patriots'. He was liberal in his outlook and stood for radical changes in Indian society, encouraging Pandita Ramabai, whose work among the unfortunate women of India was criticized by his orthodox Hindu friends. His great influence on G. K. Gokhale continued beyond his own lifetime.

Raja Rammohan ROY (1774–1833) is remembered as the morning star of the Indian renascence and the prophet of Indian nationalism. He was fluent in Persian, Arabic, Sanskrit, Bengali and

English. His first book, *A Present to the Believers in One God* or *Against the Idolatry of All Religions* (about 1903) was written in Persian with a foreword in Arabic. He wrote (both in Bengali and in English) on the Upanishads, arguing that their teaching was monotheistic, and his opposition to Marshman and the Serampore missionaries was also in the cause of monotheism, and led to his founding the Atmiya Sabha, and later the Brahmo Samaj, which was a 'theistic church'. However he co-operated with the missionaries in their educational activities and efforts at social reform, campaigning especially for English as the medium of education and for the abolition of *suttee*; he also worked for the freedom of the press. He died in Bristol while on a visit to England. See *The English Works of Raja Rammohun Roy* (one volume, including a translation of the work mentioned above, Allahabad, 1906); *The Life and Letters of Raja Rammohun Roy* by Sophia Dobson Collet (London, 1900).

Susil Kumar RUDRA (1861–1925) was Principal of St Stephen's College, Delhi, when C. F. Andrews was on its staff. Rudra's friendship with Andrews was of unique value to the latter, and helped him to see Christ in a new way. Rudra was an independent thinker and a nationalist, a friend of Gandhiji and other national leaders, and an acknowledged Indian Christian leader of his time.

Stanley J. SAMARTHA, after being Professor of Philosophy and History of Religions at United Theological College, Bangalore, and Principal of Serampore College, is now on the staff of the World Council of Churches. He is the author of *Introduction to Radhakrishnan* (New York and New Delhi, 1964).

Keshub Chunder SEN (1838–1884) unlike Debendranath Tagore, who remained always a conservative Hindu, came much nearer to Christ. After a breach in the original Brahmo Samaj he and his followers in 1866 founded the Brahmo Samaj of India, introducing elements from many religions to form an eclectic church. He was brought prominently before the European public by his lecture on 'Jesus Christ, Europe and Asia', also in 1866. He developed the idea of the 'New Dispensation of the Spirit' and sought to build the

Church of the New Dispensation round his own inspiration. See the *Life* by P. C. Mozoomdar, mentioned above, p. 81 n. 4.

Surgit SINGH is an Indian Christian theologian now teaching in San Francisco Theological Seminary. His major work, *Preface to Personality* (Madras, 1952) is a study in Christology.

Debendranath TAGORE (1817–1905) succeeded Rammohun Roy as leader of the Brahmo Samaj. When Roy died it was merely a religious platform where people of different creeds assembled for discourses and hymns; Debendranath put life into it and in 1843 provided it with a 'covenant'. He was however less liberal than Roy, and tried to receive inspiration from Hindu Scriptures only. In 1850 he published in Sanskrit and Bengali a treatise called *Brahma Dharma* giving the fundamental principles of the Brahmo faith.

Rabindranath TAGORE (1861–1941) was a poet of world-wide fame and the founder of Visvabharati University. He wrote both in English and in Bengali; his works include *Gitangali: Song Offerings* (London, 1912); *The Gardener* (London, 1913); *Sadhana: the Realisation of Life* (London, 1913); *The Religion of Man* (Hibbert Lectures, London, 1931). See also *Rabindranath Tagore: a biography* by K. R. Kripalani (London, 1962).

Naryan Vaman TILAK (1862–1919) is well known as an Indian Christian poet of Maharashastra. He was a convert from Brahminism. Some of his *bhakti* poems have been translated from Marathi into English. See the biography *Naryana Vamana Tilak* by J. C. Winslow (Calcutta, 1923).

Brahmobandhav UPADHYAYA (1861–1907), originally named Bhavani Charan Banerji, was a friend of Keshub Chunder Sen and of Sri Ramakrishna Paramahamsa; he and Swami Vivekananda were fellow-students. Though he was baptized into the Anglican Church he soon joined the Roman Catholic Church and became a Christian sanyasi. He was an advocate of indigenous patterns of theology and of monastic life, and edited a weekly paper, *Sophia*, and subsequently a monthly, *The Twentieth Century*, to propagate his views. He travelled to Rome to argue the case for indigenization, but met with discouragement. He then joined the nationalist movement in Bengal and edited a popular Bengali daily called *Sandya*. He did *prayatchita* to rejoin his caste. As he considered caste as a structure which Christianity should accept in its entirety, it is a debated question whether he thereby repudiated Christianity and rejoined the Hindu religion. He was imprisoned by the British and died in prison.

Swami VIVEKANANDA (1863-1902), originally named Narendranath, was the chief disciple of Sri Ramakrishna Paramahamsa. Unlike Ramakrishna, Vivekananda was highly educated. He became the symbol of the religious awakening of India when at the Parliament of Religions in Chicago in 1893 he presented Vedanta as the Universal Religion, reinterpreting it to suit the needs of the day and combining it with the Christian idea of social service; he thus provided a basis for social service within the framework of Hinduism. It was Vivekananda who organized the Ramakrishna Movement and made Belur its headquarters. The Ramakrishna Mission now has centres in different parts of the world. Vivekananda's writings and speeches in English are published in seven volumes (*Collected Works*, 5th edition, Almora, 1931).

Marcus WARD was on the staff of the United Theological College, Bangalore, and edited the series *The Student Christian Library*. His book *Our Theological Task* (London and Madras, 1946), based on the 'Findings' of the Indian Theological Conference held at Poona in 1942, stimulated Indian leaders like Chenchiah to set forth their own views on the same topic.

John WILSON (1804-1875) was one of the pioneer Scottish educational missionaries; his field of activity was Bombay, where he made a noteworthy contribution through Wilson College and other educational institutions, and also through the University of Bombay. Like Dr Miller he was later honoured by election as Moderator of the Church of Scotland.

APPENDIX II

Movements mentioned in the book

The Asram Movement. 'Asram' is a traditional Hindu pattern of simple community living oriented to spiritual discipline and realization. This pattern has been adopted and reinterpreted by the Christian Asrams as an expression of Christian life and service. The first Christian Asram was the *Christu-Kula* Asram (the Asram of the Family of Christ) founded by Dr S. Jesudason and Dr Forrester Paton at Tiruppattur, Tamilnad. Dr Jesudason's booklet *Unique Christ and Indigenous Christianity* (Bangalore, 1966) gives the idea behind it. Christ-centred fellowship in thought and worship, evangelism among and service to the community formed two sides of the Asram life. Following the pioneers, Christian Asrams grew up in different parts of India and there are many now active in India. The Asrams in Manganam (Kerala), Thadagom (Tamilnad), and Sihora (Madhya Pradesh) may be specially mentioned.

The Arya Samaj. Unlike Brahmo Samaj, which strove for a renewal of Hindu culture and religion in positive response to Western Christianity and humanism, Arya Samaj sought a militant revival of Hinduism in its Vedic purity in defence against Christianity. Dayananda Saraswathi was its founder. It is still a very active movement in several parts of India.

The Brahmo Samaj. This movement was founded by Raja Rammohun Roy. Its forerunner was the *Atmiya Sabha* (Spiritual Society), founded in 1815 for the purpose of religious discussion. This ceased to exist after a few years, but in 1830 Rammohun Roy, together with Dwarkanath Tagore, Prosonno Kumar Tagore and others, formed the Brahma Sabha, which was later called the Brahmo Samaj, for worship, prayer and religious discussion. Worship included recitation from the Upanishads, a sermon and hymns. The society was thus virtually a 'theistic church'. Rammohun Roy died in 1833, but the society continued under Debendranath Tagore, Keshub Chunder Sen and P. C. Mozoomdar. It was concerned with social reform and education, and for these purposes trained missionaries and published journals. It still exists but is not a powerful force in India today.

The Indian Christian Theological Association. This Association is aimed at building an Indian Christian theology. Its membership is drawn largely from the theological colleges of India. It owes its inspiration to the first Indian Christian Theological Conference in Poona in 1942, where the main theme was the indigenization of theology. The Association has held several other Theological Conferences on different aspects of the theme and also publishes a quarterly, the *Indian Journal of Theology*.

The International Fellowship. This was an organization which came to birth in the period of the national struggle for freedom under Gandhi, with a view to creating mutual understanding between men of different races and religions in India. Its ethos was religious. A. A. Paul was its founder secretary. It became a forum for inter-religious discussions and international encounters. The Inter-religious Student Fellowship of which M. A. Thomas was secretary was an offshoot of this movement. Both have gone out of active existence.

The National Missionary Society of India. In the wake of nationalism in India, Indian Christians wished to take responsibility for themselves for the work of evangelism in India. In 1905 the Society was formed at a conference in Serampore. It continues to be active with its headquarters in Madras. K. T. Paul and V. S. Azariah (later Bishop) were among its founder members.

The Movement for Church Unity. The movement for Church unity in India led the Anglican, Presbyterian, Methodist and Congregationalist Churches of South India to unite to form in 1947 the Church of South India. In North India it has led to the finalization of the Scheme of Union for a Church of North India which, it is hoped, is to come into being in the near future.

The Prarthana Samaj. In 1864 Keshub Chunder Sen, leader of the Brahmo Samaj, visited Bombay and three years later a theistic society was formed with the name Prarthana Samaj. As in the Brahmo Samaj the members met for religious worship and discussions and accepted social reform as an integral part of their work. The leader of this group was Mahadev Govind Ranade.

Ramakrishna Movement. This movement, which was founded by Swami Vivekananda, the foremost disciple of Sri Ramakrishna Paramahamsa, combines spirituality with philanthropy based on a reinterpretation of Advaita Vedanta. The Ramakrishna Order consists of monks dedicated to a life of contemplation and service and the Ramakrishna Mission has centres throughout the world.

The Rethinking Christianity Group. This group worked behind the publication of *Rethinking Christianity in India Today*. Prominent members included P. Chenchiah, V. Chakkarai, Bishop Appasamy, S. Jesudason, Devasahayam, Eddy Asirvatham and A. N. Sudarisanam.

The Serampore Missionaries. The most notable founders of the Serampore Mission were the Baptists William Carey, Joshua Marshman and William Ward. They engaged in educational work, translation of the Bible, the training of evangelists, the printing and publication of journals, etc.

The Sarvodaya Movement. This was inspired by the religious and social philosophy of Mahatma Gandhi and is dedicated to its implementation. In India today it is primarily concerned with constructive work, especially in the villages. Under the leadership of Vinobha Bhave and Jayaprakash Narain it has inaugurated the Dan-movement (*Bhoodan, Jivan-dan, Gram-dan*), aimed at revolutionizing the Indian social structure. The Sarvodaya Movement eschews politics based on party and power (*Raj Sakti*) and pursues non-party politics based on the power of the people (*Lok Sakti*). There are many

Gandhi grams in India which form centres of the Movement, and its programme is supported by the *Gandhi Smarak Nidhi*. The organized expression of the Movement is the *All-India Sarva Seva Sangh*.

The Student Christian Movement of India. Started as student departments of the YMCA and YWCA in the 1930's, it developed into one Movement independent both of the churches and of the YMCA and YWCA. A. A. Paul and later for many years A. Rallia Ram of Allahabad gave leadership to the Movement, making it sensitive to the national movement at political, cultural and spiritual levels.

INDEX OF PROPER NAMES

Abraham 24, 55, 60, 90, 145, 293
Adam, William 2, 24f., 319
Africa 75, 258, 323
Aldis, S. 228
Allahabad 250, 265
Altizer, T. J. J. 297
America 75, 130, 258
Amrit Kaur, R. 215
Andrews, C. F. 36, 100f., 110, 126–9, 143, 145f., 148, 194, 197, 215, 218–25, 235, 237f., 239, 241f., 247–9, 259–62, 267–74, 279–83, 319, 329
Andy, Parani 53
Appasamy, A. J. 138–43, 145, 149, 192, 319f., 334
Arapura, John 186f., 192, 320
Aristotle 103f.
Arius, Arianism 25, 65, 158
Arya Samaj 103, 111, 332
Aryanayagam 215
Aseshananda, Swami 129
Asia 51, 69, 75, 258, 273, 307
  See also East Asia Christian Conference
Asram Movement 276, 281, 332
Athanasius, Athanasian Creed 158, 219, 279f.
Augustine 86, 160
Aurobindo, G. 164, 207
Azariah, V. S. 77–80, 239, 257, 259, 280f., 320, 333

Baago, Kaj 54f., 103, 110
Banerjee, Kali Charan 53, 201
Banerjee, Krishna Mohan 38, 50, 52–54, 102, 320f.
Barth, Karl 162f., 170, 292, 296
Basil 279
Bengal Christian Association 53, 320
Besant, Mrs Annie 103
Bhagavadgita 130, 137, 159, 198, 201, 204, 232
Bhagavan 86, 112

Bonhoeffer, Dietrich 300, 306
Boniface 280
Bose, Mathura Nath 11
Brahman 65, 86, 112, 132, 150–2, 163, 168, 170, 182
Brahmo Samaj 1, 11, 29, 38f., 44, 56, 68, 83f., 88, 92, 95, 99f., 117, 120, 130, 255, 326f., 329f., 332–4
Brunner, Emil 312
Buddha, Buddhahood, Buddhism 70, 74, 78, 113, 120–2, 151, 156f., 161, 189, 203f., 249, 269, 305
Bultmann, Rudolf 294–6
Buri, Fritz 297

Calcutta Christo Samaj 53
Chaitanya 29, 58, 70
Chandran, J. Russell 36, 103, 110, 129–38, 145f., 148f., 306, 313, 318, 321
Chardin, P. Teilhard de 68
Chaturvedi, B. and Sykes, M. 148, 237f., 262, 282f., 319
Chenchiah, P. 68, 161–4, 312, 314f., 318, 321, 331, 334
China 130
Church of the New Dispensation 56, 65, 72, 74, 76, 82, 99
Church of South India 72, 74, 281, 327, 333
Clement of Alexandria 108, 158, 160
Cochrane, Dr 205
Collet, Sophia Dobson 24f., 32, 36, 329
Confucius 70, 74, 89
Cox, Harvey 318
Cullmann, Oscar 302, 317

Datta, S. K. 11, 36, 68, 81, 239, 259f., 263f., 275, 278f., 282f., 322
Davis, Merle 304, 317
Day, Lal Behari 38–42, 44–6, 48–55, 281, 321

Devadhar, G. K. 250
Devanandan, Paul D. 164–70, 187, 190, 229–34, 238, 286, 289, 299, 317, 322
Devdas, Nalini 116, 126, 148
Dewart, L. 318
Digby, John 8
Dodd, C. H. 291, 293–4, 317
Duff, Alexander 38, 239, 241, 246, 248, 281, 322, 325
Dyanashevar 278

East Asia Christian Conference 307–312, 318, 326
Elwin, Verrier 215
Enoch 155
Europe 57, 69, 75, 273

Farmer, H. H. 317
Farquhar, J. N. 65, 67f., 72, 81, 239, 322f.
Fuller, R. H. 36, 302, 305, 317

Gaffar Khan, Abdul 225
Gandhi, Mahatma 77, 129, 181, 187, 193–238, 240, 251f., 255, 270, 276, 319, 323–5, 327, 329, 334
Gardner, C, E. 36, 324
George, S. K. 215–18, 222, 236f., 243, 323
Gladstone, W. E. 200
Gokhale, Gopala Krishna 240, 245, 250, 255, 323, 328
Goreh, Nehemiah 11, 36, 38f., 42–4, 46–9, 51–4, 127, 143, 324

Hare, David 38
Harijans 209–14, 223, 228
Harnack, A. von 157
Hartshorne, C. 299
Heber, Reginald 259
Heidegger, Martin 299
Heiler, F. 103, 108, 153
Hodgson, Leonard 290
Hoekendijk, J. C. 294, 308, 317
Hogg, A. G. 235, 238, 304, 318, 324
Hoskyns, Edwyn 149

Indian National Congress 240f., 326

Inglis, Dr 246
Islam 2, 161

Jesudason, S. 237, 332, 334
Joad, C. E. M. 150
John the Baptist 155
John, Gospel of 7, 10, 15–19, 21, 24, 30, 122f., 127, 131–3, 140–2, 158
John XXIII, Pope 291
Johnson, E. R. 74
Jones, E. Stanley 194, 225–9, 236, 238, 324, 327

Kandy 306
Karve, D. K. 250
Keithahn, R. R. 215
Keller, Carl 163f.
Kerala 159, 218, 332
King, Martin Luther 234
Klostermaier, Klaus 109
Knox, John 58
Koran 233, 264
Kozenski 204
Kraemer, Hendrik 135, 149, 161f., 217, 285, 292, 304, 317
Krishna 30, 89, 112–14, 121f., 129, 154, 164, 189, 203f.
Kumarappa, Bharatan 215, 239, 325
Kumarappa, J. C. 215, 237, 239, 243, 281, 324f.
Künneth, W. 296

Lindsay Commission 247, 281
Lucas, Bernard 239, 325
Luke, Gospel of 17
Luther, Martin 58

Macaulay, Lord 246, 248
Macpherson, G. 55
Macquarrie, John 287f., 297, 302, 317
Madagascar 304
Madras Christian College 245, 281, 324
Maharashtra 11, 277, 324, 331
Mallich, Jadu 112
Manicheans 151
Mankar, G. A. 110
Mar Thoma Church 159
Mark, Gospel of 21

Index

Marshman, Joshua 1–37, 67, 325, 329, 334
Marx, Karl 299
Mascall, E. L. 37, 291f., 317
Matthew, Gospel of 17, 21, 133
Mayhew, Arthur 247
McNicol, Nicol 283
Mehta, Pheroz 241, 325
Meurin, Bishop 75
Miller, William 239, 242, 245–7, 281, 322, 325, 331
Milman, H. H. 156, 191
Mohammed 58, 70, 74, 89, 112, 203f.
Mohammedan, Musalman 78, 89, 113, 120, 206, 233, 262
Moses 74
Moses, D. G. 170–4, 180, 189, 228, 289, 317, 325f.
Mosheim, J. L. 27f.
Mott, John R. 207
Mozoomdar, P. C. 12, 57f., 71, 81, 82–100, 113–15, 148, 326, 333
Muller, Max 42, 62, 99, 114, 148f.
Munz, Peter 286, 317

Namdev 278
Nanak 74
Natal 272
Natarajan, K. 252
National Missionary Society 276, 281, 320, 328, 333
Nehru, J. 255
Nevinson, H. W. 240
Newbigin, Lesslie 180, 190
Nicea, Nicene Creed 28, 35
Nicodemus 16
Niles, D. T. 287, 301, 317, 327
Nobili, Roberto de 253f., 257, 282, 326

Ogden, Schubert 35, 299, 301, 317
Origen 110, 129, 135, 158, 160, 279
Otto, Rudolf 69, 82, 84, 124

Pannikar, Raymond 109, 326f.
Paradkar, B. A. 54
Paramahamsa See Ramakrishna
Parekh, M. C. 12, 29–32, 36f., 65–7, 72, 77f., 81, 96, 99f., 103, 110, 256–9, 282, 327

Paul, Pauline Epistles 18f., 21f., 24, 28, 30, 40, 85, 93f., 155, 157f., 202, 257, 261, 267f., 277, 280, 282, 285, 287, 293, 317
Paul, A. A. 210, 333
Paul, K. T. 144, 149, 239f., 243, 251–253, 259, 262f., 274–6, 280–3, 322, 327, 333
Peter, Epistle of Peter 17, 156
Philo 156
Pius XII, Pope 291
Plato, Platonism 104, 156, 169
Poona 49, 312–15, 324, 328, 331, 333
Popley, H. A. 283
Prarthana Samaj 49, 328, 334
Puranas 63, 85, 115, 159

Radhakrishnan, S. 73, 111, 147, 150–192, 276, 289, 320, 324, 327–9
Rajagopalachariar, C. 276
Raju, P. T. 187
Rama 30, 112, 114, 128, 189, 204
Ramabai, Pandita 38, 49, 52, 54, 324, 328
Ramachandran, G. 220
Ramakrishna Paramahamsa 72f., 100, 112–17, 120–2, 126, 129f., 138, 143, 327, 330f., 334
Ramakrishna Mission 79, 111, 113, 117, 144, 146, 272, 331, 334
Ramanuja 103, 132, 134
Ramayana 128
Rammohan Roy 1–37, 42–4, 56, 72, 93, 100, 123, 240, 255, 269, 273, 319, 325, 328, 332f.
Ram Tirtha 128, 269
Ranade, Mahade Govind 101, 110, 241, 250, 255f., 269, 328, 334
Rao, Mark Sunder 181–6, 189, 192, 328
Rees, T. 36
'Rethinking Christianity' Group 76, 319, 321, 334
Richter, Julius 254f., 282
Robinson, J. A. T. 34f., 37, 285, 296, 317
Rolland, Romain 99, 110, 114, 148
Round Table Conferences 275, 283, 322

Roth, W. M. 302f., 315, 318
Rudra, S. K. 34, 37, 239, 249f., 259, 264–8, 279f., 282, 319, 329

Samartha, S. J. 180f., 192, 329
Sayers, Dorothy L. 53
Schilpp, P. 190f.
Schweitzer, Albert 153
Scott, E. F. 132, 149
Seely, J. R. 58
Sen, Keshub Chunder 12, 29, 56–82, 84, 88, 93, 95–7, 99–101, 108, 112, 114, 116, 120, 123, 235, 255, 257, 269, 273, 326f., 329f., 333f.
Serampore 1f., 24, 29, 35, 274, 325, 329, 334
Servants of India Society 240, 244, 323
Shastri, Shivanath 115
Slater, R. H. L. 317
Smith, George 58
Smith, Ronald Gregor 296
Socrates 89f.
Solovyev, V. 68
Srinivasachari, P. N. 181
Streeter, B. H. 305, 318
Stokes, Samuel 271
Student Christian Movement of India 276, 279, 322, 335
Sunder Rao, Mark See Rao
Surjit Singh 174–80, 189, 330
Sykes, M. See under Chaturvedi, B.

Tagore, Debendranath 39, 44, 56, 115, 329f., 333
Tagore, G. M. 51
Tagore, Rabindranath 128, 187, 219–221, 261, 270, 319, 330
Tambaram 235, 238, 271, 324
Tattvabhushan, Sitanath 255, 282
Tennyson, Lord Alfred 128
Tertullian 280
Tilak, Balagangadhara 240, 255
Tilak, Narayana Vamana 11f., 36, 277f., 324, 330

Tillich, Paul 181, 295
Tolstoy, Count Leo 198, 221
Tukaram 277f.
Tulsi Das 128, 249, 269
Tytler, R. 2

Upadhyaya, Brahmobandhav 99–110, 239, 250f., 330f.
Upanishads 85, 127, 151f., 155, 163, 329

Vallabha 164
Van Buren, Paul 297
Vedas, Vedism 3, 39, 42f., 50, 52, 54f., 65, 85, 100, 102f.
Vedanta 3, 100, 103f., 107f., 114, 118, 120, 123, 129–34, 145, 159, 321
  Advaita Vedanta 52, 111, 113, 117f., 125, 127f., 143, 150, 153f., 165, 167–70, 182, 186–9, 327f., 334
  'Practical Vedanta' 126f., 144
Vishnu 78
Vishnu Dharmottara 93
Visvabharati University 220, 330
Vivekananda, Swami 73, 100, 103, 111, 113, 117–48, 150, 167, 269, 272, 321, 327, 330f., 334

Ward, Marcus 313–15, 318, 331
Westcott, B. F. 77, 128
Whitehead, A. N. 299
Williams, Daniel 299
Wilson, Bishop D. 259f.
Wilson, John 239, 322
Winslow, J. C. 36, 330

Yates, W. 24f., 35
Young Men's Christian Association 262, 322, 327, 335

Zacharias, H. C. E. 108, 110, 144, 149, 240, 245, 250f., 281f.
Zoroaster 70, 74, 203